Limits of Liberation

Limits of Liberation

Feminist Theology and the Ethics of Poverty and Reproduction

Elina Vuola

SHEFFIELD ACADEMIC PRESS
A Continuum imprint
LONDON • NEW YORK

First published as *Limits of Liberation: Praxis as Method of Latin American Liberation Theology and Feminist Theology* (Suomalaisen Tiedeakatemian toimituksia. Sarja Humaniora = Annales Academiae Scientiarum Fennicae. Ser. Humaniora, 289; Helsinki: Suomalainen Tiedeakatemia, 1997). Republished with permission.

Published by Sheffield Academic Press Ltd
The Tower Building, 11 York Road, London SE1 7NX
370 Lexington Avenue, New York, NY 10017-6550

www.SheffieldAcademicPress.com
www.continuumbooks.com

British Library Cataloguing-in-Publication Data

A catalogue record for this book is available from the British Library

Typeset by Sheffield Academic Press
Printed on acid-free paper in Great Britain by Bookcraft Ltd, Midsomer Norton, Bath

ISBN   1-84127-308-2 (hardback)
        1-84127-309-0 (paperback)

Contents

Acknowledgments

This book is based on my doctoral dissertation, which I wrote and defended in English at the University of Helsinki, Finland, in September 1997. Since then, the original has been translated into Spanish and published in Madrid, Spain (IEPALA Editoriales), as well as in Quito, Ecuador (Editorial Abya-Yala). It has been especially important for me that the book is being read in Latin America. Now, I am extremely happy to see the original English version become more available for a truly international audience. So, my first thanks go to Sheffield Academic Press, especially to its Editorial Director, Philip Davies, for supporting the publication of this new English version. Thanks, also, to the production editors Sarah Norman and Heidi Robbins for their work on this book.

In 1991, when I started my doctoral studies, I spent five months at the Chicago Theological Seminary. Among my Chicago area colleagues I wish to thank especially Professors Susan Thistlethwaite and Rosemary Radford Ruether for their continuing support, from the earliest stage of my research to the present day.

The most fruitful stage of this research was spent at the *Departamento Ecuménico de Investigaciones* in San José, Costa Rica, during 1991–93 and again in 1999–2000. I feel a deep gratitude to the entire *equipo del DEI* through which I have made several important contacts throughout Latin America. I especially thank Helio Gallardo, Franz Hinkelammert, Pablo Richard and Elsa Tamez for commenting on the first drafts of my work and their support ever since.

Professor María Pilar Aquino has been important for this work in several ways, as will be evident to anybody who reads my book. She was the first Latin American feminist theologian I met, and our dialogues began when she visited Finland several years ago. I thank her for her critical comments and for her ongoing support, but especially for our shared conviction that, while diverse contexts have to be taken seriously, they need not imprison us. Our dialogue is a wonderful example of going beyond the 'Third' and the 'First' worlds.

The major financial support for this work came from the Academy of Finland, which funded three years of my doctoral studies (1991–94) and another three years of my post-doctoral research fellowship (1998–2001), during which I revised both the English and the Spanish versions of the manuscript. The Emil Aaltonen Foundation funded my doctoral research during another three-year period (1994–97).

I also wish to express my gratitude to the Finnish Academy of Science and Letters, publisher of the original English version, which has also been supportive of the book's several reprints.

Finally, I am happy to thank Professor Mark Lewis Taylor for his friendship and care as well as the combination of academic work and activism that we share.

I dedicate this book to my daughters Elsa and Kerttu for two reasons. First, as a sign of a mother-daughter relationship that can give little girls courage and intellectual openness besides the care, love and nurture any mother wishes to give her child. Second, my daughters are a living example of the fullness of a woman's life, wherein mental and physical creativity are intertwined in ways that we are only beginning to explore.

Elina Vuola
Helsinki, Finland
16 November 2001
the 12th anniversary of the assassination of the six Jesuits
at the Universidad Centroamericana in San Salvador

Introduction

This work will look at the methodological presuppositions of a major theological current of our time, liberation theology (LT), by asking critical questions about the status and meaning of praxis in its method. I am interested mainly in how feminist concerns can be explicated and treated within Latin American LT. I will show that the difficulties in doing so derive largely from the praxis point of view in both Latin American LT and feminist theology (FT). Issues of sexual ethics—especially reproductive ethics—are of special interest since they offer a heuristic perspective to the limitations of praxis as the point of departure for theology.

Liberation theology is one of the most significant currents in modern theology. It can be defined either narrowly or broadly. In the former sense, it is limited to the Latin American theology of liberation (*teología de la liberación*), born out of a specifically Latin American context in the 1960s. In the latter, broader sense, LT also includes other theological currents. Most important of them are black theology—mostly in North America and South Africa—and feminist theology, of which one can no longer speak as primarily North American or Western European. Some would claim that it is even more accurate to speak of theologies of liberation. The point of departure in this research is the latter understanding of LT as a worldwide movement which, in spite of its heterogeneity, contains some central characteristics that makes it stand out, if not as a new paradigm, at least as a new moment in the history of theology. The different theologies inside the movement have had some dialogue with each other, mostly in the context of the Ecumenical Association of Third World Theologians (EATWOT), founded in 1976.[1] At the EATWOT meetings, different liberation theologies have tried to delineate both those features that they share and those where they diverge. Christianity is literally no longer 'the white man's religion'; it is not only the 'non-white' South, but also women all over the world, that look critically at the history of Christianity and claim new subjectivities within it.

A broad definition of LT stresses the inter-relatedness of different structures of oppression. Liberation of oppressive structures necessarily involves political, economic, social, racial and sexual aspects. Preferring just one of them at the expense of the others has been a reality in various liberation movements. In the LT

---

1. According to Gibellini, Latin American LT has been associated with black theology and feminist theology, which also understand themselves as liberation theologies, from 1975 on, after the conference 'Theology in the Americas' in Detroit. See Gibellini 1988: 2, 13.

movement, there is an explicit emphasis on seeing different forms of oppression and liberation of them as layers in one complicated process.

Nevertheless, as in any human activity, there is a contradiction between stated ideals and the lived reality in LT. Male liberation theologians, black and white, have not welcomed feminist critique with open arms, especially when it has been aimed at them. White, middle-class women from industrialized countries have been blind to the reality of the great majority of the world's women who are non-white and poor.

Each liberation theology, whether black, feminist or Latin American, is characterized by its distinctive viewpoint, but what they do share is their commitment to social justice.[2] To some extent, all liberation theologies are situated in contemporary political struggles, some more than others. Liberation theologians usually refer to this as praxis, not only as their aim or objective but also as their point of departure.

All liberation theologies emphasize praxis as the starting point—and, to some degree, even criterion—for theological reflection, and, because of this, they consider their theology as a wholly new way of doing theology. This is the most central single characteristic that different liberation theologies share with each other. The aim of this research is to clarify this methodological starting point in two major liberation theologies, namely Latin American LT and FT. I will do this by asking how they define praxis and what it means as a point of departure for theology. By pointing towards problems and limitations in this method, I will also ask to what extent these 'praxis theologies' can be faithful to their most central and explicit methodological characteristic.

Here the argument is that in spite of contradictions and ambiguities in the two liberation theologies, it is possible to speak of a common method that makes LT a new paradigm that indeed has serious implications for both theology and the role of it in church and society. Methodologically, Latin American LT and FT have enough in common so that we are able to speak of them together, under the label 'liberation theology'. At the same time, though, I will clarify this method by demonstrating that to a certain extent this commonality is problematic, and at least inadequately analysed and explicated. It is this tension that makes liberation theologies so vivid and open, but unfortunately also unclear and, for this very same reason, disposed to criticism.

By putting the two liberation theologies into a dialogue with each other, I want to pay attention to certain central theoretical questions in liberation theology as a paradigm. Questions of and about ethics should be *per definitum* part of any theology that claims praxis to be its most central point of reference. A natural area of dialogue between Latin American LT and FT is that of sexual ethics, because it is the area where the everyday life of poor Latin American women and progressive theology committed to defend them converge, at least theoretically. Unfortunately, no such thing as liberation theology's sexual ethics exists, nor does a dialogue that would speak of the Latin American poor and questions of sexual

2.   Thistlethwaite and Engel (eds.) 1990: 1.

ethics (especially Catholic) together. The silence, on the one hand, and the agreement with the traditional teaching of the *magisterium*, on the other hand, on the part of the liberation theologians in these issues is complicated and will be dealt with in this research. By creating a space for critical dialogue inside the liberation theology paradigm, I want to point out problems of a more general nature in the praxis starting point. Simultaneously, possibilities for new directions for liberation theologies will be shown.

Even a superficial look at the works of the most prominent Latin American liberation theologians indicates the diversity of the concept of praxis and the conceptual ambiguity of it. There are even many liberation theologians who do not explicitly analyse their method at all. This is why I concentrate on those who strive for a systematic conceptual analysis and explicitness of method. I will be speaking of LT mainly as a movement, as a whole, and thus may not do justice to individual theologians and their respective differences.

All the theologians in this research refer to praxis in the methodological sense: theological reflection starts in political, social and economic realities, then analyses them with the tools of the social sciences, philosophy and theology, and finally returns to its starting point. This is what Juan Luis Segundo calls the hermeneutic circle (Segundo 1975: 13-14). There is a definite Marxist influence in how liberation theologians understand the praxis and the relationship between theory and praxis.

The definition made by Gustavo Gutiérrez about liberation theology as 'the critical reflection of praxis in the light of the Word of God' is a classic (Gutiérrez 1990: 67). This definition also seems to refer to praxis in the methodological sense, not primarily to its object. In this sense, praxis cannot be reduced to 'the poor' or 'the society' even if they formed the central core of it.

Similar analysis will be made of FT, concentrating on those feminist theologians who define themselves as feminist liberation theologians, in both the First World and Latin America. A whole chapter is devoted to the dialogue between the two currents, analysed primarily from the perspective of the emerging Latin American feminist liberation theology.

From the perspective of 'purely' theological discourse, FT—or feminist studies in religion—forms historically and methodologically part of the wider tradition of liberation theology. However, one can also examine it as a part of academic women's studies. In that case, FT has to confront questions similar to those faced by the rest of feminist theory in other fields. It is complicated to 'locate' FT: if we analyse it as part of women's studies in the academy, the questions or at least the focal points are different from when considering it as part of the liberation theological paradigm.

Similar choices of perspective can be made in the case of Latin American LT. Liberation theologians are often 'general intellectuals' on their continent: they discuss philosophical and theological as well as economic and political issues. They have a high level of education and dialogue both with each other and with their European and North American colleagues, and not only in the field of theology. Thus, one can consider liberation theology as part of a wider critical political-philosophical intellectual tradition in Latin America (and in the Third World in general). It radically questions the Eurocentrism of our universities, churches and societies. In this sense, Latin American intellectuals, including liberation theologians, are working on much broader ground than are their European or North American colleagues. The latter are often familiar only with European or North American intellectual discourses and currents, but they may consider them as the only significant ways of thinking.

The interesting—and difficult—aspect of Latin American LT is its mobility between *theologia proper* and other disciplines. This multidisciplinarity sometimes makes it difficult to answer questions such as, 'Isn't it, after all, sociology masked as theology that liberation theologians are doing?' These sorts of questions have been the main criticisms aimed at LT, especially on the part of the church hierarchy. It is important to remember that this kind of multidisciplinarity is in no way exclusive to LT. First, theology as such has always borrowed from other disciplines: it would not even exist in its modern form without philosophy. For centuries, philosophy was called *ancilla theologiae*. Second, any theory of society—and as part of it, religion—which wants to answer such complicated questions as structural poverty, women's subordinate status, or the effects of economic changes on human well-being, cannot limit itself to the often arbitrary and out-of-date way of defining the boundaries between academic disciplines.

As a reaction and protest against Eurocentrism, LT can be seen as offering one credible explanation and means of solution for the Latin American crisis. It fills a vacuum between emancipatory social sciences and traditional 'over-metaphysical' Catholic theology. LT has offered one interpretation of the history of the continent, analysed the causes of poverty, redefined the central themes of Christianity and pointed towards possible changes and models of action. All this has happened on a deeply religious continent where the process of secularization has not taken the paths it did in Europe. Besides this, in times of military dictatorships, the church often was the only place where people could feel safe, both physically and mentally.

Further, LT can be seen as forming part of a larger intellectual and political movement in the Third World countries that seeks independent answers, rooted in their own history and culture, for political and social problems of Third World societies. Especially in Latin America, because of the historical role of the Catholic Church and Christianity there, this kind of discourse is easily channelled to theology. The role of theology and theologians there is different from that in our societies. No such thing as nonconfessional academic theology without any necessary practical connections (the Scandinavian model) exists in Latin America. Catholic theology, the predominant theology in Latin America, in general is more confessional than Protestant theology. LT is giving new meanings and interpretations to this already existing relationship between theology and (ecclesiastic, social) praxis.

This can also be seen in the contents of liberation theology: the theological and the political are interrelated in the area of language as well as in concrete action and scientific analysis. Because of this, outsiders may have difficulty in understanding LT, and they may criticize it, at least those who are not familiar with the history of the continent, the role of the church and the wider socio-political discussion there.

Further, both FT and Latin American LT are linked to the actual philosophical discourse about the interests and character of knowledge and science, as well as their objectivity and values and cultural context, and finally, the relationship between knowledge and power. Questions about contextuality of knowledge and its interests unite such simultaneous paradigm changes in Western intellectual tradition as critical social sciences, including feminist epistemologies, and various anti-Eurocentric theories, including liberation theology. Critique of false universalism is central.

In all the above-mentioned theories, 'knowing' is understood not only as a mental process in the individual mind. To use the distinction of Jürgen Habermas, different from other knowledge-constitutive interests, an emancipatory interest of knowledge aims at disclosing and overcoming forms of oppression by the help of critical social sciences and their distinctive form of critical rationality. The concern is ideology critique and liberation. There is a dialectical unity of knowledge and interest (theory and praxis).

Both objects of my research, Latin American LT and FT, are difficult to define unambiguously *per se*, and there are several different viewpoints between which I must choose. I have decided to make a choice that in my opinion does justice to both of them separately but also makes it possible to discuss them together. Taking into account all the above-mentioned possible viewpoints and their implications, I am going to analyse both feminist theology and Latin American LT as liberation theologies. Thus, the unifying factor seems to be the praxis as the starting point and method of theological reflection.

The practical commitment and the critique of 'traditional' theology in liberation theologies have been considered as more important than the creation of a theoretically solid model of thought—at least until today. It is understandable in a new tradition. However, the lack of this kind of model of thought makes it difficult to understand even the most central claims. For example, what do feminist theologians mean when talking about 'women's experience' (the praxis of FT)? Who are the subjects—'the poor'—of Latin American LT? If there is no consensus about what forms the praxis, how can it be taken as the point of departure?

A comparison between Latin American LT and FT reveals some of their respective weaknesses. The central concept 'women's experience' in most of North American and European feminist theology is contradictory in itself. The 'experience' of a European woman is much closer to the reality of the men of her society than to the reality of a woman living in a Third World country.

The concept 'women's experience' has been criticized primarily from two directions: first, by those women who see the experience FT speaks about as the experience of 'white, middle-class, educated, heterosexual women', and second, by postmodern views which reject universal truth claims. The influence of non-theological feminist theory on FT has, until recently, been scarce, and is one reason for the scant critical attention paid to the theoretical problems in the central status given to claims about experience and praxis.

Latin American LT speaks about 'the poor' as its homogeneous context, without taking into account the fact that poverty affects people differently depending on factors like their gender or race. Thus, both Latin American LT and FT, at least the FT born in industrialized countries, pass over the context of poor women who, together with their children, are the poorest of the poor.

At the moment, the greatest challenge for Latin American LT comes from the women, the indigenous peoples and the blacks of the continent—the ones who have not been included in the homogeneous concept 'the poor'. Thus, it is both theoretically and historically justified to deepen the dialogue between Latin American liberation theology (with its concept 'the poor') and feminist theology (with the concept 'women's experience').

An important issue that I will deal with is sexual ethics and its status in LT. Sexual ethics, especially reproductive ethics—or the scant attention given to it— can serve as a concrete example of the insufficient conceptual analysis and its practical consequences in LT. It is difficult to find questions of sexual ethics being treated in the works of Latin American liberation theologians. Those who do take up sexual ethics as an issue seem to agree with much of official Catholic teaching. Liberation theologians hold rather dogmatic stances in issues of sexual ethics, which also reflects their image of women, largely based on traditional Catholic anthropology.

One of the first causes of death for women of reproductive age all over the Third World, including Latin America, is the complications after an illegal abortion. Ninety-nine per cent of maternal mortality (everything related to pregnancy, birth and its complications, including abortion) in the world happens in Third World countries.

Preventing the death of poor women has not been an explicit part of liberation theologians' agenda of 'defending the life of the poor'. No doubt the reason for this can be found in the global 'invisibility' of women, but also in the exacerbated relations between Catholic liberation theologians and the Vatican. Until now, the area of sexual and reproductive ethics has been left outside the conflict, consciously or unconsciously. However, there is no notable difference between Catholic and Protestant liberation theologians in these issues, nor between male and female theologians. One of my claims is, though, that Latin American feminist liberation theology could offer adequate tools to deal with issues of sexual ethics in the Latin American context.

There are several secular women's movements in Latin American that critically raise issues of sexual ethics and reproductive rights, including contraception and abortion. These movements often consist of educated middle-class women who no longer have strong or any ties to the institutional churches. In fact, the church, especially the Catholic Church, is often considered as the archenemy. When progressive theologians, both male and female, keep silent about issues of sexual ethics, a situation is created in which the great majority of Latin American women (poor, uneducated, and to whom religion plays an important, albeit contradictory role in their lives) find no one expressing their most intimate concerns. The contradictions of middle-class feminism and women's popular movements in

Latin America have been well documented by several social scientists.[3] What is not usually explicitly stated in these studies is the missing link, Latin American feminist liberation theologians, who would speak on behalf of the praxis of women from the 'popular classes'. To be able to do so implies a critical understanding of the controversial role of religion, including its liberative potential. The Catholic monopoly in sexual ethics must be met with adequate tools of analysis. Neither secular feminist movements nor Catholic women without any formal education (especially in theology) meet this need. The same can be said of the most prominent (male) liberation theologians.

My work could be seen as divided into two major sections. The first part deals with Latin American LT and FT as liberation theologies which have methodological commonalities concerning their praxis approach. This makes their inherent problems similar as well, although the critique aimed at them comes from somewhat different directions. The second part is on sexual ethics, serving as a case study and verification of the problems stated in the first part. Since sexual ethics is an issue of utmost importance in any part of the world, it is not a trivial or marginal question—even less so, if it turns out to be a problem in a theology which has a praxical self-understanding as defending the weak and the silenced. Latin American feminist liberation theologians serve as the bridge between the two sections, Latin American LT and FT from other parts of the world. This could also be formulated as a question: How do liberation theology and feminist theology encounter one another in Latin America? How and why do they not?

In Chapter 1, I will present a historical overview of Latin American LT. Then I will sketch the liberation theological method which makes LT stand out as a 'new way of doing theology', as liberation theologians themselves claim to be doing. I will identify this method by asking how liberation theologians understand praxis and those who supposedly are the prime subjects of it, the poor. I will analyse critically liberation theologians' understanding of the poor as subjects of theology.

In Chapter 2, I will first characterize feminist theology as part of the larger framework of academic women's studies. Then I will look at FT from another angle, by defining it as part of the liberation theology movement. Here the focus is concentrated on those feminist theologians who consider themselves both liberation and feminist theologians. I will critically analyse feminist theologians' use of 'women's experience' as a central methodological concept in FT.

Chapter 3 further concentrates the focus on Latin America by looking at Latin American feminist liberation theology through its main proponents. The central concept *la vida cotidiana* (everyday life) and the concretizing of the option for the poor as an option for the poor woman brings a critical element to LT and its methodological presuppositions. Since there are some male liberation theologians who do speak more extensively on women and gender issues, I will take a critical look at how they theorize these issues as part of their overall theological project. Mariology and its reinterpretations in a Latin American context offer an example

3. See Radcliffe and Westwood (eds.) 1993.

of how gender issues can be treated in LT and how a space for alternative interpretations is also opened up in issues important to women.

In Chapter 4, which serves as a case study of what has been said in the previous
chapters, I will analyse the issue of sexual ethics in LT. It will be noted that issues
of sexual ethics, especially of reproduction, are scarcely dealt with in LT, and
when they are, they tend to be interpreted in traditional ways. In the Catholic
context, this means that many liberation theologians, willingly or unwillingly,
agree with the official teaching. Sexual ethics is a concrete example of the limits of
praxis as a theological method. It reveals that liberation theologians are not really
doing what they claim to do. This again is a challenge to the supposed commitment to praxis. The praxis starting point may even produce certain dogmatism
in theologies which give it such a central methodological status. On their part,
Latin American feminist liberation theologians offer the concrete experiences of
women, especially the poorest of them, as a critical corrective to the praxis, even
though they do not deal with issues of sexual ethics either.

My sources are primarily the writings of contemporary liberation and feminist
theologians. In practice, this means several important theologians from both Latin
America and elsewhere. Necessarily, I look at their works from a certain limited
perspective which makes it impossible to give a comprehensive analysis of each
theologian. Non-theological works, principally social scientific ones, done in and
on Latin America, as well as non-theological feminist theory, will be used when
necessary and adequate.

My method is a systematic analysis of the works considered as belonging to
liberation theology. After a historical overview, I will draw a generalized picture
of the method of one of the most important contemporary theological currents
through its main proponents. I will critically analyse and interpret some of the
most central methodological presuppositions in both LT and FT. This I will do
by asking critical questions which challenge these presuppositions, pointing
toward some necessary changes in the liberation theology paradigm, if it wishes to
be faithful to its central point of departure.

Although no systematic analysis has been done on the issue of sexual ethics in
the context of LT, there are several works on liberation theology's method in
general. There is only a handful of critical analyses of feminist theology's method,
most of them very recent works which I was able to read only in the course of
this research.

Because of the broadness of my theme, I have to make some limitations and
reservations. First, it is **not** my intention to go through the complex and long
history of the concept of praxis, or the relationship between theory and praxis, in
the history of philosophy and the social sciences. Latin American liberation
theologians borrow mostly from Marxist-orientated social sciences, the Frankfurt
School, and European political theology in their use of the concept. I will concentrate on the specificity of liberation theologians' use of the concept, namely its
interpretation in and from a Latin American context. The cutting edge of my
research is women as subjects of both theology and ethics. Thus, my analysis of

concepts such as praxis aims primarily at opening up room for a critical discussion of gender and sexual ethics in the context of LT.

Second, as was said earlier, neither am I going to present any single liberation or feminist theologian in detail. While taking into account differences among them, I will speak of LT and FT as theological currents in which certain basic presuppositions (mostly in the area of methodology, which is the focus of this research) are held by those who define themselves as liberation theologians. By this I also want to do justice to the fundamental self-understanding of LT as a collective enterprise. For the purpose of this work the most important Latin American liberation theologians are Gustavo Gutiérrez, Leonardo Boff, Pablo Richard and Enrique Dussel. Of the feminist theologians, I will concentrate on those who explicitly understand themselves as feminist liberation theologians and actively participate in the liberation theology movement, especially Rosemary Radford Ruether and Elisabeth Schüssler Fiorenza from North America and María Pilar Aquino and Ivone Gebara from Latin America. However, as will become clear, I will introduce LT and FT by quoting several authors. It is also worth noting that all the above mentioned theologians, with the exception of Aquino, are of the first generation of their respective movements. They thus represent something foundational in both LT and FT, but have also been criticized by a younger generation of scholars.

It is also important to bear in mind that neither Latin American LT nor feminist theology is an exclusively Catholic phenomenon. Actually, a kind of 'practical ecumenism' is characteristic of both of them. Traditional dogmatic disagreements or differences are not seen as being as important as the shared praxis. Confessional differences will be noted when they have relevance to the topics analysed.

Third, I am not going to analyse specific intra-theological themes in liberation theologies. Both Latin American LT and feminist theology work on classical theological questions such as God, Christology and ecclesiology. My intention is to analyse the way or the method, that is, how a different perspective evolves in LT in comparison to traditional Christian theology. It is the method that helps us understand both new interpretations of classical theological issues and new themes that were never present in earlier theology.

Fourth, in the chapter on sexual ethics, I am not going to analyse the issue theologically or trace the history and contents of sexual ethical teaching in theology. I am merely pointing out that LT would be the most appropriate context for the creation of critical and constructive sexual ethics in Latin America. It is only the Latin American liberation theologians, both men and women—but especially the latter—who can realize this task adequately. My own argument in this context is practical. I will rely on statistical facts concerning women's status in Latin America, especially when it comes to issues of reproduction. I use the concept of sexual ethics throughout this work, although I concentrate mainly on issues of reproduction. Nevertheless, the broader concept implies that there are important issues of sexual ethics other than those of reproduction which face similar problems in LT but which I deliberately choose not to deal with in this work.

Sexual ethics could have been treated more comprehensively. A study concentrating exclusively on sexual or even reproductive ethics would be important. However, I want to place questions of subjectivity and sexual ethics in the methodological context of LT. This is for two reasons. First, sexual ethics and its present role in LT is a challenge to the methodological presuppositions of LT, which claims to be a praxis-orientated theology. Sexual ethics in this research serves as a case study of what is claimed on a more theoretical level, namely that liberation theologians should pay critical attention to how praxis also excludes, turns against itself, and even becomes dogmatism, when it is given so central a status without critical questions about its premises. Second, I want to emphasize the feminist claim that 'women' and 'their' issues are not accidental or peripheral in theology, or in any intellectual enterprise. They touch the very 'core' of our often-unexplicated thinking habits and ways of seeing and ordering the world.

Fifth, even though my emphasis is on the method of LT and FT, I do not claim to have given their methodologies a systematic analysis, nor to have compared these approaches with others in the history of theology. My main interest is to ask what kind of *de facto* role or meaning praxis has as the methodological backbone of LT.

And last but not least, both the possible weakness and strength of this research is its broadness. It opens out to several theoretical discourses that in themselves are complicated and extensive: Marxism; feminist theory; recent developments in contemporary theology, including ethics; and the use of the social sciences in theology and its potential effects on the autonomy of theology (multidisciplinarity). Because of the very character of liberation theologies, they could be analysed from different angles which would do them as much—or even more— justice than the perspective chosen here. I am not pretending that my critique of LT (or FT) is the most valid and adequate one. However, I believe that my perspective offers one important point of view lacking until today in Latin American LT and studies about it. I cannot create a sexual ethical programme for others, but I can point out an existing gap at this point and the necessity of filling that gap.

Finally, there are some more practical kinds of issues that I need to point out. I have read Latin American liberation theologians primarily in Spanish and, to a lesser degree, in Portuguese. Of the books by the most-quoted Brazilian liberation theologian in this research, Leonardo Boff, I have mostly used the Spanish translations. The English translations have been consulted and partially used, when available. In this case, the English translations are mentioned in the bibliography after the original work. However, most of the direct translations are mine.

The sexism of liberation theologians' language has been pointed out by Latin American women. The English translations sometimes correct this sexism into a more politically correct, inclusive English. Since I think liberation theologians could themselves very well opt for non-sexist Spanish or Portuguese in their writings, I have not translated words such as 'hombre' as 'human being' but as a 'man'. The words have the same connotations in English and Spanish.

Personally, issues of language have been important for me in the course of this work. I have done research in both the United States and Latin America, becoming fluent in both English and Spanish. Coming from a small linguistic group, I have grown up knowing that I have to learn other languages in order to communicate with people from other cultures. After this work, I am more conscious than ever that this is both an immense richness and a limitation. On the one hand, I am convinced that in understanding a culture different from one's own, language plays a central role. On the other hand, I have often been frustrated in not being able to express myself as well as I can in my mother tongue. Having a theme as I do, I nevertheless consider it a strength rather than a weakness. The author of this work is a living example both of the difficulty and the possibility of carrying on a dialogue between very different contexts.

I am conscious of the limitations of an academic dissertation to adequately represent anybody's 'authentic voice'. When criticizing the absence of poor women's interests in LT, I present these interests through the interpretations of Latin American academic women. The question of who really can speak for others, and if it is indeed possible to do so, is a complicated issue and which is being dealt with in several contexts, including feminist and postcolonial theory. Because of the nature of this work, I have made a deliberate choice of engaging in debate on a theoretical level where participants with similar presuppositions— that is, with a similar level of education—can enter into dialogue. It would be arbitrary for me to claim that I speak for poor Latin American women. This does not mean, though, that I cannot participate in the discussion on the basis of my own presuppositions.

I have always believed that participating in a discussion is the best way to recognize the other participants as subjects worth listening to. After my experiences in Latin America, having befriended several of the colleagues who are introduced and analysed in this research, and recognizing the influence they have had on my intellectual development, I do not consider myself a total outsider in the discourse in which I aim to participate. My critique rises from an empathetic demand that the praxis starting point in LT be taken more seriously than has actually been done. My own analysis is as provisional as anybody else's analysis. By revealing and pointing to certain weaknesses and problems in contemporary liberation theology, I participate in the same process as those whose thinking I analyse: looking seriously at what our present religious, economic and social systems are doing factually to large parts of the human community.

Chapter 1

Latin American Liberation Theology

1.1 How to Explain Liberation Theology

It would be against the most basic intentions of LT to try to present it separate from the surrounding society—and the church, as well—as a purely academic or intellectual innovation. The rise of a specific Latin American theology is not understandable without the events and changes in the political, economic and ecclesiastical history of the continent, especially during the last 30 or 40 years.

Our thinking and the possibilities of knowing—thus, also the possibilities of creating knowledge—are always intrinsically bound to personal and general history, society and culture and, within these categories, to class, gender, age, race and so on. Explaining a phenomenon like LT, in an ideal situation, one should be able to take into account many different perspectives: political, economic, social, cultural, intellectual, ecclesiastical, and even personal, in the case of individual theologians. Since this is neither possible nor necessary (considering the purpose of this study), I will drastically limit my presentation to a brief overview. There is a lot of literature available on Latin American history in general, the history of the church in Latin America, and the more immediate political and ecclesiastical background of LT.[1]

According to the Venezuelan sociologist of religion, Otto Maduro, 'It might be reasonably hypothesized that LT represents, albeit to a limited degree, the intellectual, religious and theological crystallization of a new movement of social, economic, political and properly religious protest and dissent by the Latin American oppressed.'[2] He also considers LT an integral, central part of an emergent social, cultural and religious movement that has economic, political, intellectual and scientific implications. All this because LT is simultaneously a result of, a reflection on, and a stimulating rationale for the emergence of new social groups striving for the radical transformation of the entire Latin American socio-religious

---

1.   Representative works on the general history of Latin America are *The Cambridge History of Latin America*, I–V (1986); Keen and Wasserman 1988; Navarro García (ed.) 1991. On the history of the church in Latin America, see Dussel 1981; Levine (ed.) 1986; Mecham 1936; Prien 1978; Richard (ed.) 1981; Rivera Pagán 1991.

2.   Maduro 1991: 2.

14   LIMITS OF LIBERATION

scene. I would add that if LT is seen not just as a Latin American phenomenon
(Asian and African theologies of liberation), this is true for the Third World in
general. 'The emergence of LT has contributed to the desacralization, deconstruction, and delegitimation of many perspectives which have enjoyed a presti-
gious, predominant place in the prevailing Latin American perception of what is
real, legitimately desirable, and reasonably possible', says Maduro. At the same
time, LT is generating 'new perspectives on what can be considered as legitimately real, possible, and/or desirable' and promoting 'a mode of approach to the
interpretation of reality which is remarkably different from the "traditional"
ones'.[3]

Social scientists most often analyse liberation theology in the context of
'religion and politics'.[4] Latin America has become one of the major arenas for
contemporary changes in church and state relationships, on the one hand, and in
the revitalization of traditional religion in modern secular culture, on the other
hand. One has to remember, though, that liberation theology and the ecclesial
base communities (*comunidades eclesiales de base*, CEBs)[5] are but one facet of this
phenomenon. There has been a tendency to see them as the most significant
religious change in Latin America in recent decades. To some extent, of course,
this is true, but liberation theology and its supporters in the church never were a
majority in any Latin American country. Even more importantly, since the 1970s,
the 'golden age' of LT, significant changes have occurred in both the political and
religious arena. LT itself has changed, which is not always taken seriously by its
analysts.

Some social scientists analyse LT in the context of new social movements.[6]
This offers a fruitful perspective, because it is impossible to understand LT separate from the wider social and political changes that took place on the continent
in the 1960s and 1970s. LT has both practically and theoretically been linked to
such wide-ranging phenomena as Marxism and the New Left, the guerrilla
groups inspired by them (in some countries), different human rights organizations, the grassroots organizations of both urban and rural poor (including the
CEBs), and the post-Vatican II changes in the Catholic Church with their special
consequences in Latin America. In the 1980s and 1990s, new social movements
have emerged while old ones have lost some of their significance. Among these
new movements are the women's movement (in all its forms), gay and lesbian
rights movements, different indigenous peoples' movements, and ecological and
anti-racism movements. It is difficult to place LT as such among these as one

3.   Maduro 1991: 2-3.
4.   See Burdick 1993; Casanova 1994: 114-34; Keogh (ed.) 1990; Mainwaring and Wilde
1989.
5.   I will be using the Spanish- and Portuguese-language acronym (CEB).
6.   See several articles in Escobar and Alvarez (eds.) 1992. The writers in this volume do not
view social movements only as 'survival struggles' but also as cultural struggles over the
production of meaning and as collective forms of cultural production. The emergence of these
movements also entails the construction of collective identities. See Alvarez and Escobar 1992:
319-20. This is very much true of LT as a movement as well. See also Slater 1994.

movement among others—even more so in the context of the newer movements, with which LT has created no such strategic alliances as it did with the movements of earlier decades.[7]

Those who are not social scientists—theologians, for example—tend to see LT too easily as a principally intellectual trend and explain it through its main ideas and proponents. Although this perspective is more suitable to this study than is the former social scientist kind of analysis, I maintain that LT is best understood as a complex theory and praxis in explaining social power structures of contemporary Latin America. What makes this possible is, on the one hand, LT's close—albeit often insufficient and contradictory—relationship with different social movements. On the other hand, the powerful traditional status of the Catholic Church on the continent makes its recent changes, including the social and political repercussions of these changes, noteworthy. LT forms an important part of this process.

According to Jorge Castañeda, the CEBs—not LT—as a movement is the most important of the new social movements in Latin America.[8] In many countries, the official church emerged as the most important and often the only voice of the subaltern classes and defence of human rights. This is especially true in Brazil and El Salvador.[9] In the latter, Castañeda explains the strength of the phenomenon by three rarely converging tendencies: the church, the left, and the popular movements.[10] The relationship of the CEBs to the new social movements is often indirect. For example, many activists in human rights movements, women's

7. According to Daniel H. Levine, LT is not to be understood as a 'movement' in the narrow sense of the term. It has no organizational structure, no identifiable leadership or members. Rather, LT's political impact lies not in direct political outcomes, but in its role in changing Latin American Catholicism. See Levine 1990: 231.

On recent changes and crises and new definitions of Latin American leftist social movements, see various articles in Beverley and Oviedo (eds.) 1993; Castañeda 1993; Lehmann 1990.

8. 'Los nuevos movimientos provenían en parte de la nueva pobreza en América Latina. El movimiento más importante, por estar tan bien anclado en la historia y en el inconsciente de la región, es sin duda la eclosión de las llamadas comunidades eclesiales de base (CEB), que transformó radicalmente el papel de la Iglesia en varios países del hemisferio. Aunque se vincula con la teología de la liberación, dicha eclosión no se puede reducir a, ni tampoco confundir con ella' (Castañeda 1993: 244).

9. Castañeda 1993: 246-49, 254-57.

10. 'El tema crucial era la fusión de tres tendencias siempre presentes en la sociedad y la política latinoamericanas, pero que raras veces han convergido: la Iglesia, con la autoridad moral, la historia y la devoción que inspira; la izquierda, perenne pero muchas veces carente de una base de masas; y por último, los movimientos populares, siempre presentes, pero a menudo sin dirigentes e indefensos ante la represión' (Castañeda 1993: 256-57). According to him, in El Salvador, it became clear how threatening the eventual change of the church as a social factor can be to the Latin American elites. 'La muerte de Romero y, nueve años después, la de los seis jesuitas de la UCA, simplemente confirmaron lo que era manifiesto en El Salvador desde el principio. Cuando la Iglesia deja de ser una defensora del *status quo* y se convierte en una fuerza de cambio social, las consecuencias son aterradoras para las élites latinoamericanas' (Castañeda 1993: 256).

'survival movements' and the urban movements in general come from the CEBs.[11]

In a more nuanced way, David Lehmann describes the relationship between LT, the CEBs, and the social movements with the term *basismo*.[12] According to him, it is among the contemporary social movements that we can find the most important influence of LT and where we can also assess the potential of *basismo*.[13] He traces the origins of *basismo* to the Brazilian educator Paulo Freire, whose ideas played an important role in early LT.[14]

Even though LT may not have transformed the institutional church as fundamentally as its protagonists would have liked, in the wider world its influence has been enormous. For Lehmann, 'The informal church has provided an institutional and ideological framework for popular movements after the decline, or repression, of Marxism'.[15] This is, of course, a very strong statement, and many would disagree, at least partially, with it. He does not take into account the later decline of LT and the CEBs themselves, nor does he discuss reasons for this. What is interesting is his point that one consequence of the importance of LT has been to place the theme of citizenship—that is, of the human and civil rights of persons—at the forefront of popular movements, avoiding the assumption of earlier radicalism that there could be no citizenship without a total transformation of society.[16] Here he comes close to Castañeda, who stresses the importance of the CEBs and LT in human rights organizations and the 'survival movements' of the urban poor. Lehmann, too, recognizes the important role of the Catholic Church in providing protection and even encouragement to the new forms of popular organization, especially when it comes to the defence of human rights and guaranteeing basic welfare to the poor.[17]

Nevertheless, even though liberation theologians and sectors close to it in the church have tried to create alliances with social movements such as the women's movement and the ecological movement, these movements have no such weight

11.   Castañeda 1993: 259, 276-77.
12.   'Although Liberation Theology did not meet with its unqualified approval, and occasionally met with open hostility, the official Church came to the fore in the defence of human rights (except in Argentina) while under hierarchical protection a vast informal Church of Base Communities, Human Rights Organizations and *Pastorales* (Pastoral Missions) regrouped, in new ways and on a large scale, the social base which repression had tried to demobilize... But a new type of mobilization grew up from 'below', especially in Brazil, whose progenitors were armed with the Theology of Liberation and financed by a growing international community of non-governmental organizations. To these were joined another network of centres and institutes of social research, and later of social action, in which the intelligentsia in their turn regrouped, aided by those same clerical and international supports, but expounding a variety of ideological positions. *It is the combination of these institutional forms and levels which I describe as* basismo' (Lehmann 1990: xiii [emphasis added]).
13.   Lehmann 1990: xvi.
14.   Lehmann 1990: 96-101.
15.   Lehmann 1990: 147.
16.   Lehmann 1990.
17.   Lehmann 1990: 150.

or space in LT as did other movements at the dawn of LT. It could even be claimed that the present crisis of LT is very much due to its inability to include these new discourses. LT has largely remained unaffected by such recent developments in social theory as gender theory and postcolonial discourses, of which at least the former has an explicit expression in theology. It is important to bear in mind that these theories were developed in a political praxis which did not put theory and praxis into rigid opposition to each other. Prominent liberation theologians such as Enrique Dussel, Pablo Richard and Leonardo Boff, among others, grasp the need for these 'new subjectivities' within LT, but are unable to include them because of the radical critique these new forms of social critique entail to certain traditional positions held by liberation theologians themselves.

Thus, it may well be that the influence of LT has been central in the creation of new social movements, as Castañeda and Lehmann claim, but the reverse may be more complicated. What has happened to LT itself? Has it done its job by creating new spaces of discourse and new alliances?

If liberation theologians have largely remained unaffected by new social movements and discourses produced by them, the same is true on a more practical level as well. The CEBs are clearly losing ground to a very different kind of religiosity all over the continent. Why do people, mostly poor people, turn to Pentecostalism? Some even claim that Latin America is turning Protestant.[18] Recent empirical studies search for answers to this latest phenomenon in Latin America's religious arena. Anthropologist John Burdick pays attention to the issues of gender, age and race as partial explanations for the loss of credibility of the CEBs.[19]

Recent critical studies start from three premises. First, there is an undeniable crisis within the progressive Latin American Catholic Church. Second, there is a diversity within the CEBs and their support for the popular church. Third, related to the former, it must be accepted that LT was always only one faction, even among the CEBs. LT never had such an enduring and wide influence in the Latin American church as has often been claimed. According to most authors, though, this does not mean that LT and the popular church have been a 'fad' or illusion. Rather, their real influence, in the future as well, can best be traced when analysed objectively and critically. This is of special importance for this study, since one of the claims of these authors is that much of the failure of LT among

18. Stoll 1990. Phillip Berryman quotes a Brazilian evangelical leader: 'The Catholic Church opted for the poor, but the poor opted for the evangelicals'. See Berryman 1995: 109. Berryman makes an implicit reference to Stoll's book by the title of his article 'Is Latin America Turning Pluralist?'

In a later article, Stoll claims that 'Ten percent or more of the Latin American population identifies itself as *evangélico*, with the percentage substantially higher in Brazil, Chile, and most of Central America... But if the growth of the last several decades continues, Latin Americans claiming to be *evangélicos* could still become a quarter to a third of the population early in the twenty-first century' (Stoll 1993: 2).

19. Burdick 1992 and 1993 on Brazil. See Levine 1992 for Colombia and Venezuela. Both of them make the point that the number and strength of CEBs have usually been overestimated. See also Stoll 1993: 4-8.

the CEBs is due to the clericalism and authoritarian way of their promoters. This has special implications for the question of women.[20]

It may be that it is, for example, not only the 'discourse' on gender that is lacking in LT on a more substantial level, but that the practices of the Catholic Church—*both* the traditional *and* the popular church style Catholicism—may push women to search for solutions to their problems in other contexts. According to Burdick, 'Progressive Catholic discourse presents domestic problems as secondary to the "really important" issues of the world beyond the household'.[21] Of the same issue, says Stoll, quoting the research of Elizabeth Brusco in Colombia, 'born-again religion helps Latin American women resocialize their men away from the destructive patterns of machismo in ways that may be far more effective than secular feminism'.[22]

All the above-mentioned perspectives on LT—LT as an intellectual current, LT as a social movement, or LT as a new way of ordering religion in relation to politics—offer ways of 'explaining' LT. Since the present work is consciously theological, I will give only a brief account of the political and ecclesiastical context of LT and then concentrate on more substantial—albeit not exclusively theological—issues, being well aware of the insufficiency of my approach in giving a comprehensive picture of a phenomenon as diverse and multifaceted as LT.

1.2 The History of Liberation Theology

1.2.1 *History of the Church in Latin America*

To understand Latin American history, especially the history of the church, it is indispensable to understand how Latin America became part of European expansion and Western Christianity in the first place. The roots of both contemporary conflicts on the continent and the different liberation movements and discourses, including LT, can be traced back to the conquest and the colonial period following it. Latin America is the largest area—a whole continent, or at least sub-continent—in the so-called Third World that has become both colonized and predominantly Christian.[23] According to Enrique Dussel, Latin America occupies a unique place in the history of Christianity, representing a new kind of Christianity: colonial or dependent Christianity. The peripheralization of Latin America, in general, is concomitant with its peripheralization within Christianity.[24]

Even the possibility of speaking of Latin America as one entity, with all its cultural richness and variation, is due to the conquest. Although the Spaniards did

20.   Burdick 1993 and 1994; Drogus 1995.
21.   Burdick 1992: 176; Stoll 1993: 8.
22.   Stoll 1993: 8.
23.   'We live at the same time in one of the most Christian lands and in one of the most inhuman ones. We cannot escape the question of the connection between both facts' (Segundo 1985a: 20).
24.   Goizueta 1988: 62.

not 'discover' America, 'America' as we know it did not exist before the Spanish colonization. Probably the best grounds for speaking of *one* Latin America are economic: the continent was made by force part of the global economy in the sixteenth century. The economic and political structures were made for the system to serve mainly people overseas, not the local inhabitants. This is why the conquest of America has been considered the single most important event in the birth of the modern global economy or the first event of the modern era in general.[25]

The administrative centralization was realized through the Council of the Indies (*Consejo de las Indias*) in Seville, Spain, where all the issues of the Spanish colonies were treated.[26] There was a very limited possibility for direct communication or trade among the colonies; everything happened through Spain. At the local level, the centralization was made effective through the viceroy and the *audiencias*, and the *encomienda* and *mita* systems, which made possible the use of the indigenous labour force practically without any limits.[27]

From the very beginning of the conquest, the Catholic Church acted as the 'Second Estate', as the moral protector and legitimizer of the state, and as one of the principal agents of the civil power for over three centuries. It was really as late as the 1960s when a radical change took place in the relationship between the church and the state. It was preceded, though, by a break in the alliance between the church and the state during the independence of the Latin American countries, and by a respective weakening of the church. Thus, even a limited autonomy of the church is historically a quite recent phenomenon in Latin America.[28]

A central and indistinguishable element of the conquest was the missionary mentality of the Spanish Catholic monarchs and the Pope. This mentality functioned not only as the central motive of the conquest but also as a legitimization of it. In the 'Spanish messianism', the Spanish state and the Catholic monarchy, became God-chosen vehicles for the expansion of Christianity and evangelization of other cultures.[29] The leadership of the church voluntarily gave all power to the Spanish and Portuguese crowns in the questions of the American continent, in religious as well as secular matters. This total fusion of religious and secular power is known as the *Real Patronato de las Indias*, the Royal Patronage of the Indies. According to Mecham, 'Never before or since did a sovereign with the consent of the pope so completely control the Catholic Church as did the Spanish kings in their American possessions'.[30]

---

25.   The world-system theorist Immanuel Wallerstein speaks of the 'long' sixteenth century (1450–1640) as the period of the emergence of the European world economy (Wallerstein 1980: 2). See also Dussel 1995: 9-12; Pakkasvirta 1992: 23-45; Teivainen 1992: 183 and 1994: 81.

26.   Keen and Wasserman 1988: 97.

27.   Keen and Wasserman 1988: 78-80, 97-99.

28.   Bethell 1986: 229-33; Lynch 1986: 527-30.

29.   Prien 1978: 73.

30.   Mecham 1936: 200.

Three papal bulls 'gave' the 'discovered' regions to the property of the Spanish crown. The church also conceded to the state the right and responsibility for the expansion of Christianity in America. This means that in all possible matters, the crown was above the church. The most important of these bulls are *Inter Caetera* (1493 by Pope Alexander VI), which conceded to the Catholic Kings the dominion of the Indies and the exclusive privilege of christianizing the natives, and *Universalis Ecclesiae* (1508 by Pope Julius II), which throughout the sixteenth century was interpreted as the principal documentary evidence of the legal right of the Spanish sovereigns to exercise jurisdiction over the Catholic Church in America.[31]

Modern discussion over which was the most central motive for the conquest—economic, military or religious—does not take into account how these are blended in the fifteenth-century mentality. The cross and the sword were the two arms of the conquest both theoretically and practically. Converting the native Americans to Christianity was simultaneously a juridical justification of the conquest.[32]

The church in America was thus totally, including economically, dependent on the Spanish state. The church leaders could not even communicate directly with Rome but had to do it through the Council of the Indies.[33] The preservation of Spanish power in America depended largely on the vitality of Catholicism which explains the constant preoccupation of the Spanish kings in protecting the patronage.[34]

It is not always remembered that since the early days of the conquest there were different opinions concerning the legitimacy and nature of the conquest, and especially the nature of the indigenous inhabitants of America. This debate, which was mostly of a theological and philosophical character, lasted throughout the sixteenth century.

It was the Dominican friars who started to question the use of force and violence by the Spaniards. They never questioned the conquest itself, not to speak of evangelization, but they did question the means of realizing it. In fact, their complaints had some, albeit minimal, effect, such as the so-called Burgos Laws (1512–14) and the so-called New Laws (*Leyes Nuevas*) in 1542. The most famous of these churchmen was Bartolomé de las Casas (1484–1566), who was later to be called 'the Apostle of the Indians'.[35]

---

31. Mecham 1936; Barnadas 1986: 512-13; Prien 1978: 124-26.
32. The discussion over the motives of the conquest and the nature of the 'Indians'—as they were erroneously called—and even how we should talk about the events 500 years ago (conquest, discovery, or encounter of two cultures) reached its peak in the *Quinto Centenario* debate in 1992. See Meléndez (ed.) 1992; Mires 1991; Pakkasvirta and Teivainen (eds.) 1992; Quesada and Zavala (eds.) 1991; Rivera Pagán 1991; Vuola 1992.
33. Mecham 1936: 201, 207; Prien 1978: 135.
34. Mecham 1936: 213.
35. Barnadas 1986: 513-14; Prien 1978: 170-79. It should be noted that there is a tendency among liberation theologians and historians sympathetic to LT to idealize personalities such as Bartolomé de las Casas. See Gutiérrez 1993 and Rivera Pagán 1991. A more critical

Both sides in the struggle for Spanish American independence (1808–25) sought the ideological and economic support of the Catholic Church. From the beginning, the church hierarchy for the most part supported the royalist cause and identified with the interests of Spain. The lower clergy were predominantly Creole and though divided, more inclined to support the independence.[36]

Notable among the individual priests who played outstanding roles in the struggle for independence were the subsequent national heroes Miguel Hidalgo y Costilla and José María Morelos in New Spain (Mexico).[37] Throughout most of the period of the revolutions and wars for independence, the papacy maintained its traditional alliance with the Spanish crown and its opposition to liberal revolution.[38]

The Catholic Church in America emerged from the struggle for independence seriously weakened: its intellectual position undermined, its colonial Spanish-dependent roots exposed and internally divided.[39] The new independent states, secular and liberal, confiscated church property, secularized education, restricted missionary work and separated the church and the state. The church lost much of its earlier legal, political and economic power. Latin American anticlerical liberals considered the church an enemy: the colonial and antiliberal Catholicism was the major obstacle to the creation of modern democratic states. This led to open hostilities in Mexico. In this chaotic situation, the church turned to the conservative parties in search of support. Thus, Catholicism became the main ideology of Latin American conservatives.[40]

Gradually, in the last quarter of the nineteenth century, the church adjusted itself to the secular state and began a process of independent development. The conservative trend which culminated in the *Syllabus of Errors* in 1864 (condemning liberalism, secularism and freedom of thought and religion) and in the First

historiography on Latin America tends at least to problematize the activities of the early critics of the Spanish conquest. See Hanke 1965. The most critical attitude considers the 'Lascasian' kind of theology and activity as an intrinsic part of the colonializing, paternalistic European mentality that served as the spinal column of the conquest itself. According to this view, it is impossible to be different and equal at the same time. See Seed 1993 and Todorov 1984.

36.   Bethell 1986: 229.

37.   Anna 1986: 61-68. Hidalgo is remembered in modern Mexico as 'the father of independence'. Both priests made the Virgin of Guadalupe the rebellion's guardian and protectress. See Chapter 3.4.

38.   Bethell 1986: 230; Lynch 1986: 528.

39.   Lynch 1986: 527. See also Batllori 1967: 441. It could even be claimed that Latin American Creole intellectuals participated in the *birth* of modernization. The counter-revolutionary Europe in the spirit of the Holy Alliance was not the centre of modernization. Europe was still a continent of monarchies when the Latin American republics were born. See Pakkasvirta 1996.

40.   Lynch 1986: 528-31. The major disagreements between Latin American liberals and conservatives concerning religion were on the separation of the church and the state and the secularization of education and marriage. Conservatives generally were for the preservation of Hispanic traditions and values, seeing the Catholic Church as the main defender and representative of them.

Vatican Council in 1869–70 (reinforcing papal authority) nevertheless had to give way to more reformatory ideas at the end of the century. This is the time when Social Catholicism was born.[41] The encyclical *Rerum Novarum* in 1891 by Pope Leo XIII was a new statement of Catholic social thought, opening the way to lay activism, concern for social justice and political parties inspired by Catholicism.[42] The Catholic Action (*Acción Católica*) lay movement, formed at the end of the First World War in Europe, was to have a great influence on the early formation of LT.[43]

The alliance of the altar and the throne, of the church and the state, was gone forever, thanks less to Catholics themselves than to liberals, but in any case leaving the church free for future development. A colonial, dependent church had started to become independent. This process also partly enabled the church to speak more clearly for the poor and the oppressed.[44] In this way, the efforts of liberation theologians in the second half of the twentieth century to create a truly Latin American indigenous theology can be said to have its early roots in these dramatic changes in the church and state relations half a century earlier.

By 1900, a new structure of dependency, or colonialism, called neocolonialism, had arisen, with Great Britain and later the United States replacing Spain and Portugal as the dominant power in the area. This is why it may be called 'neo-colonial'.[45] The neocolonial order evolved within the framework of the trad-itional system of land tenure and labour relations. Indeed, it led to an expansion of the *hacienda* (great landowners) system on a scale far greater than the colonial period had known.[46] The unresolved questions of uneven land tenure and agra-rian reform have been the key issues in social and political conflicts up to the

41. Lynch 1986: 531, 562, 584-85.

42. Lynch 1986: 586-87; Lehmann 1990: 88-90. According to Lehmann, the encyclical laid the foundations of both Catholic Action and Christian Democracy.

43. See Lehmann 1990: 91-92.

44. Lynch 1986: 595. According to Keogh, 'The struggle by the Church to distance itself from the State has been a feature of a Catholicism reacting to the liberalism of the nineteenth century. There was a clerical comfort with political conservatism which formed a bridge between colonial Latin America and twentieth-century oligarchical rule. The profundity of the present conflict within the Catholic Church in Latin America is traceable to a religion which has ceased to play its traditional role in society. The traditional alliance between conservatism and Catholicism has been challenged by the new theological visions ' (Keogh 1990: 398-99).

45. Keen and Wasserman 1988: 172, 208. In 1900, the Uruguayan writer José Enrique Rodó published a short essay which had an immense influence on Spanish American intellectuals for two decades. Rodó's 'Ariel' evoked a Latin American 'spirit', and, identifying it with a revised sense of race, the essay inspired a reaffirmation of the humanistic values in Latin American culture. It included an indictment of the utilitarianism and pragmatism of the United States. It provided Latin American intellectuals with a basis for differentiating 'their' America. The 'arielists' did this by referring to the superior values of the Hispanic, that is, European, culture, of which, obviously, the Catholic religion forms an essential part. Whether this turn 'back to the roots' against North American imperialism by the Latin American intellectuals also served the recovery and re-strengthening of the Catholic Church from its nineteenth-century crisis is an issue to be investigated. On arielism, see Hale 1986: 414-22.

46. Keen and Wasserman 1988: 208.

present day. The demand for land for the vast impoverished rural population has been at the heart of both the Mexican and Nicaraguan revolutions, as well as of the Central American wars of the 1980s.

The first decades of the twentieth century were a time of the consolidation of North American hegemony in the region: several military interventions, the building of the Panama Canal and its falling into the hands of the United States, and the spreading of North American corporations to different parts of the continent. The first of Latin America's three revolutions in this century started in Mexico in 1910. The new Mexican constitution in 1917 had devastating effects for the Catholic Church.[47]

In the 1930s and 1940s a strong wave of populism[48] rose in Latin America. The roots of this populism were national, based on claims for social reforms and larger political participation. In the background, there was a strong belief in 'development' and the possibility of a national capitalist economy. Increasing capital and developing technology in the post-war European way would bring prosperity and 'development' to the poor countries as well. In Latin America, the foreign capital has always worked together with local landowning upper classes (oligarchies). Thus, in many countries a rise in the gross national product has been accompanied by impoverishment in the living standards of the people. Practically nothing was done to promote agrarian reforms.[49]

The failure to modernize archaic agrarian structures and improve income distribution also held back industrialization. The new industrial and financial oligarchies were fearful of social change. In the 1950s, a number of leading Latin American countries moved to the right.[50] The crisis of populism and the loss of belief in development, together with the Cold War political situation, prepared the path for military dictatorships backed by the United States, legitimized by the ideology of national security. Their main characteristics were a strong military,

47.   On the Mexican revolution and the church, see Beteta 1950: 80, 233-34; Lynch 1986: 590-94; Meyer and Sherman 1987: 543, 574; Prien 1978: 942-64.

48.   In Latin America, populism refers primarily to the Brazilian *Estado Nôvo* (New State) project of the president Getulio Vargas in the 1930s and Argentinian Peronism from the 1940s onwards (President Juan D. Perón), and to a certain extent also to reformist movements such as APRA (*Alianza Popular Revolucionaria Americana*) in Peru and Evita Perón in Argentina. Through these projects and their charismatic leaders, politics became more personalized and was brought closer to the masses. The liberal politicians sought a broader popular base for their political power by appearing as the defenders of the poor masses. According to Prien, 'Der "*populismo*" ist ein Ausdruck der Krise der Oligarchie, die, gezwungen durch die sozio-ökonomischen Umwälzungen, sich die Macht durch die Freigabe eines gewissen Demokratisierungsprozesses zu sichern suchte. Zugleich ist der "*populismo*" Ausdruck der Schwächen der herrschenden urbanen politischen Gruppen in der Auseinandersetzung mit den oligarchischen Gruppen im nationalistischen, kapitalistischen Entwicklungsprozess. Schliesslich ist der "*populismo*" vor allem Ausdruck der Entstehung organisierter, unterprivilegierter Gruppen der städtischen Massen, um deren Unterstützung sich die herrschenden Gruppen bemühen' (Prien 1978: 513-14). See also Keen and Wasserman 1988: 268.

49.   Keen and Wasserman 1988: 267.

50.   Keen and Wasserman 1988: 268.

often directed against the national opposition, cooperation with multinational corporations, anticommunism, and the military and economic support of the United States. This became especially clear after the Cuban revolution.[51]

Violations of human rights, increasing poverty and repression led to the rise of peasant revolts and, later, insurgent movements all over the continent.[52] The only remaining solution was seen to be in radical structural changes. After 'developmentalism' (*desarrollismo*) and ECLA's structuralism,[53] the dependency theory became the main intellectual analysis of the Latin American situation. According to the dependency theory, the Third World countries are not really economically and politically independent in spite of a formal political independence. The main reason for the poverty of the periphery—the Third World—is its dependency on the centre, the industrialized countries. The economic development of the countries of the centre and the 'underdevelopment' of the countries of the periphery are in fact two sides of the same coin. It is not possible to get rid of the dependency by 'development' but by radical changes in the international economic system.[54] The dependency theory has had a strong influence on most liberation theologians in their analysis of the oppression of their people. According to Hugo Assmann, 'the starting point for a "theology of liberation" is the historical situation of dependency and domination in which the people of the "Third World" live'.[55] It could even be claimed that the dependency theory is the single most important political theory in the formation of LT.

Many Christians, even some priests, joined the insurgent guerrilla movements of their countries. In this process, some lost their faith and left the church, being unable to combine their religious and political commitments, not in the reformatory way of the Christian democratic parties but in the service of a revolutionary process. For some, this kind of political, even military, activity appeared as a central ethical demand of the Christian faith. The most famous of the so-called guerrilla priests was the Colombian Camilo Torres who died in combat in 1966. Without doubt, the birth pangs of LT can partially be traced back to the inner conflict of these people.

Most liberation theologians claim that LT was born out of concrete experiences of Latin American Christians, most of them both poor and Christian. 'Liberation theology was born out of a pastoral mission, in other words, it was not conceived of a theory or in a laboratory, either. It was born out of a concrete necessity, to

51. Comblin 1979: 54.
52. Keen and Wasserman 1988: 268.
53. The Economic Commission for Latin America, a United Nations agency established in 1947 and located in Santiago, Chile. On the Latin American structuralist school of development, see Kay 1989: 25-57.
54. For a standard presentation of dependency theory, see especially Frank 1969. See also Kay, according to whom 'A key contribution of the Latin American school [of dependency] was the emphasis on the specificity of the peripheral countries and the insistence that new theories were required to explain their different structures, dynamics, and realities' (Kay 1989: 4).
55. Assmann 1971: 50. On the influence of the dependency theory on liberation theologians, see Cerutti Guldberg 1992: 68.

give theological and Christian support to committed Christians'.[56] LT was not seen as a direct religious legitimation of certain political practices, even though they would have been seen as just.

Certainly, LT can be seen as part of a larger liberation movement in Latin America. In no way does this mean only armed insurgent movements. In most cases the armed struggle was seen as the last resort. 'The original and constitutive fact of the Popular Church (*Iglesia Popular*) is the conscious participation of Christians in the popular movements of workers and peasants'.[57] Recent studies emphasize the fact that, seen from the perspective of the 1990s, LT and the popular church never became as influential—neither qualitatively nor quantitatively— as sources close to them have wanted to claim.[58]

56.   Segundo 1976: 93. In a later article, Segundo takes a slightly different point of view. In this (self)critical article, he states that the first stage of LT was born among the university students' movement in the early sixties. Thus, the context was the university, the middle-class people. It was not the oppressed people, but the middle classes, beginning with students, who received the first features of LT. See Segundo 1985a: 18-21. An opposite view is presented by Gustavo Gutiérrez: 'It is mistaken to maintain that this intelligence of faith was born in the middle classes, and that only years later was the experience of the poor themselves introduced. The truth is that their commitments, intentions to organize themselves, their models of living the faith, were present from the very beginning' (Gutiérrez 1990: 32-33).

I think most liberation theologians share the latter rather than the former view. However, the truth may lay somewhere between the two extremes. The wish of liberation theologians to present themselves as 'organic intellectuals' sometimes leads to an idealization of the role of the 'people' in discussions that simultaneously have their roots in immediate reality *and* are directed principally at other intellectuals, at home and abroad. Whatever the true balance between social classes in the creation of LT, it certainly is a complicated reality which should not be reduced to one or two principal factors.

Speaking of Latin America as a totality also has its dangers. There are great differences between Latin American countries. For example, the history of LT and the Church of the poor in Central American countries differs from that of the Andean and *Cono Sur* countries. It is neither possible nor meaningful in the context of this study to go into these differences in detail. Historically, the birth of LT coincides with the impoverishment of the middle classes all over the continent. Thus, putting 'the middle classes' and 'the poor masses' into total opposition with each other is unnecessary.

57.   Richard 1990: 66. The popular movement (*movimiento popular*) could also be translated as grassroots movement(s). According to McGovern, both LT and liberation movements grew out of the same historical context, but they had different origins and have different identities. LT and the base community movement had parallel but distinct histories of development. However, in Latin America, the developments in theology and in social movements cannot be separated entirely. McGovern 1989: 228.

58.   See Levine 1992. Levine realized an empirical study on base communities (CEBs) in Colombia and Venezuela. He presents a view of CEBs which is more nuanced than that usually offered, especially by researchers close to the LT movement. According to Levine, in practice the CEBs are much more conventionally religious than is commonly realized. To understand the phenomenon in all its richness (the CEBs are not just the stereotyped radical, liberation theology orientated religio-political groups) he creates a typology of CEBs. There are three types of CEBs: conservative, radical and sociocultural. Of these, the last is the one most likely to have a long-term influence on both the Latin American Church and society, as well as among the poorest of the population (Levine 1992: 46-51, 356-62. See also Burdick 1993 and 1994; Drogus 1995).

According to Lehmann, there are several elements of the ideological watershed of the late 1960s that aided the 'return of the church to centre stage': the renewal of Marxism, the rise of dependency theories, their attack on developmentalist economics and reformist politics, and the attack on mainstream bearers of Catholic social and political thought from a dissident Christian left. The Second Vatican Council and its effects in the Latin American church completed the picture.[59]

The successful revolution in Cuba in 1959 became the great inspiration for the insurgent and other revolutionary movements all over the continent. They no longer believed in the post-war developmentalist populist project. The Cuban revolution marks a turning point in Latin American modern history.[60] At the same time, preventing 'another Cuba' became the main motivation for US foreign policy in the region, especially in Central America and the Caribbean.[61] In countries such as Nicaragua, El Salvador, Guatemala, Colombia and Peru, this meant an open war between the government and the insurgent groups and also an increasing internal repression of opposition groups such as leftist and liberal reformist political parties, human rights organizations, churches and trade unions.

The 1970s was a decade of violence and military dictatorships in Latin America. From 1964 (the military coup in Brazil) until mid 1978, there were only six formal democracies left on the continent. The succession of military coups led to the most violent human rights violations. Thousands of persons 'disappeared' and were killed, many left their countries as political refugees, and any organized opposition, even in the form of moderate social-Christian parties, was met by even stronger measures of government and army violence. Imprisonments, torture, disappearances, killings and exile became reality even for many priests and nuns, as well as bishops.[62]

This kind of extreme violence fueled the tendency in the churches to move towards opposition to repressive governments and a stance in defence of human rights. The activities of the churches, or sectors of them, were increasingly defined as subversive by national military governments. At the same time, the church was often seen by the people as the only organization they could look to for support and assistance.[63]

Some outstanding bishops, such as Dom Evaristo Arns and Dom Helder Câmara of Brazil and Oscar Romero of El Salvador, became internationally

---

59.   Lehmann 1990: 108.
60.   Keen and Wasserman 1988: 269.
61.   Keen and Wasserman 1988: 269-70.
62.   See Bruneau 1979: 335.
63.   Bruneau 1979: 333. According to Alain Touraine and Sergio Spoerer, 'It is as if the Latin American Church today is going through a third phase in its history. In the first phase, the Church was an instrument of social and cultural control, particularly in the rural areas. In the second phase, the Church came closer to the people, showed aspirations for social change…and was very close to a particular political party (the Christian Democrats). In the third phase, the Church, living under dictatorships, is practically a surrogate for democracy and all that democracy stands for' (Touraine and Spoerer 1978: 11).

known for their defence of human rights. Nevertheless, the opposite also is true. In other countries, the leadership of the church either stayed outside the conflict or even openly supported military juntas. This inner conflict of the church went through the whole institution, from the top down to the grassroots level.[64]

In 1979 the Sandinista Revolution in Nicaragua marked a new turning point. Compared to the Cuban revolution, the Sandinistas represented ideologically a new kind of revolutionary thinking.[65] The triumph of a popular insurrection against one of the most dreaded dictators of modern Latin America was backed by almost all sectors of society. It gave new hope for possibilities of a radical change in other parts of the continent as well. The Sandinista revolution also marks the start of a process of democratization in Central America.[66]

The 1980s saw the gradual process of democratization in practically all of the Latin American countries. In Central America, former guerrilla organizations now participate in democratic elections as political parties. The changes in international relationships and the final end of the cold war have had their effect in Latin America, too. Politically, the United States has lost its security policy argument on Latin America, especially Central America and the Caribbean, as the 'Soviet satellite'. Since there are no internationally legitimate reasons for supporting anti-democratic tendencies in Latin America, in the 1990s the US government has opted for the support of local peace processes.[67] The prominent role of the church in the establishment of democracy in various countries is recognized. This is especially true in the issues of human rights and objection to repressive military governments, often by protecting grassroots democratic organizing under the auspices of the church's own structures.[68]

Economically, there has not been much change for the vast majority of Latin Americans. In the 1990s, the strong tendency towards structural adjustment

64. According to Mainwaring and Wilde, 'As it [the Church] identified more closely with suffering in society, it took more of that suffering into itself and became more sharply divided internally... As it distanced itself from established power, it gained both political visibility and social authority' (Mainwaring and Wilde 1989: 1-2).

65. 'The originality of the Sandinista regime, with its mix of socialism and private enterprise, of Marxism and progressive Catholic thought, suggested the varied forms that social revolution could assume in Latin America' (Keen and Wasserman 1988: 272). Or 'Los objetivos medulares del nuevo gobierno eran la construcción de una democracia pluralista, mantener un sistema económico mixto y una política internacional de no alineamiento a ninguna de las potencias entonces imperantes' (Fonseca 1996: 278-79). According to Cleary, the Nicaraguan revolution can be characterized as nationalist, Marxist and Christian in inspiration, even though it did not employ these three elements in equal measure (Cleary 1992: 212). On the Sandinista revolution, see Castañeda 1993: 125-32; Dunkerley 1990; Hodges 1986: 184-96; Torres-Rivas (ed.) 1993: VI, 67-78.

66. See Fonseca 1996: 280.

67. The Central American peace process, culminating in the peace treaty Esquipulas II in 1987, was a Latin American initiative which the Reagan administration did not support. See Torres-Rivas (ed.) 1993: 25-26.

68. See Cleary 1992: 203-204, 209.

programmes and economic integration has meant a process of ever-deepening poverty for the poorest people.[69]

1.2.2 *The Birth of Liberation Theology*
The Argentinian historian and philosopher-theologian Enrique Dussel presents the history of Latin American theology in six stages. First, during the time of the conquest and Christianization of America, there was on the one hand the dominant Catholic theology and on the other hand the prophetic theology against it—for example, Bartolomé de las Casas (1492–1577). Secondly, there was the colonial Christendom (1533–1808) and, thirdly, the practical-political theology (1808–31). The fourth phase was the conservative neocolonial theology (1831–1931), the fifth the theology of 'Neo-Christendom' (1930–62) and, finally, the phase of liberation theology (1962–).[70]

The purpose of Dussel is to 'rewrite' the history of the church in order to periodize it after models other than the dominant European perspective on other peoples' history. The problem with the specific case of Latin America is that it is practically impossible to 'separate' the interests of Spain from the interests of 'the Latin Americans'. Several historians who are also 'rewriting' the history of Latin America are much more critical than Dussel of personalities such as Las Casas.[71] The early Spanish critics of their fellow countrymen were critical of *some* aspects of the conquest but never questioned the enterprise as such. The evangelization of the natives should happen without violence, but it should happen anyway.

Similarly, it is questionable if one can give LT such a post-1960s hegemonic status as to name a whole period after it, because LT and its practical dimensions (the CEBs, the so-called popular church) never were a majority tendency in the church. Without doubt, LT presents a new phase in the relations between the church and the state, between theology and society, and in the reorientation of Christian churches in the modern world. Still, it has always remained a minority voice in the church and in theology as well as in Latin American societies.

Speaking about the social and political participation of the Christians in the 1960s, one also has to take into account the changes within the Catholic Church and developments in modern theology, both Catholic and Protestant. Modern European theology, especially the political theology of Johann Babtist Metz (Catholic) and the theology of hope of Jürgen Moltmann (Protestant), as well as the theology of revolution, have had their intellectual influence on LT, as developed both in Europe (Trutz Rendtorff and Heinz Eduard Tödt) and in

69. See Castañeda 1993: 11-13.
70. Dussel 1981: 332-33. In another text, speaking about the history of the church in Latin America, Dussel reduces these stages to three: (1) Colonial Christendom (1492–1808), (2) Crisis of the Christendom (1808–1950) and (3) The popular church (1950–). 'The Christendom' (*la cristiandad*), distinguished from 'Christianity' (*el cristianismo*), is a model of relationships between the church and the society, especially the state, where the church defines itself basically through the state (the colonial model). Dussel 1982: 93-95.
71. See Seed 1993; Teivainen 1994: 81-83; Todorov 1984, especially 162-67; Vuola 1992.

North America (Richard Shaull).[72] It did not take much time before liberation theologians started a major dispute with their European colleagues.[73]

The Second Vatican Council (1962–65) was the culmination of a process of 'modernization' in the Catholic Church and of a 'theology of development'. The Council was going to have its strongest effect in Latin America,[74] but 'the great ecclesiastical and theological events in the universal church of the years 1962–68 were taken up and interpreted in Latin America from a different social and political practice than the Central European one'.[75] The new active role of the church in society and the empowering of the laity evoked a strong response in the Latin American church. At Vatican II, it was insisted that the church stand in defence of human rights, that authority lines within the church be redrawn to give greater responsibility to the laity, and that the church actively promote social justice as an integral part of its mission.[76] All Catholics were urged to scrutinize 'the signs of the times'.[77]

The most important Council document for the Latin Americans has been the Dogmatic Constitution on the church, *Lumen Gentium*, where both the poverty of the church and its option for the poor have a Christological foundation.[78] Also, the papal encyclicals of Pope John XXIII (*Pacem in Terris*, 1963) and Pope Paul VI (*Populorum Progressio*, 1967) were interpreted as new moments in the Catholic social teaching.[79]

The most immediate response to both the Council and the participation of Christians in revolutionary movements in Latin America came from the second Latin American Bishops' Conference (*Conferencia Episcopal Latinoamericana*,

---

72. 'Nachdem der revolutionäre Kampf in Lateinamerika in 1965 seinen Höhepunkt erreicht hatte, tauchte 1966 im Zusammenhang mit der Genfer Konferenz für Kirche und Gesellschaft der Begriff der "Theologie der Revolution" auf, einer Theologie, die ursprünglich nicht von lateinamerikanischen Theologen entwickelt war, die aber in Lateinamerika Widerhall fand' (Prien 1978: 897).

Shaull is still a well-known and respected theologian in Latin America. He participates in conferences and meetings, as well as teaches at theological institutions there. His latest book is on reformation and LT, based on the 'new ecumenism' between Latin American Catholics and Protestants, inspired by LT, who 'find that they are closer to each other than they are to members of their own confession'. See Shaull 1991: 21.

73. See Chopp 1989 for a qualitative comparative study between European political theology and Latin American LT. According to her, one point of convergence between them is anthropocentrism: the content and meaning of the Christian faith are interpreted in response to problems of modernity, both at the individual and collective level.

74. Levine 1986: 8-13; Bruneau 1979: 332.

75. Lois 1988: 31, quoting Pablo Richard.

76. Mainwaring and Wilde 1989: 8. See also Lehmann *et al.* 1977: 108-109; Levine 1986: 8-9; Nash 1975: 85-91, 112-13. On Vatican II and its meaning for LT, see also Hennelly (ed.) 1990: 39-42.

77. Lehmann *et al.* 1977: 176.

78. Lois 1988: 25. See also Nash 1975: 192-93. Hennelly states that 'Of primary importance was The Pastoral Constitution of the Church in the Modern World (*Gaudium et Spes*)' (Hennelly [ed.] 1990: 40).

79. Lehmann *et al.* 1977: 176; McGovern 1989: 5; Prien 1978: 895.

CELAM) in Medellín, Colombia, in 1968. Even though it is not totally correct to consider this conference the starting point for LT—as is often done—nobody can doubt the tremendous significance the conference has had on the Latin American church up to the present.[80] It is perhaps best understood as a culmination point and Latin American interpretation of a process in the Catholic Church worldwide started at Vatican II.[81] At the Medellín conference, for the first time in the history of Latin America, the Catholic Church as an institution critically analysed the socio-economic and political reality of the continent.[82] The documents of Medellín, and to some extent those of the CELAM Puebla conference (1979), are the only official church documents along liberation theological lines that the Latin American Catholic Church *as a continental institution* has produced and accepted.

The bishops declared the situation of injustice to be a situation of *institutionalized violence*.[83] The church itself has been an accomplice in this situation. Liberation from the sin of poverty implies that the church itself has to become a church of the poor.[84] In Medellín this commitment was called *the preferential option for the poor (opción preferencial por los pobres)*. Pastorally, the primary obligation of the church must be the poor and the oppressed.[85] Theoretically, this means openness

80. 'Diese Konferenz, die an Bedeutung sogar das berühmte *Limense III* (1582–83) übertrifft, ist als das wichtigste konziliare Ereignis in der Geschichte der lateinamerikanishen Kirche anzusehen' (Dussel 1992b: 30). See also Bruneau 1979: 333; Hennelly (ed.) 1990: 89.

81. According to Gutiérrez, in the concrete question of poverty, Vatican II was a disappointment: 'desde la primera sesión conciliar el tema de la pobreza estuvo presente. […] El resultado final no correspondió a las expectativas. El Vaticano II alude varias veces a la pobreza pero no hace de ella una de sus líneas de fuerza' (Gutiérrez 1990: 321-22). He hints that it was the Medellín conference of Latin American bishops in 1968 that made the qualitative leap forward in the issue of poverty and the church. See Gutiérrez 1990: 155-74, especially 172.

82. On the Medellín conference, see Berryman 1987: 22-24; *Documentos de Medellín* 1969; Hennelly (ed.) 1990: 89-119; Levine 1986: 10-12. According to Lois, 'Sin Medellín y el impulso que su celebración supuso para la vida de la Iglesia y para la reflexión teológica, toda la posterior vitalidad del cristianismo en América Latina sería difícil de explicar' (Lois 1988: 39).

83. 'No deja de ver que América Latina se encuentra en muchas partes ante una situación de injusticia que puede llamarse de violencia institucionalizada, porque las estructuras actuales violan derechos fundamentales, situación que exige transformaciones globales, audaces, urgentes y profundamente renovadoras' (*Documentos de Medellín* 1969: 23). On the Medellín documents, see also Dillon 1979: 399; Hennelly (ed.) 1990: 89-119.

84. *Documentos de Medellín* 1969: 84-88.

85. 'Frente a las tensiones que conspiran contra la paz, llegando incluso a insinuar la tentación de la violencia; frente a la concepción cristiana de la paz que se ha descrito, creemos que el Episcopado Latinoamericano no puede eximirse de asumir responsabilidades bien concretas. Porque crear un orden social justo, sin el cual la paz es ilusoria, es una tarea eminentemente cristiana' (*Documentos de Medellín* 1969: 25).

The International Theological Commission puts it this way: 'Der Christ sieht in diesen "Zeichen der Zeit" im Lichte des Evangeliums elementare Herausforderungen, um im Namen des christlichen Gewissens alles zu tun, um diese Brüder aus ihren unmenschlichen Lebensbedingungen zu befreien. Diese Option für die Armen und die Solidarität mit allen Unterdrückten gewinnen eine besondere Leuchtkraft und Verdichtung in einigen Schlüsselworten, die

to the social sciences and their analysis of the structures that produce poverty, at that time especially the 'situation of dependency'. Theologically, it means going back to the Bible, its prophetic tradition and, above all, Jesus' teaching and practice.[86]

According to the bishops, peace is above all justice. It is something that has to be realized permanently. In Latin America a situation of 'institutionalized violence' prevails, since actual structures of society are violating fundamental human rights. This situation requires transformation, which is also a Christian responsibility.[87] According to Gustavo Gutiérrez,

> The denunciation of social injustices is certainly the most constant theme in the texts of the Latin American church... The denunciation of injustice implies the rejection of the use of Christianity to legitimize the established order. It also implies, in fact, that the church enters into conflict with those who wield power.[88]

The bishops also denounce imperialism and the excessive inequalities between the rich and the poor.[89]

If poverty is understood as a structural injustice, one also has to accept the logical consequences: poverty is not going to disappear with charity but through structural (that is, political and economic) changes.[90] There is an obvious influence of liberation theologians such as Gustavo Gutiérrez in the final document of the conference, especially in the section on poverty.[91]

Obviously, Medellín is a landmark in the history of the Latin American church. 'From a church that was theologically and pastorally dependent on Europe, it changed over to a church with theological and pastoral themes and elaborations of its own, at least in an initial form'.[92]

---

der biblischen Sprache angehören: Gerechtigkeit, Befreiung, Hoffnung, Friede' (Lehmann *et al.* 1977: 176-77).

86.   '...habrá que recalcar con fuerza que el ejemplo y la enseñanza de Jesús, la situación angustiosa de millones de pobres en América Latina, las apremiantes exhortaciones del Papa y del Concilio, ponen a la Iglesia Latinoamericana ante un desafío y una misión que no puede soslayar y al que debe responder con diligencia y audacia adecuada a la urgencia de los tiempos. Cristo nuestro Salvador, no sólo amó a los pobres, sino que "siendo rico se hizo pobre", vivió en pobreza, centró su misión en el anuncio a los pobres, de su liberación y fundó su Iglesia como signo de esa pobreza entre los hombres' (*Documentos de Medellín* 1969: 85).

87.   *Documentos de Medellín* 1969: 22-23.

88.   'La denuncia de las injusticias sociales es ciertamente la línea de fuerza más constante en los textos de la Iglesia latinoamericana... La denuncia de la injusticia implica que se rechace la utilización del cristianismo para legitimar el orden establecido; implica también, de hecho, que la Iglesia entra en conflicto con quienes detentan el poder' (Gutiérrez 1990: 168-69).

89.   *Documentos de Medellín* 1969: 21, 25.

90.   Though not expressed literally in this way, this emphasis is clear in the document. 'Debemos agudizar la conciencia del deber de solidaridad con los pobres, a que la caridad nos lleva. Esta solidaridad ha de significar el hacer nuestros sus problemas y sus luchas, el saber hablar por ellos. Esto ha de concretarse en la denuncia de la injusticia y la opresión, en la lucha contra la intolerable situación que soporta con frecuencia el pobre' (*Documentos de Medellín* 1969: 86).

91.   Berryman 1987: 24; Lois 1988: 38; Schutte 1993: 266.

92.   Oliveros 1989: 91. Oliveros divides the development of LT into three stages: (1) Genesis

In spite of the tremendous historical weight of Catholicism in Latin America, since its origins LT has had a Protestant presence and influence. Some of the first liberation theologians were Protestants: for example Rubem Alves (whose doctoral dissertation, *A Theology of Human Hope*, from Princeton Theological Seminary was published in 1969, two years before Gutiérrez' *Teología de la liberación*), Julio de Santa Ana, and José Miguez Bonino. Institutionally, there were changes in the historical Protestant churches[93] similar to those on the Catholic side. Of special importance have been the First Latin American Congress on Evangelization (*El Congreso Latinoamericano de Evangelización*) in 1969, in Bogotá, something like 'the Protestant Medellín', and the Third Latin American Evangelical Conference (*Conferencia Evangélica Latinoamericana*), also in 1969, in Buenos Aires.[94]

Some ecumenical groups of Protestant origin were important in the development of modern Protestantism, also in liberation theological directions, in Latin America, one example being *Iglesia y Sociedad en América Latina* (ISAL). The Council of Latin American Churches (*Consejo Latinoamericano de Iglesias*, CLAI), the coordinating ecumenical body of the historical Protestant churches on the continent, was founded in 1982 and has since its foundation seen as one of its duties the promotion of justice.[95]

Internationally, the influence of the World Council of Churches (WCC) has been important. At its general assembly in Uppsala in 1968, the same year as

(1968–70), (2) Growth (1971–79) and (3) Consolidation (1979). According to him, other important moments, besides Medellín, in the development of LT are the El Escorial meeting in 1972 between Latin American and European theologians, the meeting in Mexico in August 1975 where the methodology of LT was discussed, the Detroit meeting the same year between North American and Latin American theologians, and the first EATWOT meeting in Dar es Salaam in 1976 (Oliveros 1989: 89-107). All the papers presented at these conferences have been published as books. With a slightly different emphasis, Rosino Gibellini presents the same process as: (1) The preparatory phase (1962–68), (2) The formative phase (1968–75), and (3) The systematizing phase (from 1976–). The last phase starts with the formation of EATWOT in 1976, when LT found a place in the broader context of Third World theology. Published for the first time in 1987, Gibellini's book does not give any characterizations of later developments (Gibellini 1988: 1-2). See also Boff and Boff 1989: 84-87.

93. The term *iglesias históricas* refers to the 'old' Protestant churches that arrived in Latin America with European immigrants in the late nineteenth century, in contrast to the 'new' Protestant, especially Pentecostal, missionary churches.

94. Alvarez 1987: 255-56.

95. Alvarez 1987: 259; Adolf 1992: 41-42. It would make an interesting research to compare some of the Catholic and Protestant liberation theologians. Until now, the most important methodological, ethical and political viewpoints have been shared over confessional limits. The same is true in all liberation theologies, including feminist theology. It is tempting to think that while the churches in the First World are struggling with questions of orthodoxy, there is a living ecumenical orthopraxis in large parts of the Third World which may bridge the classical confessional disagreements on a practical level. Does this 'practical ecumenism' have implications on a more institutional and theological level, in the attempts of the churches at greater rapprochement?

Medellín, the theology of revolution played a central role.[96] Another important WCC meeting in this respect was the 'World Conference on Church and Society: Christian Response to the Technical and Social Revolutions of Our Time' (Geneva 1966).[97] The WCC has also given economic support for decades to both institutions and individuals (theological training with the help of WCC scholarships) close to LT.

The first big meeting of liberation theologians was held in 1972, the same year that a group called Christians for Socialism (*Cristianos por el socialismo*) came into being in Chile.[98] A little earlier, Gustavo Gutiérrez had published his *Teología de la liberación*, which came to be the founding text of LT. The concept 'liberation theology' was uttered for the first time in Chimbote, Peru, in 1968, by Gutiérrez himself. The seventies was the time of military dictatorships, increasing violations of human rights, and the 'disappearances' and the martyrdom of many committed Christians. But it was also the time when the 'popular church' or 'church of the poor' became more organized and LT became a strong and well-formulated theological movement. If LT was created and formulated between 1968 and 1972, the period from 1973 to 1979 was the time of its definite sedimentation and consolidation.[99]

After the Medellín conference, an influential part of the Catholic Church distanced itself from LT and the Church's commitment to the poor.[100] The inner division of the Catholic Church became more visible. In some countries, the ecclesial base communities and the bishops worked together; in others the Catholic hierarchy strongly condemned both the CEBs and LT as Marxist, incompatible with the Christian faith and the tradition of the church.[101] In 1972, the Colombian Alfonso López Trujillo was elected general secretary of CELAM. He represented the theological opposition to LT.[102] Under his leadership, CELAM has played a central role in the development of new directions for the

96. Nash 1975: 269-75, 314-30.

97. Nash 1975: 269-81.

98. Dussel 1981: 327.

99. Lois 1988: 46, 50. According to Hennelly, 'As regards liberation theology, I would evaluate this epoch [1968–1973] as the most creative in its entire history' (Hennelly [ed.] 1990: 121).

100. It is worth noting that there were sectors of the Church that never adhered to the conclusions of Medellín, the Colombian bishops, for instance. See Bruneau 1979: 333. According to Hennelly, 'It is more illuminating to view the period [1968–1973] as a time of extraordinary paradox or…of a curious dialectic between diffusion and resistance to the documents of Medellín… This was a period of enormous activity and vitality in order to spread the liberating message of Medellín from the Río Grande of Mexico to Cape Horn. At the same time, however, the period witnessed the emergence from the very beginning of a powerful and well-organized opposition to key directions of Medellín and to liberation theology, which had followed those directions' (Hennelly [ed.] 1990: 121).

101. Dussel 1982: 112-17.

102. See Beozzo 1992: 39-40; Hennelly (ed.) 1990: 123, 175-76; Keen and Wasserman 1988: 557; McGovern 1989: 12-15.

Catholic Church by becoming a force in support of the 'new restoration'.[103] CELAM became the main base of opposition to LT.[104]

The growing conflict between 'traditionalists' and 'progressives' concerning the role of the church prepared the way for the third CELAM conference in Puebla, Mexico, in 1979.[105] It was characterized by a conflict between these different groups.[106] The new Pope, John Paul II, opened the conference. According to some, the final document of the Puebla conference is a compromise,[107] while for others it clearly continued the line of Medellín.[108] The preferential option for the poor continued to be the option of the Latin American church. On the level of means, though, the church opts more for reforms than structural changes. This is also the basic line of the social doctrine of the Catholic Church.

The unity of the church emerged as an issue. It later became the main issue for the Vatican in Latin America. The church of the poor, that is, the CEBs, is seen as a parallel church, a threat to the unity that rests on the traditional hierarchy of the church (the pope, the bishops as the symbols and preservers of the unity) and on obedience to this hierarchy. This division or conflict inside the Latin American Catholic Church has since become very visible (for example in countries like Nicaragua in the 1980s where the Catholic hierarchy was directly opposed to the Sandinista revolution whereas the CEBs were some of the strongest foundations of the revolution itself, or Brazil, where the Vatican policy of nomination of bishops has been aimed at getting rid of bishops supportive of LT and the CEBs). Nevertheless, the Brazilian Leonardo Boff affirms that 'If Medellín was the baptism of our church, consecrated for the poor, for their organization in the ecclesial base communities and for their liberation, I believe that Puebla has been its confirmation'.[109]

The year 1979 marked the inception of a new period, politically as well as religiously. On the one hand, it saw the triumph of the Sandinista revolution in Nicaragua, in which Christian base communities played an important role. On the other hand, in the 1980s, Latin America seemed to be swept by a wave of democratization.[110] In the Catholic Church, the new Pope was elected. His

103.   Keogh 1990: 399.
104.   Houtart 1990: 78.
105.   Costello 1979: 337; Hennelly (ed.) 1990: 175.
106.   See Berryman 1987: 43-44, 77-78, 103-104; Dussel 1992b: 30; Keen and Wasserman 1988: 557; Levine 1986: 12-13. According to Berryman (1987: 103-104), the Puebla meeting could be seen as a clash between three mindsets among the bishops: the conservatives (stressing hierarchical authority and doctrinal orthodoxy and combatting LT), the liberationists (stressing the role of the CEBs), and the centrists, which was the largest group (concerned with church unity).
107.   Berryman 1987: 104; Dussel 1982: 116; McGovern 1989: 14.
108.   Keen and Wasserman 1988: 557. The final document of the conference is reprinted in Spanish in *Puebla: La evangelización en el presente y en el futuro de América Latina* 1979 and in English in Eagleson and Scharper (eds.) 1980. See also Hennelly (ed.) 1990: 225-58.
109.   Quoted by Lois 1988: 69.
110.   Mainwaring and Wilde 1989: 29.

influence in Latin America has been of major importance. When it comes to LT, the period after 1979 is marked both by theological maturation and a growing cooperation with other Third World and liberation theologies, especially in the forum of the EATWOT, founded in 1976. This globalization of the liberation theology movement has meant, among other things, new challenges for Latin American LT, especially as presented in the critique of some feminist and black theologians.

In August 1984, the Vatican Congregation for the Doctrine of the Faith, led by the German Cardinal Joseph Ratzinger, issued a document on 'certain aspects of liberation theology' that many groups and individuals interpreted as a virtual condemnation of LT.[111] A year later, the Vatican officially silenced Leonardo Boff, at that time still a Franciscan brother, for almost a year.[112] The critical reactions all over the Catholic world to these measures were somehow balanced in another Vatican document (1986) where both the theme of liberation and LT are seen in a more positive light.[113] Finally, a letter by John Paul II to the Brazilian bishops in April 1986 was seen as a conciliatory gesture, arousing a lot of enthusiasm among liberation theologians and the CEBs. The letter states that 'Liberation theology is not only opportune, but useful and necessary'.[114]

In practice, the actual Pope has strengthened a conservative tendency in the Latin American church.[115] One of his most powerful methods has been the nomination of bishops, which in countries like Brazil has meant the removal of almost all 'popular bishops' supportive of the CEBs and LT. They have been replaced by bishops who tend to emphasize the hierarchical structure of the church and want to avoid what they see as the politicization of religion.[116] Some scholars have

111. *Libertatis Nuntius* 1984. Among several other commentaries around the world, the always thorough Segundo wrote an entire book as a response to the accusations made by the Vatican. See Segundo 1985b. See also Hennelly (ed.) 1990: 393-414.

112. See Cox 1988; Hennelly (ed.) 1990: 425-34, where both the Vatican notification regarding Boff's theology and his response to it are reprinted.

113. *Libertatis Conscientia* 1986. See also Hennelly (ed.) 1990: 461-97. According to Anselm K. Min, the differences between the two documents are minor or accidental and should not be praised as a radical change in the Vatican policy concerning LT. Since the Vatican has been the most persistent critic of LT since 1978, and because of the institutional weight of the highest teaching authority of the Catholic Church, these documents should be taken seriously and analysed carefully. This is what Min does. According to his study, there is really no essential change between the two documents, especially theologically. The Vatican views and LT continue to be two irreconcilably opposed theologies. See Min 1989: 117-22.

114. Hennelly (ed.) 1990: 498-506; Oliveros 1989: 104; Min 1989: 119. Also here Min's interest is to show how minor and in fact superficial the possible change of attitude of the Vatican was.

115. According to Stewart-Gambino, the Pope's primary preoccupations with the Latin American church have been the defence of theological orthodoxy and the maintenance of traditional institutional authority patterns (Stewart-Gambino 1992: 4).

116. See Cleary 1992: 201; Keen and Wasserman 1988: 557; Mainwaring and Wilde 1989: 31; Stewart-Gambino 1992: 8. The conflicts and tensions between liberation theologians and the church hierarchy have been widely documented and commented on. Well-documented studies on different kinds of critique aimed at LT are McGovern 1989 and Min 1989. On the

noted, though, that the Vatican's influence has not been uniform. In several instances, John Paul II has called the church's attention to social issues as well as supported the 'preferential option for the poor'.[117]

The fourth Latin American Bishops' Conference organized by CELAM was held in Santo Domingo in October 1992, in the conflictive atmosphere of the 500th anniversary of the 'discovery' and evangelization of America. The final document is a mixture of opposing elements where it is difficult to find the main theme. The deep division inside the church was clear in the conference itself and is also reflected in the final document. LT is not mentioned in the document at all, nor does the document quote well-known liberation theologians.[118]

According to some observers, the inner division that had already been visible in Puebla was now added to by a conflict between Rome and the Latin American church, the North and the South. An attempt by the Vatican to control the conference caused protest and confusion.[119] This control was expressed, among other ways, in how the Vatican selected the three presidents of the assembly, all well known for their conservative tendencies. Additionally it controlled the editing commission and it also blocked the use of the text Second Report (*Secunda Relatio*, the most 'Latin American' of the document drafts, containing the proposals of national bishops' conferences for changes to the first draft) as a basis for the debate.[120]

Nevertheless, the Santo Domingo document itself, as well as the latest declarations of the Pope, affirm the preferential option for the poor and condemn

relationship of the Vatican to the Latin American Catholic Church, see several articles in part one of Keogh (ed.) 1990.

117.   Cleary 1992: 202.

118.   *Nueva evangelización, promoción humana, cultura cristiana*. IV Conferencia General del Episcopado Latinoamericano, Santo Domingo, 12–28 October 1992. Conclusiones. (A conference draft). See also Hennelly (ed.) 1993.

119.   Richard 1992: 2 and 1993: 2. According to Richard, in spite of the pressures, the Latin American church was successful in affirming its own identity and consciousness in Santo Domingo, against the rigid and authoritarian attitude of the Vatican. It must be asked, though, if this vision is too optimistic. Richard's own intention is to show how the Santo Domingo conference can be interpreted as being on the same continuum as Medellín and Puebla. He says: 'The fundamental issue of the Santo Domingo conference was the affirmation of the identity of the Church in Latin America and the Caribbean. This identity is in clear and explicit *continuity* with the earlier conferences of Medellín and Puebla, and it responds to the *practice of our churches of the last 30 years*' (Richard 1993: 2 [emphasis in original]). There are other more critical evaluations of the conference, with the Venezuelan Gladys Parentelli, one of the Latin American lay persons present in Vatican II, referring to the enthusiasm of earlier conferences: 'Medellín and Puebla documents contrast with the total indifference of the conclusions of the IV CELAM conference. This document does not respond to our reality, and there is an evident intervention of Rome in it' (Parentelli 1993: 5). She is especially critical of the document's view on Latin American women.

See also Hennelly (ed.) 1993 and Serbin 1992. According to the latter, 'Diverging from the line of Medellín and Puebla, many of the official conclusions of Santo Domingo have a decidedly spiritualist and abstract message' (Serbin 1992: 403).

120.   Sobrino 1993: 170-71.

the negative impacts of neoliberal politics on the poorest sections of the population.[121]

On the one hand, the great changes in theology and the church in Latin America during the last thirty years have been produced by the social, political, religious and economic conditions of the continent. On the other hand, these changes undoubtedly have had their share in the recent processes towards pacification and democratization in the region. Whatever the future directions in the religious field of Latin America will be, including the developments in LT, three issues are central.

First, the Catholic Church as an institution has forever lost its privileged but also dependent status in relation to the state. Its eventual role in the formation of civil society and democracy in Latin America, as well as internationally, depends much on its inner development, including theological development.

Second, the rapid change in religious power balance in Latin America is a well-known, albeit unpredictable, fact. What kind of effects will the rise of Protestantism have on the Catholic Church, the CEBs and liberation theology? How will they react to these changes?

Third, the fundamental issues that gave rise to LT—widespread poverty, human rights violations, and the globalization of a market economy with all its implications for ecology and the poorest sectors of Latin American societies—have not disappeared. Social scientists, liberation theologians and grassroots activists all agree that there is an urgent need for new, creative responses.

1.3 The Method in Liberation Theology

All liberation theologians emphasize that the innovation of LT lies not as much in its content as in its method. LT is 'a new way of doing theology'. What do the liberation theologians mean by that? What was the 'old' way?

One of the arguments of this work is that in spite of the diversity in how liberation theologians understand the praxis and the relation between theory and praxis, it is possible to speak of a liberation theological method that is different enough from the tradition. It is this method that defines LT as a theological paradigm. The praxis starting point, as elaborated in liberation theologies, represents a fundamental shift in the history of theology.[122]

---

121.   'El creciente empobrecimiento en el que están sumidos millones de hermanos nuestros hasta llegar a intolerables extremos de miseria es el más devastador y humillante flagelo que vive América Latina. Así lo denunciamos tanto en Medellín como en Puebla y hoy volvemos a hacerlo con preocupación y angustia… La política de corte neoliberal que predomina hoy en América Latina y el Caribe profundiza aún más las consecuencias negativas de estos mecanismos. Al desregular indiscriminadamente el mercado, eliminarse partes importantes de la legislación laboral y despedirse trabajadores, al reducirse los gastos sociales que protegían a las familias de trabajadores se han ahondado aún más las distancias en la sociedad' (*Nueva Evangelización* 1992: 52-53). 'Hacemos nuestro el clamor de los pobres. Asumimos con renovado ardor la opción evangélica preferencial por los pobres, en continuidad con Medellín y Puebla' (*Nueva Evangelización* 1992: 81).

122.   For example, according to Rebecca S. Chopp, in comparison to modern European

I shall first present the central methodological issues in LT as liberation theologians themselves understand them (Chapter 1.3) and then go into a more critical discussion of their possible limitations (Chapter 1.4).

1.3.1 *Theory and Praxis*
The relation between theory and praxis is central in LT's method. There is diversity among liberation theologians in how they understand this relation. There is no explicit consensus about it, and none of the different approaches can claim to be definitive. But all of the diverse viewpoints have something in common, and that is their attempt to employ the resources of the Christian tradition to come to grips with the present historical reality of Latin America.[123] In spite of the difficulty of presenting an overarching definition of how praxis is understood in LT, it is possible to characterize some of the general recurrent methodological elements that liberation theologians employ in their work.

In spite of my emphasis on methodology, hence the importance of praxis for liberation theologians, my aim is not to go into detail about the extensive and complex discussion on praxis. It is evident that since all the most influential liberation theologians spent several years in Europe in the political-intellectual atmosphere of the 1960s, the impact of those experiences is present in their work. LT's emphasis on praxis is not intelligible without the influence of the evolution in modern European philosophy and the social sciences.

The whole post-1960s discussion on praxis is interpreted in LT in the context of the socio-political and religious situation of Latin America and especially in the perspective of the marginalized poor masses of the continent. Thus, whatever the intellectual heritage liberation theologians have concerning their discussion on praxis, their specific and innovative perspective is that of the poor of Latin America. LT claims to *start* from this praxis and *return* to it by being pragmatic in

theology, 'Latin American liberation theology continues modern theology's concern for the subject, the representation of freedom by Christianity, and the experience of faith in history but, in a radical reformulation, defined the subject as the poor, reinterprets the freedom to include political self-determination, and envisions history as the arena for both liberation and redemption' (Chopp 1989: 19). She also says: 'Perhaps the most significant area of both agreement and disagreement between German political theology and Latin American liberation theology was the vision of faith acting in a *critical* relationship to the world... Latin American liberation theology located its disagreement with political theology in the dual issues of *how* the church should be a critical institution and the *nature* of theology as a political activity. Locating the critical activity of the church through its political, educational, and social activity with the poor, Latin American liberation theology committed itself not only to interpreting critically the world, in the tradition of its German counterpart political theology, but also to transforming that world' (Chopp 1989: 20 [emphasis in original]). Thus, she affirms that LT both continues and radically departs from modern theology (Chopp 1989: 153).

123. Nessan 1989: 56-57. According to McGovern, 'The differences [between liberation theologians], however, more often involve questions of emphasis rather than of conflicting approaches. All the major liberation theologians include some mention of praxis, of the use of social analysis, and of the need to question ideological elements in traditional presentations of the Christian message' (McGovern 1989: 24).

its application. Thus, *praxis is both a point of departure and an objective of LT.*[124]

Liberation theologians both use the concept praxis in the classical Marxist sense and specify it to connote Latin American historical, political and economic conditions, seen from the point of view of those most affected by them. Other theologies of liberation work in a similar way, when applying specific non-theological theories in theology. Black theology uses different theories of racism, feminist theological analysis of sexism is based on social theories of sexism, and so on. What different theologies of liberation have in common is their conviction of the need for some theory of society in order to bring about social change.[125]

In Marx, praxis refers to

> the free, universal, creative and self-creative activity through which man creates (makes, produces) and changes (shapes) his historical, human world and himself; an activity specific to man... In this sense man can be regarded as a being of praxis, 'praxis' as the central concept of Marxism, and Marxism as the 'philosophy' (or better: 'thinking') of 'praxis'.[126]

According to Richard Kilminster, praxis in Marx and in the writings of a number of philosophers in Western Marxism is

> (a) a type of creative practical activity peculiar to human beings whereby they construct their world, an idea basic to Marx's model of human nature; (b) an epistemological category describing the practical, object-constituting activity of human subjects as they confront nature, that Marx called 'practical, human sense activity'; and (c) as 'revolutionary praxis', the putative point of fundamental social transition.[127]

124.   Since LT is predominantly Catholic, it must be remembered that Catholic theology in general is more praxis-orientated or confessional than Protestant theology. The relationship between academic theology and Church practices is closer and more direct than in Protestant countries. My own context, non-confessional Scandinavian academic theology, is the other extreme, where academic theology has much less practical relationship or implications to the church or the society.

125.   On feminist theological understanding of praxis, see Chapter 2.3.

126.   Bottomore (ed.) 1988: 384. In Marx's writings, the concept is most pregnantly expressed in his *Theses on Feuerbach*, in which the term 'revolutionary praxis' is central. Sometimes he seems to suggest that theory should be regarded as one of the forms of praxis, but then he reaffirms the opposition between theory and praxis and insists on the primacy of praxis in this relationship. For a long time, Marx's original concept of praxis was forgotten or misinterpreted, largely because of Engels, who made only one of Marx's theses on praxis widespread, namely that praxis is a guarantee of reliable knowledge and the ultimate criterion of truth. This initiated the view that Marx was not a philosopher but a scientific theorist of history and a political economist. Later, the interpretation of Marxism as a 'philosophy of praxis' was put forward by Labriola, Gramsci, Lukács, Marcuse, the Yugoslavian Praxis Group, and the Frankfurt School (Bottomore [ed.] 1988: 386-89).

127.   Kilminster 1993: 507. He also says that 'Although the three separate Marxist senses [of praxis] have come to be established in modern social thought, the concept generally remains imprecise, obscure and elastic in its application' (Kilminster 1993).

The Cambridge Dictionary of Philosophy states that 'The central philosophical issues addressed in the current literature on praxis have to do with the theory-praxis relationship and the problems associated with a value-free science. The general thrust is that of undermining or subverting the

All three of these usages of praxis can be found in LT as a current of thought, albeit not necessarily in individual theologians. According to Kilminster, usage (b) has made a contribution to the growing realization of the social nature of the knowledge process,[128] which, again, has had its influence on liberation theologians.

According to Francis P. McHugh, Christian social theory can be viewed as a 'praxis', meaning that voluntarism and the purposive character of human conduct are stressed, which makes it primarily a theory of action. He mentions political theology and liberation theology as two recent forms of Christian social theory which have been developed in an attempt to break with received styles of political and economic thought, the former as a critical corrective to the tendency of contemporary theology to concentrate on the private individual, and the latter as an attempt to recover the social meaning of the Gospel for Third World countries engaged in the struggle for justice. Both of these have appropriated some existing forms of social theory (from Marx or Habermas, for example), along with the secularization which they usually entail.[129]

According to Craig L. Nessan,

> Praxis in liberation theology refers to a method which is exercised in a fluid interchange between thought and action, theory and practice. It is not the application of a preconceived theory upon practice but instead an encounter with historical reality which itself gives rise to thought within the context of engagement.[130]

For Stephen B. Bevans, 'the praxis model' is one of the five models of contextual theology as employed in modern theology today. These models point to various approaches being used in constructing contextual theology, but no model is exhaustive or applicable to all situations.[131] He warns of not confusing the term *praxis* with the words *practice* or *action*. Praxis is a technical term that has its roots in Marxism, in the Frankfurt School, and in the educational philosophy of Paulo Freire.[132] According to Bevans, in the praxis model 'Theology is done not simply by providing relevant expressions of Christian faith but also by commitment to Christian action. But even more than this, theology is understood as the product

---

traditional bifurcation of theory and praxis via a recognition of praxis-oriented endeavors that antedate both theory construction and the construal of practice as a mere application of theory. Both the project of "pure theory", which makes claims for a value-neutral standpoint, and the purely instrumentalist understanding of practice, as itself shorn of discernment and insight, are jettisoned' (Audi [ed.] 1996: 639).

128. Kilminster 1993: 508.

129. McHugh 1993: 70-73.

130. Nessan 1989: 119. Similarly, Goldstein says: 'Die Neuartigkeit der Theologie der Befreiung gegenüber anderen Theologien besteht in ihrem fünffachen Bezug zur Praxis: Der Theologe, der sie betreibt, steht (zumindest mit einem Teil seiner Arbeit) *in* der Praxis. Ein guter Teil ihrer Intuitionen erwächst *aus* der Praxis. Als Reflexion *über* die Praxis aus dem Glauben muss sie sich verantworten *gegenüber* dieser Praxis. Und schliesslich soll sie der Veränderung der Verhältnisse dienen: sie arbeitet also *für* die Praxis' (Goldstein 1991: 181 [emphasis in original]).

131. Bevans 1994: 26-28, 64-71.

132. Bevans 1994: 64.

of the continual dialogue of these two aspects of Christian life'.[133] Praxis is action with reflection.[134]

Although most writing about the praxis model has been by those who have taken liberation as a main concern, the model has wider applications, and it does not necessarily have to take on liberation themes.[135] Its strength lies in its potential to give ample room to cultural expressions of faith, while providing new understandings of the scriptural and older theological witness. It has deep roots in theological tradition, even though it has been criticized for its use of Marxist categories.[136]

According to Robert J. Schreiter, liberation theologians' usage of the term praxis goes back to Hegel and Marx. The modern usage of the term was begun by Hegel, and it is primarily he and Marx who have shaped the understanding of praxis prevalent in contemporary theology.[137] Schreiter says:

> As understood today, praxis is the ensemble of social relationships that include and determine the structures of social consciousness. Thus thought and theory are considered sets of relations within the larger network of social relationships. Theory represents a dialectical moment within practice, as does action. Theory's task is to illumine the exact nature of those social relationships. By so doing, theory can point to false and oppressive relationships within the social fabric... Since oppressive relationships occur in every society, and in many societies characterize the larger part of social life, praxis can come to be defined as a revolutionary or transformative praxis, aimed at the changing of those patterns.[138]

In theology, the theoretical moment includes reflection on how God is active in human history, bringing judgment and a transformative moment to history. Theology cannot be mere reflection nor can it be reduced to practice. According to Schreiter, this way of understanding theology is what is called liberation theology.[139] According to Schreiter, theology as praxis has three tasks. First, theology as praxis helps to disentangle true consciousness from false consciousness. Technically this is known as ideology critique, 'ideology' being a Marxist term for false consciousness. Second, theology as praxis has to be concerned with the ongoing reflection upon action. And third, theology as praxis is concerned with the motivation to sustain the transformative praxis.[140] Sociology of theology can clarify to us how theology as praxis is one way of responding to the question of how to be faithful both to the contemporary experience of the gospel and to the tradition of Christian life that has been received.[141]

---

133. Bevans 1994: 65.
134. Bevans 1994, quoting Phillip Berryman.
135. Bevans 1994: 66, 70.
136. Bevans 1994: 71.
137. Schreiter 1986: 91.
138. Schreiter 1986: 91.
139. Schreiter 1986: 91-92. Here he uses the term liberation theology in the wide sense, including black, feminist and other Third World theologies.
140. Schreiter 1986: 92.
141. Schreiter 1986: xi, 80.

According to Walter Kasper, most liberation theologians are not clear and explicit in their use of the central concept praxis, which, as we know, has a long history and several meanings.[142] Nevertheless, I am not going to 'locate' liberation theologians' use of praxis in the long historical perspective. The above quoted references to the specific liberation theological use of the concept should make clear that there is an evident influence of Marxist understanding of praxis in LT, filtered especially through such First World theological currents as theology of hope, theology of revolution and political theology.[143] In economic analysis, this influence is best seen in the use of the dependency theory in early LT.[144]

Also, the understanding of the contextual nature of knowledge as well as the hermeneutical circle between revelation and situation as constitutive of the religious praxis are some of the most discussed themes in modern European, especially German, Protestant theology (Tillich, for instance). Thus, the emphasis on contextuality and praxis is as such not something that the liberation theologians would have taken up for the first time in the history of theology. Instead, they give it a specific meaning in a specific context and, to a certain extent, radicalize it as a theological method. They give more importance to the community than to the individual, to the society in its entirety than to the role of the church in society. Further, in their analysis of society, liberation theologians reject any perspective that pretends to be ethically neutral. There are no neutral perspectives, since all perspectives are bound to certain interests. Liberation theologians make their perspective explicit: the poor and their interests.

142.   'Bei dem Begriff Praxis handelt es sich nämlich um einen äusserst vielschichtigen und vieldeutigen Begriff mit einer langen Begriffsgeschichte, angefangen von Aristoteles über die Patristik und Scholastik (besonders Duns Scotus) bis hin zu Kant, Hegel, und nicht zuletzt Marx. Leider wird dieser für sie zentrale, aber äusserts vieldeutige Begriff Praxis von meisten Befreiungstheolpgen kaum erklärt' (Kasper 1986: 85). With the Marxist use of the concept, the liberation theologians would, according to Kasper, make a far-reaching decision against metaphysics on behalf of the social sciences (Kasper 1986: 86).

143.   J.B. Metz sees both political theology and liberation theology as representatives of the same theological paradigm, that of a post-idealistic (nachidealistisch) paradigm, which competes with Neo-Scholastic and transcendental-idealistic paradigms in Catholic theology. There are three crises which have given birth to this paradigm: (1) the challenge of Marxism, (2) the challenge of the Third World, and (3) the challenge of the catastrophe of the poor. According to Metz, the first challenge, that of Marxism, has not been taken seriously enough in (Catholic) systematic theology. Thus, he presents a somewhat different view from those who claim that Marxist elements have a too extensive role in modern theology, especially in liberation theology. The challenge of Marxism to theology is in the question of truth (Wahrheitsfrage)—for example the relationship between knowledge and interest (Erkenntnis und Interesse)—and in the question of history, which along with that of truth is a foundational theme in Christianity (Metz 1986: 147-51). 'Die nachidealistische Theologie, zu der die Befreiungstheologie gehört, sucht sich zentralen Herausforderungen des Marxismus zu stellen, ohne sich ihm zu unterwerfen. Sie ist nicht dadurch politisch, dass die Religion einer fremden politischen Ideologie ausliefert, sondern dadurch, dass sie in der Religion die gefährliche Erinnerung an den messianischen Gott buchstabiert' (Metz 1986: 149).

144.   The philosophy and ethics of Emmanuel Levinas are also of special importance for many liberation theologians, most notably Enrique Dussel.

According to Rebecca S. Chopp,

> The rupturing claim of theological method [in LT] is twofold: liberation theology
> must find a way to uncover the distortions within modern theology and a way to
> transform theology in light of its new understanding of human existence and its new
> interpretation of Christianity. *Theological method in liberation theology is, then, nothing else*
> *than the double demand to think in new ways on a new subject.*[145]

There is a different theological method in LT, but it has a preliminary status and
it is in the first stages of formulation. For Chopp,

> Liberation theology is much more than some new variation of methodological
> finesse; rather, it is a paradigm shift in the context, the content, the experience, and
> the interpretation of Christianity... Indeed, rather than reading theological method
> in liberation theology as either a well-established, easily imitated operation or a non-
> substantive, popular-activist fad, it seems preferable to locate the initial steps of
> liberation theology's method within the broader attempts among a variety of
> disciplines for practical reflection. The status of 'newness' in liberation theology's
> method shares much in common with the status of current trends in a variety of
> disciplines seeking to understand their own foundations in praxis and concentrating
> attention on practical reason, reason as itself shaped by social practices.[146]

Although Chopp does not say it explicitly, the location of LT among other
similar approaches in other disciplines is exactly the point of convergence of LT
with feminist theory, including feminist theology. The anthropocentrism and
turn to praxis are shared as methodological starting points in all liberation
theologies.

Chopp's central claim—that LT presents a new paradigm shift in theology—
rests on four assumptions. First, LT asks a quite different question from that of
modern theology, the question of massive public suffering. Historical, human
suffering is the focus of attention in LT. In this question of suffering and this
speaking of God, a new paradigm shift is formed. LT risks a wager that only by
standing with those who suffer shall we see the reality of human existence
through their eyes and experience in their suffering a God of grace, of hope, and
of love.[147]

The second reason why LT is a new paradigm shift of theology is its orientation toward transformation rather than understanding as the reconciliation of
human existence and reality.[148] Together the question of suffering and the reality
of transformation lead to the third reason whereby LT differs from modern
theology: the emphasis on praxis.[149] Fourth, LT is a different understanding of
theological reflection. LT sees theology as *practical hermeneutics*, the ongoing appropriation of Christian tradition and human existence. Theology is also a *critical*

---

145.   Chopp 1989: 134 (emphasis added).
146.   Chopp 1989: 134-35.
147.   Chopp 1989: 151.
148.   Chopp 1989.
149.   Chopp 1989.

theory, a theory of emancipation. In LT, theology is also understood as a *social theory*, a theory of a definite praxis.[150]

The first and the most well-known definition of LT is made by the Peruvian Gustavo Gutiérrez, 'the father of liberation theology'. According to him, theology is *'the critical reflection on the praxis in the light of the Word of God accepted in faith'*.[151] Theology is reflection, a critical attitude to reality as it presents itself to us. For liberation theologians, this reality is first of all the massive poverty in Latin America and in the Third World. The reality challenges us to bring about a change. The specific challenge for Christians is in the relationship of faith and reality. The commitment to a change is what liberation theologians usually mean by praxis. In LT, faith is experienced historically as the praxis of liberation, which is 'the first step'. Theology is a second step.[152] The first step, the commitment, is not just any commitment, but the commitment to the Latin American poor and oppressed for their liberation. This was called 'the preferential option for the poor' at the Medellín conference.

To take the historical praxis—with all its possible aspects, including the political and the economic spheres—as the conscious starting point for theologizing is what the liberation theologians mean by 'the new way' of understanding and doing theology. LT is not as much 'new theology' or a 'genitive theology' that would take up 'liberation' as one theme among others as it is a 'new way of doing theology'.[153] The praxis—in Latin America, especially the commitment to the historical struggle of the poor and the oppressed for their liberation, is not just an ethical choice. It is the perspective, the 'from where' (*desde donde*) one thinks and acts as a theologian. 'To know' is to 'know from'. In the case of LT, from the perspective of the Latin American poor. Praxis is both the starting point and the aim for liberation theologians. There are practical and emancipatory interests that LT wants to serve, even though it would not see them as the only meaning and criterion of theology.

The praxis that Latin American theologians speak about is the liberating historical praxis. The existence of the millions of poor and oppressed is a fact, but

150.   Chopp 1989: 152-53 (emphasis added).

151.   'La reflexión teológica sería entonces, necesariamente, una crítica de la sociedad y de la Iglesia, en tanto que convocadas e interpeladas por la palabra de Dios; *una teoría crítica, a la luz de la palabra aceptada en la fe*, animada por una intención práctica e indisolublemente unida, por consiguiente, a la praxis histórica' (Gutiérrez 1990: 67 [emphasis added]).

What is meant by 'the Word of God' is not much explicated in LT. Other liberation theologies, most notably feminist theology, take a much more critical perspective on how the Word of God (the Scripture) has been influenced by surrounding culture and how it has been interpreted by the church during history. A critical study of biblical interpretation in LT is, however, beyond the scope of this research.

152.   'La teología es reflexión, actitud crítica. Lo primero es el compromiso de caridad, de servicio. La teología viene *después*, es acto segundo' (Gutiérrez 1990: 68 [emphasis in original]).

153.   'Por todo esto la teología de la liberación nos propone, tal vez, no tanto un nuevo tema para la reflexión, cuanto una *nueva manera* de hacer teología' (Gutiérrez 1990: 72 [emphasis in original]).

it is not this fact as such that forms the praxis. It is above all the struggle for liberation of these people, the commitment to the transformation of oppressive social structures, that forms the praxis. The reflection or theory, which for liberation theologians is theology, has to surge from this praxis.

According to Pablo Richard, Gutiérrez' use of the concept praxis has gone through three stages. At first it referred to the *pastoral practice of the church*. At a second stage, the focal point of reflection was not so much the pastoral practice as the *political practice of Christians*, the involvement of lay people, priests and the religious in the popular movement, in leftist parties, and even in guerrilla movements. At a third stage, theological reflection focused not only on the political practice of Christians but also on the *political practice in which the agent or subject was simply the popular class*. This last stage is when LT's theological method was developed: political practice was not a new object for theological reflection, but its starting point.[154]

For Gutiérrez, praxis is the conscious human action characterized as political activity that affects, not without conflict, the economic and sociocultural structures, aiming at the liberative transformation of human history, for which a historical project is required.[155]

Theory and praxis are not separate. Thus, the 'first' and 'second' steps LT speaks about are not to be understood in chronological order. The image of steps refers instead to the primacy of praxis over theory, orthopraxis over orthodoxy, and to the intimate, inseparable relation between the two.[156]

The dialectical nature of the theory-praxis relation is illustrated by Juan Luis Segundo in what he calls the *hermeneutic circle*. There are two preconditions for such a circle: profound and enriching questions and suspicions about reality; and a new interpretation of the Bible that is equally profound and enriching.[157] There are four decisive factors in the hermeneutic circle. First, there is our way of experiencing the reality, which leads us to ideological suspicion. Second, there is the application of the ideological suspicion to the whole ideological superstructure in general and to theology in particular. Third, there is the new way of

154. Richard 1987b: 147 (emphasis in original). In the years since this book was written, the praxis concept has inevitably gone through further modifications as LT has had to revise itself. As will become clear later in this work, 'the poor' as a concept has been changed from simply a class term to include types of oppression other than the economic. 'The praxis' must come to include a wide array of human experiences and activities. This does not have to mean giving up its primacy in intellectual reflection.

155. 'En efecto, si la historia humana es, ante todo, una abertura al futuro, ella [la praxis histórica] aparece como una tarea, como un quehacer político' (Gutiérrez 1990: 65). He also says: 'Entre la denuncia y el anuncio está, al decir de Freire, el tiempo de la construcción, de la *praxis* histórica. Es más, denuncia y anuncio sólo se pueden realizar *en* la praxis. Eso es lo que queremos decir cuando hablamos de la utopía como movilizadora de la historia y subversiva del orden existente' (Gutiérrez 1990: 280 [emphasis in original]). See also Gutiérrez 1990: 312-13.

156. Gutiérrez 1990: 66.

157. Segundo 1975: 13. Segundo borrows the term 'hermeneutic circle' from Rudolf Bultmann.

experiencing theological reality that leads us to exegetical suspicion, that is, to the suspicion that the prevailing interpretation of the Bible does not take important pieces of data into account. Fourth, we have our new hermeneutic, that is, the new way of interpreting the fountainhead of our faith (the Scripture) with the new elements at our disposal.[158]

The key to Segundo's method is what may be called an ideological dialectic, that is, an exposure of unconscious and conscious ideologies that sacralize the status quo, while at the same time clearing the ground for the creation of new and more efficacious ideologies that will be open to change.[159] Segundo himself says that to complete the hermeneutic circle in itself is not a sufficient criterion of truth. What it does is to prove that a theology is alive, that is, connected to the vital fountainhead of historical reality.[160] For him, the ultimate criterion of truth (orthodoxy) is orthopraxis, not only in theology in general but in truth interpretation as well. He recognizes the 'dangers' in this kind of approach, but concludes that 'There is no reason to rule out a coherent theological method, just because it entails dangers'.[161]

If theory and praxis are not opposites but intrinsically bound, the same is true for faith and praxis. Gutiérrez says: 'Theology is an intent to read the faith from a

158.   Segundo 1975: 14. The concept of hermeneutical suspicion is derived from Paul Ricoeur. See Hennelly 1977a: 717.

159.   Hennelly 1977a: 718. The relation between faith and ideology (which Segundo understands positively) is more elaborated in Segundo's *Fe e ideología* (1982).

160.   Segundo 1975: 34.

161.   Segundo 1975: 44. Segundo does not problematize in which sense he uses the concept 'truth' (*verdad*) here. He says, though, that the primacy of orthopraxis over orthodoxy is based on 'doing the truth' (*hacer la verdad*). It seems that his way of using 'truth' stems from its Marxist usage.

According to Marsha A. Hewitt, Segundo shares both explicitly and implicitly certain general basic traits with critical theory (the Frankfurt School). In the light of critical theory, Segundo's writings become more intelligible but, at the same time, closer to social theory than theology. Hewitt claims LT to have the same goal as critical theory: practical, transformative activity with an emancipatory intent aimed at liberation. This takes Segundo close to 'the end of theology' (Hewitt 1990: 5). 'how can a theology, however critical or progressive, seek to become a practical, emancipatory force in the historical process without transforming itself utterly into a theory that is not theology in its classical definition? This is an urgent question that most liberation theologians do not raise, and in not doing so, fail to confront one of the deepest contradictions inherent in liberation theology' (Hewitt 1990: 4). And 'liberation theology, by virtue of its "subversive" methodology, especially as elaborated by Segundo, indeed bears the seeds of its own negation as theology *per se*' (Hewitt 1990: 167 [emphasis in original]). She also says: 'the question remains, whether Segundo can still be called a *theologian* as such, since in the works under study here, his preoccupation is not with God, nor religious concepts, but with humanity and society, and the historical project of liberation' (Hewitt 1990: 10 [emphasis in original]). I will not try to answer the questions raised by Hewitt in this study. However, it is crucial to bear in mind that LT consciously moves on a multi- or interdisciplinary level that may lead to its transformation 'in its classical definition'. The 'anthropological turn' in modern theology does not necessarily mean that theology ceases being theology, if it speaks more consciously from and of the human point of view.

determined situation'.[162] Theology is a 'critical reflection *from within* and *upon* historical praxis, in confrontation with the Word of the Lord as lived and accepted in faith'. Theology is also 'a reflection *in* and *on* faith as liberative praxis'.[163] Thus, it is not just theory and praxis that have to be interrelated, but faith and praxis as well. In a way, faith in LT is understood as faith *in* praxis.[164] Theory (theology) is a reflection, but inseparable from this praxis-as-faith. Since history is one (there is no separation between salvation history and world history) and the human existence is by definition historical, faith also has to be understood in these terms. There is a dialectic of transcendence and history, of faith and praxis.

> Faith and praxis are not, as the Vatican would have it, two independent, mutually external realities that must be brought together following their constitution as independent realities, where the one is conceived of as the 'consequence', 'implication', or 'expression' of the other. Their relation is mutually internal and 'constitutive'.[165]

Thus, praxis is not an application of faith but the realization of faith's own intrinsic demand.[166] Faith must demonstrate its effectiveness by being tested in praxis. Faith *is* existential and praxical.

The importance of praxis in LT can also be seen in how the idea of *orthopraxis* is being developed. It not only refers to the critique of European theology as being profoundly deductive, but also to the self-understanding of LT as *fides quaerens intellectum*, the normativeness of faith sentences. Thus, orthopraxis means both

162.   'La teología es en efecto un intento de lectura de la fe desde una situación determinada' (Gutiérrez 1982: 52). Also, 'la teología de la liberación es un intento de comprender la fe desde la praxis histórica, liberadora y subversiva de los pobres de este mundo, de las clases explotadas, razas despreciadas, culturas marginadas' (Gutiérrez 1982).

163.   'En este contexto la teología será una reflexión crítica *desde* y *sobre* la praxis histórica en confrontación con la palabra del Señor vivida y aceptada en la fe… Será una reflexión *en* y *sobre* la fe como praxis liberadora' (Gutiérrez 1982: 81 [emphasis added]).

According to Lehmann *et al.*, ' "Praxis" bedeutet selbstverständlich nicht einfach Teilnahme an den religiösen Vollzügen der Kirche. Diese Forderung bezieht sich überhaupt nicht auf das Individuum, vielmehr geht es bei der "Entprivatisierung" des Glaubens um eine geschichtliche Praxis der Befreiung im sozio-ökonomischen Kontext. Die theologische Reflexion über den Glauben wandelt sich in eine kritische Reflexion über die geschichtliche Praxis' (Lehmann *et al.* 1977: 21). They point out how the relationship between theory and praxis in all its complexity and radicality has not been sufficiently analysed in LT. There are tendencies in LT which are not free of 'theory hostility' and 'actionism'. This is especially serious, if the 'efficiency' of a theory is made the criterion of truth (Lehmann *et al.* 1977: 24-25).

164.   'En la raíz de toda teología está el acto de fe, pero no en tanto que simple adhesión intelectual al mensaje, sino como acogida vital al don de la palabra escuchada en la comunidad eclesial, como encuentro con el Señor, como amor al hermano. Se trata de la existencia cristiana tomada en su totalidad… Ese es el sentido de *credo ut intelligam* de san Anselmo… La vida de fe no es, pues, sólo el punto de partida; es también el punto de llegada del quehacer teológico' (Gutiérrez 1982: 75).

165.   Min 1989: 46, quoting Jon Sobrino.

166.   Min 1989. According to Hofmann, 'nach diesem Verständnis, ist die Theologie der Befreiung selbst nichts anderes als ein Glaubensgehorsam in der konkreten Form einer reflektiven Glaubens-Praxis' (Hofmann 1978: 165).

fidelity (practice should match beliefs) and efficacious love (service to others).[167]

LT affirms the 'primacy of praxis' as something constitutive for the starting point of theology. Praxis is the *locus* of LT. This does not exclude a critical reflection on the praxis itself, as is made clear in Gutiérrez' classical formulation. Being inseparable, theory and praxis together constitute the method, the theological knowledge. Praxis is not a mere theme of theology but the hermeneutical perspective of all theologizing. In interpreting LT, European theologians (including the Vatican) constantly 'accuse' liberation theologians of 'reducing' theology to 'mere' praxis or sociology or politics. LT has to be understood not only as interpretative but also as having a profoundly transformative interest. This interest leads to a new affirmation of the importance of praxis. It is the very 'reduction' of either theory or praxis that liberation theologians criticize. There is a strong critique of any kind of dualism in LT.

1.3.2 *Critique of Dualism and the Unity of Salvation and Liberation*

According to the Salvadorean (originally Basque) Jesuit Jon Sobrino, the most fundamental difference between European theology and LT lies in their different ways of solving the problem of dualisms in theology. The basic dualisms of Western philosophy and theology have been the oppositions spirit–body, person–society and transcendence–history. LT has tried to overcome 'the most radical dualism of all: that between the believing subject and history, between theory and praxis, not on the level of mere thinking, but on the level of real existence'.[168] According to the Brazilian Hugo Assmann, these dualisms have a tremendous ideological function. They imply a contempt of the human being and history and dislocate the axis of ethics on an ideal level. For him, the dualisms are political ideologies of 'order' and 'status quo'.[169]

Because of the historical situation in which LT was born and its selective use of the social sciences (emphasis on economic and political analysis), the critique of dualisms is concentrated in the oppositions profane vs spiritual or sacred and history vs transcendence.[170] According to Gutiérrez, the distinctions temporal

---

167. Cleary 1985: 94.

168. 'En este sentido la diferencia más fundamental entre ambos modos de hacer teología consistiría en la superación de los dualismos. Ciertamente en la teología europea se ha avanzado mucho en esa superación, en el desenmascaramiento de la dicotomía espíritu-cuerpo, persona-sociedad, fe privada-fe pública, transcendencia-historia... Lo que la teología latinoamericana ha pretendido es la superación del dualismo más radical en la teología: el de sujeto creyente e historia, el de teoría y praxis, pero no ya dentro del mismo pensamiento, sino dentro de la existencia real' (Sobrino 1976: 207).

169. Assmann 1971: 92.

170. Other liberation theologies, most notably black theology and feminist theology, take this critique further in the area of (Christian) anthropology. Among the basic dualistic oppositions are thus seen man-woman, white-black, good-evil and spirit-body. In a later text, Gutiérrez writes: 'Tenemos que someter a una radical revisión las nociones corrientes de materia y espíritu, imbuidas del pensamiento griego y filosofía idealista que poco tienen que ver con la mentalidad bíblica. Como decía Berdiaeff, reinterpretando términos frecuentes en los ambientes cristianos a

vs spiritual and sacred vs profane are founded in the distinction natural vs supernatural. It is only the *historical* and *existential* viewpoint that overcomes these dualisms. The historical viewpoint allows us to leave behind the narrow individual angle.[171] In fact, he presents the question 'What relation exists between salvation and the historical process of liberation of the human being?' as *the* problem of his theology.[172]

Gutiérrez emphasizes *the unity* of history as his starting point. He says: 'concretely, there are not two histories, one profane, the other sacred, "juxtaposed" or "closely related", but only one human happening assumed irreversibly by Christ, Lord of history'.[173] Thus, this affirmation of one and only human history (*una sola historia*) has a christological foundation (incarnation). Human history and salvation history are united in Jesus' person. God's auto-revelation happens in human history. Here liberation theologians lean mostly on the Exodus story (Old Testament) and Jesus' incarnation (New Testament). In the history of theology, 'salvation' has almost exclusively had transcendental, spiritual connotations. Thus, liberation theologians prefer the concept liberation—not only in opposition to economic and political dependency but also as a more accurate term than salvation that bears the weight of other-worldly and exclusively spiritual connotations.

The historization of salvation is the theological 'backbone' of LT.[174] Central to the biblical roots of this claim is the concept of the Kingdom of God. According to the Brazilian brothers Leonardo and Clodovis Boff, no other theological or biblical concept is as close to the ideal of integral liberation as this. Seeing the Kingdom as God's absolute and universal project helps us to understand the link joining creation and redemption, time and eternity. The Kingdom of God is something more than historical liberations, which are always limited and open to further perfecting, but it is anticipated and incarnated in them in time.[175]

Thus, because of its eschatological dimension, salvation is always 'more' than historical liberation. But if the relation between final, full salvation is denied and concrete historical liberation are denied, the historicity of God's action is also denied, as is the ultimate sense of human life. Creation and redemption are united. In LT, on the one hand, the creation of the human being as the image of God (spirit, body) is taken seriously. On the other hand, the ultimate meaning of life and historical liberation are never fully realized. Between the two is human history in which God acts, even though not against the free will of human beings.

que aludimos, "si yo tengo hambre, ése es un problema material; si otro tiene hambre, ése es un problema espiritual."' (Gutiérrez 1982: 267).

171. Gutiérrez 1990: 118-21.
172. Gutiérrez 1990: 95, 189.
173. '...en concreto, no hay dos historias, una profana y otra sagrada "yuxtapuestas" o "estrechamente ligadas", sino un solo devenir humano asumido irreversiblemente por Cristo' (Gutiérrez 1990: 194).
174. Silva Gotay 1983: 73-74.
175. Boff and Boff 1989: 64-65. See also Gutiérrez 1990: 203-14.

The two elements that best define liberation theologians' understanding of the Kingdom of God are *historicity* and *totality*.[176] To exempt history from God's salvific activity would be in fact to deny God's sovereignty.[177]

The Kingdom of God is eschatological and cannot be reduced to history. But the only realm where it can manifest itself is human history. Participation in processes of human liberation is not only ethically justifiable, but it is also an essential part of our incomplete knowledge of God and the Kingdom of God. History has its autonomy and human beings are its subjects. Christian faith means, on the one hand, waiting and hoping for the Kingdom of God, and on the other hand, concrete commitment to the promotion of love and justice in history. This tension between utopia and reality is what marks LT as a spiritual-theological movement among all the other liberation movements. There is a concrete, living hope in an eschatological utopia that gives meaning both to present-day struggles (so that they are not without sense) and to a larger horizon for human insufficiency.

The question of the relation between history and the Kingdom of God, between liberation and salvation, has been one of the main disputes between European and Latin American theologians. According to Sobrino, the 'eschatological reserve' (*reserva escatológica*) in European theology has meant the relativization of any intrahistorical future (concrete liberation) that does not coincide with the Kingdom of God. For LT, even partial solutions for human suffering are essential in the concept Kingdom of God.[178] For Gutiérrez, Moltmann's theology of hope, for example, is not sufficiently rooted in the concrete historical experiences of oppression.[179] In the political theology of Metz, there is 'an impression of a certain insufficiency in the analysis of the contemporary situation...that does not permit him to penetrate deep into the situation of dependency, injustice and despoliation in which the majority of humanity lives'.[180]

The dialectic of salvation and liberation can also be illustrated by Gutiérrez' definition of the three dimensions of liberation. In fact, it is his definition of the concept of liberation. First, there is the dimension of economic, social and political liberation of the oppressed, the historical praxis (political order). Second, there is the personal and cultural transformation, the construction of the 'new human being' in a qualitatively different society (ethical order). Finally, there is the dimension of liberation from sin, which is the ultimate root of all injustice

---

176.   Min 1989: 89.
177.   Min 1989: 90.
178.   Sobrino 1976: 204.
179.   Gutiérrez 1990: 257. This critique of European theology for its supposed restriction in metaphysics and abstractions corresponds with liberation theologians' view of how the social sciences in LT have replaced philosophy as the most adequate non-theological element in theology.
180.   '...la impresión de una cierta insuficiencia en su análisis de la situación contemporánea... [que] no le permite calar hondo en la situación de dependencia y de expoliación en que se encuentra la mayor parte de la humanidad' (Gutiérrez 1990: 266).

and reconciliation with God and other human beings (theological order).[181] This last dimension is the 'orientating pole' of the global process of liberation.[182] These three dimensions are not parallel or chronological processes. They are 'three levels of signification of one complicated process that finds its profound meaning and full realization in the salvific work of Christ'.[183] They imply each other mutually. The first dimension is the realm of scientific rationality (social sciences), the second that of utopia of human self-liberation (ethics and philosophy), and the third that of faith (theology).[184]

The third dimension gives ultimate meaning and transcendent motivation to the first. The ultimate motive for participating in the struggle for liberation is the conviction of the radical incompatibility of evangelical demands with an alienating and unjust society.[185] Faith also provides a self-critical principle to the praxis of liberation. It keeps us from any confusion of the Kingdom of God with any historical event and from any absolutizing of revolution. Faith simultaneously demands and judges our political praxis.[186] In LT, 'The theological dimension of salvation and faith mediates the historical dimension of the utopian struggles for political and cultural liberation as the unifying or *totalizing* principle of the latter, while the latter mediates the former as its *concretizing* principle'.[187] Gutiérrez answers the question 'What is the use of changing social structures if the human heart is not changed?' by saying that this juxtaposition is only half true because it ignores the fact that the human 'heart' is also being transformed by changes in social and cultural structures. According to him, 'the one who thinks that a structural transformation automatically brings about different human beings is not being less "mechanical" than the one who believes that a personal change guarantees social transformations'.[188]

The rejection of dualism can also be found in the theology of Pablo Richard. 'This dualism between temporal and supernatural orders permits theology, Christianity and the church to postulate their universal, spiritual and supernatural mission above the historical contradictions', he says.[189] The basic dialectic or oppositions in LT cannot be reduced to the oppositions between abstract and concrete or deductive and inductive. The proper opposition is between dom-

---

181.   Gutiérrez 1990: 43-44, 91-92, 283. Here Gutiérrez refers to the human being as 'man' (*hombre*). *El hombre nuevo* is literally 'the new man'.

182.   Gutiérrez 1990: 44. He refers to the Kingdom of God as the eschatological finality of human existence.

183.   Gutiérrez 1990: 92.

184.   Gutiérrez 1990: 283.

185.   Min 1989: 100, quoting Gutiérrez.

186.   Gutiérrez 1990: 286; Min 1989: 100.

187.   Min 1989: 101-102 (emphasis in original).

188.   Gutiérrez 1973: 236.

189.   'Este dualismo del orden temporal y del orden sobrenatural permite a la teología, al cristianismo y a la Iglesia postular su misión universal, espiritual y sobrenatural, por encima de las contradicciones históricas' (Richard 1990: 26-27).

ination (oppression) and liberation, between interpretation and transformation.[190] 'It is not enough to move from the abstract to the concrete, but to explain the abstract as a practice of oppression or as a false practice of liberation'.[191] Even though LT is clearly closer to an inductive methodology (taking the non-theological analysis of reality as its starting point), it 'makes a qualitative leap forward and produces a radical *epistemological rupture* (*ruptura epistemológica*) by proposing not the analysis or interpretation of reality, but the transformation of reality as the starting point for theological work'.[192]

1.3.3 *Theological Knowledge and the Epistemological Rupture*
The question of (theological) knowledge and how it is being constituted is central for all liberation theologians, for some more explicitly than for others. This is historically understandable. Liberation theologians ask questions such as 'What is the ultimate interest of theological knowledge?' and 'For whom and from whom is theology done?'[193] According to Sobrino,

> when comparing different ways of theological knowledge, it is more fundamental to investigate the practical and ethical option of that knowledge and discover what in that understanding of knowledge exists of the practical and ethical option than to investigate methodological details of theological analysis. This is why, for us, the key question for establishing comparisons between different theologies is to ask what the interests are that, factually and not intentionally, direct different ways of theological knowledge.[194]

Trying to answer these questions, Sobrino analyses the two moments of Enlightenment. These two moments can be symbolized in Kant and Marx. The first moment, aiming at liberation from theological dogmatism and authoritarianism, has been foundational for modern European theology in its critical function. The main interest has been to demonstrate the truth of faith before natural and historical reason and to liberate theology from its historical errors. The second moment does not conceive liberation as autonomy of reason but as liberation from the miserable conditions of reality. It is not as much orientated to interpretation as to transformation (as Marx's phrase about philosophers states). If modern European, especially Protestant, theology has tried to respond to the challenge of the first Enlightenment, LT has taken up the challenge of Marx by trying to respond to the historical situation of Latin America.[195] Here again,

190.   Richard 1990: 18-21.
191.   Richard 1990: 21.
192.   Richard 1990: 22.
193.   Sobrino 1976: 179.
194.   'Creemos por lo tanto que más fundamental para establecer una comparación entre diversos conocimientos teológicos que investigar en detalle métodos de análisis teológicos es investigar la opción práxica y ética del mismo conocimiento y descubrir lo que en la misma intellección del conocimiento existe de opción práxica y ética. Por ello nos parece una pregunta clave para establecer comparaciones entre diversas teologías el preguntar qué interés mueve real y no intencionalmente a los diversos conocimientos teológicos' (Sobrino 1976: 179).
195.   Sobrino 1976: 181-84.

theological knowledge appears inseparable from the ethical and the practical. The influence of Marxism on liberation theologians can also be seen in the way they use concepts such as truth and epistemological rupture.

Sobrino says, maybe somewhat simplifying: 'European theology has tended to accede and confront reality as something *thought*, while Latin American theology tends to confront reality as such, even if, in doing this, has not been able to set aside interpretative schemes'.[196] This is how Sobrino explains the use of the social sciences (instead of primarily philosophy) in LT. Finally, Sobrino claims that LT is more conscious of its status as knowledge, that is, that knowledge is never neither practically nor ethically neutral. Here he comes back to the question of the factual use and consequences of theology in society.[197] European theology, even in its more 'progressive' forms, is experienced as profoundly ahistorical.[198] There is an apparent tension in Sobrino's thought: on the one hand, liberation theologians emphasize the contextual and provisional nature of all truth claims, including their own; on the other hand, in the statement above, Sobrino seems to believe in the possibility of confronting reality 'as such', whatever this could possibly mean. Taking his Marxist influences into account, it seems that Sobrino believes in the possibility of a correspondence between reality and truth claims about it.

This tension in LT is also evident from the ways that the classical tasks of theology—theology as wisdom, *sapientia*, and theology as rational knowledge, *scientia*—are portrayed within LT. They are considered to be indispensable for all theological reflection, including LT.[199] Gutiérrez' own definition of theology would point towards a third task of theology, arising from a totally different context from that of earlier theologizing. The history, culture and political and economic situation of Latin America are unique. What has traditionally been understood as something universal thus appears as something contextual and particular. There is no abstractly universal theology. European theology since its earliest days has always been European theology. To start consciously from a different context— Latin America, for instance—naturally changes the perspective. More than perhaps any other theology past or present, LT is self-consciously historical and contextual. It does not claim to be *the* universal truth for all times and for all societies.[200]

The themes of LT are basically the same as of any theology. Questions about God, salvation, grace, creation, and so on are also questions of LT. But the chosen point of view, the 'from where', the method, gives new and different answers to

---

196.   '...la teología europea ha tendido a acceder y enfrentarse con la realidad más en cuanto *pensada*, mientras que la teología latinoamericana tiende a enfrentarse con la realidad tal cual es, aun cuando para ello no puede prescindir de esquemas interpretativos' (Sobrino 1976: 186 [emphasis in original]).

197.   Sobrino 1976: 189.

198.   Sobrino 1976: 206.

199.   Gutiérrez 1990: 58-61.

200.   Min 1989: 3.

these age-old questions of theology.[201] They also shed new light on theology itself, its task and its meaning. The critical attitude of LT makes clear how the basic questions of theology have been defined and interpreted for centuries according to certain interests. There is no 'pure' theology because there is no abstractly universal theology. Thus, LT's 'reformatory' potential is inside the theological discourse itself and, consequently, the church and its structures. According to Gutiérrez' definition, theology as *critical* activity should be critical both of society and of the church, including the history of theology. 'Theology must be critical thinking over against itself, its own foundations... We refer also to a gracious and critical attitude in respect to the economic and sociocultural conditioning of the life and reflection of the Christian community'.[202]

If classical theology, both Catholic and Protestant, has considered the Christian praxis primarily as a moral and pastoral issue—in a way, as an application of fundamental theology—in LT the focus is shifted. The praxis, especially the Christian praxis, becomes the starting point for theological reflection. Thus, among other things, LT could be seen as a serious intent to bridge dogma and morality, faith and Christian praxis. Even though there is really no distinctive ethical theory in LT, the ethical questions are present in the very starting point of LT. The emphasis on praxis is in itself an ethical choice. The understanding of faith as emancipatory praxis, or rather, the emancipatory praxis as an essential aspect of faith, is at the root of LT. Faith and ethics are inseparable in LT. Theory (of truth and theology) and praxis are two sides of the same coin, the inevitable historicity of human existence. Theological knowledge stops being primordially interpretative and acquires an essentially ethical and practical (transformative) character.

The basic ethical nature of LT is well reflected in the words of Raúl Vidales:

> If the political situation of dependency and domination of two thirds of humanity, with the millions of deaths caused by hunger every year, does not become the starting point for Christian theology, it cannot situate and concretize historically its most fundamental themes with credibility either.[203]

As the history of LT, presented at the beginning of this chapter, makes clear, the solidarity with these millions of poor is the cornerstone of LT. Without it, all the other insights and challenges of LT are not understandable. For liberation theologians, this solidarity is not just a question of ethics and morality—as in traditional Western theology—but of epistemology as well. This is what liberation

201. Vidales 1974: 426.
202. 'La teología debe ser un pensamiento crítico de sí misma, de sus propios fundamentos... Nos referimos, también a una actitud lúcida y crítica respecto de los condicionamientos económicos y socioculturales de la vida y reflexión de la comunidad cristiana' (Gutiérrez 1990: 67).
203. 'Si la situación política de la dependencia y dominación de dos tercios de la humanidad con sus millones anuales de muertos de hambre no se convierten en el punto de partida de la teología cristiana, ésta no podrá situar y concretizar históricamente sus temas fundamentales con credibilidad' (Vidales 1985: 72).

theologians mean by the epistemological rupture. For Jon Sobrino, it is not as much a traditional question of theodicy as of anthropodicy:

> The epistemological rupture does not happen opposing natural theology and theodicy as different ways of theological knowing, but in the concept of theodicy itself: the fundamental scandal does not consist of the existence of misery in spite of the existence of God, but simply of the existence of misery... Thus, the fundamental question is how to justify the man.[204]

For LT, it is the moral perspective of the poor and the oppressed which enables us to perceive the moral dimension of oppression (in any of its forms). Without that perspective moral problems are not even recognized as moral problems, since the oppressed 'see' the reality differently.[205] This 'seeing' implies a different kind of 'knowing'.

It seems that liberation theologians presuppose that the perspective of the poor offers a 'truer' picture of both reality and of Christian revelation. As was said, they are not very explicit in which meaning they speak of truth and the truthfulness of reality. In relation to what has been said earlier, I would claim that there is a twofold understanding of 'true knowing' in LT.

First, there is an undeniable influence of the Marxist and neo-Marxist understanding of the historical character of knowledge.[206] Secondly, we have the classical Christian understanding of knowing God (the truth) through loving other people, especially the weakest and the most dispossessed and unworthy of them. This would come close to what Gutiérrez means by poverty as spiritual infancy.[207] The particularity of the perspective would not deny the universality of the Christian message: the option for the poor is a *preferential* option, which does not exclude but prioritizes.

1.3.4 *Multidisciplinarity*
According to the liberation theologians, the interaction with the social sciences is a logical consequence of the commitment to praxis. Theology is reflection, yes, but in the light of the Word of God and faith. The need to understand, analyse and act on the complicated social, political and economic phenomena can be an

204. 'La ruptura epistemológica se da entonces no sólo contraponiendo la teología natural y la teodicea como diversos modos de conocimiento teológico, sino en la misma concepción de la teodicea: el escándalo fundamental no consiste en que exista la miseria a pesar de que existe Dios, sino simplemente en la existencia de la miseria... Por ello la pregunta fundamental es cómo justificar al hombre' (Sobrino 1976: 200). The historical facts of reality as the starting point for theology are also reflected in Sobrino's analysis of the 'death of God' theology. If the death of God is the expression of a crisis of meaning (in Europe), then the death of a human being is the expression of a crisis in reality itself. The real and widespread death of innocent human beings in Latin America is not experienced primarily as the loss of meaning but as a triumph of injustice and sin. Thus, the epistemological rupture is not formalized so much in the concept 'death of God' as in 'the death of the oppressed' (Sobrino 1976: 201-202).
205. Min 1986: 548.
206. On Marxist theory of knowledge, see Bottomore (ed.) 1988: 254-63.
207. See Chapter 1.4.1.

inspiration and starting point for theology, but theology *as* theology never has the necessary tools for realizing this task. Thus, the need for the analysis made by the social sciences that explain the causes of poverty and oppression is raised. Obviously, this interaction with and the use of the social sciences could as well be called multi- or interdisciplinarity.

If for centuries it was philosophy that gave theology its conceptual coherence and the necessary tools for making itself intelligible, now the liberation theologians claim that in their situation they have more use of the social sciences. Of course this does not mean rejecting philosophy, even though 'traditional' philosophy, and more specifically, its use in theology, has principally been aimed at intellectual understanding and defence of the dogma (orthodoxy) rather than at historical action (orthopraxis). Multidisciplinarity in this sense is no invention of LT. It is instead the extensive use of new disciplines, mainly the social sciences, in theological analysis that could be seen as an innovation of LT.

Why, then, call this critical reflection on the historical praxis theology, if there are better means (the social sciences) to realize that reflection? Hugo Assmann says: 'A critical reflection on the historical praxis by men (*los hombres*) is theo-logical to the extent that it examines in this praxis the presence of the Christian faith. This is *what distinguishes* theology from other possible ways of critical reflection on the same praxis'.[208] According to Gutiérrez, 'The theological work, properly understood, begins as we intend to read reality in the light of the Word. This implies returning to the foundations of revelation'.[209] And 'The ultimate criteria for theology are to be found in the revealed truth that we receive in faith, not in the praxis itself'.[210]

It is interesting that Gutiérrez does not discuss what a 'return to the found-ations of revelation' would mean if liberation theologians tried to apply the meth-ods of modern historical critical exegesis to biblical studies. In general, the use of the Bible in LT is orientated more to expressions of faith than to critical analysis.

The liberation theologians are unanimous in their affirmation of the need of social analysis as an integral element of their theological method. What, then, is the relationship between theology and the social sciences? According to Clodovis Boff

> The interfacing of theology with praxis through the medium of socio-analytic mediation has as its objective the safeguarding of theology from the empty 'theorism' that, in certain circumstances, is a trait of *academic cynicism* that ignores the crying scandal of the starving and suffering multitudes of our world.[211]

208. 'Una reflexión crítica sobre la praxis histórica de los hombres será teológica en la medida en que ausculte en esta praxis la presencia de la fe cristiana. Es esto *lo que distingue* la teología de las demás posibilidades de reflexionar críticamente sobre la misma praxis' (Assmann 1971: 65 [emphasis in original]).

209. '...el trabajo teológico propiamente dicho comienza cuando intentamos leer esa realidad a la luz de la Palabra. Ello implica ir a las fuentes de la revelación' (Gutiérrez 1990: 27).

210. 'Los criterios últimos en teología vienen de la verdad revelada que acogemos en la fe y no de la praxis misma' (Gutiérrez 1990: 38).

211. C. Boff 1987: 7 (emphasis in original).

The social sciences enter into theology as a constitutive part, as 'raw material'. Theology has its own proper object, but it can be enriched by other disciplines.

> The text of a theological reading with respect to the political is prepared and furnished by the sciences of the social. Theology receives its text from these sciences, and practices upon it a reading in conformity with its own proper code, in such a way as to extract from it a characteristically, properly, theological meaning. Consequently, it must be denied that the sociological and the theological subsist in the same continuum.[212]

Thus, the role of the social sciences is pre-theological.

Gutiérrez, for his part, says that the use of the social sciences 'helps us to understand better the social reality. The attitude in front of them must be that of discernment'.[213] This includes a critical attitude and respect for the autonomy of different disciplines.[214] Theology works on its own sources, but for this it needs the critical analysis done by the social sciences.[215]

According to Juan Luis Segundo,

> It is obvious that the Christian message impels us to realize this path [of deideologization of faith] but does not offer us the concrete scientific tools for the task. With all logic, we can suppose that if these tools need to come from somewhere, it is sociology, the science of collective behavior, that provides them.[216]

He does not explain why sociology best serves this purpose.

For Leonardo Boff,

> In the labor to detect the mechanisms that produce poverty, the theology of liberation has been urged to look for a more relevant rationality than the one offered in traditional theology by philosophy. This has not lost its function: it has obtained other tasks. The human sciences, especially the social sciences, have offered an analytical tool able to discover the structural causes of oppression and to elaborate alternative models.[217]

212.   C. Boff 1987: 30-31.

213.   Gutiérrez 1984: 258.

214.   Gutiérrez 1984: 259, 262. Also Juan Carlos Scannone points out the instrumentality of the use of the social sciences in LT. It is intrinsic but instrumental. See Scannone 1990: 307. He also differentiates between three different practical and theoretical dimensions of 'the option for the poor'. They are the theological (theology), the human-ethical (philosophy) and the historical-empirical dimension (social sciences). These dimensions are distinct but united. See Gutiérrez 1984: 322-36.

215.   Gutiérrez 1984: 263-64.

216.   'Es obvio que el mensaje cristiano nos impulsa a realizar ese camino [de desideo-logización de la fe] pero no nos brinda los instrumentos científicos concretos para dicha tarea. Con toda lógica podemos suponer que si éstos deben venir de alguna parte, es la sociología, la ciencia de los comportamientos colectivos, la que debe proveernos aquí' (Segundo 1973: 285-86).

217.   'En el afán de detectar los mecanismos generadores de la pobreza, la teología de la liberación se vio urgida a buscar una racionalidad más pertinente que aquélla que ha ofrecido la tradición teológica por la filosofía. Esta no ha perdido su función; ganó otras tareas. Las ciencias humanas, especialmente sociales, han ofrecido un instrumental analítico capaz de descubrir las causas estructurales de la opresión y de elaborar modelos alternativos' (L. Boff 1976: 143).

Hugo Assmann says that

> 'the Christian faith', 'the Gospel', or 'the Revelation' do not exist clearly bestowed as
> such as realities (or criteria), because they only exist mediated historically... We do
> not possess Christianity 'as such' as a criterion of comparison a priori—above all in
> Latin America today, when the critique of the legitimizing functions of the church in
> relation to the defects of 'status quo' is a constant.[218]

These references make it clear that liberation theologians share the basic
acceptance of the use of the social sciences in LT, with the emphasis varying.[219] A
closer analysis would even reveal contradictions or at least great differences
between different liberation theologians in how and what they understand by the
use of the social sciences in theology. If it is 'raw material' for Clodovis Boff, a
'tool of analysis' for Gutiérrez, Segundo and Leonardo Boff, and 'instrument' for
Scannone, there is a need for a much greater differentiation in what is really
meant by these concepts. Again, I think, this conceptual confusion can be overcome to some extent if we speak simply of multidisciplinarity.

Multidisciplinarity is in no ways exclusive to LT, as we will see in the chapter
on feminist theology. Neither is it exclusive to modern theology in general. It
seems that the complexity of the modern world, and our ever-growing consciousness of it, inevitably leads to greater multidisciplinarity in all disciplines.[220] LT
uses *selectively* some of other disciplines.[221] The status of the social sciences in

218. '...la "fe cristiana", "el Evangelio", la "Revelación" no existen como realidades (o
criterios) tan claramente conferibles en sí, porque *sólo existen históricamente mediatizados...el
cristianismo "como tal" no lo poseemos como criterio de comparación a priori*—sobre todo hoy en América
Latina, cuando la crítica a las funciones legitimadoras de la Iglesia en relación a los vicios del
"status quo" es una constante' (Assmann 1971: 62 [emphasis in original]).

219.   Fernando Castillo presents three different models of how the relationship between
theology and the social sciences is seen in LT. Firstly, there is the model represented best by Juan
Carlos Scannone. Theology has to make a choice between different analytical alternatives. There
must be a theological differentiation between them, depending on how these alternatives coincide with the concept of integral liberation. Secondly, Juan Luis Segundo sees the role of the
social sciences as critique of ideology that must become an inner moment of any theology. The
third model is represented by Hugo Assmann. Theology is 'the second step' not only in relation
to the praxis but also in relation to the social sciences. See Castillo 1978: 31.

220.   Interestingly, Juan Carlos Scannone shows how the theoretical and practical mediation
of the social sciences is also applied in the social doctrine of the Catholic Church. This is
inevitable, if the doctrine wants to be historically concrete and orientate towards concrete actions.
His argument is supported by several quotations from papal encyclicals. See Scannone 1991.

Anselm K. Min shows how John Paul II presents terms and ideas such as 'alienation',
'proletarianization' and 'exploitation' that are undoubtedly Marxian in origin. So much of
Marxism has become part of the very intellectual culture of today that we use its categories
without even noticing their origin. In spite of the use of Marxian concepts, the 'abstract
personalism' and dualism of the Pope's thinking waters them down. See Min 1989: 18-19, 152-
55.

221.   There are other disciplines, even among the social sciences, that LT could take much
more seriously to be able to be faithful to its basic insights. The emphasis on economics and
political science in LT is due to its historical development—as such, understandable, but
nevertheless open to criticism. Feminist theory has criticized the 'ideologization' of *all*

LT and how they are applied to a certain historical situation, that is, the poverty and dependence of Latin America, has until now been the cornerstone of LT's self-understanding as multidisciplinary theology. As Hugo Assmann says, 'The greatest merit of LT lies perhaps in the insistence on the historical starting point of its reflection: the situation of "the dominated (Latin) America"'.[222]

Concretely, the most important non-theological theories for LT have been the dependency theory and Marxism.[223] In general, the use of the social sciences has been quite selective, concentrating on economic and political analysis. Some liberation theologians have also seen the need for anthropology.[224] Even though the option for social scientific analysis or multidisciplinarity remains a constant in LT, a need for new fields is felt. Pablo Richard says that the traditional dialogue of LT with sociology and philosophy has been enlarged in recent years to include economics, ecology and anthropology.[225]

Gutiérrez, too, states that

> It is clear, for example, that the dependency theory, so widely used during the first years of our encounter with the Latin American reality, today results—in spite of its contributions—in an insufficient tool. It does not sufficiently take into account either the internal dynamics of different countries or the vastness of the world presented by the poor.[226]

knowledge, including the social sciences that liberation theologians have too easily judged as 'scientific' and 'objective'. There is also critique of the 'scientificity' of the social sciences that does not come from the feminist perspective but from modern sociology of knowledge and critical theory. For a critique of LT from this perspective, see Rubiolo 1990. A similar point of view is taken by Raúl Vidales: 'Al admitir la hipótesis moderna de que no hay ciencia "neutra", la teología latinoamericana no puede ser indiferente ante las ciencias, como si por igual le prestaran el mismo aporte' (Vidales 1978: 29).

222. Assmann 1971: 24.

223. The question of the influence of Marxism in LT is one of the major disagreements between the Vatican and the Latin American theologians. There is a lot of confusion, misunderstanding, uncriticalness and of course differing political opinion on this issue. It is not necessary to deal with these complex issues in this study.

224. See L. Boff 1976: 137-38; Richard 1991: 8.

225. Richard 1991: 8. By this, he refers to works that combine economic and theological analysis (e.g. Hugo Assmann and Franz Hinkelammert), ecology and theology (e.g. Fernando Mires) and anthropology and theology, especially in relation to the indigenous people. Hinkelammert, who combines economic analysis with theology and philosophy, says that 'The theological discourse as such does not have much importance in itself, but any concrete analysis has a theological aspect, and this indeed is important. To reflect on theology is scientific, but to reflect on Trinity, for example, is not' (personal communication, 31 March 1993, San José, Costa Rica). The need for economic analysis has always been central in LT. But a change has occurred. Theory of dependency and Marxism were influential at the dawn of LT. A later discourse between theology and economics has moved onto a more philosophical level. The basic contradiction is now seen between the 'God of life' and idolatry, not between theism and atheism. Idolatry produces victims. A (political, economic) system that produces victims needs 'a theology of sacrificiality'. This sort of theology is criticized by LT. The sacrificiality of the economic system in Latin America needs to be analysed with theological as well as economic tools. See especially the works of Franz Hinkelammert.

226. 'Es claro por ejemplo que la teoría de la dependencia, tan usada en los primeros años de

He mentions psychology, ethnology and anthropology as new fields of cooperation.[227]

The incorporation of these disciplines into LT in recent years reflects and coincides with a change in how the liberation theologians understand the concept of the poor. 'The poor' are not a faceless and nameless mass, not even a class in the Marxist sense, but a large group of people who have poverty as one common denominator. They may differ from each other in all other aspects, such as race and gender. To be able to understand racism, for example, one cannot remain in a mere class analysis. The selective use of the social sciences and the concentration primarily on economic and political aspects of oppression in LT has been criticized by other liberation theologians from other contexts. The Africans and Asians, as well as women and racial and ethnic minorities, have criticized their Latin American (male, of European descent) colleagues of ignoring other forms of oppression. It has been mostly this interaction with other liberation theologies that has first called into question, then enlargened and deepened, the Latin Americans' use of other disciplines.

It is important to bear this development in mind, since LT is often understood as something done in the 1970s, the later development being only a sort of application of that 'more foundational' work. The more recent understanding of LT as a global, wide and heterogeneous movement, where the multiplicity of oppression is taken into account, puts LT in a different framework. In this process, the Latin Americans are but one group. In the 1970s the influence of both Marxism and the dependency theory, of economics in general, was strong. It may well be that LT has become diluted as *theologia proper* since the 1970s, but there are new themes and areas being developed that often are ignored, since this work is not mainly—or only—done by the 'founding fathers' of LT.

Since the 1970s LT has sometimes been called the 'theology of life' (*teología de la vida*).[228] This too reflects the need for the enlargement and reformulation of such basic concepts as 'the poor' and 'liberation', and even 'praxis'. A 'theology of life' may speak more easily of the heterogeneity of the poor. To speak of 'defending the life of the poor' means speaking of their concrete life conditions.

The poor as 'a class' that needs 'liberation' reflects the heavy emphasis on economic analysis of the LT of the 1970s. The understanding of the poor as the multiply marginalized and excluded, deprived of the fullness of life, in need of economic, political, racial and sexual liberation, reflects better the reality of the Latin American majorities.

nuestro encuentro con la realidad latinoamericana, resulta hoy—pese a sus aportes—una herramienta corta por no tener suficientemente en cuenta la dinámica interna de cada país, ni la vastedad que presenta el mundo del pobre' (Gutiérrez 1990: 25).

227. Gutiérrez 1990: 26.
228. See Richard 1987a. For a critical perspective, see Chapters 1.4.1 and 4.1.1.

1.4 The Subjects of Liberation Theology

The *locus* of LT is the poor and exploited Latin Americans. As we have seen, this is very much the common denominator for all liberation theologians. The poor are understood as active subjects for their own liberation;[229] they are 'the new historical subjects'.[230] The question about the subjects of LT is central for at least two reasons. First, it is the explicit claim of practically all liberation theologians that it is the poor, the exploited, the popular classes, who are ultimately the subjects of LT. Second, the emergence of 'new subjectivities'—women, blacks, Indians—has been excluded from the above-mentioned definition. They bring up critical questions about how seriously their subjectivity—that is, the construction of their specific identity—is really taken into account in LT. If LT has largely been 'the voice of the voiceless', now those without voice are finding it and expressing it themselves. The process of enlarging the concept 'the poor' in LT is parallel with the emergence of new subjects in LT.

In this chapter, I will examine who actually are the *subjects* of praxis in LT, or, in other words, who form the praxis. In Chapter 1.3, I drew a general picture of liberation theologians' understanding of praxis. The ambiguity and vagueness of their definitions of praxis is not only due to the lack of explicity in their writings but also to the limited discussion about who really are the poor, in all their diversity, who supposedly are the locus of LT. This, again, is very much due to selective use of the social sciences, traditionally with an almost exclusive emphasis on economics and political science. Asking explicitly for the subject may help us clarify how such central concepts as 'praxis' and 'the poor' form the methodological backbone of LT. There is no 'praxis' without 'the poor' in LT.

By asking who the subjects of LT really are, I want to point to certain deficiencies in LT that may turn out to be partial reasons for its present crisis of credibility. Whose is the crisis if there is one? There are new subjectivities within LT claiming a different understanding of the most central concepts of LT.

I will first explain briefly how I will use the concept 'subject'. I am **not** using it in the sense of being under authority or control ('subject peoples'), or as the opposite of object (the mind or ego as distinguished from everything outside the mind) or as a theme or topic ('subject matter').[231] Instead, I use it in the sense of an *agent*, an *active actor*, as it is used in contemporary feminist theory, postmodern discourse and post-colonial theory.[232] Even in these discourses, the meaning of

---

229.   'El "locus" de la teología de la liberación es otro. Está en los pobres del subcontinente, en las masas indígenas, en las clases populares; está en la presencia de ellos como sujeto activo y creador de su propia historia, en las expresiones de su fe y de su esperanza en el Cristo pobre, en sus luchas por liberarse' (Gutiérrez 1982: 249).

230.   See Gallardo 1992.

231.   See Guralnik (ed.) 1984: 1417-18.

232.   See Braidotti 1994; Eriksson 1995: 43-44, 68, 127-44; Fulkerson 1994, especially 8-12, 27-30; the various articles in Nicholson (ed.) 1990; Slater 1994; Spivak 1994.

the concept varies.[233] What is usually referred to in European political theory as 'subject' translates into 'agent' in the USA. The continental tradition is strong in feminist and post-colonial theories, as well as in Latin American political and philosophical tradition (the Spanish equivalent of 'subject' is literally *sujeto*). Thus, by wishing to display the subject of LT, I want to search for the agent, the collective 'maker' of LT, which is sometimes explicit, sometimes implicit, in liberation theologians' texts. I want to take a critical look at what is meant by 'the poor as subjects of LT'.

Being interested in the absence and/or presence of the female subject within LT, I will explore the limits of liberation theologians' understanding of praxis primarily from this perspective. This analysis will be done mainly in Chapter 3.

According to Gustavo Gutiérrez, the subjects of the epistemological rupture in LT are the *non-persons*, the ones who are not totally valued as human beings. The best of the modern Western theology after the Enlightenment has tried to respond to the challenges of the non-believer.[234] Sobrino agrees with Gutiérrez:

> The fundamental problem of Latin American theology has not been the recovering of the meaning of threatened faith but recovering the meaning of reality, not only threatened but in the misery. Doing theology in its liberating sense has helped to transform the reality of sin. The adversary of theology has not been as much 'the atheist' as 'the non-man'.[235]

According to Gutiérrez, the challenge to theology is something else in Latin America.

> On a continent like Latin America, the challenge does not come principally from the non-believer, but from the *non-person*. That is, from somebody whom the existing social order does not recognize as human: the poor, the exploited, the one who is systematically and legally deprived of his humanness (*su ser de hombre*), the one who hardly knows that he is a person. The non-person puts in question not so much our religious world as our *economic, social, political and cultural world*.[236]

---

233.   Tuija Pulkkinen draws a distinction between the liberal and Hegelian-Marxist use of transcendental subject-assumptions in modern political theory. The liberal ontology assumes a transcendentally singular individual agent, the Hegelian-Marxist ontology a transcendental communal will. In the latter, the social subject is logically prior to any other conceptualization in the construction of political space including individual agents, who are conceivable as agents only when the social is already assumed. She argues that both of these modern political ontologies are bound by subject-philosophy which the postmodern thought needs to question in order to fight modern universalism and in order to address difference. Feminist theory carries distinctive traits descending from both traditions. See Pulkkinen 1996, especially 1-2, 27-31, 151-63.

234.   Gutiérrez 1990: 31 and 1982: 77.

235.   'El problema fundamental de la teología latinoamericana no ha sido en directo recobrar el sentido de una fe amenazada, sino recobrar el sentido de una realidad no sólo amenazada, sino en la miseria. Hacer teología en su sentido liberador ha significado ayudar a transformar la realidad de pecado. El adversario de la teología no ha sido tanto el "ateo" como el "no-hombre"' (Sobrino 1976: 206). As with most liberation theologians, Sobrino refers to 'human being' as 'man' (*hombre*) that has the same sexist connotations in Spanish as it does in English. In this specific context, Gutiérrez does speak of non-person whereas Sobrino speaks of non-man.

236.   'Pero en un continente como América Latina el reto no viene en primer lugar del no

These non-persons are 'the exploited classes, marginalized races, and the despised cultures'.[237]

Who are these 'non-persons' Gutiérrez talks about? There has been a shift in LT in defining them. Let us first see what liberation theologians have said about poverty, which is the necessary condition for there being poor persons.

1.4.1 *Poverty*

Again, it was Gutiérrez who among the liberation theologians first gave a systematic definition of poverty. His insights were taken up at the Medellín conference and in its final documents and were universally accepted by other liberation theologians.[238] He starts with the biblical understanding of poverty.

First, poverty is material poverty, the lack of the economic goods necessary for a human life with dignity.[239] Ultimately, poverty means death.[240] In the Bible, material poverty is a 'scandalous condition' that goes against human dignity, and consequently, against the will of God. It is clearly denounced in the Bible. Poverty is not a fatality, because it is produced in human relationships. There are poor because there are rich, the former being victims of the latter.[241] The existence of poverty reflects a lack of solidarity in human relations and in the communion with God. Poverty is an expression of sin, of lack of love.[242]

Second, poverty can be seen as spiritual infancy. According to Gutiérrez, there is a double aspect of poverty in the Bible. It is not only a 'scandalous condition', but also 'an ability to receive God, a willingness to be used by God, and a humility in front of God'.[243] It is openness to God, spiritual infancy. In this sense, poverty can be understood as an ideal that reaches its clearest expression in the Beatitudes in the New Testament.[244]

Third, poverty is a commitment of solidarity and protest. The theological foundation for this Christian ideal is Christological. It is a question of following Jesus. Poverty as solidarity and protest assumes concrete forms, politically and economically, since it has to be effective to be true.[245] According to Gutiérrez, 'Only an authentic solidarity with the poor and a real protest against poverty as it

creyente, sino del *no persona*, es decir, de aquel a quien el orden social existente no reconoce como tal: el pobre, el explotado, el que es sistemática y legalmente despojado de su ser de hombre, el que apenas sabe que es una persona. El no-persona cuestiona, ante todo, no nuestro mundo religioso, sino nuestro *mundo económico, social, político, cultural*' (Gutiérrez 1982: 77 [emphasis in original]).

237.   Gutiérrez 1982: 248.
238.   Lois 1988: 104.
239.   Gutiérrez 1990: 323.
240.   Gutiérrez 1990: 22.
241.   Gutiérrez 1990: 325-27.
242.   Gutiérrez 1990: 330.
243.   Gutiérrez 1990: 330.
244.   Gutiérrez 1990: 330-32.
245.   Gutiérrez 1990: 334-38.

appears in our times can give a concrete and vital context for a theological discourse about poverty'.[246]

Thus, the principal preoccupation of LT is to avoid confusing poverty with a mere internal attitude that is not connected to the historical reality of real poverty.[247] The later development of Gutiérrez' theology—and LT in general—seems to concentrate more on 'the poor' than on 'poverty', more on the subject than on the structures. This development is at least partially due to a later tendency in LT that places more emphasis on spirituality. The second definition of poverty, poverty as spiritual infancy and openness, becomes a condition for the third, for the solidarity and the protest.[248] This development is well reflected in Gutiérrez' introduction (1990) to the new edition of his *Teología de la liberación*. When one moves from mere structural analysis to a more specified analysis, it implies a greater differentiation. Poverty gets a human face. 'Poverty' as a concept is much more abstract than 'the poor'. The latter adds substance and concreteness, as well as diversity, to the first.

As was said earlier, there is new emphasis in LT on the concept of poverty that is based on the dichotomy life–death. Poverty is negation of life, not just materially, but culturally and spiritually as well. LT must become a *theology of life*, of defence of life. According to Pablo Richard, 'The death of millions of human beings is not a mere economic, political or technical problem. It is also an ethical and spiritual problem. This religious dimension is especially visible in the Third World, since we are a poor world, but also a profoundly religious world'.[249] And

> The fundamental contradiction is between the *centers of power*, situated mostly in the developed world, and the *poor and oppressed masses* of the Third World. This is usually called the *North–South conflict*. It is a contradiction between life and death, between the Third World masses that fight for *life* and the economic, financial, technological, political, cultural and ideological centers of *death* of the developed world. The conflict is not with the *people* of the industrialized world, but with the *centers of power and death* in that world.[250]

246. 'Solamente una auténtica solidaridad con los pobres y una real protesta contra la pobreza tal como se presenta en nuestros días, puede dar un contexto concreto y vital a un discurso teológico sobre la pobreza' (Gutiérrez 1990: 338).
247. Lois 1988: 122.
248. Lois 1988: 124-25.
249. 'La muerte de millones de seres humanos en el Tercer Mundo no es sólo un problema económico, político o técnico. Es también un problema ético y espiritual. Esta dimensión religiosa se hace especialmente visible en el Tercer Mundo, pues somos un mundo pobre, pero también profundamente religioso' (Richard 1987a: 44).
250. 'Esta contradicción fundamental se da entre los *centros de poder* ubicados fundamentalmente en el Mundo desarrollado y las *masas pobres y oprimidas* del Tercer Mundo; es lo que se llama normalmente *contradicción Norte-Sur*; es una contradicción entre la vida y la muerte, entre las masas del Tercer Mundo que luchan por la *vida* y los centros económicos, financieros, tecnológicos, políticos, culturales, ideológicos de la *muerte* localizados en el mundo desarrollado. La contradicción no es con los *pueblos* del mundo industrializado, sino con los *centros de poder y muerte* ubicados en ese mundo' (Richard 1987a: 93 [emphasis in original]).

When Gutiérrez says that the challenge of the non-person does not put into question our religious world so much as our economic and political world, the tendency presented by Richard claims that it does. Massive poverty is seen as a challenge to the 'religion of the North' and its credibility. Enrique Dussel, too, points out that 'Rather than secularization we are seeing the divinization of the whole [European, North American] system and the conversion of money into a fetish'.[251] Thus, 'Those who do not serve the poor are "atheists" with respect to the creating and redeeming God because they think that the poor should serve them and that "god" (their fetish) is with them. Those who serve the poor are "atheists" with respect to themselves and the system.'[252]

The emphasis on idolatry rather than faith vs atheism has appeared in LT especially as a result of the multidisciplinary research team of the *Departamento Ecuménico de Investigaciones* (DEI) in San José, Costa Rica.[253] According to this way of thinking,

> The central issue is idolatry, the worship of the false gods of the system of oppression... All systems of oppression are characterized by the creation of gods and of idols that sanction oppression and anti-life forces... The search for the true God in this battle of the gods brings us to an anti-idolatrous discernment of false gods, of those fetishes that kill and their religious weapons of death. Faith in God the liberator...necessarily passes through the negation and apostasy of false gods. Faith becomes anti-idolatrous.[254]

This is why LT has often been called a theology of life, as was noted earlier. 'God of life' (*el Dios de la vida*) is another name for 'God of the poor' (*el Dios de los pobres*). In Latin America, the basic question about God arises from the radical alternative between life and death. The most radical opposition to the God of life is not atheism but idolatry, the cult of gods who produce death and demand victims.[255]

According to Franz Hinkelammert, 'In the 1970s, LT was elaborated more and more as a theology of life. Liberation was conceived as a situation in which the right to life is guaranteed to everybody, securing the satisfaction of basic needs for everybody, by means of work'.[256]

At the latest EATWOT general assembly, in 1992, Pablo Richard gave a paper that reflects this new understanding of Latin American LT as the theology of life.

251. Dussel 1980: 199.
252. Dussel 1980: 201.
253. See Araya 1987, especially 91-104; Hinkelammert 1990 (especially part III), 1991a, 1991b, 1995; Richard *et al.* 1989.
254. 'El problema central es la idolatría, como culto a dioses falsos del sistema de opresión... Todo sistema de opresión se caracteriza precisamente por la creación de dioses y generar ídolos sacralizadores de la opresión y la anti-vida... La búsqueda del Dios verdadero en esta lucha de los dioses, nos lleva al discernimiento anti-idolátrico de los dioses falsos, de los fetiches que matan y sus armas religiosas de muerte. La fe en el Dios liberador...pasa necesariamente por la negación y la apostasía de los dioses falsos. La fe se torna anti-idolátrica' (Richard *et al.* 1989: 7).
255. Lois 1988: 182-83.
256. Hinkelammert 1988: 27.

It is exactly in the EATWOT context where Latin American theologians have
been challenged by other Third World theologians on their too exclusive emphasis on class analysis. Thus, it is not without significance that it is this very same
context where Latin American LT of the 1990s is presented as the theology of life.

According to Richard, the major reality challenging LT in the new international order is the massive death of the poor. There are two facts behind this.
First, the failure of 'historic socialism' in the East, and second, the failure of
'development capitalism' in the South. The former has shaped the latter: what we
now see in the Third World is a 'savage capitalism', excluding the great majority
of people and destroying nature.[257]

Richard says:

> In this situation of death, liberation theology raises questions about the credibility of
> life: about life for all and the life of nature. More radically, it raises questions about
> the very credibility of God as the God of life, as the God who creates and saves.
> Liberation theology responds to that question by *taking the radical and absolute option for
> life*.[258]

He refers to a phrase by St Irenaeus, '*gloria Dei vivens homo, gloria autem hominis
visio Dei*'.[259] Against this background, what Richard sees as the most pressing task
for LT is the rebuilding of hope and utopia. The foundation of that utopia is 'the
faith in the God of life as a transcendent God'.[260]

He says in a prophetic tone:

> The South exists and has its own theology. The South refuses to accept its own
> death and destruction. The South refuses to allow itself to be run over and treated
> unequally. The South refuses to surrender the sovereignty of its peoples or to forego
> democracy. The South has a culture, an ethic, a spirituality, and an identity. The
> South wants to live and to live in abundance. The South wants the whole world
> (including the North) to have life and the cosmos to be recreated and saved in its
> entirety. This is the context in which liberation theology is seeking to redefine itself
> as the theology of the South.[261]

1.4.2 *The Poor*

'The poor' (*el pobre, los pobres*) have been named as the subjects of LT since its
earliest moments. 'The epistemological rupture' is the 'irruption of the poor' in
history. According to Gutiérrez, 'What we have often called "the major fact" in
the life of the Latin American Church, the participation of the Christians in the
process of liberation, is nothing but an expression of a vast historical event: *the
irruption of the poor*'.[262] The solidarity with the poor, the option for them, is a result

257.   Richard 1994: 93.
258.   Richard 1994: 94 (emphasis added). Of the potential dangers of this kind of discourse,
especially for creating a constructive sexual ethics inside LT, see Chapter 4.1.1.
259.   Richard 1994: 95.
260.   Richard 1994: 101-102.
261.   Richard 1994: 104.
262.   'Lo que hemos llamado con frecuencia el "hecho mayor" de la vida de la Iglesia
latinoamericana: la participación de los cristianos en el proceso de liberación, no es sino una

of the existence of millions of human beings without the most fundamental human rights (right to life, education and health). The poor and the oppressed, and their perspective ('from where', '*desde*'), are the main single starting point for all liberation theologians.[263]

According to Julio Lois, Ignacio Ellacuría[264] offers the most complete synthesis about the concept of the poor in LT.[265] First of all, the poor is a socio-economic concept that refers to two thirds of humanity, the so-called Third World. The poor are a historical reality; their existence is not so much due to natural as historical causes. The poor are a collective, conflictive and ethical subject. This is the sociological perspective of the concept.[266]

From a theological perspective, there are principally four ways to 'define' the poor. First, the *theo-logical* perspective. The theological backbone of LT is in the affirmation of the mystery of God as the God of the poor.[267] The poor are the 'place' (*lugar*), the 'sacrament' and the 'presence' of a crucified and suffering God that is hidden and absent. But at the same time, the poor are also the presence of a liberating God who intervenes actively and salvifically in history. The eschatological tension between the 'not yet' and the 'already' of the Kingdom of God is concretely present in the poor.[268]

Second, according to Ellacuría, there is the *christological* perspective. Not only was Jesus himself poor, but he also put his life into the service of the poor. The poor had a special place in his life and mission. Jesus announced the Kingdom of God from the poor and for the poor, and he shared their destiny to its ultimate consequences by dying on the cross, at the hands of the powerful of his time.[269]

Third, the poor have a specific *soteriological* significance, since it is for them the Good News is announced (the 'passive' practice of salvation). The poor are also the carriers of the Good News and have a special 'evangelizing ability' by having been elected by God (the 'active' practice of salvation). Since Christian

expresión de un vasto acontecimiento histórico: *la irrupción de los pobres*' (Gutiérrez 1990: 21 [emphasis in original]). The introduction for this latest edition of *Teología de la liberación*, written by Gutiérrez himself, almost twenty years after the first edition, reflects the changes both in his thinking and in LT in general. The language reflects this change: 'irruption of the poor' and 'irruption of the Third World' are concepts adopted at the international meetings of Third World theologians.

263.   This fact is well reflected in the titles of their books. See Gutiérrez' *Teología desde el reverso de la historia*, Leonardo Boff's *Teología desde el cautiverio* and *Teología desde el lugar del pobre*, and Hugo Assmann's *Teología desde la praxis de la liberación*.

264.   This Salvadorean (originally Basque) theologian was one of the Jesuits brutally murdered by the Salvadorean Army in November 1989.

265.   What follows is based largely on Lois' work, a good synthesis of Ellacuría's concept of 'the poor'. See Lois 1988: 146-75. See also Tamayo-Acosta 1990: 229.

266.   Lois 1988: 147-49.

267.   Lois 1988: 149-50.

268.   Lois 1988: 156-57.

269.   Lois 1988: 157-61.

soteriology is always historical, the poor are a privileged instrument of God's salvific power in history.[270]

Fourth, the *ecclesiological* understanding of the poor is most remarkably expressed in what is called the church of the poor in Latin America. The option for the poor is one of the marks of the true church, a church that is poor and of the poor. In this church, especially in the ecclesial base communities, the poor are active subjects.[271]

The theological understanding of the poor aims at determining the significance of the (sociological) reality of the poor for the Christian faith. The sociological and the theological are two different perspectives which are not mutually exclusive but complementary.[272] According to Lois, the merely sociological perspective on the poor is deepened and enriched by the theological analysis. The social reality of the poor does the same to the theological categories, 'illuminating each other mutually'.[273]

As has been said earlier, the notion of the poor has become more differentiated or specified. The poor are not only the economically oppressed (as a class) but there are also cultural, ethnic, racial and sexual aspects to poverty.[274] The poorest among the poor are the indigenous people, the blacks and the women, a black or indigenous woman being the most oppressed of all because of the triple burden of oppression (material poverty, racism and sexism). According to Gutiérrez, the extension of the concept in this direction is due to the popular movements that take up these causes and to the international dialogue of the Third World and other liberation theologians.[275] Yet it has been the Latin American women themselves, both theologians and lay women, who have expressed the demand to be included *as women* among the constitutive subjects of LT. They have been the protagonists of their liberation.

Gutiérrez himself, in his earlier works, referred to the poor as 'the absent of history' (*los ausentes de la historia*),[276] and 'the exploited classes, marginalized races, the despised cultures'.[277] The 'rupture' between traditional and progressive

270. Lois 1988: 161-67.
271. Lois 1988: 170-74.
272. Lois 1988: 149, 175.
273. Lois 1988: 175.
274. See Gutiérrez 1990: 22-27.
275. Gutiérrez 1990: 24-25. In an earlier article, Gutiérrez says: '*Only* the overcoming of a society divided into classes, *only* a political power in service of the popular majorities, *only* the elimination of the private appropriation of the richness created by human labor, can offer us the bases of a more just society' (Gutiérrez 1973: 240-41 [emphasis added]). There is an obvious change both in the language used and in what he considers the way to a more just society. He also changed the title of one of the last chapters of his *Teología de la liberación*—'Faith and class struggle' in 1972, to 'Faith and social conflict' in the 1990 edition. It is important to note, though, that the change is neither merely semantic nor superficially political (for instance, the crisis of socialism, the disintegration of Soviet Union or the 'loss of meaning' of a socialist discourse). The change implies substantial changes and conceptual deepening inside LT itself.
276. Gutiérrez 1977: 35, 43. Thus the title of the book, *Teología desde el reverso de la historia*.
277. Gutiérrez 1977: 43, 54. 'The exploited social sectors, the despised races, the marginalized

theology is not only theological. According to Gutiérrez, there is first a political rupture (*ruptura política*).[278] The perspective of the poor does not automatically make theology more scientific or serious, but 'the direct participation in a historical process, in the struggles of the poor, in the popular expressions of faith, *permits us to perceive aspects in the Christian message that escape other perspectives*'.[279]

As can be seen, the racial and ethnic perspective is already present in Gutiérrez' earliest works. The perspective of gender has been the last to be included in the category of 'the poor' in the writings of the liberation theologians.

According to Pablo Richard,

> In the last ten years, LT has deepened and extended the concept *poor* using the term *oppressed*, not only in its economic dimension, but also in its racial, cultural and sexist dimensions. The concept of class was overemphasized at the cost of that of race, nation and sex… [This] new form of poverty hits children, youth and women especially hard, and it hits them doubly if they are indigenous or Afro-Americans… The preferential option for the poor acquires a qualitatively different radicality.[280]

The new challenges to LT are thus women's theology of liberation, the Afro-American theology of liberation and the indigenous theology of liberation.[281] He also mentions the new ecumenical and universal (global) perspective in LT. All this means a historical opportunity (*kairos*) for a new birth of LT.[282]

The same observations are made by the Uruguayan Protestant theologian Julio de Santa Ana.

> [There is] a necessity for a response to the expectations of *all* oppressed *social* groups in Latin America. It is impossible to generalize the poor. They have concrete faces. The specificities of these faces cannot be left aside… These concrete faces of the poor are challenging the liberation theologians to develop new ways of reflection, to make their arguments more substantial and concrete.[283]

cultures are the historical subject of a new intelligence of faith' (Gutiérrez 1977: 59). And, 'Liberation theology is an intent to understand faith from the historical, liberating and subversive praxis of the poor of this world, of the exploited classes, despised races and marginalized cultures' (Gutiérrez 1982: 52 [originally written in 1973]).

278. Gutiérrez 1977: 35.

279. 'la participación directa en un proceso histórico, en las luchas de los pobres, en las expresiones populares de la fe, *permite percibir en el mensaje cristiano aspectos que escapan a otras perspectivas*' (Gutiérrez 1977: 38 [emphasis added]).

280. 'En los últimos diez años la TL ha profundizado y ampliado el concepto de *pobre* utilizando el término *oprimido*, no sólo en la dimensión económica, sino también en lo racial, cultural y sexista. El concepto de clase fue sobredeterminado por aquellos de raza, nación y sexo… Esta nueva forma de pobreza golpea especialmente a los niños, los jóvenes y las mujeres, y los golpea doblemente cuando son indígenas o afro-americanos… La opción preferencial por los pobres adquiere una radicalidad cualitativamente diferente' (Richard 1991: 4 [emphasis in original]).

281. Richard 1991: 6.

282. Richard 1991: 8.

283. '…la necesidad de dar respuestas a las expectativas de *todos* los grupos *sociales* oprimidos en América Latina. No cabe generalizar sobre los pobres. Tienen rostros concretos, cuyas especificidades no pueden ser dejadas de lado… Estos rostros concretos de los pobres desafían a los teólogos de la liberación a desarrollar nuevas líneas de reflexión, a hacer más sustantivos y

He too mentions specifically women, Indians (the indigenous people) and blacks. According to his judgment, LT has become more inclusive in recent years.[284]

Leonardo and Clodovis Boff affirm this as well. The overarching characteristic of the oppressed in the Third World is the poverty in socio-economic terms. This conditions all other forms of oppression. It is necessary to start from this infrastructural oppression if we want to understand correctly all other forms of oppression.[285] But, they continue, 'We cannot confine ourselves to the purely socio-economic aspect of oppression, the "poverty" aspect, however basic and "determinant" this may be. We also have to look to other levels of social oppression, such as racial oppression..., ethnic oppression...and sexual oppression.'[286]

For Enrique Dussel,

> Salvation, redemption, and liberation are meant to apply to the whole human being. One-sided 'spiritualization' is as idolatrous as one-sided 'historification'... People are 'flesh', bound up with history, politics, economics, culture, and sexuality; by nature people are not 'spirit'.[287]

Thus, we can see that there is a strong emphasis on the poor as a class in the Marxist sense, on the one hand, but that this emphasis has been shifting toward a more inclusive definition, on the other hand. There are differences between liberation theologians, as well. Some stress the spiritual and biblical aspects of the poor and poverty more than others do. New subjects within LT are bringing with them critical elements, especially in the issues of race and gender, pointing to the insufficiency of previous definitions.

1.4.3 *Option for the Poor*

As has been said earlier, since the Medellín conference the 'preferential option for the poor' has been *the* option of the Latin American Church, at least formally. It is a concept created by liberation theologians which was introduced into official church documents.[288] What do liberation theologians really mean by that option?

According to Lois, 'The option for the poor consists, first of all, of a voluntary decision that leads to an incarnation in the world of the poor, to assume with

concretos sus argumentos' (Santa Ana 1988: 235 [emphasis in original]).

284. Santa Ana 1988: 237-39.

285. Boff and Boff 1989: 35.

286. 'Es imposible quedarse en el aspecto puramente socio-económico de la opresión, el aspecto "pobre", por más fundamental y "determinante" que sea. Es preciso ver también los otros planes de opresión social, la opresión de tipo racial..., la opresión de tipo étnico..., la opresión de tipo sexual' (Boff and Boff 1989: 39). The Boffs also include feminist theology in the concept 'liberation theology worldwide' (Boff and Boff 1989: 93-98).

287. Dussel 1980: 211.

288. It is interesting to note how this concept has become the connecting thought of the three bishops' conferences (Medellín, Puebla, Santo Domingo). Those who wish to see a continuity between the conferences stress the significance of 'the option for the poor' as a concept being present in all three official documents. Those who are more doubtful point out how the meaning of the concept has actually changed from Medellín to Santo Domingo.

historical realism their cause for integral liberation'.[289] It is always a Christian option founded in faith.[290] This option is a duty of all Christians, whatever their socio-economic status. This includes the poor themselves.[291] The option must be realized both at a personal-individual level and at a communitarian-ecclesiastical level. Individual believers, Christian groups and communities, different ecclesiastical sectors and the church in its entirety are all responsible for the realization of the option.[292]

Liberation theologians have not given clear definitions of 'the option for the poor', but let us take a look at the ways some of them understand it.

For Leonardo Boff, the option for the poor is threefold. First, it is a *political option*. Second, it is an *ethical option* (since the situation is not accepted as it is), and third, it is an *evangelical option* (because the poor were the first addressees of Jesus' message).[293] He says:

> this preferential option for the poor has produced the great and necessary Copernican revolution in the bosom of the Church. Its significance exceeds the Latin American ecclesiastical context and affects the universal Church. I sincerely do believe that this option signifies the most important theological and pastoral transformation occurred since the Protestant reformation in the 16th century.[294]

For Gutiérrez, the term 'preferential' rejects all kinds of exclusion and refers to the universality of God's love, giving preference to those who must be the first. The word 'option' refers to the free and committing character of a decision. In the ultimate instance, the option for the poor means an option for God—it is a theocentric and prophetic option.[295] This is also the basic line of the Puebla document. The Christian message is universal, but universality can be affirmed and realized only from particularity (the poor).[296]

This is emphasized by Sobrino, too. 'Partiality and universality are not opposed. Liberation theology stresses the principle of partiality because..., methodologically, better and in a more Christian way one recovers the universality better and in a more Christian way from partiality than vice versa'.[297] For

289. '...la opción por los pobres consiste en la decisión voluntaria que conduce a encarnarse en el mundo de los pobres para asumir con realismo histórico su causa de liberación integral' (Lois 1988: 195).

290. Lois 1988: 195.

291. Lois 1988: 195-96.

292. Lois 1988: 196.

293. L. Boff 1981: 74-75.

294. '...con esta opción preferencial por los pobres se ha producido la gran y necesaria revolución copernicana en el seno de la Iglesia, cuyo significado desborda el contexto latino-americano y concierne a la Iglesia universal. Sinceramente creo que esta opción significa la más importante transformación teológico-pastoral acaecida desde la Reforma protestante del siglo XVI' (L. Boff 1981: 193).

295. Gutiérrez 1990: 28-30.

296. Lois 1988: 199, quoting the Puebla document.

297. 'Parcialidad y universalidad no se oponen, pues. La teología de la liberación recalca el principio de parcialidad porque...metodológicamente, mejor y más cristianamente se recupera la universalidad desde la parcialidad que a la inversa' (Sobrino 1988: 253). It is unclear whether he

him, the option for the poor acts as a precomprehension for theology when it comes to understanding both the Scripture and today's reality.[298] LT is, above all, *intellectus amoris*, in contrast with the classical notion of theology as *intellectus fidei*. And this is the major novelty of LT.[299]

According to Julio Lois, the subjects of the option for the poor are all the believers, including the poor themselves. But it is notably different if the subject of the option her/himself is among the non-poor or the poor.[300] To opt for somebody else is different from opting for oneself.[301]

More than in the case of the homogeneous 'poor', the oppressed themselves are now becoming the subjects of theology. This is the very point of contact between Latin American LT and feminist theology. The encounter/disencounter with the poor is constitutive for the praxis liberation theologians speak about. As we have seen, the option for the poor, the solidarity with 'the Other', is at the heart of LT. Still, it is another matter when this 'Other' announces her/himself as a subject and wants to participate in the very definition of theology. From the point of view of 'the Other', she or he is no 'Other'.[302] Thus, the whole discourse on solidarity with the poor and the option for them is deepened, and to some point, challenged, when the objects of this option become subjects. To put it bluntly, the oldest 'Others' of Western theology have very much continued being Others in LT, as well.

One could illustrate this by taking an example. Clodovis Boff speaks about the epistemological and methodological questions in LT. He says: 'The "liberation theologian"…is a person *inserted* concretely in the cause of the oppressed. This is why it is said that liberation theology was born and is born out of *compassion with* those who suffer.'[303] He also says that the '*encounter with* the poor' is the indispensable condition for LT.[304] The same kind of citations could be taken from all liberation theologians. Besides the 'epistemological rupture' in LT, the citations

uses *parcialidad* (partiality) on purpose, instead of *particularidad* (particularity) as opposed to *universalidad* (universality).

298.   Sobrino 1988: 249.

299.   Sobrino 1988: 259.

300.   Lois 1988: 195-96. See also Lois 1991: 9.

301.   The option liberation theologians talk about is reminiscent of liberation theologians seeing themselves ideally as 'organic intellectuals'. Those of them who really have opted for becoming poor themselves are few. Liberation theologians are not necessarily unfaithful to their message if they stay in their middle-class lifestyle. Rather, it is a question of tension between the stereotypical and idealized image of liberation theologians being immersed in the life of the poor (an image they themselves have been eager to promote) and the reality.

302.   Leonardo and Clodovis Boff observe this when they say that 'The poor do not usually refer to themselves as "poor", which would offend their sense of honor and dignity. It is the non-poor who call them poor' (Boff and Boff 1989: 41-42). On the concept of the Other, see Chapter 1.4.4.

303.   'El "teólogo de la liberación"…es una persona *metida* concretamente en la causa de los oprimidos. Por eso se dice que la teología de la liberación nació y sigue naciendo de la *com-pasión con* los que sufren' (C. Boff 1991: 89 [emphasis added]).

304.   C. Boff 1991: 90 (emphasis added).

reflect the complicated subject-object relationship that exists between 'the poor' or 'the Other' and the liberation theologians (or any intellectual). The option for the poor is another reflection of these problems, even though Gutiérrez says that the poor themselves have to realize this option, too.[305] Beyond mere rhetoric, it is different if the option is made by a poor or a non-poor person.

In the above-mentioned article, C. Boff presents a diagram that illustrates the distinction between three different levels in LT: the professional, the pastoral and the popular. The distinction itself makes it easier to understand how professional theologians, the base communities and the clergy interrelate in LT. But it is the description of these levels that reflects a certain dualism and even elitism in his thinking. He says that the major difference between these different kinds of theological levels is in the logic or, more concretely, in the language.

The professional theologians are described as 'elaborated and rigorous' and their logic more 'systematic'. The pastoral level has a 'logic of action' in contrast to the scientific professional logic. The popular level is 'spontaneous and oral' and produces 'commentaries' and has a 'logic of life'.[306] These kinds of descriptions are almost synonymous to the definitions that for centuries have been made about men and women, on the one hand, and about whites and blacks on the other hand. The implicit ordering categories are rationality vs emotions and theory vs practice. This could also be seen as being in total contradiction with other affirmations of liberation theologians where the ideal is, as we have seen, the overcoming of dualisms.

Similar problems arise in Pablo Richard's metaphor of a tree for different levels of LT. According to him, as a tree, LT too has its roots, its trunk and its branches. The roots of LT are in the spirituality of Latin American people, in how they combine the fight for their rights with a deep and rich spirituality. The trunk is formed by the ecclesial base communities in which the popular spirituality gets its communal and concrete form. This is the level in which most of the priests and nuns work. Finally, the academic theologians form the branches of the tree. This level consists of explicit and systematic theological work, mostly in written form. As a tree, LT too is an integrated whole in which one element does not exist without the others. Without a trunk, there are no branches; the roots generate the trunk.[307] These levels correspond with the popular, pastoral and professional levels of LT presented above.

In spite of the vegetal (and not historical or cultural) character of the metaphor, it nevertheless presupposes an organic whole and does not characterize the 'non-professional' levels in as stereotypical terms as does C. Boff's scheme. Still, the problem remains: Who can represent 'the people', the poor? What does it mean that liberation theologians speak for the poor?

Academic liberation theologians prefer understanding themselves as 'organic intellectuals' in the Gramscian way. According to Juan Luis Segundo, liberation

---

305.   Gutiérrez 1990: 28.
306.   C. Boff 1991: 92-93. The same diagram is presented in Boff and Boff 1989: 22.
307.   Richard 1987a: 59.

theologians have accepted being organic intellectuals, accepting as their tasks the representation of the community, the articulation of a foundation for their intra- and extra-communal demands, and the providing for them of the fundamentals of a conscientization that is appropriate to their possibilities of knowledge and analysis of reality.[308] According to him, 'There is no doubt that liberation theology, in its simplest and most basic forms, plays an important and, in some extraordinary cases, decisive role in satisfying these needs'. He himself 'translates' this role of a theologian into 'teaching to analyse reality'. This, according to some, is a crucial shift in the role of the intellectual (theologian) from individual scholarly authority to reflective community advocate.[309] Even if true, it also entails problems which have to do with the question of who speaks for whom, and in what way.[310]

According to Lois, there are four fundamental elements in 'the option for the poor'. First, there is the element of rupture (*ruptura*) with one's own social, cultural and political status. Second, there is the element of incarnation or identification with the poor that expresses itself in the 'encounter with the poor'. This means entering the world of the poor and assuming it as one's own. Third, there is the element of active solidarity with the poor and the defence of their rights. This equates to the historical praxis of liberation. Fourth, one has to assume the destiny of the poor as one's own. Often this means persecution and martyrdom. This is the final criterion for the verification of the authenticity of the second element.[311] Naturally, all this is quite different for those who are poor and for those who are not poor themselves.

Obviously, the option for the poor and its theological, epistemological, spiritual and political consequences can be seen as the major innovations of LT. But,

308.   Segundo 1985b: 150. On the theologian as an 'organic intellectual', see also L. Boff 1986b: 137-42, 227-52.

309.   Engel and Thistlethwaite 1990: 2.

310.   According to Horacio Cerutti Guldberg, the theoretical problems and difficulties included in the option for the poor have generally been obviated. If most liberation theologians' claim that 'only the exploited and those who side with them can see the perversity of the system' (referring to José María Vigil), how can one change position or place (*lugar*), asks Cerutti Guldberg. He criticizes the option for the poor in LT (with the exception of Raúl Vidales) as some kind of guarantee of orthodoxy and orthopraxis, which is not far from 'the unsustainable uncriticality of a proletarian science' (Cerutti Guldberg 1996: 10-12). He also says: 'Esta opción, que en verdad es un conjunto de opciones o decisiones existenciales renovadas en diversas coyunturas, no garantiza nada. Posibilita, sitúa, brinda perspectiva, abre horizontes pero exige una permanente alerta racional y autocrítica para seguir avanzando' (Cerutti Guldberg 1996: 13). According to Cerutti Guldberg, liberation theologians confuse different levels of analysis, which represents a question of cardinal importance and is difficult to resolve (Cerutti Guldberg 1996: 14).

Cerutti Guldberg takes up the same issue in another text in a little different way: '...habría una identificación cuasi natural entre teoría de liberación y pueblo pobre, una especie de armonía preestablecida y de relación no conflictiva entre el pueblo y el pensamiento de su liberación efectuado por otros' (Cerutti Guldberg 1997: 3).

311.   Lois 1991: 11-12.

as was said, a radical and critical question about the subject of theology goes further. The differentiation and extension of the concept 'poor' is accepted nowadays by practically all liberation theologians. But still they speak from a context that *is not* that of a woman, of an Indian, of a poor person.[312]

The critique from race and gender perspectives is making itself present in Latin American LT, too. More recently, most liberation theologians have included these perspectives, at least formally, and as will be shown, in most cases superficially.

The supposed collective subject (the poor, the Other) of LT certainly has changed the role of an academic intellectual. Nevertheless, the majority of the most prominent liberation theologians are clerics (with a special meaning in the Catholic Church where women's ordination is out of the question and priests do not marry), highly educated, male and of European descendancy, that is, 'white' in the eyes of the black and indigenous population. The critique of the pretended universality and neutrality of European theology must be extended to LT itself, especially in questions of race and gender.

Earlier in this chapter, I presented different ways of periodizing LT. It is usually done by referring to historical stages that of course to some extent are always arbitrary. This way of presenting the development of LT reflects external causes, such as political and economic ones, more than internal causes as well as ecclesiastical changes. Another way to understand how LT has changed and evolved during the last thirty years is to take a more thematic or internal perspective. Tamayo-Acosta describes the internal development of LT by referring to 'first and second generation' liberation theologians (the latter since 1975). He sees the development as a process of evolving (new) themes, such as ecclesiology, Christology, spirituality and popular religiosity. Among these new themes the concept 'the option for the poor' (Indians, blacks and women) is dealt with more deeply.[313] I would argue that a more radical difference between 'first and second

---

312.   As will be shown in forthcoming chapters—mainly Chapter 4—this has practical consequences. Liberation theologians have consciously taken 'the dominated and dependent Latin America' as their starting point, but they have not been as critical of other 'places' that define their theologizing, such as race and gender. This is why the growing dialogue between different liberation theologies is so important. It does not mean weakening the basic options and innovations of LT or ridiculing them. On the contrary, it means taking them more seriously. This is why we should be critical of idealizing statements such as this, by the Spanish theologian Juan José Tamayo-Acosta: 'the theologies developed in the First World are "theologies *of*" (*de*) while Latin America is the cradle of "theologies *from*" (*desde*). This means that the liberation theologians are conscious of the limits and conditionings of their theologizing' (Tamayo-Acosta 1990: 68, quoting J.I. González Faus [emphasis in original]). He says next: 'This is something of capital importance, since these conditionings constitute "an indispensable hermeneutical factor"' (Tamayo-Acosta 1990: 68). If by limits and conditionings is only meant economic, political and overall social factors, it is true, especially when comparing LT with European and North American theology. But surely there are other limits and conditionings, of which Latin American liberation theologians are not much more—or even less—conscious than their European or North American colleagues.

313.   Tamayo-Acosta 1990: 120-23. It is true that the 'second generation' liberation

generation' liberation theologians lays in the specification of the subject of theology (the concept of the poor, who form the praxis of LT, for instance). Or maybe we can even talk about 'third generation' liberation theologians, among which there are many women.

The poor as subjects of LT carry the Marxist heritage, referring primarily to production and class consciousness. Recent social scientific research on Latin American social movements stresses the importance of moving beyond the centrality of class concept in interpreting the success or failure of these movements.[314] According to Slater, the major problem with Marxist class analysis concerns the failure to theorize subjectivity and identity.[315] He reminds us that nowhere has the critique of a notion of a unified subject been so effectively developed as in feminist theory.[316] Referring to Chantal Mouffe, Slater states that each social agent is inscribed in a range of social relations connected to gender, race, nationality, locality, and so on. Every social agent is the site of many subject positions. An oppressed subject can also, simultaneously, be an oppressing subject.[317] This kind of perspective offers us one explanation of why there are conflicting interests and power struggles inside social movements. This can very well be applied to LT, too. The poor as a too one-sided (seen primarily as a class) and homogeneous concept needs to be challenged by the 'multiple subject positions of each agent in the struggle'.

1.4.4 The Other

The above-mentioned differentiation in the concept of 'the poor' can be examined from still another perspective. Several liberation theologians use the

---

theologians have gone deeper into classical theological questions—such as Christology—than their predecessors, even though there is also an internal development in each individual theologian. Gutiérrez, for example, has been developing a spirituality of liberation in his later works. Juan Carlos Scannone sees LT as one movement, but with four currents within it. These are: (1) Theology on the basis of the pastoral praxis of the institutional church (several bishops); (2) on the basis of the praxis of revolutionary groups (socialist orientated liberation theologians); (3) on the basis of historical praxis that stresses the poor themselves as subjects of their own liberation (most liberation theologians); and (4) on the basis of the praxis of the peoples of Latin America (popular religiosity and cultural aspects). Quoted in McGovern 1989: xvi-xvii; Gibellini 1988: 12. McGovern sees problems in this set of distinctions. He pays attention to the heterogeneity of LT and does not speak of it as a static entity.

This is a fresh perspective among many studies done on LT. He, too, sees the changes mostly reflecting changes within society and within the church. By this he means the changing historical context of LT—for example the democratization of Latin American states. This is correct, of course, but according to my view, he does not pay sufficient attention to more internal causes, such as the critique presented by women or ethnic minorities. He mentions these but does not elaborate them further (McGovern 1989: 19, 229-32).

314. See Slater 1994: 12-13.
315. Slater 1994: 13.
316. Slater 1994: 15.
317. Slater 1994: 15-17.

concept 'the Other' (*el Otro*) to clarify the basic difference of LT from 'traditional' theology.

The question of the Other is most systematically elaborated by Enrique Dussel. He is usually counted among the liberation theologians, and rightly so, but his most important contributions are in the area of philosophy and history. He is one of the founders of the Latin American philosophy of liberation (*filosofía de la liberación*) that has close affinities with LT—a movement that since its beginning has been divided into several camps, Dussel presenting only one of them.[318] One of the basic—if not the most important—concepts and starting points for the philosophy of liberation is the concept of the Other, the question of alterity,[319] and related to this, the question of who is the philosophizing subject.

Dussel says:

> a philosophy of liberation is rising from the periphery, from the oppressed, from the shadow that the light of Being has not been able to illumine. Our thinking sets out from non-being, nothingness, otherness, exteriority, the mystery of no-sense. It is, then, 'barbarian philosophy'.[320]

Another important term in Dussel's philosophy is 'Totality' (*Totalidad*). It is not merely understood in the classical sense of 'the ordered Whole' or as the *a priori* ultimate horizon of meaning without which it is impossible to attach meaning to any object, including the human being. His anadialectical (*ana-*, beyond)

---

318.   For a systematic analysis of the philosophy of liberation, see Cerutti Guldberg 1988–89 and 1992. He differentiates four versions or manifestations of the philosophy of liberation. The first two, the ontologicist and analectic (*ana-*, beyond) manifestations, he characterizes as antihistoricist populism. According to the first version, Latin American thought can only be such [Latin American] if it starts from zero, from the explicit and voluntary ignorance of the whole world-philosophical tradition, elaborating a new rationality capable of expressing what belongs specifically to Latin American culture. The subject of this 'Latin America's own essential rationality' must be the Latin American 'people'. The second version is reflected by a point of departure which is denominated the criticism of a 'Eurocentric' or 'North Atlantic modernity'. Analectical philosophy of liberation claims to begin with the reality of Latin America. The role of the philosopher is that of a prophetic teacher who 'informs' and 'opts for' the poor people. Cerutti Guldberg does not say it explicitly, but it is obvious that he places Dussel in this group (as well as most liberation theologians by virtue of their reasoning). The third, historicist, version of the philosophy of liberation aims at developing a systematic Latin American historiography, in order to trace the history of ideas of the continent. The last, the problematizing modality, refuses any search for originality as a prerequisite. It claims back every human tradition as 'useful and critically instrumental for the affirmation of what is genuinely ours'. The problem for this philosophy is the real urgencies generated by the Latin American socio-historical and political praxis. What matters is the 'process of liberation' (Cerutti Guldberg 1988–89: 46-56).

Finally, Cerutti Guldberg says that it is practically impossible to speak of a philosophy of liberation. One would instead have to speak in plural of philosophies *for* liberation (Cerutti Guldberg 1988–89: 57). This corresponds to similar developments in theology where it is nowadays more accurate to speak of theologies of liberation.

319.   Dussel bases his use of the concept on the philosophy of Emmanuel Levinas. According to Ofelia Schutte, Dussel manipulates the principle of alterity of Levinas. See Schutte 1991: 282.

320.   Dussel 1985: 24.

method is a way to go beyond the dominant Totality that in a historical sense is that of Europe and North America. He says:

> 'The Same' (Lo Mismo), as a Totality, is closed in a circle that rotates eternally without novelty. The apparent novelty of a moment in its dialectic, in its movement, is accidental... 'The Same' devours historical temporality and ends up being the Neutral 'since always'.[321]

Modern thinking has been introducing 'the Other' in 'the Same' so much that the Totality, as the only possible substance, makes any real alterity impossible.[322]

What makes it possible to think—or rethink—the Totality outside its boundaries, outside its logic, is the Otherness. The irruption of the Other into the Totality reveals not just its boundaries, but also its irrationality and, ultimately, its violence. The dominant Totality is incapable of acknowledging the existence of the Other in his alterity/difference.[323]

For Dussel, the basic concretizations of the alterity are to be found in the relationships male–female, parent–child (also teacher–student) and brother–brother (including nation–nation). These correspond to three different levels: the erotic, the pedagogical and the political.[324]

For Dussel, Otherness is basically a category that refers to domination, or to the dominant–dominated relationship where the Other is the dominated party and to the potential liberation of this oppressive relationship. For example, women are the Other not just in relation to men but in relation to 'the Totality' as well. For the historical reasons of their oppression and domination, women are the principal protagonists of liberation, at least in the realm of female–male relationships.[325]

Since ethics and philosophy are not separable for Dussel,[326] his basic ethical thesis is: 'To affirm the Other and serve him is the good act, and to dominate him is the evil act'.[327] This is the absolute criterion of metaphysics and ethics.[328] 'The Same', as Totality, is the *being* and its knowledge the *truth* (for example, the *ego cogito* of Descartes, the Absolute Knowledge of Hegel, and the Eternal Return of the Same of Nietzsche). Thus, the one who-is-not (the Other) has to be dominated and, ultimately, eliminated.[329] If the negation of the Other is the ultimate wrong, the ultimate good is his affirmation through love-for-justice (*amor-de-*

---

321.   Dussel 1987: I, 97.
322.   Dussel 1987: I, 108.
323.   Dussel 1987: I, 118-27.
324.   Dussel 1987: I, 128.
325.   Dussel 1988: III, 115. It is the woman who concretizes the alterity in a more radical way because of her historical submission. There are contradictions in Dussel's thought which will be analysed in Chapter 3.3.1.
326.   Dussel 1988: III, 163.
327.   Dussel 1988: III, 183. In the original Spanish text, the Other is defined in male terms (*el Otro*) in spite of the explicit affirmation of women's alterity and their necessary liberation.
328.   Dussel 1988: III, 183.
329.   Dussel 1987: II, 14 (emphasis in original).

justicia).[330] The radical goodness for Dussel is the conversion to the oppressed Other—be it in racial, political, economic or sexual terms. To have 'ethical conscience' is to listen-to-the-voice-of-the-Other, the voice that demands justice. Not to have ethical conscience means killing the Other. This is the same as to say that the Other is silent.[331] The 'illiteracy' of the dominant culture interprets the Other as a 'silent thing', without taking into account the necessity of listening.[332]

The Other manifests himself as a face exterior to the ontological horizon: beyond the established and institutionalized Totality. 'The Other', as exteriority, is a condition for a metaphysical possibility of an authentic, creative, new future.[333] In a specific Latin American context, this means that 'the Other, for us, is Latin America in respect to the European Totality, the poor and oppressed Latin American people in respect to the dominating oligarchies'.[334] Dussel's anadialectical method starts from the Other as somebody oppressed but free, as somebody *beyond* the Totality.[335] He puts it very concretely: 'The face of the dominated poor Indian, of the oppressed mestizo, of the Latin American people, is the "theme" of Latin American philosophy'.[336] This means 'the end of the pretended universality of Europe',[337] the ability to 'judge the Totality as overcome and dead',[338] and a justification of the liberation of the oppressed. The Totality now appears as an ontic system, one more system, a given system at one moment of history, one of many, and, finally, as an ideological system.[339]

Thus, in many ways 'the Other' appears as a more open and inclusive category than 'the poor'. Implicitly, they are congruent in the writings of most liberation theologians. 'The poor' become more particularized and specified as 'the Other'. Nevertheless, it does not solve the problem of identity: Who is the Other to whom? Who is the one defining others as Others? Is the Other also a subject for himself and herself?

The Finnish philosopher Sara Heinämaa explains how, for Simone de Beauvoir, the absolute alterity of a woman—the absoluteness of her alterity— means the attempt of man to negate his own carnality, the 'impurity' of his existence. Thus, woman as the absolute other is a male projection. In this situation, the man in fact does not encounter the woman. Woman's alterity is not equivalent to woman's being for herself.[340]

330. Dussel 1987: II, 37.
331. Dussel 1987: II, 56.
332. Dussel 1987: II, 56-57.
333. Dussel 1987: II, 59-60.
334. Dussel 1987: II, 161.
335. Dussel 1987: II, 161.
336. Dussel 1987: II, 162.
337. Dussel 1987: II, 173.
338. Dussel 1987: II, 176.
339. Dussel 1987: II, 176-77.
340. Heinämaa 1996: 150-51.

Many feminist theorists take a critical distance to Dussel's kind of use of the term Otherness or alterity. Stanley and Wise reject a notion of 'self and Other' that the self supposedly defines itself against and in opposition to.[341]

Horacio Cerutti Guldberg has criticized Dussel, among other issues, for homogenization (there is no *one* school of philosophy of liberation), for defining the role of the philosopher as that of a prophet (messianism and elitism), for creating a 'new ontology' which is theoretically untenable, for confusing theology and philosophy, and for authoritarianism.[342] According to Cerutti Guldberg, the methodological centre of Dussel's philosophy, the existence of the space (*ámbito*) of anthropological otherness, is very close to a proposal of an ontological difference between 'the Third World' and 'the centre' (Europe).[343]

Of special interest for this study is Cerutti Guldberg's critique of the 'people' as the supposed subject of the philosophy of liberation. It is worth remembering that Dussel himself participates in both the theological and philosophical formulations of the Other, the poor, and the people as the starting point for Latin American thinking. According to Cerutti Guldberg, the role of the intellectual as the prophet is problematic. The intellectual is the master, the knower, the thinker, whereas the Other (the poor and so on) is necessarily in the role of the disciple, incapable of thinking for himself or herself.[344] The gap between the philosopher (or theologian) and the Other (the poor, the oppressed) is evident. If philosophy is understood as *ancilla theologiae*, as Dussel according to Cerutti Guldberg understands it, and theology as the ultimate verification of truth ('philosophy as access to transcendency' in Dussel's words), this results in 'salvationalist philosophy', which for Cerutti Guldberg is unacceptable.[345]

In short,

> Philosophy, as it is understood by this sub-sector [of philosophy of liberation] is a specific activity of a philosopher, the only one capable of opening himself to the interpellation with the Other, but who does not open himself to the interpellation with social and human sciences. Rather, he dictates to them their epistemic limitations and possibilities... Primary philosophy (*filosofía primera*) is servant of a theology which responds to the unconditional supreme Alterity. The *counter image* of this philosophy is the dominating North Atlantic thinking and its dominating subject. The subject is not questioned and the philosopher-ethicist appears in his own real life as the norm according to which one can reach alterity and justice. The *self-image* of this philosophy is not far from perennial philosophy... The difference is in that instead of exercising metaphysics as primary, this function is assigned to

341.   Stanley and Wise 1993: 195. See also Benhabib 1992: 148-77; Code 1992: 86, 324 (in which she speaks of women's refusal to remain the Other); Smith 1989: 145-61.

342.   Cerutti Guldberg 1992: 42-43, 46, 230-37, 256-61, 277.

343.   Cerutti Guldberg 1992: 236-37. Ironically, seeing Latin America only as a repetitive reflection of Europe in need of liberation, may result in the negation of the history of Latin American thinking (Cerutti Guldberg 1992: 238). See also Cerutti Guldberg 1988–89: 49.

344.   Cerutti Guldberg 1992: 256-58, 277-78; Cerutti Guldberg 1988–89: 50-51.

345.   Cerutti Guldberg 1992: 279-81.

ethics-politics. And this, even though it may appear so, is no alteration from the dominating dimension of philosophy.[346]

According to Cerutti Guldberg, this kind of thinking makes itself immune to criticism, since it

> conceives itself as the most profound level of all criticism and as incapable of being criticized because it is 'exteriority' (*exterioridad*)... the only guarantee possible for a permanently renewed interpellation is to postulate an absolute 'exteriority' (God). All 'analectical' philosophy is a philosophy in the service of a theology redefined as a 'popular theology'.[347]

Cerutti Guldberg calls for self-criticism and historicity, and not for 'a philosophy *of* (*de*) liberation' but for 'philosophies *for* (*para*) liberation'.[348] Critique similar to Cerutti Guldberg's is presented by Ofelia Schutte. According to her, the philosophy of liberation is an intellectual movement based on a phenomenological analysis of reality, but politicizes it and involves specific Catholic influence as well.[349] Somewhat differently from Cerutti Guldberg, Schutte argues that Dussel's philosophical system rests on the primacy of a fusion of ethics and metaphysics, ultimately based on the premise of the origin of all things in God, the Absolute, as 'wholly Other'.[350] This appeal to God and religion makes it possible for Dussel to 'justify his vision of the moral superiority of the periphery over against the center, since the periphery represents the voice of the poor and the oppressed'.[351] The postulation of an absolutely untainted source for truth claims is problematic. Ethically, of Dussel's two principles, totality (evil) and alterity (good), the latter ceases to refer to an otherness or a difference in the post-

---

346. 'La filosofía, tal como la entiende este subsector es una actividad específica del filósofo, único capaz de abrirse a la interpelación del Otro pero que no se abre a la interpelación de las ciencias sociales y humanas, sino que más bien les dicta sus límites y posibilidades epistémicas... La filosofía primera es sierva de una teología que responde a la suprema Alteridad incondicionada. La *contra-imagen* de esta filosofía es el pensamiento nordatlántico y su sujeto dominador. El sujeto no es cuestionado y el filósofo-ético aparece en su propia vida como la norma por la cual se puede llegar a la alteridad y la justicia. La *auto-imagen* de esta filosofía no dista mucho de la filosofía perenne... La variante está en que, en lugar de ejercer la metafísica como primera, la función se la adjudican a la ética-política. Y esto, aunque parezca, no es ninguna alteración de la dimensión dominadora de la filosofía' (Cerutti Guldberg 1992: 283-84 [emphasis in original]). I have translated the philosopher as 'he', since in the original Cerutti Guldberg uses the male pronoun *el* for the philosopher.

347. Cerutti Guldberg 1988–89: 51-52.

348. Cerutti Guldberg 1988–89: 56-59.

349. Schutte 1991: 275. Actually, Schutte argues that Dussel is aiming at 'replacing Marxism theoretically with something else—that something else being a theory of "liberation" based on a religious metaphysics derived from the Catholic patriarchal tradition and an ethics of "alterity" borrowed in large part, yet also departing significantly, from the work of the French phenomenologist, Emmanuel Levinas' (Schutte 1991: 276).

350. Schutte 1991: 276.

351. Schutte 1991: 277. She also says that 'In effect, Dussel here makes the Third World the symbolic ethical representative of God on earth' (Schutte 1991: 276).

modern sense, but comes to designate the ground for a new absolute.[352] Dussel's philosophy seeks to derive its fundamental principles from faith rather than scientific knowledge.[353]

Schutte warns of authoritarianism in Dussel's philosophical system, since before one is entitled to speak or to make an ethical claim, one must portray oneself as *representative* of the Other (God, the Third World, the people, and so on).[354] Also, the 'people' (*el pueblo*) is represented as weak and in need of help from superior forces, such as God and his prophets. The people remains an object that is thought about rather than a group of persons endowed with the capacity to think for themselves.[355] Here Schutte coincides with Cerutti Guldberg's critique of Dussel and with my critique of the liberation theologians, whose understanding of themselves as 'organic intellectuals' may result in positioning themselves above and outside the people they want to speak for. She even says:

> The subject of liberation, in his or her ethical and metaphysical condition as 'other', is always in need and helpless in Dussel's theory... Thus the structure of Dussel's theory is built around a subject who must show his or her pain, who must say 'help me'.[356]

The 'people' as a singular collective subject fails to denote the diversity and/or conflicting interests of those who make up 'the people'. The meaning of 'the people' can easily slip from the context of an empirical reference to that of a normatively constructed ideal.[357]

In short, Schutte's critique of not only Dussel but certain tendencies in the philosophy of liberation and, implicitly, in LT, rests on the assumption that

> The theoretical apparatus they [Dussel and others] bring to the problem of the oppression of the Latin American people is not sufficiently liberated *itself* to guarantee the liberation of others. We need a good (critical) theory which can also serve as a theory of liberation. Such a theory cannot rest essentially on the principle of alterity and on the conflict between the center and the periphery, for we have seen that these principles alone do not escape the dualistic, hierarchical, authoritarian, and dogmatic structures which have characterized other oppressive ideological systems in the past.[358]

According to Schutte, there are three levels of absolutism in Dussel's thinking: political, religious, and a combination of these two into an absolute ethics of

---

352. Schutte 1993: 178-79.

353. Schutte 1991: 278.

354. Schutte 1991: 280-82. Schutte does not discuss a further difficulty in this configuration: How does one become a representative of somebody else? Who gives the philosopher/the theologian the legitimacy of representing somebody else besides him/herself?

355. Schutte 1991: 281-83.

356. Schutte 1991: 283. For Schutte's critique of Dussel's ethics from a feminist point of view, see Chapter 3.3.1.

357. Schutte 1993: 162.

358. Schutte 1991: 287 (emphasis in original). There are similar difficulties in feminist theology when 'women's experience' is uncritically raised as *the* sole criterion of theology and ethics, which I will discuss in Chapter 2.3.

service to the Other.[359] Dussel's 'yes-to-the-Other' is the *absolute criterion* of a political ethic.[360]

Even though both Schutte and Cerutti Guldberg discuss primarily the philosophy of liberation, not LT, and concentrate especially on Dussel, much of their critique can be extended to (other) liberation theologians as well. The problem here is that only a few liberation theologians have even tried to theorize these issues from perspective other than their own, which, as we have seen, grants 'the poor' or 'the other' a status that raises critical questions. Dussel is important here, since he is both a philosopher and a theologian of liberation.

1.4.5 *The New Historical Subject*

In the discourse over the subject in LT, we also have the concept 'new historical subject' (*nuevo sujeto histórico*), developed mostly in the 1990s by the team of researchers at the *Departamento Ecuménico de Investigaciones* (DEI) in Costa Rica. This concept comes close to the other mentioned concepts, but implicates a more concrete and active subject, compared, for example, with 'the Other', who by definition is always somebody seen and defined by one other than the Other him/herself. The new historical subject as a concept also allows more diversity than do the rest of the concepts. It is a communitarian, not individual, subject, growing from concrete social and political movements.

The new historical subject is the popular subject, a political actor in the popular (liberating) sense, being constituted in close relationship to a radical critical theory that has as its object the social structures that produce exploitation and oppression. The new historical subject can be used as a category of analysis inside a wider conceptual scheme that aims at confronting systems of domination. Thus, the concept announces the meaning and content of a utopia for a more just society. Finally, the new historical subject is radical hope.[361]

The question of the subject (*el sujeto*) is an important concept in actual Latin American theorizing—be it philosophical, theological or socio-political. It is elaborated as the ultimate instance for a radical alternative. The term 'Alternative' with a capital A is usually presented without adjectives, referring to a totalizing concept that has both political and economic, as well as philosophical and theological, consequences. It refers to an alternative for a capitalist, patriarchal and racist society. The 'subject' translates into 'real life' (*la vida real*) in its biological, material and corporal meaning. Human beings are not 'subjects of preferences' (Max Weber) but 'subjects of necessities' that again goes back to the 'real life'. Thus, the concept of subject is used similarly to that of 'the Other'. The Other and the new historical subject are concepts that refer to the confrontation oppression/domination–liberation. They are constituted both by oppression

359. Schutte 1993: 187-88.
360. Schutte 1993: 187, quoting Dussel (emphasis in original).
361. See Gallardo 1992: 40-42.

(which can be concretized in racism, poverty, sexism and so on) and by resistance (liberation). Thus, both ultimately refer to a utopia.[362]

According to the Chilean philosopher Helio Gallardo,

> Latin American liberation theology pays attention to the poor as a *subject*, with the double meaning of both as somebody who endures and suffers from the social sin of unsolidarity and as the one who is capable of his own initiatives and acting for himself. The impoverished (*el empobrecido*) as a subject is, consequently, not somebody insignificant, but a *radical interpellator* (*interpelador*) *of fellow beings,* the reference of all humanity, and, for the believers, of the presence of God. Saying it with an image: we are the poor when we deny our neighbor recognition and justice.[363]

For Gallardo, the poor is an (auto)transformative subject which refers not as much to lack (*carencia*) as to plenitude, or aspiration to plenitude. Because of this open and wide understanding of the poor *as a subject*, it is possible for Gallardo to make an explicit reference to other theologies of liberation, including women as subjects of theology. In their lack of full subjectivity, as well as in their aspiration for it, women, too, are 'poor'.[364] According to Gallardo, the option for the poor has a socio-historical basis that gives it corporality, temporality and politicality. At the same time, it is a radical demand of humanity (universalism).[365] Thus, for him, LT is 'theology of the poor as subject', not just one theology *of* something among others like, for example, theology of hope or theology of revolution, but in the sense of 'theology of the human subject', in his or her aspiration to plenitude and liberation.[366] Thus, we can see that 'defining' the poor as a collective historical subject at least potentially is more flexible than Dussel's use of 'the Other' or the mainstream liberation theological use of 'the poor'.

According to another member of the *equipo del DEI*, Franz Hinkelammert, LT is concrete, historical theology. Its option for the poor must be an option of the poor themselves. He says,

> [that the option for the poor]…is not as an act of others who have the obligation of liberating the poor, seen as an object. Without mutual recognition of subjects, in which poverty is the real denial of this recognition, there is no option for the poor. Human subjects cannot recognize each other mutually, without recognizing each other as corporal and natural beings with necessities… From the point of view of the theologians of liberation, the human being cannot liberate himself [*sic*] to be free without this mutual recognition of subjects. Thus, the poor as a subject, found in

362.   See Acosta 1992.

363.   'La Teología latinoamericana de la Liberación se ocupa por el pobre como *sujeto*—con el doble contenido del que soporta y sufre el pecado social de la insolidaridad, y de quien es capaz de iniciativas propias, de quien es capaz de actuar por sí mismo. El empobrecido como sujeto es, por consiguiente, no alguien insignificante, sino un *interpelador radical de prójimos*, la referencia de toda humanidad y con ello, para los creyentes, de la presencia de Dios. Diciéndolo con una imagen: el pobre somos nosotros cuando negamos el reconocimiento y la justicia al prójimo' (Gallardo 1994: 15 [emphasis in original]).

364.   Gallardo 1994: 15.

365.   Gallardo 1994: 15-16. Gallardo also notes that there is a variety of criteria for defining this option for the poor in LT.

366.   Gallardo 1994: 16.

this relation of recognition, is the place (*lugar*) in which it is decided if such a recognition is made effective or not.[367]

Thus, it is the poor who make present the absence of mutual recognition between human beings. According to LT, God is there where this recognition is made reality. The presence of the poor, therefore, also reveals the absence of God. More exactly, the absence of God is present in the poor. The poor are the presence of an absent God.[368] For Hinkelammert, this is the great starting point of LT, even though different theologians may use different expressions. In this analysis, we also come back to praxis, or more specifically, to how praxis is understood in LT from the point of view of the Latin American poor. The opposite of poverty is not abundance of things, but plenitude of life constituted by the mutual recognition of corporal subjects.[369]

The poor as the subjects of LT can be maintained at the same time as its definition is extended and made more diverse and concrete. Defining the poor as subjects in their own right has made it possible to both universalize and particularize the praxis starting point in LT. It is interesting that this kind of turn in LT is not as much the result of well-known individual liberation theologians as of concrete multidisciplinary work[370] and of recognizing the existence of new social movements and new subjectivities within them, including the women's movement, which by their very presence bring a critical and heterogeneous element to the intellectual discourse inside LT.

1.5 Conclusions

At the beginning of this chapter it was stated that Latin American LT is not intelligible without its political, economic, social and religious context in post-Second World War Latin America, and more specifically, the violent and repressive decades of the 1960s and 1970s. The various human rights organizations, anti-repression opposition movements, including armed guerrilla groups, church-based organizations and, more widely, Latin American social movements are the immediate practical reference point of LT. Later, the dialogue between the churches, the theologians and the social movements opened up globally, aiming at the creation of Third World theologies.

367. 'No como acto de otros que tengan el deber de liberar al pobre, visto éste como objeto. Sin reconocimiento mutuo entre sujetos, en el cual la pobreza resulta ser la negación real de este reconocimiento, no hay opción por el pobre. Los sujetos humanos no pueden reconocerse mutuamente, sin que se reconozcan como seres corporales y naturales necesitados... Desde el punto de vista de los teólogos de la liberación, el ser humano no puede liberarse para ser libre sin este reconocimiento mutuo entre sujetos. Así, el pobre como sujeto que se encuentra en esta relación de reconocimiento, es el lugar en el que se decide si este reconocimiento se hace efectivo o no' (Hinkelammert 1995: 2).

368.   Hinkelammert 1995: 2.

369.   Hinkelammert 1995: 3.

370.   Hinkelammert is an economist; Gallardo is a philosopher who considers himself an atheist. This is but one example of how LT is an intrinsic part of intellectual discourse in Latin America. LT is an important point of reference in the work of non-theologians as well.

Because of the political, social and religious changes in Latin America, LT faces three challenges in its immediate future. First, the role of the Catholic Church in the formation of civil society and democracy depends largely on its inner development, as well as on its ability to face challenges from within its own ranks, such as the various liberation theologies. The second challenge is the rapidly growing Protestantism all over the continent. And third, the very reason that gave birth to LT, widespread poverty, seems to be deepening throughout the Third World. There is an urgent need for both local and global responses, in which religion(s) can play a crucial role.

The reality of poverty and the immersion of Christians in different actions in order to change the situation is very much what has been called the praxis starting point in LT. The analysis showed how liberation theologians borrow mostly from Marxist-orientated social theories and philosophies in their use of the concept. There is not much originality in liberation theologians' use of the concept as such. However, in spite of the diversity in how liberation theologians understand praxis and the relation between theory and praxis, it is possible to speak of a liberation theological method which has praxis as its most important starting point. Thus, to a certain extent, LT can be said to present a paradigm shift in theology.

Since my interest has been not so much tracing the intellectual debts and heritage of the liberation theologians as seeing how they apply their stated methodology in their specific context, more emphasis was given to areas which raise critical questions about the praxis starting point in general. This was done by analysing not only the overall method of LT—as presented by liberation theologians themselves—but by looking at it from another angle. The question of the subjects of LT is critical for several reasons.

First, 'the poor' as the subjects of LT turned out to be a vague and homogenizing concept. This has nowadays been acknowledged by most liberation theologians themselves, and they are eager to enlarge the concept in order to include more specific subjects within the poor, such as women and indigenous peoples. This new phase in LT has nevertheless very much remained on the level of mere inclusion.

Second, the poor as the radical vanguard subjects have implicit Marxist connotations—for instance, being defined primarily as a class. The shortcomings of this kind of analysis have been made clear in recent social scientific research, feminist theory being one of the most critical of them. The implications of the interrelatedness of different identities—race, gender, ethnicity and so forth—have been worked out in feminist theology as well. The challenge they pose to LT will be presented in forthcoming chapters.

Third, the narrow way of defining the poor principally in economic terms sees them primarily as a productive and political collective subject. In LT, there is an obvious lack of theorizing an integral subject which is also individual, corporal and reproductive. The critique aimed at liberation theologians and philosophers as well as some elaborations in recent dialogue between liberation theologians and Latin American social scientists has taken LT more into this direction. The definitions of the subject have become more flexible and differentiated. Nevertheless, there is still a yawning gap in LT which has to do with human corporality, sexuality and sexual ethics. The right of a female subject to her body and 'bodiliness' has been absent in LT, as it has also very much been in Latin American feminist liberation theology, as we will see in Chapters 3 and 4.

There are concepts other than the poor being elaborated within LT to connote the supposed subject of LT, such as the Other and the new historical subject. Though conceptually more open and diverse than the poor, they face similar problems. It is very much the role of the liberation theologians as 'organic intellectuals' that make them speak for others. This entails the danger of elitism and authoritarianism, which becomes clear when those groups being represented by liberation theologians start to represent and speak for themselves.

LT has been critical of the 'false universalism' of Western intellectual traditions. Stressing the importance of the particular, the practical and the contextual has been central in all those theories (in the social sciences as well as in theology and ethics) that consider the universalizing aspirations of Western scientific ideals detrimental. It seems that liberation theologians do not abandon universalism as such but, instead, abstract universalism. The emphasis on the particular gives birth to new concrete universalism, rooted in particularities.[371]

Juan Carlos Scannone, a Jesuit philosopher of liberation, calls this *situated universalism*. According to him,

> Since the reflection is done from the point of view of a new particular experience, this discovers dimensions of the faith and the Word which, from the point of view of other experiences, particular as well, have not yet been completely grasped. The universality of theology is not negated. On the contrary, it is supposed and encountered more fully. But the question is not of a mere abstract universalism, nor of a concrete universalism in the Hegelian meaning, but of a *situated* universality.[372]

When criticizing false universalisms, particularist or contextual theories paradoxically created new universals. This has been the case of 'the poor' as a concept in LT, as well as 'women's experience' in FT. Thus, we can critically analyse 'the universalist poor' from a feminist point of view, claiming that the particularities of female existence tell us something essential about human existence in general (universally). This critical spiral between universalism and particularism implies that the two cannot be separated. 'Particularist theories', such as LT and much of feminist theory and FT, are for the first time in the fruitful position of being able to dialogue critically.

In the next chapter, I will show how a process of differentiation, similar to that in LT, has evolved in feminist theological discourses.

371. According to Anselm K. Min, this 'concretely universal' perspective avoids both sheer particularism and ahistorical universalism. LT locates such a concretely universal perspective in the poor and oppressed who, as victims of the injustice of the economic structure, embody and suffer in their own life situation the universal human crisis of the time. The poor embody the universal ethically, structurally and economically. See Min 1986: 545-46.

372. Scannone 1990: 316 (emphasis in original). For a critique of Scannone's philosophical and theological positions, see Cerutti Guldberg 1992: 278-84.

Chapter 2

Feminist Theology

It is perfectly possible to consider feminist theology both as part of modern *women's studies*—applying feminist analysis in religious studies, especially in Christian theology—and as part of the *liberation theology paradigm*. As was said in the introduction, a wider definition of liberation theology permits us to include not just the Latin American LT but also other theologies in the concept 'liberation theology'. This is the opinion of those liberation and feminist theologians who have participated in the global dialogue of Third World and First World theologians, especially in the EATWOT process. Among the feminist theologians, it is a specific group that defines itself as feminist liberation theologians. Not all Third World women theologians are feminists, and even fewer First World feminist theologians consider themselves liberation theologians as well. In this research FT is primarily understood as part of the liberation theology paradigm.

As will be made clear in the course of this chapter, it would be more correct to speak of *feminist theologies in the plural*.[1] North American womanist and mujerista theologies point towards the difference race or ethnicity produce inside the FT paradigm. Those feminist theologians from Latin America who are relevant to this study prefer to call themselves Latin American feminist liberation theologians. It is only for the sake of convenience that the abbreviation FT refers to feminist theology in the singular. The contents of this chapter will make it clear that I understand FT as a heterogeneous and multifaceted phenomenon.

In this chapter, I will analyse FT from two different perspectives. On the one hand, it is impossible to imagine the birth of FT without the secular women's movement and women's studies in other disciplines. Thus, I will shortly describe the intellectual debate concerning feminist theory and the place of FT in it (2.1). This discussion continues in Chapter 2.3 on methodological issues. Seen from a more intra-theological discourse, the most natural context of FT is the liberation theology movement or paradigm (2.2.1). This is based on methodological reasons which will be explicated later. Both theological currents have as their intellectual

---

1.   A recent theological dictionary on FT is called *Dictionary of Feminist Theologies*. The editors take the plural for granted because of the abundance of perspectives and points of view, as well as cultural contexts. See Russell and Clarkson (eds.) 1996.

foundation the reference to praxis, even though they may use different words for it. Latin American liberation theologians prefer speaking of 'praxis' and feminist theologians of 'experience', while some call both approaches 'contextual'. The discussion on the points of contact between different liberation theologies, especially FT and Latin American LT, will go on in Chapter 3. Further, there is no one feminist theology nowadays, but FT is defined by its heterogeneity (2.2.2) and plurality (2.2.3). In the last part of the chapter, I will analyse how 'women's experience' as a central methodological concept is understood in FT, especially by some feminist liberation theologians (2.3).

2.1 Feminist Theology, Feminism and Feminist Theory

Feminist theology was born as one aspect of the 'new feminist movement' of the sixties, principally in Western European countries and the United States. FT has its immediate roots in extra-ecclesiastical and extra-academic reality.[2] This is true globally, even though First World white women have had an earlier and easier access to education and political participation. But the women's movement—or feminist movement—is a truly global phenomenon that naturally has as many faces as there are different cultures. The practical and political connection of FT to the women's movement, both in and outside the churches, is closest to what Latin American liberation theologians call the inseparability of theory and praxis. Feminist praxis informs feminist theory and vice versa.

Women's studies have been the 'academic arm of the movement for the liberation of women'.[3] The construction of feminist theory in various academic disciplines has been an innovative and fast-growing phenomenon, especially in the social sciences and humanities. It has challenged the major paradigms of our time, such as Marxism and Freudianism, for their distorted image of women,

---

2.   As in LT, there are feminist theologians who seek to 'reconstruct' a 'feminist theological historiography' which goes beyond the last couple of decades. In history, in the Bible itself, there are women who could be called 'proto-feminists.' The same is true of the monastic era, the Middle Ages, the Reformation and different nineteenth-century religious movements. The suffragette movement produced leaders who took up the question of women's rights in the church and theology as well. In the United States, one of the most well-known of them was Elizabeth Cady Stanton, who wrote *The Woman's Bible* in 1890, and several black women, such as Sojourner Truth and Jarena Lee, who were leaders both in their religious communities and in the anti-slavery movement. Very much the same could be said of the English suffragettes at the end of the nineteenth century. In Latin America, 'the first feminist of America' was Sor Juana Inés de la Cruz, a seventeenth-century nun, poet and intellectual.

But it is only in this century that women have gained their formal civil rights and access to higher education in most regions of the world. Theology and religious communities have been the great exceptions. Formal theological education has been one of the last careers opened to women. They still lack 'civil rights' in many religious communities, including Christian churches, not only because they cannot be ordained but because they form the biggest part of the large grassroots laity in a hierarchically formed community where it is either exclusively or predominantly men who hold the positions of power and prestige.

3.   Carr 1990: 64.

demanded women's presence in the academic world and created new concepts, new methods and new practices. Women's studies are interdisciplinary or multi-disciplinary.

Feminist theory is a concept for a wide array of issues.[4] Broadly stated, it 'aims to create a deeper understanding of women's situation' and 'begins with women's experience of oppression and argues that women's subordination extends from private circumstances to political conditions'.[5] This is, of course, a definition as wide and general as possible.

It is common that feminist theologians apply psychological, sociological and philosophical feminist research to theology and are generally more familiar with feminist theory in other disciplines than non-theologians are with FT.[6] The reason for this may be the general nature of different disciplines. For example, the philosophical question of the possibility of a feminist epistemology is of major importance for all disciplines. Another reason may be the marginalization of questions concerning religion in secularized societies. In a global perspective, the situation is different. In countries like the Latin American ones, it is important to be able to critically analyse the role religion plays in society and culture.[7]

---

4.   In this study, I refer mainly to philosophical and social scientific discourses which discuss, among other things, the nature, basis, and central concepts of feminist theory, such as woman, sex and gender. These theories also have the most direct relation to theological issues. Even of the most central concepts, there is today a wide array of definitions which may contrast with each other. Since my aim is not to analyse feminist theory as such, I cannot go into detail in this discussion. Thus my presentation does not do justice to the richness of the reality.

5.   Humm 1990: 223-24. According to Humm, feminist theory is simultaneously political and scientific because feminist theorists use a complex network of conceptual, normative, empirical and methodological approaches (Humm 1990: 224).

According to a European feminist dictionary, 'die feministische Wissenschaftskritik analysiert und entschlüsselt die Logik und Praxis einer Wissenschaftskultur, die sich durch den Ausschluss all dessen definiert, was in unserer Kultur als weiblich gilt: Gefühl, Leiblichkeit, Kontingenz. Die Aufgabe einer feministisch orientierten Wissenschaft ist es, praktische und theoretische Alternativen für eine Wissenschaft im Interesse von Frauen zu entwickeln... Sie [feministische Wissenschaft] wählt die Kategorie des Geschlechts als kritischen Ausgangspunkt ihrer Forschung, um den politischen Gehalt und die Herrschaftsfunktion traditionellen Konzeptionen des Männlichen und Weiblichen sichtbar zu machen' (List 1991: 101).

In the *Dictionary of Feminist Theologies*, the plural is also used for feminist theories. 'These theories provide a critical analysis of the forces that subordinate women to men...feminist theories tend to be interdisciplinary and to employ various methods of inquiry and analysis... Through these various approaches, feminist theories interrogate structures of male dominance and of patriarchy, and their accompanying systems of gender' (Brock 1996: 117).

6.   This seems to be the case in Europe as well as in the United States. My own personal experience in Latin America points to a far greater interest and openness to theological issues in Latin American social sciences and in women's studies as well. This may be due to a lesser degree of secularization in Latin America and the importance of religion in the society.

7.   On the importance of feminist critique of all religious traditions, see O'Neill 1990. According to her, 'for women, as for other people seeking liberation, there is a vital connection between social justice and religion. This connection demands that a discussion of one includes a discussion of the other...many women are realizing that an understanding of religious issues is basic to changing the situation of women. A culture's religious traditions are its basis for

According to Elisabeth Schüssler Fiorenza,

> Much feminist theological writing accepts the twofold presupposition: that the root of women's oppression is dualistic thought or patriarchalism as a mind set or projection, and that the monotheistic religions of Judaism and Christianity constitute the bedrock of Western patriarchalism.[8]

This statement contains an implicit assumption of the relevance of FT to feminism and feminist theory in other disciplines.

Similarly, Daphne Hampson says: 'It is conservative Christians who, together with more radical feminists, perceive that feminism represents not just one crisis among many. For the feminist challenge strikes at the heart of Christianity'.[9] She also says: 'Women realize, as feminists, the extent to which this Christian story has hurt women, indeed how far the fact that God has been seen as "male" in the West has served to undermine a sense of women as also made in the image of God'.[10]

According to Anne-Louise Eriksson, 'Christian feminist theology aims at understanding how women are subordinated in theological contexts, and its goal is to initiate changes whereby theology is transformed so that it does not subordinate women'.[11]

What has been called 'the identity crisis of feminist theory'[12] is in fact the existence of different responses to the question of the possibility of a feminist epistemology. These differences have also been characterized by such definitions as 'essentialism' on the one hand and 'poststructuralism' or 'constructivism' on the other hand. The initial emphasis of feminist theory (including FT) was on a commonality or universality of women's experiences. Women were all alike in both their femaleness and their oppression. The universals or essentialisms were 'femaleness' and 'oppression'. In the 1980s, these were increasingly criticized through an emphasis on differences among women.[13] The poststructuralist or postmodern feminist critique focuses on the very criteria by which claims to

---

meaning-making, image-making, and creating an ordered world and an ethos...the fight for women's rights in the secular arena will be weakened if it fails to acknowledge the religious dimension of the problem' (O'Neill 1990: 55).

8.   Fiorenza 1984c: 296.

9.   Hampson 1990: 1. And 'The revolution in religion will affect human society, for religion constitutes an underpinning of our lives' (Hampson 1990: 6). This, too, implies the necessity and importance of feminist theological critique for feminist theory.

10.   Hampson 1990: 45. 'It is precisely at the level of symbolism that the Christian story has hurt women' (Hampson 1990: 46). Elizabeth A. Johnson also emphasizes the importance of symbols. Insofar as 'the symbol gives rise to thought' (Paul Ricoeur), feminist critique of religious symbolism calls into question prevailing structures of patriarchy (Johnson 1994: 6).

11.   Eriksson 1995: 12. She also says that 'Feminism concerns questions about gender and dominance, and feminism applied to theology focuses on gender-related issues in theology' (Eriksson 1995: 12).

12.   Alcoff 1988: 405-36.

13.   Code 1992: 299-300; Fraser and Nicholson 1990: 27.

knowledge are legitimized.[14] For the poststructuralists, feminism has become a sort of philosophical metanarrative or at least a very large social theory that presupposes some commonly held but unwarranted and essentialist assumptions about the nature of human beings and the conditions for social life.[15] The postmodern feminist theory would thus replace unitary notions of woman and feminine gender identity with plural and complexly constructed conceptions of social identity, treating gender as one relevant strand among others, attending also to class, race, ethnicity, age and sexual orientation.[16] This sort of feminist analysis could logically include 'men's studies', the critical analysis of the social construction of masculinity. Furthermore, this kind of feminism and feminist theory can best be spoken of in the plural as the practice of feminisms.[17]

There are also those feminist theorists who refuse to locate themselves either in the essentialist or in the postmodernist camp. For them, postmodernism entails the danger of dissolving different subjects into 'a perplexing plurality of differences, none of which can be theoretically or politically privileged over others'.[18] In the case of women, '*she* dissolves into *he*'.[19] Postmodernism leads to (ethical and epistemological) relativism.[20] Rosi Braidotti, speaking of the deconstruction of the modern subject, says 'One cannot deconstruct a subjectivity one has never been fully granted'.[21]

Many feminist theorists are reluctant to subscribe to the view that affectivity, bodily specificity, intersubjectivity, and cognitive 'location' can have no part in informing the construction of knowledge. They are caught between a recognition of the productive, emancipatory worth of cognitive postures commonly devalued as 'feminine' and a recognition of the source of these postures in the oppressive positions reserved for women.[22]

This conflict in feminist theory has also been defined as a conflict between two traditions, the 'humanist' and the 'gynocentric'.[23] The first is based on the supposition that there are no significant differences between men and women, whereas the latter at least implicitly states that there is an essential difference between men and women, and that this difference is reflected in their different ways of knowing.

In the 1990s, there has been a tendency in feminist theory to try to theorize 'sex' and 'gender' in new ways, in order to overcome the potential mind–body dualism in this categorization where 'sex' refers to biology (as something given

---

14. Nicholson 1990: 3.
15. Fraser and Nicholson 1990: 26-27.
16. Fraser and Nicholson 1990: 34-35.
17. Fraser and Nicholson 1990: 35.
18. Di Stefano 1990: 77.
19. Di Stefano 1990: 77 (emphasis in original).
20. Benhabib 1990: 107-30.
21. Quoted in Eriksson 1995: 54. See also Braidotti 1993 and 1994.
22. Code 1992: 121.
23. I.M. Young 1985: 173.

and natural) and 'gender' to socialization, somehow 'attached' to this unaltered biology.[24]

The 'identity crisis of feminist theory' superficially presented above has not been resolved, but it has made clear how problematic it is to speak of 'experiences' without taking into account the 'differences'. And how can one speak of 'differences' without falling into 'essentialisms'? How can one build a moral theory and political agenda that serves women's liberation without falling into false essentialism and universalism? In the words of a feminist theologian,

> How can women transcend our being socially constructed as *women* and at the same time become historical subjects as *women* struggling against patriarchal domination? If subjectivity is seen as totally determined by gender, one ends up with feminine essentialism; if it is understood as genderless, then one reverts to the generic human subject of liberalism for whom gender, class, or race are irrelevant.[25]

Or, how can one simultaneously defend real women of flesh and blood (or oppose sexism) and deconstruct the Woman?[26]

Inside FT, one can identify positions similar to those in recent feminist theory, even though not in a clear-cut way. A 'gynocentric' kind of feminism is most clearly present in post-Christian, radical FT. Post-Christian feminist theologians tend to place more emphasis on women's biological specificity.[27]

The concept 'woman' itself has dissolved into the differences between women. The difference between an educated, white, First World woman and a Guatemalan Maya Indian *campesina* woman, for example, is probably far greater than their respective differences with the men of their communities. It is no wonder that the critique of essentialism and universalism in 'women's experience' has mostly come from economically, socially and racially disadvantaged women, whose culture is defined as less or worse compared with the technologically advanced, homogeneously white and supposedly superior First World culture.

2.2 The Versatility of Feminist Theology

2.2.1 *Feminist Theology as Liberation Theology*
According to the broad definition of LT, different liberation theologies were born more or less at the same time. Even though they were not developed totally

---

24.   Recent works that problematize the distinction are Butler 1990 and 1993; Gatens 1991 (originally 1983); Grosz 1994; Heinämaa 1996. In a theological context, see Eriksson 1995, especially 33-41.

25.   Fiorenza 1989: 317 (emphasis in original).

26.   See Braidotti 1993 and 1994.

27.   Anne-Louise Eriksson sees strong tendencies towards gynocentric positions also in reformist feminist theologians such as Ruether and Fiorenza (see 2.3). 'The humanist/gynocentric duality catches an inbuilt tension within much feminist theological work' (Eriksson 1995: 18). And 'The feminist theoretical debate in recent decades has problematized such concepts as woman, sex, and gender in ways that need to be considered also in feminist theology' (Eriksson 1995: 16). Eriksson's own work is a response to the neglect of feminist theoretical elaborations in much of FT.

independent from each other, it is not correct to claim that the other liberation theologies are 'derived' from Latin American LT. This becomes clear when one notes when the first books on black theology, Latin American LT and FT were published.[28] This historical fact is one argument for speaking about liberation theologies in the plural. The global economic, political, ecclesiastical and socio-cultural changes of the 1960s are the major single factor behind all liberation theologies. As we saw in Chapter 1.1, liberation theologies can be seen as 'social movements', as they often correspond to factual processes in churches and societies and have strong and effective ties to grassroots groups and movements for social change. In FT, this is especially true in the Third World countries, and to a more limited degree in the United States (where there are forums such as the Women-Church movement). In Europe and the Scandinavian countries, there is not necessarily a connection between academic FT and feminist activists in and outside the church.

All liberation theologies take concrete life situations, seen through the lenses of human suffering, individually and collectively, as their starting point. Different words and concepts are used to refer to this methodological principle: praxis, experience, context, and so on. This standpoint of speaking of liberation theologies in the plural as well as assuming that they have enough methodological commonalities in order to speak of them together as a paradigm is shared nowadays by most liberation theologians themselves.[29]

According to the *Dictionary of Feminist Theologies*,

> Theologies of liberation developed in the midst of global armed and negotiated struggles for cultural and social justice that were initiated and sustained by the poor, the colonized, the vanquished, the segregated, the marginalized, the disenfranchised, the invisible women, men and children of the Third World.[30]

---

28.   For example, James Cone's first books on black theology (*A Black Theology of Liberation* in 1970 and *Black Theology and Black Power* in 1969) were published before Gutiérrez published his *Teología de la liberación*. There were also feminist theological publications in the sixties.

29.   According to Ferm, liberation theology as a term stresses the liberation from all forms of oppression: social, economic, political, racial, sexual, environmental and religious. Different liberation theologies share the conviction that theology must be truly indigenous. Thus, African and Asian liberation theologies are not mere offshoots of Latin American LT (Ferm 1986: 1-2).

Tissa Balasuriya, a Catholic theologian from Sri Lanka, offers the most inclusive and broad definition of liberation theology. Among other things, traditional Christian theology has been: (1). culture-bound and implicitly ethnocentric, a handmaid of Western expansion; (2) church-centered, tending to equate the universal kingdom of God and the common human good with the expansion of the church; (3) male-dominated, without the acceptance of the fundamental equality of men and women. For him, the whole planet earth must also be seen as a context for theology (thus the name of his book, *Planetary Theology*). He also proposes an ecumenism of all religions (Balasuriya 1984: 3-5, 15, 140). He is one of the few Third World liberation theologians to include a radical gender perspective in his theology: 'The world system, in its social aspects, has many interrelated lines of affinity and division based on color, class, and sex. They are global, as well as local and personal. An understanding of their interrelationships is essential for the cause of integral human liberation' (Balasuriya 1984: 45-46). See also Balasuriya 1986.

30.   Copeland 1996: 284.

Also, 'Feminist theologies, like other forms of liberation theology, not only reflect on praxis but seek actively to be a form of praxis: to shape Christian activity around the norms and visions of emancipation and transformation'.[31]

According to Ruy O. Costa, 'A methodological premise common to all liberation theologies is that no theological production is free from mediations of its socio-historical locations'.[32] José Míguez Bonino states:

> Thus one important fact for the relation of theologies of liberation is this: The point of departure of an awareness of oppression and a struggle for liberation can take place anywhere in this wide spectrum (economic, institutional, juridical, cultural, religious), but, if pursued in depth and extension, one will lead to the others.[33]

According to Phillip Berryman's definition, liberation theology is (1) an interpretation of Christian faith out of the suffering, struggle and hope of the poor; (2) a critique of society and the ideologies sustaining it; and (3) a critique of the activity of the church and of Christians from the angle of the poor. 'The poor, nonwhites, and women are finding new meaning in Christian faith as well as revealing the shortcomings of interpretations made by white Western males'.[34]

Theo Witvliet refers to a statement by the first EATWOT assembly in 1976 that there are three basic methodological questions that liberation theologies raise. These questions can be distinguished, but they nevertheless overlap. First is the question of contextuality, which is much more than a mere recognition that all theological language is socially and culturally conditioned. Contextuality presupposes a creative interaction between the reading of Scripture and the reading of present-day social reality, the mediating authority between these two elements not being an individual theologian but the praxis of a community.[35] The second question is that of the relation between theory and praxis and the definition of theology as critical reflection of the praxis. The third question is that of criticism of ideology, which includes self-criticism.[36]

All analysts and liberation theologians themselves seem to share these basic assumptions as the common base for different liberation theologies: the context of oppression, experienced both individually and collectively; an active transformation of that context and its analysis (theory-praxis relationship); the critique of both society and religious institutions, including theology, from this context; and reinterpretation of the religious texts and traditions. The last instant happens

---

31. Chopp 1996: 222.
32. Costa 1992: 18.
33. Bonino 1992: 34. Between these different instances of oppression and liberation, there is a clear interconnection. Nevertheless, each of them has a certain autonomy and cannot simply be reduced to a mechanical effect of another. This means that theology can be done today only as an interdisciplinary exercise (Bonino 1992: 34).
34. Berryman 1987: 6. This definition, even though broad in including feminist theology, for instance, is narrow when speaking only of the poor and when limiting liberation theology only to Christianity. Many Asian liberation theologies, even those formally Christian, are syncretist and take the ecumenical dialogue between religions as a starting point.
35. Witvliet 1985: 26-29.
36. Witvliet 1985: 29-31.

in a tension between the oppressive and liberative elements in a given religious tradition.

Liberation theologies have influenced each other to some extent since their very beginning, and this has been a growing tendency in recent years when liberation theologians from all continents have come together to define the liberation theological paradigm and practice. Theoretically, this corresponds with the liberation theological claim that different forms of oppression (economic, cultural, racial, sexual) are intrinsically intertwined and cannot be separated. Nevertheless, most feminist liberation theologians agree that in practice the gender perspective has been the last to be included in the 'liberation theological agenda', and that to a great extent, it is still a question of merely formal inclusion.[37] There is an apparent conflict between stated common ideals and real dialogue in the global liberation theology movement.

Feminism needs to be understood not only as a struggle against sexism but also 'against racism, classism, colonialism and militarism as structures of women's exploitation and oppression'.[38] Feminism's self-understanding and analysis must therefore shift from a preoccupation with gender-dualism in order to attend to the interstructuring of sex, race, class, culture and religion in systems of domination. Only when patriarchy is understood not as a universal transcultural structure but as a historical political system of interlocking dominations can it be changed.[39] Theologically, if liberation theologians insist that God is on the side of the poor, it is necessary to ask what it actually means that God is on the side of poor women and children dependent on women.[40]

For most Latin American feminist liberation theologians, as well as for the black and Hispanic women theologians in the United States, this interstructuring of oppressions is their explicit starting point. The Colombian Ana María Bidegain, a church historian, says that 'Racial discrimination, sexism and capitalist exploitation in Latin America constitute the triad that keeps women in subjection'.[41]

A serious dialogue between different liberation theologies and between First World and Third World feminist theologies is a quite recent phenomenon. There have been international meetings, mostly in the context of EATWOT. Third World women theologians' works are becoming internationally more well-known. But still, First World feminist theologians communicate mostly with feminist theorists of other disciplines and with the 'tradition'; Third World feminist theologians dialogue mostly with other liberation theologians in their countries or continents. Male liberation theologians talk with the 'tradition'

37. See Cone for how North American black theology lacked gender analysis in its beginning and for the meaning of black feminist theology (Cone 1984: 122-39).
38. Fiorenza 1989: 316.
39. Fiorenza 1989: 316.
40. Fiorenza 1989: 323.
41. Bidegain 1989: 116. On Latin American feminist liberation theology, see Chapters 3.1 and 3.2.

(considered 'European') and with each other. According to Tissa Balasuriya, the greatest limit of Latin American LT is its remaining within the framework of Western white male domination of the world. It does not seriously take into account the situation of indigenous peoples and women of Latin America.[42]

Male liberation theologians have been slow and even reluctant to include poor women's problems as part of their 'preferential option for the poor'. This situation is changing not so much because of well-known liberation theologians' revision of their opinions, as necessary as it is, as because of a growing body of feminist theological writing within LT. The differentiation in the concept 'the poor' in LT has been a process similar to that of the concept 'woman' or 'women's experience' in FT. These concepts have been necessary and central in the construction of a critical paradigm (feminist theory, liberation theologies, other non-Eurocentric critical theories). Postcolonialist Third World feminist theory is one powerful intersection between these different discourses.[43]

Questions about the relationship between power and knowledge, interests of knowledge, and the contextual character of knowledge bring together these different theories. In all liberation theologies, the critique of abstract universalism is raised from the experience of being in the margins of 'Christian' understanding of humanity. Praxis as a starting point emphasizes the importance of everyday life and human bodiliness, as well as holistic anthropology, in order to overcome the dualisms private–public (individual–community) and body–soul (matter–spirit). A strong ethical demand for concrete changes in society and the church is a further factor that different liberation theologies have in common.

Nevertheless, those feminist theologians who define themselves as liberation theologians—those who call themselves *feminist liberation theologians*—both agree with other liberation theologians and have serious disagreements with them. A multiracial group of North American feminist theologians[44] says:

> The significant difference between the claims made by liberation theologians and those made by theologians who presume themselves to be theologically objective— those whose ideas are 'unpolluted' by ideology—is that the former admit readily the extent to which their daily lives provide the substance of their theologies, while the latter seldom do. Put simply, liberation theologians claim they theologize in praxis; most other theologians fail to acknowledge explicitly that they have a praxis, as if their doctrines somehow float free of the contingencies of human life... We have been influenced by Latin American liberation theology. Most of us have learned much from this theological movement about praxis as context of theology.[45]

42. Balasuriya 1978: 131-34. In the years after this article was written, it is exactly the issues mentioned by Balasuriya that have become critical for Latin American LT.

43. Writers such as Gayatri Spivak, Chandra Talpade Mohanty, Trinh Minh Ha and Chantal Mouffe.

44. The Mudflower Collective, as they call their collective work, is formed by the womanist theologian and ethicist Katie G. Cannon, the ethicist Beverly Wildung Harrison, the Hispanic feminist theologian Ada María Isasi-Díaz, and Bess B. Johnson, Mary D. Pellauer, Nancy D. Richardson and Carter Heyward.

45. Cannon *et al.* 1988: 18.

They then explain the two main disengagements they have from Latin American (male) LT and North American (male) black theology. First, there is a failure of nonfeminist liberation theologians to take sexism and heterosexism seriously as fundamental political and theological issues. This is a flaw in the vision, theology and process of liberation. Secondly, according to these feminist theologians, most male theologians of whatever color, culture or continent tend to overlook the 'small places' of their lives as theological praxis. There is a dangerously superficial comprehension of the struggle for racial and economic justice, as well as of the movements for sexual liberation.[46] Liberation theologians, too, should look at what is going on in their own backyard.

These feminist theologians then define the conditions of their own praxis. The first condition is *accountability*, which means that their theologizing is done in relation to the interest of certain particular people—for example, black and Hispanic women. Second, *collaboration* conditions the feminist theological praxis. This distinguishes feminist theologians from the classical model of the lone researcher as think tank. It also means that theories are not only confirmed or critiqued by others but conceived in the praxis of collaboration. Third, they believe all research, teaching and learning should begin *'with our own lives-in-relation'*. That means they cannot lift themselves, as individuals, outside their communities. We do not begin as isolated individuals but rather as members of particular communities of people. To begin with one's own life is to make a pedagogical and epistemological claim. Knowledge is both relational (born in dialogue with others) and relative (contingent upon the difference it makes to our lives and the lives of others). The fourth condition for the feminist theological praxis is the *diversity of cultures*. FT does not operate on the assumption that any theology can be applied universally. It wants to criticize the arrogance in the assumption that theology constructed on the basis of men's experiences has a universal significance lacking in theology constructed on the basis of women's experiences. The fifth and last condition is *shared commitment*. The feminist theological praxis is strategic and action oriented.[47]

According to sociologists Liz Stanley and Sue Wise, 'Radical feminism argues that there must be a relationship between theory and praxis which not only sees these as inextricably interwoven, but which sees experience and practice as the basis of theory as the means of changing practice'.[48] They propose a similar relationship between theory, experience and research. In this configuration, theory and practice are not separate but are instead in a constant and dialectical relationship with each other.[49] This is a view of the relationship between theory and praxis very similar to that of Latin American LT, and implicitly, of FT—implicitly, because none of the feminist theologians I am analysing, such as

    46. Cannon *et al.* 1988: 19-21.
    47. Cannon *et al.* 1988: 23-27.
    48. Stanley and Wise 1993: 58. This book, one of the classics of feminist sociology, first came out in 1983.
    49. Stanley and Wise 1993: 56.

Rosemary Ruether and Elisabeth Schüssler Fiorenza, are as explicit about their method as Stanley and Wise, and feminist social scientists in general. The difference to LT, if there is one, lies in the feminist use of 'practice' and 'experience' interchangeably, synonymously.

For Stanley and Wise, experience 'is the basis of all analysis'.[50] For a theory about oppression, it is the experience of oppression itself that becomes normative.[51] They also note how the oppressed cannot simultaneously be oppressors.[52] This notion has been criticized by black and Third World feminists. Feminist liberation theologians, in spite of similar understanding of the relationship between theory and praxis presented here, base their analysis of oppression on a quite different view. For them it is the interlocking of oppressions which makes it possible for an individual to be both oppressed and oppressor simultaneously. This is the very starting point for their critique of the male liberation theologians, as well as for their self-critical attitude to their own generalizations of 'women's experience'.

In an afterword ten years later, Stanley and Wise review some of their earlier presuppositions, as a response to the critique directed at them in the rapid developments of feminist theory in the 1980s. Their feminist ontology 'rejects binary and oppositional notions of "the self" and its relationship to "the body" and "mind" and "emotions"'.[53] They reject, in contrast to some feminist ethicists, such as Nancy Chodorow and Carol Gilligan, a different pattern of psychological development for men and women. Feminist theologians have not theorized much about methodological questions. Their presuppositions concerning the relationship between theory and praxis and 'women's experience' are based both on feminist theory in other fields, on the one hand, and liberation theology, on the other. The problem lies in the meagreness of feminist *theological* theorizing which would make these connections explicit.

In FT, the relationship between theory and praxis is understood very much in the same way as in other liberation theologies. Gutiérrez' classical definition of theology as 'the critical reflection on the praxis in the light of the Word of God accepted in faith' is naturally true only for those feminist theologians who are committed to the Christian tradition and who consider themselves feminist liberation theologians. Nevertheless, it is important to bear in mind feminist theologians' much more critical relationship to the Bible and standard biblical interpretation within LT.

The praxis in FT is *both more inclusive and more specific* than in Latin American LT. The praxis is not merely understood as the liberative praxis of the oppressed for their liberation. When praxis is translated into 'women's experience'—this is the term that most feminist theologians use—new aspects of praxis appear which escape the more 'abstract' or general definitions of the Latin American liberation

50. Stanley and Wise 1993: 89.
51. Stanley and Wise 1993: 87.
52. Stanley and Wise 1993: 58.
53. Stanley and Wise 1993: 195.

theologians.[54] The feminist theological praxis is more inclusive in the sense that it explicitly includes (and starts from) issues such as sexuality and reproduction, everyday life, children, the relationship between humans and the rest of nature and a theological critique much more radical than that of the other liberation theologians. For most feminist theologians, 'human being' explicitly includes *both men and women*, and human liberation is by its very definition understood as the liberation of both men and women from oppressive economic, social and sexual structures.

At the same time, the feminist understanding of praxis can be said to be more specific. This is not in contradiction to the former. If the very possibility of a universal human experience is questioned, FT does not even claim to express abstract universals. All liberation theologies are self-consciously praxical, con-textual and historical. This *implies* difference and particularity. If the praxis and the subject of LT do not reflect the reality of Latin American women, what kind of praxis is it? It is as if the liberation theologians would say: 'There is no universal male experience, there are different male experiences'.

However, as will be clarified in forthcoming chapters, 'women's experience' in FT has gained the status of a 'new universal', raising important questions about the role of experience and praxis in liberation theologies.

The role of the Bible as the foundation for potentially liberating Christian praxis is quite different in FT than in other liberation theologies. For example, it is less complicated for Latin American LT to lean on the Bible than for FT to do so. Feminist theologians have more difficulties in reinterpreting the tradition, especially certain biblical texts, than do their Latin American (male) colleagues. The classical definition of LT as 'critical reflection on the praxis in the light of the Word of God' is not as easily acceptable for feminist hermeneutics. The 'theology of poverty' of Latin American LT has a strong biblical basis. It is much more difficult—if not impossible—to create a theology in favour of women's liberation based on biblical texts.[55]

To take another example, the Exodus story as a paradigm of liberation is complicated for a feminist eye.[56] The Bible is still today frequently used to legitimate

54. 'La teología feminista representa ante todo una ampliación del concepto de teología. La teología es aquí una reflexión sobre la praxis que la precede y que forma parte de ella; una reflexión sobre las experiencias recogidas, sobre el análisis de las estructuras injustas, en este caso sexista... Así, la teología feminista es un instrumento analítico para comprender mejor lo que ha acontecido en el curso de la historia y un medio estratégico para ahondar, enriquecer y ampliar todo lo que es Iglesia, ministerio, carisma y profecía. De este modo puede contribuir a la aparición de una nueva realidad' (Halkes 1980: 126-27).

55. 'Feminist theologians do not find an explicit feminist-critical principle or tradition in the Bible. Instead we are faced with the fact that the Bible is written in male language, which mirrors and perpetuates patriarchal culture and religion' (Fiorenza 1984b: xxi).

56. Even the language and concept of liberation may appear to be 'male' to some feminists, or 'Western' or 'white' to somebody outside the Western culture. The Korean feminist theologian Kwok Pui-lan says: 'Trying to articulate a new paradigm for Asian theology, I have benefitted from the insights of Delores S. Williams. In her study of black women's literature, she

women's secondary status. There are no post-Christian Latin American liberation theologians. On the contrary, even the Catholic liberation theologians are often almost uncritically 'biblical', although they may use the insights of modern historical-critical exegesis.[57]

In spite of feminist critique, liberation theological language remains sexist and exclusive. This is as much true at least in Spanish as in English.[58] Androcentrism in theological anthropology and image of God is but one example of difficulties that feminist liberation theologians face.[59] Ethical issues have remained mostly on the level of economic and political ethics. The notable lack of sexual ethical reformulations in liberation theologies is one of the points in this study (see Chapter 4). According to Hugo Assmann, one of the most serious errors of past theologies has been 'the theological totalization' as an opposite to historicity. The social location of a theologian has not been considered important. Now, what feminist theologians do is to extend this demand to further social 'locations', such as gender. Liberation theologians have been reluctant to see gender as one formative part of the social location, which they in more general terms accept as constitutive for one's theologizing.

Feminist theologians ask liberation theologians to take their methodological presuppositions more seriously, not to give them up. To Sobrino's claim that 'The key question for establishing comparisons between different theologies is to ask what the interests are that, factually and not intentionally, direct different ways of theological knowledge',[60] feminist theologians respond by asking the same question of liberation theologians themselves, claiming that gender is one of the 'factual interests' that direct our theological work. Sobrino brings up this question in the context of his critique of modern European theology. He wants to ask 'of what and for what the theological knowledge of different theologies has liberated and liberates'.[61] From a gender perspective, there may be less difference between European theology and mainstream liberation theology than liberation theologians believe.

As was said in Chapter 1.4, the enlargement of the understanding of the poor as the subjects of liberation theology has partly been produced by feminist critique. A simple 'adding' of women into the collective poor is not enough. The epistemological rupture that liberation theologians claim in relation to their

has found that black women don't use the language of liberation. Instead they speak of creating a context for survival and of the importance of quality of life' (Kwok 1992: 104).

57. For the feminist interpretation of the Bible in the LT context, see Tamez 1988 and Fiorenza 1984a and 1989. According to Ruether, feminist theologians have a much more ambivalent relationship to biblical origins than do male liberation theologians, who often consider liberation theology simply as the recovery of true biblical faith (Ruether 1988: 2).

58. The sexist language of Latin American liberation theologians is frequently 'corrected' in the English translations of their works. This makes them appear as more 'politically correct' to a North American audience than they actually are.

59. On the image of God in Latin American LT, see Araya 1987.

60. Sobrino 1976: 179.

61. Sobrino 1976: 180.

European heritage is challenged by the 'contextualized ways of knowing in which one knows through emotional and discursive connectedness to others'[62] of a feminist epistemology. The emotive dimension of knowing is recognized to be constitutive of consciousness in feminist ethics,[63] which does not mean that abstracted interpretations are not needed.[64] The acceptance of individual experiences, including emotions and personal relationships, in feminist ethics and theology is an implicit critique of liberation theologies' 'collectivism' in which only collective subjectivity is valued and a critique of 'Western individualism' is sometimes done in rather uncritical ways. The oppression both liberation and feminist theologians speak about is often also a more intimate personal kind of experience for the latter than for the former—in the area of sexuality, for instance.

As will be explained in Chapter 2.2.2, the relationship of feminist theologians to religious institutions and traditions is much more complex than that of most liberation theologians. There is, of course, an obvious reason for this: women as a group have been—and in many churches still are—excluded from the most valued positions, especially from ordination. It is only recently that women have been allowed to study theology. Personal experiences of sexism in the churches are deep in most feminist theologians. Most male liberation theologians are ordained priests and pastors, and in spite of conflicts of authority and orthodoxy, continue to be so. Especially in Latin America, formal church documents affirm many positions of LT. The denouncing of poverty and the option for the poor are official church teachings in the Catholic Church. No such denouncements of sexism and improvements in women's position *in the church* have been made.

According to Elisabeth Schüssler Fiorenza,

> Since feminist theology deals with theological, ecclesial, and cultural criticism and concerns itself with theological analysis of the myths, mechanisms, systems, and institutions which keep women down, it shares in the concerns of and expands critical theology... But because Christian symbols and thought are deeply embedded in patriarchal traditions and sexist structures, and because women belong to all races, classes, and cultures, its scope is more radical and universal than that of critical and liberation theology.[65]

In another text, Fiorenza says: 'But a critical feminist theology of liberation does not speak of male oppressors and female oppressed, of all men over all women, but rather of patriarchy as a pyramidal system and hierarchical structure of society and church.'[66] Thus, a critical feminist theology of liberation 'seeks to enable Christian women to explore theologically the structural sin of patriarchal sexism'.[67]

62. Tomm 1992: 107.
63. Tomm 1992: 107.
64. Tomm 1992: 108.
65. Fiorenza 1975: 616-17.
66. Fiorenza 1984b: 5.
67. Fiorenza 1984b: 7.

One evident, and not at all trivial, problem is the low educational level of women all over the Third World. In many regions, women with doctorates in theology can be counted on one's fingers. The fact that so many female Third World liberation theologians are including gender issues in their theologizing points to a positive correlation between higher education and feminist consciousness in liberation theologies as well. Women's theological education is of major importance in regions such as Latin America, where the arguments concerning women's status are largely theological or at least based on Catholic moral codes.

Here it is important to note the significance of the ecumenical movement, especially the World Council of Churches, for Third World women theologians. The WCC has made the higher education of many Third World women theologians economically possible. The WCC has been a forum of international solidarity and of concretizing new ideas for those Protestant feminist theologians who have decided to remain in their religious traditions.

On the Catholic side, the Second Vatican Council has had the same effect in FT as in other Catholic liberation theologies, especially in Latin America. The radicalization of Catholic nuns in gender issues dates from the post-Vaticanum years of *aggiornamento* ('bringing up to date' or 'renewal'). These contacts have to be taken into account when we speak of the non-academic references of FT. For theologians, the ecumenical contacts bear a specific meaning, which no other discipline has. Especially in the case of Third World feminist theologians, it is thus not only the secular women's movement that is seen as the socio-political base of feminist theorizing.

According to Ruether, Third World liberation movements, based on socialist theory, have shown their ambivalence towards women. This ambivalence combines the feelings of injured masculinity of colonized males, taking out their resentment on women, with the traditional Marxist hostility to any feminism that does not subordinate itself to the class revolution. Feminism is decried as merely a white, Western, middle-class movement having no relevance to Third World women. This hostility to feminism has also been reflected in the liberation theology produced by black and Third World male theologians.[68]

There are feminist theologians in all major Christian churches, and nowadays also in non-Christian traditions (for example, Jewish or Buddhist feminist theology).[69] As in other liberation theologies, doctrinal and confessional differences between churches are of less significance than is a shared practice. One concrete example is Mariology. Both Catholic and Protestant feminist theologians are interested in the Virgin Mary and have participated in the creation of an ecumenical feminist Mariology.[70] Between Catholic and Protestant women, the major differences probably lie in the question of women's ordination and the church

68.   Ruether 1988: 55-56.
69.   See Cooey *et al.* (eds.) 1994; Eck and Jain (eds.) 1986; O'Neill 1990; various entries in Russell and Clarkson (eds.) 1996.
70.   See Chapter 3.4.

hierarchy/authority in general, and possibly, to a lesser degree, in questions of sexual ethics.

It is a fact today that widespread poverty in the Third World as well as different 'development projects' to improve the situation affect women differently from men. Third World feminist theologies imply the need of critical analysis of religion(s) in the context of poverty. For example, gender analyses of Islam made by Muslim women themselves point both to the hegemony of 'Christian' interpretations of Islam, including First World feminists, and the necessity of the reinterpretation of religious traditions.[71]

The term 'feminization of poverty' points to three realities. First, both in the Third and First World, women are generally economically disadvantaged. Second, mothers with dependent children are additionally at risk. And third, women of colour who live in historically poor communities where social institutions have deteriorated are especially likely to be poor.[72] In the forthcoming chapters of this work, I will return to these issues in more detail.

2.2.2 Feminist Theology as a Heterogeneous Movement

Like other liberation theologies, FT has both its critical, deconstructive aspect in relation to the tradition and a constructive aspect that aims at creating a more inclusive, non-sexist theological discourse and practice. The first covers practically every aspect of the history of Christian theology, and concomitantly, much of Western philosophy. Revealing sexism and androcentrism in Christian theology has been one of the first and most important tasks of FT since its very beginning. By taking gender as the hermeneutical criterion, FT reveals not only how women

---

71.   According to Bonino, '[Religion] functions as an instrument of domination by creating in the oppressed a "religious" acceptance of domination as a sacred duty and even as a means of salvation. The religion of the oppressed, like their consciousness, is split... This ambiguity of religion as the privileged instrument of ideological domination, but also the place where the split in consciousness finds the deepest expression, makes religion an important field in the struggle for liberation' (Bonino 1992: 32-33).

Similarly, Maura O'Neill says: 'In current interreligious dialogues, participants are becoming increasingly aware of the need to explore ways in which abstract religious beliefs both affect and are affected by the social situations in which the religions are practiced... The past decade has indicated what an important and powerful role religion can play, for better or for worse, in bringing about socio-political transformation'(O'Neill 1990: 53-54). Many women are not only seeking a vital connection between social justice and religion but understanding that religion, including religious images, is profoundly influential in determining attitudes toward women even in the most secular societies (O'Neill 1990: 55).

See Ahmed for a critical analysis of the role of early British feminism in the imperialist endeavours of the British government. 'The Victorian colonial paternalistic establishment appropriated the language of feminism in the service of its assault on the religions and cultures of Other men, and in particular on Islam, in order to give an aura of moral justification to that assault at the very same time as it combated [sic] feminism within its own society' (Ahmed 1992: 152).

72.   Couture 1996: 121.

as a group have been excluded from theology, but also how androcentrism permeates the very inner structure of Christian theology.

In exegetics, the use of historical-critical interpretation combined with a feminist hermeneutic is of major importance. Insofar as feminist biblical interpretation has been motivated by an apologetic retrieval of biblical authority, it has focused on biblical texts about women, on male injunctions for women, on the biblical teaching on womanhood, on the great women of the Bible, or on feminine biblical language and symbols.[73] Feminist hermeneutics has attempted to reduce the historical particularity and pluriformity of biblical writings to a feminist 'canon within the canon' or a liberating 'organizing principle' as the normative centre of the Bible.[74] Fiorenza herself takes the contemporary liberation struggle as the starting point for exegetics, seeking

> to shift the focus…away not only from the discourse on 'women in the Bible' to the feminist reconstruction of Christian origins, but also from the drive to construct a unifying biblical canon and universalist principle to a discussion of the process of biblical interpretation and evaluation that could display and assess the oppressive as well as liberating functions of particular biblical texts.[75]

In church history, on the one hand, it is important to display the sexism in the teaching and practice of the church. Thus, no important Christian theologian has escaped feminist critique. On the other hand, women as well are the 'underside of the history', and it is necessary to reconstruct the forgotten and often unwritten history of women. Women have always been present in history. 'Feminist theological historiography' has made the life and work of women of previous generations more visible.

In systematic theology, the feminist critique goes deepest into the structures of Christian theology. The teachings of the church, Catholic, Orthodox and Protestant, and its main dogmas seem to be sexist to an extent that was invisible before feminist analysis. The most important single issues have been the image of God, Christology, theological anthropology, ethics and, to some extent, Mariology. Women have been both excluded from the sacred, concretely and symbolically, and included in a 'female principle' that serves as the lower, carnal and immanent/profane part in a dualistic construction of theological dogmas.

In practical theology, feminist theology has concentrated on the issues of language and symbols and their importance to theology and practice of the church. Of course, all the above-mentioned questions are intertwined, so that one cannot separate the issue of language from the question of God, for example. Our understanding of human nature in its sexual differences affects ecclesiology. As the Catholic discourse on women's ordination makes clear, theological anthropology cannot be separated from either Christology or soteriology.

---

73. Fiorenza 1989: 313. Without doubt, the single most important work in feminist exegetics is Fiorenza's *In Memory of Her* (1983).
74. Fiorenza 1989: 314.
75. Fiorenza 1989: 313.

Feminist scholarship within the Christian context is unified in its critical perception of sexism as a massive distortion in the historical and theological tradition and in its attention to the interpreted experience of women as a source of religious and theological reflection.[76]

But, as was said earlier, there is no one FT. First, feminist theologians are divided in their relation to tradition and their respective religious communities. Second, there has been a development of inner critique in FT that has led to theologies that do not want to be called 'feminist' even though they share many of the basic insights of what has come to be called FT.

Since the very beginning of FT, a great disparity was to be observed between different feminist theologians in their relation to tradition. The standard way of presenting this division nowadays is to put them into two groups called 'the reformists' and 'the radicals'.[77] Sometimes the latter are also called 'the reject-ionists' or post-Christian feminist theologians.

The reformists are those feminist theologians who continue to have a living relationship with the Christian (or Jewish) tradition. The Christian message continues to be authentic revelation for them, even though seriously distorted by sexism and other social injustices. But there are elements in the Scripture and in the tradition that can serve human, including women's, liberation. These women often claim that the core message of the Bible is that of liberation. Here they coincide with other liberation theologies. These feminist theologians believe that it is more important and wiser to try to 'reform' the tradition than to 'ignore' or 'reject' it.[78]

---

76. Carr 1990: 95.

77. See the Introduction in Christ and Plaskow (eds.) 1979: 9-13.

Rosemary Ruether sees three, not just two, different groups in FT. First, there are the 'evangelical feminists' who believe that the message of Scripture is fundamentally egalitarian. What is needed is better exegesis. The second is the 'liberationist' position that takes a more critical view of Scripture. The vision of redemption of the biblical tradition transcends the inadequacies of the past. This could be called the normative prophetic tradition. Biblical sexism is not denied, but it loses its authority. Ruether herself is closest to this group. The third group would then be what others call the 'revolutionaries', the Goddess religion (Ruether 1981a: 399-400).

It is important to note, though, that Elisabeth Schüssler Fiorenza would most easily fall into the second group (and defines her theology as critical feminist theology of liberation) but does not agree with Ruether's 'prophetic principle' and 'usable past'. According to Fiorenza, exegetically probably the most rigorous feminist theologian, Ruether draws an idealized picture of the biblical and prophetic traditions and overlooks the oppressive androcentric elements of these traditions. This is because Ruether does not analyse the prophetic tradition as a historical phenomenon, but uses it instead as an abstract critical interpretative pattern. See Fiorenza 1983: 16-17.

78. 'It is my view that the feminist option will be able to develop much more powerfully at the present time if it secures footholds in existing Christian churches and uses them to communicate its option for larger groups of people... Feminists who claim to have rejected all "male" institutions fail to appreciate how much their ability to function is based on a constant use of institutions that they have neither created nor maintained' (Ruether 1988: 39).

The radicals or 'the revolutionaries', as they are also called, deny the validity of both the Jewish and Christian tradition. According to them, the core message and symbolism of these traditions are so sexist that there is no hope for reform or transformation. Women should not waste their energy in hopeless efforts to change their religious heritage. These feminist *thea*logians[79] and religious feminists have been creating new religious traditions for women. Goddess worship has re-emerged in a feminist context. In it, a prebiblical matriarchal Goddess religion is often combined with the women's witchcraft tradition (Wicca).

In this group, there are also women who deny any personal deity, be it female or male. For them, there are other, more authentic sources for a feminist and woman-centred spirituality—women's bodily processes or natural phenomena, for instance. It is interesting that the post-Christian feminist theologians usually give up one religious tradition in favour of another. The strong spiritual ethos is channelled into the creation of a new religious community, rather than becoming 'post-religious'. Historically seen, there is nothing especially radical or transformative in the move itself. That is how all the existing religious traditions and sub-traditions have been born. Nevertheless, the existential religious choices of certain individuals and communities should not be mixed up with academic feminist research, even though a total separation of the two would appear arbitrary as well.

The very existence of these two groups, after only a couple of decades of FT, makes clear the depth of the conflict that religious feminists have with their traditions. Latin American LT, with all its radicality and criticism of its roots, has not produced a similar split. As far as I know, there are no post-Christian liberation theologians in Latin America, even though some of the Catholic liberation theologians (for example, Leonardo Boff) have left their religious orders and priesthood—but not the church—because of their continuous conflicts with the Vatican.[80] Basically, the difference between these two groups is crystallized in the question of whether the inferiority of women (and other oppressed groups) is seen as built-in in the Christian tradition or whether it is possible to find unconditional support for equality between all human beings in the tradition.

79.   The term *thealogy* is sometimes used to describe feminist reflections on the Goddess. In Greek the word *thea* is the feminine of the word for the divine.

80.   There is a women's network based in Chile called *Con-Spirando*, which is the closest I know in Latin America to post-Christian Goddess-orientated feminist groups. This group has not disassociated itself from its religious traditions, but its journal (*Con-Spirando*) shows a clear interest in ecofeminist goddess spirituality. Of course, Latin America abounds with syncretistic religious cults which contain similar elements, also by being more affirmative about women than the Christian tradition, but they are not to compare with groups which consciously distance themselves from Christianity for feminist reasons.

In Africa and Asia, where there are other strong and ancient religious traditions, the situation is somewhat different. African and Asian (Christian) liberation theologians are searching for liberative elements in the pre- and non-Christian religions of their continents as well. For Asia, see for example Chung 1990; Koyama 1974 and 1985; Song 1989 and 1991. For Africa, see Gibellini (ed.) 1994; Mbiti 1970 and 1990; Pobee 1996.

The reformist feminist theologians usually criticize the radicals for lack of historical analysis and historicity (when claiming, for instance, a matriarchal past that probably never existed), of dualism ('female' and 'male' are turned upside down—now women are the 'good' and men are the 'evil') and of essentialism (all women, because of their common biology, are seen as having some common 'women's experiences' that men cannot have). The radicals, for their part, accuse the reformists of lack of courage (women remain in the churches for convention- alities or psychological security) and lack of intellectual honesty (if Christianity and Judaism are really as sexist as FT has revealed them to be, the only logical consequence is to leave them to men, for and by whom they were really created).[81]

This rather black-and-white division between the two groups does not, of course, do justice to individual feminist theologians. Many reformist feminist theologians draw on pre- and non-Christian sources, including Goddess reli- gions—for example, when creating non-sexist liturgies.

Many current post-Christian feminist theologians were once Christians and have traditional theological education. One should take seriously their painful and real conflict with the tradition, not just theologically but institutionally as well. If women are actively excluded from full participation in the church, who is it then who really leaves whom? Psychologically, for most feminist theologians there are times when one believes in a *metanoia* of the church and theology; at other times, one feels a frustration so great that leaving religion altogether seems to be the best option.

The division of feminist theologians into these two groups was born in the United States and, as such, reflects the reality of that country. The relationship between academic theology and churches is different in the US from that in the Scandinavian countries and in many other European countries where the aca- demic work of an individual theologian does not necessarily have to reflect his or her religious convictions.

By maintaining the Christian/post-Christian division or by grouping themselves according to religious affiliations in general, feminist theologians themselves may be an obstacle to the further development of non-confessional feminist research of religion and continue a quite unfruitful either-or dualism. To 'locate' oneself as a researcher is another typically North American feature, especially in feminist research. In FT, this 'localization' has as one of its criteria religious conviction, which for somebody outside of that culture may appear strange. Those who criticize FT—as well as other liberation theologies—are often demanding religious criteria for theological research. It may be possible that with the Christian/post-Christian division, feminist theologians are subjecting their work to similar criteria.

---

81. See Chapter 2.3 for Anne-Louise Eriksson's claim that from a feminist theoretical perspective, the two groups may actually not be so different from each other, even in the question of essentialism.

Nevertheless, the United States has been the centre of FT both quantitatively and qualitatively. Thus, the classification is helpful in illustrating the internal differences of FT, as well as the development of FT up to now. It may be, though, that this kind of classification no longer serves, as FT becomes more global. In Europe as well as in Third World countries, the development is necessarily different from that of North America.

According to the British, currently post-Christian Daphne Hampson, the question as to whether feminism and Christianity are compatible is that of whether the equality of women is compatible with a religion that has come from a past patriarchal age.[82] There are different answers to this question.

First, there is the conservative response, which takes the past as normative: God's plan is set for all time, including different roles for men and women.[83] Second, there are those liberal theologians, including many feminists, who try to bridge the gap between past and present. Inside this response, there are three kinds of approaches. The 'Kairos' approach claims the past to be normative, but there can be development and changes since Christianity is a historical religion. For Hampson, this position is ethically incoherent, since sexism is not seen as evil, and the past is whitewashed.[84] Another approach inside the second kind of response is what Hampson calls the 'golden thread' approach, which has been popular especially in Lutheran theology and liberation theology. Hampson places Rosemary Ruether in this group, since she takes as the norm 'the prophetic-liberating tradition of the Biblical faith' (criticized by Elisabeth Schüssler Fiorenza).[85]

Third, there is the 'ethical a priori' position, which claims God's will to be one with what is good. According to Hampson, this position, like the two former ones, does not take sexist history seriously.[86] The third response is of those Christian feminists who deny the existence of any 'gap' or discontinuity. They write a 'feminist herstory'. Among these theologians, Hampson counts feminist exegetics Fiorenza and Phyllis Trible.[87] The fourth and last response to the question of the compatibility of Christianity and feminism is the post-Christian position which takes only the present as normative. This is the position of Hampson herself. Since theology has the same relation to the past as all other human sciences, Christianity cannot be qualitatively different or exceptional.[88]

82. Hampson 1990: 11.
83. Hampson 1990: 12-21.
84. Hampson 1990: 22-24.
85. Hampson 1990: 25-29.
86. Hampson 1990: 29-32.
87. Hampson 1990: 32-40.
88. Hampson 1990: 41-46. Hampson takes seriously the fact that there are central elements in Christian tradition, such as christological arguments against women's ordination, which make it logically impossible for a feminist to define herself as a Christian. Before ending up in a post-Christian position, she was one of the most active proponents of women's ordination in the English Anglican Church.

From now on, I will concentrate exclusively on reformist feminist theologians. This is reasonable, because liberation theologies as a worldwide movement are Christian theologies and have a living—even if critical—relationship to the institutional churches, and my point is to analyse FT as part of this movement. Also, those feminist theologians who explicitly consider themselves feminist liberation theologians are all from the reformist camp.

2.2.3 *Feminist Theologies in the Plural*

From the perspective of non-white and Third World feminist theologians, the above-mentioned differences between reformists and post-Christians may appear to be insignificant. Both positions represent mainstream theology, if factual relations of power in society are taken into account.

In the 1990s, FT has grown into a worldwide, global ecumenical movement. There are feminist theologians in all major religious traditions, including non-Christian. This globalization of FT has been a process similar to that of LT. It is a process of simultaneous globalization and particularization. A false abstract universalism is replaced by particularism and concrete universalism.

There are the women from racial minorities in the United States who have raised their voice against the empty universalism of 'women's experience' in FT. If FT in its beginning accused 'traditional' theology of reflecting really only the experience of white, educated, middle- and upper-class males, and denied its claim to universality, now it is African-American women who say that the 'experience' feminist theologians are talking about is really the experience of white, educated, middle- and upper-class women.[89] Historically, black women never have been able to separate sexism from racism. They have been, and still are, victims of both, and they do not want to construct 'hierarchies of oppression' (if they are 'more oppressed' as women or as members of a despised race) and thus political preferences. Even though there was a strong female presence in both the North American anti-slavery movement and the later civil rights movement, the issues of black women were treated as secondary. The North American feminist movement has been markedly white since the last century. 'Feminist universalism' is now criticized by women who have suffered not only from sexism but from racism and economic disadvantage as well.

According to Rosemary Ruether, FT is increasingly entering into a pluralistic situation. There is now a multicontextual expression of feminist religious reflection. The same critique of cultural imperialism that feminism has applied to white male theology also needs to be applied to white Western Christian feminist

---

89. 'Through the 1970s and 1980s, the women's experience claimed as source and substance was, more often than not, white, European-American, middle-class, heterosexual women's experience. The classism, heterosexism, racism, etc., of white women's theologies have been exposed as African-American women, Native American women, working-class women of various ethnic identities, Latina women, lesbians in diverse racial and class locations, Asian-American women, women living with unique physical and mental abilities, etc., have begun to speak up and speak out of their own unique experiences' (May 1996: 107).

theology.[90] Nevertheless, what all Christian women, whether white, black, Asian, Latin American, or whatever, have in common is that they have the same basic problems with Christian Scripture and tradition. They face the same androcentric and misogynist Christian past. Thus, according to Ruether, the work of feminist biblical hermeneutic and theological critique done by feminist scholars in a white Western context is relevant to all Christian women,[91] keeping in mind that it is also of primary importance for feminists to consider the effects of Christianization and Westernization on women of the Third World.[92]

Similarly, Elisabeth Schüssler Fiorenza says:

> There exists not one feminist theology or *the* feminist theology but many different expressions and articulations of feminist theology. These articulations not only share in the diverse presuppositions and perspectives of feminist studies but also function within the frameworks of divergent theological perspectives.[93]

In its beginning, black theology also reproduced this sexism against black women.[94] Black women's theology was born out of a critique of both black theology and mainstream (white) feminist theology. To mark their distinctiveness, black women do not use the term 'feminist theology' but 'womanist' of their theologizing. The term is taken from Alice Walker's book *In Search of Our Mothers' Gardens* (1983) where she explains why 'womanist' is a more correct term for black women's consciousness than is 'feminist'.[95] According to Jacquelyn Grant, a womanist is a strong black woman who has sometimes been mislabelled

---

90.   Ruether 1992: 49. This pluralistic and inclusive definition of FT has been the distinctive mark of Ruether's theology. Already in 1975, she wrote: 'any women's movement which is *only* concerned about sexism and no other form of oppression, must remain a women's movement of the white upper class, for it is *only* this group of women whose *only* problem is the problem of being women, since, in every other way, they belong to the ruling class... Thus it seems to me essential that the women's movement reach out and include in its struggle the interstructuring of sexism with all other kinds of oppression, and recognize a pluralism of women's movements in the context of different groupings. Otherwise it will tend to remain a women's movement of the ruling class that can be misused to consolidate the power of that ruling class against the poor and nonwhite of both sexes' (Ruether 1975: 125 [emphasis in original]).

91.   Ruether 1975: 50.

92.   Ruether 1975: 59.

93.   Fiorenza 1984b: 3 (emphasis in original).

94.   Cone 1984: 132. James Cone, probably the most well-known North American black theologian, admits his own sexism and that of the black churches and black theology in general, in this later work. According to him, the blindness to black women's situation has been a great lack and weakness in black theology.

95.   Grant 1989: 203-204. Alice Walker says: 'Womanist from womanish. (Opp. of "girlish", i.e. frivolous, irresponsible, not serious.) A Black feminist of color. From the Black folk expression of mothers to female children, "You acting womanish", i.e. like a woman. Usually referring to outrageous, audacious, courageous or willful behavior. Wanting to know more and in greater depth than is considered "good" for one. Interest in grown-up doings. Acting grown-up. Being grown-up. Interchangeable with another black folk expression: "You trying to be grown." Responsible. In charge. Serious"' (Walker 1983: xi). See also Cannon 1988 for another womanist theological work. For a white feminist theologian's response to womanist theology, see Thistlethwaite 1989. As far as I know, black women in other disciplines do not use the term 'womanist'.

as a domineering, castrating matriarch, but who has developed survival strategies in spite of the oppression in order to save her family and her people.[96]

A related term is 'mujerista theology', which some North American Latina women theologians, also unwilling to use the word 'feminist', use. 'Mujerista' comes from the Spanish word *mujer*, woman. One of the most well-known mujerista theologians is Ada María Isasi-Díaz, of Cuban origin, who says:

> the fact that the word 'women' refers only to middle- and upper-strata white women shows who decides what is normative. All the rest of us, in order not to be totally invisible, have to add adjectives to the word: *poor* women, *Black* women, *Hispanic* women.[97]

The distinctions feminist/womanist/mujerista, as well as the distinction between rejectionist and reformist feminist theologians, are products of North American culture and history. They have become a standard way of 'defining' FT and its heterogeneity, but they may also be confusing, especially for somebody who does not share the historical and cultural presuppositions (for instance, the history of slavery in the US) which they entail.

It is important to note that only some North American black feminist theologians want to call themselves 'womanists'. The concept is not derived from a concrete social or religious movement or intellectual current with a special impact on black women. Latin American black women theologians prefer to call their work 'black feminist theology of liberation' (*teología negra feminista de la liberación*). The Latin American black community has a history of its own. The term 'womanist' refers to a particular context of the literary and theological tradition of North American black women.[98]

The same can be said of mujerista theology in the United States. There are Latina theologians in the US, including María Pilar Aquino, who has been one of the major proponents of both Latin American feminist liberation theology and Hispanic feminist theology, who do not want to be called mujeristas. There are problems with *mujerismo* which have been criticized by Aquino, among others.[99]

One important area where the normativity of universal women's experience has also been called into question is that of sexual preference and orientation. Lesbian and bisexual women claim an 'experience' that is not that of heterosexual

---

96.   Grant 1989: 205.
97.   Isasi-Díaz 1988: 97 (emphasis in original).
98.   Aquino 1997: 11-12, 26-27.
99.   As a term, *mujerismo* carries essentialist notions of women. The term was coined by a group of Peruvian women who distanced themselves from the feminist movement at the end of the 1970s. Thus, the term mujerista has a specific connotation in the history of Latin American feminism and cannot as such be used to refer to an explicitly feminist project. Nor does 'mujerista theology' surge from any social movement which would call itself a mujerista movement or its participants themselves mujeristas (Aquino 1997: 11-12). According to Raquel Rodríguez, the translation of 'womanist' as 'mujerista' in Spanish has a different meaning with negative connotations for the Latin American feminist movement (Rodríguez 1991: 11). Similarly, Virginia Vargas says: 'Esta idea de la unidad natural de las mujeres—el mujerismo—ha sido el fantasma que recorre el feminismo' (Vargas 1989: 146-47).

women in a patriarchal society. In theology, these women have paid special attention to the critical analysis of sexuality and (hetero)sexism in the Christian tradition and the positive affirmation of human bodiliness and sexuality, in all its richness, as expressions of the divine.[100]

Globally, there is Latin American, Asian and African feminist theology, mostly inside and as part of the larger liberation theological movement, both worldwide and in their respective contexts.[101]

What these theologies have in common is an analysis of sexism and patriarchy in the larger context of class and race. It is not only gender but also their race, the economic situation and belonging to the Third World that define their 'experience'. For them, the interstructuring of oppression is a fact, in a way different than for those feminist theologians who first defined what it is 'to be a woman in a sexist society'. Third World women are suffering from triple oppression—being women, being citizens of the impoverished Third World (imperialism, colonialism) and often belonging to a despised race, especially if they are black or indigenous. On the one hand, they suffer from the traditional sexist attitudes of the men of their cultures; on the other hand, they are the ones (together with their children) who suffer most from the neocolonial economic and political structures typical of the Third World. In their critique of both sexism and unjust economic structures, they are critical of both male liberation theologians and First World feminist theologians. The great majority of the poorest of the poor, women and children, have not been included in either 'the poor' or 'the women' in LT and FT.

In many ways, liberation theology as a worldwide movement, in its broader definition, is not only an innovative modern theological movement but also one of the most self-critical. In spite of its short history, an inner critique which is moving the 'original paradigm' into new directions has already appeared. Feminist critique of male liberation theologians, black theologians' critique of Latin American and white liberation theologians, the mutual critique between Asian, African and Latin American liberation theologies and, finally, the womanist, mujerista and Third World women theologians' critique of their white, First World colleagues makes LT a living, dialoguing and open theological paradigm that is best defined as a process or as a movement rather than 'a school'.

---

100. See Harrison 1985: 135-51; Heyward 1989a and 1989b.

101. In the *Dictionary of Feminist Theologies*, there are separate entries for Asian, European, Jewish, North American, Pacific Islands, South Asian, African and Latin American feminist theologies. See Russell and Clarkson (eds.) 1996: 100-16. Third World women have written collective books which aim at defining a Third World feminist theology. Culturally and racially, of course, there are vast differences between different Third World countries. See Fabella and Oduyoye (eds.) 1988; King (ed.) 1994; Russell *et al.* (eds.) 1988; Thistlethwaite and Engel (eds.) 1990. For collective works by Latin American feminist theologians, see Aquino (ed.) 1988; Foulkes (ed.) 1989; *Mujer Latinoamericana* 1981; Tamez *et al.* 1986; Tamez 1989. On Asian women's theology, see Chung 1990; Fabella and Sun Ai Lee Park (eds.) 1990; Katoppo 1979; Mananzan (ed.) 1992. On African feminist theology, see Oduyoye 1986 and 1995.

2.3 Women's Experience in Feminist Theology

If, for feminist theologians, praxis translates into 'women's experience', what do they really mean by that? Is it some biological experience only women can have? Is it an essentially female experience, and thus unchangeable? What makes an experience a specifically female experience?

When theology is understood as the critical reflection of praxis, the historical, concrete, even bodily human experiences, especially those of oppression and suffering—since they reflect the deprivation of full humanity—are placed at the centre of theology. But, as has been said, experience or praxis as the norm for theology does not mean reducing theology to experience or praxis. In liberation theologies, including FT, experience becomes a critical tool for critique and reconstruction of reality.

In its widest possible meaning, 'women's experience' refers to women as a group defined by their biology. Here we face the problems concerning sex-gender distinction and the meaning of 'woman' in feminist theory, referred to in Chapter 2.1.

Since feminist liberation theologians such as Ruether and Fiorenza want to stress the historical and cultural—not so much biological—aspects of women's experience (even though they do not always succeed in being consistent, as we will see), they tend to give emphasis to the particularities of the situations in which women live. Women are oppressed in numerous ways in all societies, but these ways differ historically and culturally. Thus, women need to develop critical conscience as women but not detached from their social, cultural and racial specificity. This is what was referred to as the plurality of different feminist theologies.

This makes it possible to speak of women as a group, on the one hand, and of the great diversity and differences between them, on the other hand. Among feminist theorists, including feminist theologians, there is a broad agreement about the situation of women as subordinate in the context of patriarchy and sexism, both in the private and the societal dimensions of human life. Feminists are united in efforts to analyse the fundamental injustice in this situation and in discussion of strategies for overcoming it.[102]

According to Beverly Wildung Harrison, a North American feminist ethicist who can very well be counted among the feminist liberation theologians,

> given historical-cultural differences in male and female socialization, we must at the very least suspend any imputation of an irreducible difference between men and women rooted in biological distinctness. It is especially critical to avoid equating the cultural concepts 'masculinity' and 'femininity' with the concrete identity of women and men as individuals or as groups because the notions of femininity and masculinity are especially freighted with cultural stereotype. Gender is culturally and historically important but it is not of ontological significance.[103]

102. Carr 1990: 118.
103. Harrison 1985: 29-30.

It makes more sense to analyse historical rather than biological differences since no conceivable biological or psychological differences can justify gender-based distinctions in social power, prestige and wealth.[104] It is important, though, to analyse biology and biological differences as an ideology or argument for women's subordination.

Harrison is ready to do without the notion of 'femininity' because it is a male construct and always an ambivalent term.[105] What feminists must do is to take up and defend concrete female experiences, female modes of being, and women's culture, not 'femininity'. In this tension between 'giving up femininity' and 'celebrating femaleness', Harrison proposes concreteness—feminists need to 'celebrate women's concrete lives without lapsing back into gender dualism'.[106] For Harrison, 'women's experience' is very much the same as women's concrete everyday experiences, both negative and positive. The sources of women's experience in FT and feminist ethics are women's actual historical struggles. Refusing to use biological femaleness as an adequate base for FT does not mean contempt of bodiliness, especially of female bodiliness. Harrison proposes the term 'embodiment' to mean overcoming the body/mind split and recognizing that all our knowledge is body-mediated knowledge.[107]

For Rosemary Ruether, the principle of 'experience' is not unique to FT, as if classical theologies would have more 'objective' sources of truth. In fact, all theological reflection has its base in experience. According to her, 'What have been called the objective sources of theology, Scripture and tradition, are themselves codified collective human experience'.[108] She says:

> The uniqueness of FT lies not in its use of the criterion of experience but rather in its use of *women's* experience, which has been almost entirely shut out of theological reflection in the past. The use of women's experience in FT, therefore, explodes as a critical force, exposing classical theology, including its codified traditions, as based on *male* experience rather than on universal human experience.[109]

Here she comes methodologically very close to Latin American liberation theologians in their critique of 'European theology'. Religious traditions fall into crisis when the received interpretations of the redemptive paradigms contradict experience in significant ways[110] or when the total religious heritage appears to be corrupt and a means of enslavement and alienation.[111] But still, Ruether proposes staying in the tradition, because there is a human need to situate oneself

104. Harrison 1985: 30.
105. Harrison 1985: 34.
106. Harrison 1985: 31.
107. Harrison 1985: 12-13. She says: 'Ironically, no dimension of our Western intellectual heritage has been so distorted by body/mind dualism as has our moral theology and moral philosophy, which is why a feminist moral theology is so needed' (Harrison 1985: 12-13).
108. Ruether 1983: 12. Here she, in fact, coincides with the commonly accepted liberal theological tradition that gave birth to historical-critical biblical exegesis.
109. Ruether 1983: 13 (emphasis in original).
110. Ruether 1983: 16.
111. Ruether 1983: 17.

meaningfully in history.[112] Women's experience of oppression and their becoming conscious of it surely represents one of the major sources for the actual crisis of religion. FT, among other liberation theologies, reveals both the contradictory character of most Christian theology and the high level of theological corruption in the Christian churches.

According to Ruether,

> *The critical principle of FT is the promotion of the full humanity of women.* Whatever denies, diminishes, or distorts the full humanity of women is, therefore, appraised as not redemptive. Theologically speaking, whatever diminishes or denies the full humanity of women, must be presumed not to reflect the divine or an authentic relation to the divine... This negative principle also implies the positive principle: what does promote the full humanity of women is of the Holy.[113]

Again, as experience is not something unique to FT, neither is 'the principle of authentic, full humanity'. The uniqueness of FT is the fact that *women claim this principle for themselves*, naming themselves as subjects of authentic and full humanity.[114]

There are probably many who would say that this full humanity was never denied women. A careful study of the history of theology reveals that this is not true. Throughout the history of Christian theology, women (and other Others) have been defined as less or different from the authentic *imago dei* that only (free) men normatively present. This question over the full humanity of women is still at the centre of the Roman Catholic ordination debate.[115]

Androcentrism and *misogyny* are the two main targets of feminist critique in theology. The first takes the male to be the normative and dominant representative of the human species. Women never appear in patriarchal theology as

---

112. Ruether 1983: 18.

113. Ruether 1983 (emphasis added).

114. Ruether 1983: 19 (emphasis added).

115. According to the Roman Catholic view, women are incapable of being ordained because they cannot represent Christ, be images of Christ. If women are fully equal with men as *imago dei*, how can it be they cannot be *imago Christi*? Nowadays, according to the official Vatican view, women are equals in the natural, created order (and this has not always been so in the history of theology), but this has no implications for the ecclesial, sacramental order. According to Ruether, earlier theology (St Thomas, for instance) was at least coherent in claiming full human nature only to men and, consequently, it is only men who can represent Christ, who had to be born a male to fully possess humanity. The modern teaching of the Church 'gives' full humanity to women and supports their full human rights in civil society. The great exception is the Church itself. The modern Catholic anthropology is 'anthropology of complementarity' that implies two opposed ontologies. If earlier theology said women were inferior in nature but equal in grace, a contradiction prevailed between creation and Christology (soteriology). Today, the direction of the contradiction is the opposite: women are equal by nature and fully *imago dei*, but still they cannot represent Christ. If this incapacity is of the order of grace, does it mean that the grace brought by Christ does not fully include women? If women cannot be ordained, on the basis of this sort of theologizing, they cannot be baptized either. The affirmation of the full humanity of women *both* in nature *and* in grace would collapse the theological arguments against women's ordination in the Catholic Church. See Ruether 1991.

representatives of humanity as such. When women challenge this definition, patriarchal theology becomes not only androcentric (male-centred) but overtly misogynist, that is, defending the male right to define and control women.[116] The first is more difficult to unmask than the latter because it is so unconscious and taken-for-granted in Western culture. What feminist theologians do is to throw the authority of this theology into question and to name patriarchalism as evil. This is again very much a process similar to that in LT, where poverty is proclaimed a sin.[117] This could be said to be the critical, negative side of FT.

The constructive, positive side aims at seeking alternative traditions, both in and outside Christianity, which support the full and autonomous personhood of women. It could be said that much of the earlier feminist theological work was concentrated in the critical aspect whereas the best contributions of later FT are critical-constructive. According to Ruether, the third moment or aspect of FT is restatement of the norms and methods of theology itself in the light of the critique and alternative traditions. This is also the most constructive moment of FT even though (or because) it means the re-envisioning of the basic categories of theology. This allows new visions, such as experiencing the divine in places where it has not been allowed to be experienced before, new symbols and stories, although they do not have to be in total discontinuity with the past. But neither is there any 'original good moment' in the past, since no such period can be discovered for women. This means a much more critical attitude to Scripture and tradition than in other liberation theologies. For the reformatory FT, Scripture is *both* sexist *and* liberative.[118]

Ruether does not enter into a detailed discussion on what she understands by 'women's experience'. But in the light of her writings, it becomes clear that, for her, women's experience is not based on an essential feminine nature. It is a hermeneutical, analytical principle in the critique of sexism in the church and society. It *may* include biological, psychological experiences in the most traditional understanding of the word, but principally it is closer to what liberation theologians understand by praxis, by 'the place' or *locus* (the 'from where') and the human context of theology. Therefore, for Ruether, there is no normative, archetypal women's experience that would be common for all women over racial, cultural and other boundaries. If FT should be spoken of in the plural, so should women's experience as a methodological starting point be characterized by plurality and multiplicity.[119]

---

116. Ruether 1985a: 704-705.

117. It is important to remember that in spite of the conflicts between Church hierarchy and LT in Latin America, these kinds of proclamations are official proclamations of the Church (Medellín, Puebla). The Church has never proclaimed sexism to be a structural sin and evil.

118. Ruether 1985a: 707-11. As an example of new ways of experiencing the divine, Ruether tells the story of her student who, after having been raped, experienced a vision of Christ as a crucified woman: 'I would not have to explain to a male God that I had been raped. God knew what it was like to be a woman who had been raped' (Ruether 1985a: 710-11).

119. There is only one article by Ruether where she deals explicitly with what is meant by women's experience in FT. See Ruether 1985b. See also Young 1990.

According to Ruether,

> we are not talking about women's experiences primarily in terms of experiences created by biological differences in themselves but, rather, women's experiences created by the social and cultural appropriation of biological differences in a male-dominated society. In such a society, women experience even their biological differences in ways filtered and biased by male dominance and by their own marginalization and inferiorization.[120]

What feminist theologians *do* mean by women's experience is

> a key to hermeneutics or theory of interpretation...which arises when women become critically aware of these falsifying and alienating experiences imposed upon them as women by a male-dominated culture... It is this process of the critical naming of women's experience of androcentric culture that we refer to when we say that women's experience is an interpretative key for feminist theology.[121]

Rosemary Ruether acknowledges, as do the other feminist liberation theologians, that women's experiences of sexism differ, both individually and collectively. Nevertheless, for her, 'Patriarchy by its very nature provides enough of a common body of experiences that women, even from different cultures and religions, find commonalities'.[122] This is a response to the critique of universalizing women's experience, but it does not answer the more theoretical questions mentioned above.

Some second-generation feminist theologians who are more influenced by recent developments in feminist theory have criticized the notions of experience in Ruether and other 'older generation' feminist theologians. In a recent study, Anne-Louise Eriksson discusses the use of this concept in FT in relation to non-theological feminist theory.[123] According to her, FT as represented by Rosemary Radford Ruether and Elisabeth Schüssler Fiorenza—both of whom have relevance for this study as well—elaborates women's experience as a norm in ways that imply an epistemologically privileged position for women. Ruether and Fiorenza thus would come close to a standpoint feminism and a gynocentric approach, which claim that women's experiences provide a potential grounding for more complete and less distorted knowledge claims than do men's.[124]

According to Eriksson, Ruether is not claiming women's experience *per se* as a norm, but the norm is a principle that Ruether claims to be present as 'glimmers of truth' in history, such as women's alternative traditions within dominant patriarchal traditions.[125] It is the equality between women and men that is given an ontological status in Ruether's theology.[126] Nevertheless, since women's

---

120. Ruether 1985b: 113.
121. Ruether 1985b: 114. Women's experience is, thus, 'itself a grace event' or 'conversion experience' (Ruether 1985b: 114).
122. Ruether 1985b: 115.
123. Eriksson 1995.
124. Eriksson 1995: 42, 46-47.
125. Eriksson 1995: 110-11.
126. Eriksson 1995: 112.

experience is explicitly given an epistemological privilege (as a source and criterion of truth), this experience must, according to Ruether, somehow correlate with what is ultimately true.[127] According to Eriksson, Ruether proposes a kind of standpoint feminism where an epistemological privilege is given to women marginalized as a 'gender' (even though what she understands by 'gender' remains unclear).[128] So even though Ruether explicitly speaks against defining women's experience primarily in terms of biological differences, she nevertheless, according to Eriksson, has a strong tendency towards gynocentrist claims, which tend to see 'women's difference'—femininity—as essential.

This kind of reading of Ruether is possible. However, I would claim that since Eriksson interprets Ruether exclusively in the theoretical framework of non-theological feminist theory, she does not pay attention to how Ruether's position appears in a more theological context. This context is liberation theology and its understanding of praxis as a starting point for theology. A more nuanced reading of Ruether would point out that the openly 'political' nature of feminist liberation theology gives 'women's experience' a tactical or rhetorical, not merely epistemological, character. What feminist theory clearly reveals in FT is how little attention is given to the kind of theoretical reflections presented above. Nevertheless, this is not the same as to claim that feminist theologians neatly fit into the non-theological categories that feminist theorists themselves attack as too narrow and rigid.

The lack or meagreness of theoretical reflection concerning the truth claims in FT are similar to those in LT. This is why I would claim that these problems arise as a result of grounding the concept of theology in praxis. There is an obvious lack of a more theoretical discussion within the liberation theology paradigm, including FT, which would look critically at its own premises. Further, it seems that if this kind of critical analysis is not done, a theology wishing to be liberative may end up being dogmatic and uncritical. The epistemological status assigned to 'women' and their 'experience' in FT is analogical to the role of 'the poor' in Latin American LT. Their inherent problems are similar, as well. I will come back to these issues later in this chapter.

According to Eriksson, Elisabeth Schüssler Fiorenza, another feminist liberation theologian, uses women's experience to refer first and foremost to women's feminist and historical experience, even though the concept is far from being univocal in Fiorenza's work.[129] There is an apparent ambivalence in her work between 'humanist feminist' and 'gynocentric' approaches which creates incoherencies and dilemmas. On the one hand, Fiorenza sees gender as funda-mental and of decisive importance.[130] On the other hand, because she does not want to give exclusive preference to gender oppression (the experience of oppres-sion because of poverty, race, and so forth is an experience women share with

127. Eriksson 1995: 112-13.
128. Eriksson 1995: 118-19.
129. Eriksson 1995: 96-98.
130. Eriksson 1995: 100.

many men), Fiorenza conceptualizes patriarchy in a way that undermines the primacy and epistemological significance of gender.[131] According to Eriksson,

> Schüssler Fiorenza's pretensions for 'women's experience' as not only source but also norm in theology (that is, 'women's experience' theorized into an epistemologically privileged standpoint) forces her to abandon the humanist feminist model and embrace gynocentric notions of gendered experiences as a separating category.[132]

What both Ruether and Fiorenza do, according to Eriksson, is to maintain an epistemologically significant difference between women and men (Ruether) and between nonpersons—mostly women—and other persons (Fiorenza). They are claiming for women what they criticize men for having claimed for themselves, thereby maintaining physical gender as a separating category.[133]

The positioning of Ruether and Fiorenza by Eriksson close to the gynocentric approach is interesting, since both are usually defined as non-essentialists in relation to women's experience. I believe that conflicting interpretations are very much due to the modest level of theoretical reflection in FT in relation to non-theological feminist theories. Feminist theologians have most often been categorized as either reformist or radical (or Christian/post-Christian), and not so much according to their theoretical background in feminist theory. As has been said earlier, the post-Christians have been defined as having an essentialist tendency whereas the reformists such as Fiorenza and Ruether have been seen as representing a non-gynocentric approach.

Eriksson proposes refraining from all claims of a privileged position that set some people apart from others, not privileging one physical gender over the other when it comes to the question of verifying or falsifying theological claims.[134] Nor are women's experiences limited to the restricted area that is culturally constructed as feminine, even though feminists tend to emphasize those life experiences of women that men do not have (biological functions such as pregnancy and menstruation, everyday experiences due to the gendered division of labour, and women's experiences of marginalization in a patriarchal culture).[135]

Eriksson claims the experience of marginalization because of physical gender to be of the utmost importance in FT, but *this does not mean claiming the marginal position as an epistemologically privileged standpoint*.[136] Women's marginal position says nothing about what women *are*, but a lot about how women are treated and how female and femininity are constructed within a given frame of meaning. People on the margin are not objects but knowers and subjects in their own lives.[137]

131. Eriksson 1995: 101-102.
132. Eriksson 1995: 105.
133. Eriksson 1995: 131-32.
134. Eriksson 1995: 132.
135. Eriksson 1995.
136. Eriksson 1995: 134 (emphasis added).
137. Eriksson 1995 (emphasis in original).

According to her,

> we need a conception of 'women' that does not separate women from men, but still
> makes it possible to situate women 'as women' in the masculine domain (and men in
> the feminine domain). 'Women' must not be perceived as a homogeneous group,
> denying diversity among women, and 'women's experience' not understood as
> universal.[138]

She suggests not women's experience in general but the 'inner experience' of an 'I' which is historical and social and open in its identity as a point of departure for FT.[139] Women form part of this group of people sharing the experience of being marginalized because of their physical gender whether they accept or resist 'the viewer's view' which constructs women as subordinated and supposedly submissive.

Those women who resist are partaking in a systematic destabilization of the given frame of meaning that structures gender into a value-laden hierarchy.[140] For Eriksson, *resisto ergo sum* ('I resist, therefore I am', to rephrase Descartes' *cogito ergo sum*) summarizes a coherent feminist theological position which neither pre-supposes an epistemological privilege nor gives up speaking of women's realities as women.[141]

Eriksson is one of the few to analyse FT in a feminist theoretical framework. By doing this, she is able to reveal important, largely unresolved, theoretical issues in FT. It seems that the problems in Ruether's and Fiorenza's theology derive from the scarcity of these sorts of reflections. It is the lack of explicit theorizing of epistemological issues—with the help of non-theological feminist theory—that makes their theology vulnerable and open for different readings.

According to Morny Joy, neither Ruether nor Fiorenza believes in an essential form of womanhood. They must be read within the framework of feminist hermeneutics, which incorporates present self-understanding in a way that over-comes the subject/object split.[142] Joy wants to present a 'bridging' view: in (feminist) hermeneutics,

> allowance is made for women to speak from their own experience, without resorting
> to unsubstantiated generalizations. All this occurs within an overarching acceptance
> of continuous critique and correction of the contents and methods one employs.
> This in turn presumes many different approaches by women… Such an approach
> appears to avoid the extremes of both relativism and essentialism that hover around
> postmodernism and its remedies.[143]

Concerning the role of 'women's experience' in FT, Rebecca S. Chopp, for her part, admits—referring to the process philosopher A.N. Whitehead—that the word 'experience' is 'one of the most deceitful', having a certain inextricable vagueness that can never be fully explained. When applying the word to FT,

138. Eriksson 1995: 135.
139. Eriksson 1995: 141-42.
140. Eriksson 1995: 143.
141. Eriksson 1995: 143-44, 150.
142. Eriksson 1995: 132.
143. Eriksson 1995: 133.

Chopp wants to locate it in its own praxis, that is, the practical, historical experience of Christian feminism. This *location* of experience is established on three observations: first, the critique of women's oppression and its effects (the daily experience of being other and of lived oppression); second, the experience of women in the realm of the practical (the practical religious experiences of women in all their paradoxicality); and, third, the anticipation of change in practical experience (ideology critique).[144]

According to Chopp, FT approaches experience through a claim to historicality: experience should be conceived as *particular and concrete* rather than as absolute and general. An example is women's experience of physical abuse and sexual violence. Further, experience, in FT, is always understood as both *structural and individual*, social and personal, natural and historical. Besides particularity and interconnectedness, experience is also defined by *pluralism*, the variety of experience.[145] The difference of this kind of understanding of experience from classical theology is not just that FT substitutes women for men. The feminist construct of experience also both criticizes and opposes the way experience is viewed in 'theology proper'.[146] Chopp concludes that the location and themes of experience in feminist theory demand a 'pragmatics of inquiry', a way of interpreting and transforming experience. But a new vision of reality is needed as well, and this is the very radicalness of FT.[147]

A similar position to that of Eriksson's, in which the reformists and the radicals are shown to have much more in common than usually thought, is presented by Sheila Greeve Davaney, albeit for different reasons. Davaney bases her critique of FT on postmodern feminist claims against FT's

> Enlightenment-inspired quest for certain truth and the countermodern recognition of the historical and, hence, relative character of all claims to truth…these themes have reemerged in feminist theology's claim of a normative vision and in its assertion of the perspectival and conditioned nature of all human knowledge.[148]

These, again, stand in problematic and unresolved relation to one another within much feminist theory.[149] She is critical of the rejectionist as well as the reformist feminist theologians who 'do not adequately uncover the understandings of truth and knowledge operative within feminist theology'.[150] According to her, between the two 'camps' of FT, there are profound similarities in their 'continued

144. Chopp 1987: 242-43.
145. Chopp 1987: 244-45. See also Chopp 1993, where she locates feminist theology as practised in the US in the tradition of American pragmatism and its theological counterpart, public theology. These have been discourses of the dominant culture that attempt to include others in the centre of that culture, trying to develop or correct or improve those 'others' to ensure successful inclusion. She argues that women's experience should be understood as a pragmatic rather than an ontological norm.
146. Chopp 1987: 246.
147. Chopp 1987: 252.
148. Davaney 1988: 79-80.
149. Davaney 1988: 80.
150. Davaney 1988: 84.

assumption of the correspondence between feminist visions and ontological reality'.[151] By this she means that both groups have continued to search for onto-logical validation for their positions, be this 'divine reality' or 'God' (Fiorenza), 'the primal matrix' (Ruether), or 'Ontological or Elemental Reality' (Daly).[152]

This is very similar to the critique that was aimed at LT and philosophy of liberation by Ofelia Schutte and Horacio Cerutti Guldberg. What kind of truth claims can be made from an oppressed position? What kind of epistemological status do these claims have? A tendency in the philosophy of liberation and much of LT which has been criticized by Horacio Cerutti Guldberg is that of giving the Latin American 'people' a position as the 'subject of philosophizing' ('the poor' in LT), which presupposes Latin America's own essential rationality of some kind.[153] Cerutti calls this mildly 'low level of theoretical elaboration'.[154] Similarly, the elitist tendency in philosophy of liberation (especially Dussel) founds a 'new ontology',[155] which presupposes the acceptance of a divine and creational origin.[156] Cerutti criticizes another Catholic philosopher of liberation who also is counted among the theologians of liberation, Juan Carlos Scannone, for similar reasons. According to Cerutti, Scannone offers the possibility of situating oneself beyond all ideologies in order to judge from outside all projects.[157] This is equi-valent to giving a divine or transcendent status to one's political claims where philosophy only serves as *ancilla theologiae*.

Ofelia Schutte has also criticized LT, especially Dussel, for the 'postulation of an absolutely untainted source for, or undisputed authority at the origin of, its [Dussel's approach] claims to truth or justice'.[158] This approach allows Dussel to be critical of many things, but not of the view that an absolute criterion of truth is available to the philosopher 'of liberation'.[159] The 'alterity' (otherness) ceases to refer to an otherness or a difference thought to lie 'beyond absolute knowledge', as interpreted by postmodern writers. It also ceases to refer to the marginalized. It comes to designate the ground of a new absolute, but one constructed in the name of the poor, the exploited, the oppressed.[160]

Both Cerutti's and Schutte's critique of LT is similar to that of the critique concerning the status of women's experience and appeals to universal trans-cendent truths in FT. Schutte is actually very critical of the possible political applications of Dussel's ethics, not least concerning women.[161] It seems that the

151. Davaney 1988: 92.
152. Davaney 1988: 88-90.
153. Cerutti Guldberg 1988–89: 48-49. See also Chapter 1.4.4.
154. Cerutti Guldberg 1988–89: 49.
155. Cerutti Guldberg 1992: 52.
156. Cerutti Guldberg 1992: 42.
157. Cerutti Guldberg 1992: 279.
158. Schutte 1993: 178.
159. Schutte 1993. See also Schutte 1991, esp. 276-77.
160. Schutte 1993: 179.
161. Schutte 1993: 200. I will deal with Schutte's critique of Dussel concerning women in Chapter 3.3.1.

praxis starting point in the liberation theology paradigm—including FT, espe-cially feminist liberation theologians—is becoming a weaker and weaker point of reference, if these theologies want to be both theoretically coherent and politically emancipatory.

Concerning the latter, of central importance are notions of diversity, difference and plurality. Also, absolutizing one praxis—whether that of the poor or that of women—ironically contradicts the very claim to the praxis. If poor women's 'praxis' or 'experience' is not voiced either in the mainstream liberation theo-logical praxis of the poor or in the mainstream feminist theological women's experience, what does it tell of the overall use of praxis as a central point of reference?[162]

In addition, as we saw, liberation theologians in general give the perspective of the poor an epistemological status which supposedly gives a 'truer' understanding of reality and, theologically, of the revelation. The epistemological rupture of Latin American liberation theology, that is, the central role given to praxis, and the status of women's experience in FT, are thus subject to a similar critique con-cerning universal truth claims. The meagreness of self-critical theoretical reflec-tion concerning praxis in FT and LT makes it possible to interpret them both in ways that contradict their stated ideals. Both may in practice end up with a dog-matism contrary to the liberative and open character they claim to be based on.

If FT would give up the appeal to ontological reality as a grounds of validation for its positions, it would be understood as a thoroughly human construction sharing the same ontological status as male perspectives. Davaney proposes a new pragmatism instead of measuring which of the perspectives is closer to 'truth' or 'reality'.[163] The same would happen with religious symbols: they would be com-prehended as solely products of the human imagination, not as referents of an objective truth.

Davaney's critique of the tensions and contradictions within FT may be valid, but much of what she says concerns theology in general, not just FT or other liberation theologies. What is the character of theological claims at all? It seems that what she is proposing is that since FT is necessary, or at least important, for women's liberation and feminism, it should become consciously profane and stop pretending that there are any transcendent foundations for theology in the modern world. This, of course, is a question that goes beyond this research and which theologians would answer very differently depending on their overall worldview.[164]

---

162. Nevertheless, if Schutte's critique of Dussel is correct in that he intends 'to create a "space" free of error, blame, or guilt, out of which the truth may emerge, dramatically con-fronting an "evil" and oppressive system' (Schutte 1991: 281), it must be noted that this sort of tendency is explicitly denied by most feminist theologians, especially those who consider themselves feminist liberation theologians. They all stress the importance of not reversing the positions (women over men) and the necessity of liberating the oppressor as well, be it 'the white', 'men' or 'the First World'.

163. Davaney 1988: 93.

164. The post-Christian feminist theologian, Carol P. Christ, has published a response to

In a book where several North American feminist theologians explore the influence of French feminism on their thought, FT is seen as being challenged simultaneously from two directions, both of which I have already mentioned. First, FT's failure to acknowledge the diversity of women, resulting in complicity with discrimination by race and gender, is brought up mostly by non-white women. Second, FT has been challenged by postmodern views that reject modernity's claims to universal truth.[165] Both critiques point to methodological assumptions in FT.[166] Feminist theologians have tended to make 'women's experience' the ontological standard of theological sources and interpretations (Davaney).[167]

This implies two tasks for FT in the future. First, feminist theologians must attempt to uncover any hidden metaphysical assumptions underlying the methodologies they use. Second, given the centrality of the category 'women's experience', FT must rethink the anthropological assumptions that inform it. How do we understand the subject 'woman' whose perception of the divine is of such importance? And, more tellingly, how do we understand and account for the diversity of subjects which are indicated by the name 'woman?'[168]

The problems of the appeal to women's experience in FT have also been clarified by Mary McClintock Fulkerson. According to her, FT has failed to offer theories of language, social location, power and gender capable of displaying difference. She wants to radicalize the feminist appreciation of the constitutive character of social location—class, race, sexual preference. For her, experience is not the *origin* of theology in the sense of evidence for our claims, but the reality that needs to be explained.[169] There is a danger that FT reproduces the Cartesian 'universal subject' when basing its methodology on the appeal to women's experience. The point is not to lose the subject 'woman' but to *change the subject* in the sense that the complex production of multiple identities becomes basic to our thinking.[170] She is not proposing a feminism without women, as some critics of poststructuralism fear.[171]

McClintock Fulkerson argues that taking seriously the challenge of feminist theory to the subject—that there is no 'real woman'—is crucial to our ability to

Davaney in which she names Davaney's position 'nihilist' and, thus, warns feminists not to embrace that position (Christ 1989: 14).

165. Introduction in Kim *et al.* (eds.) 1993: 2.

166. Introduction in Kim *et al.* (eds.) 1993: 3.

167. Introduction in Kim *et al.* (eds.) 1993: 4.

168. Introduction in Kim *et al.* (eds.) 1993: 5. On questioning the concept of 'woman' and 'women's experience' in mainstream FT, see especially the articles by Rebecca S. Chopp and Ellen T. Armour in Kim *et al.* (eds.) 1993.

169. Fulkerson 1994: vii-viii.

170. Fulkerson 1994: 6-7. She herself uses discourse analysis to map different modes of women's existence in such diverse locations as Appalachia and Presbyterian women's groups. Like Eriksson, she too identifies most feminist theological positions theoretically close to feminist standpoint theories. See Fulkerson 1994: 53.

171. Fulkerson 1994: 11.

speak for the situation of different women. An approach to difference must offer categories that take seriously the way in which subjects are constructed out of social relations that feature multiple forms of gender oppression. Feminist theological reflection is thus *not* liberating praxis based upon women's experience (as feminist liberation theologians such as Ruether and Fiorenza would claim) but is itself a produced cognitive practice inextricable from social relations. This means that the site of feminist theology is part of its meaning.[172]

According to Fulkerson, the problem with feminist liberation theologies has been that the question of difference among women has thus far only produced an 'endless list of the excluded'. It has been successful in blocking the hegemony of white Euro-American women's experience but is not sufficient. How can one value both the multiplicity and diversity of the oppressed subject and 'women' as a group?[173] Her analysis of the use of women's experience in FT reveals how most feminist theologians implicitly assume a prelinguistic realm of experience, which is shared by all humanity (in Ruether's terms 'authentic humanity'). When women's experience is used as a warrant for a claim, this implicitly grants that experience the status of a universal, shared consciousness. Those with the power to produce knowledge can claim a common identity as human.[174] This is hardly what feminist theologians want.

Fulkerson proposes a provisional description of an ideal liberationist epistemology which is consonant with feminist commitments. There are five elements in it. First, the term 'liberationist' indicates that theology itself has ideological or oppressive possibilities. Knowledge is not *tainted* by interest: it *is* interest. Second, interests are connected to social conditions, which include the economic, political, and civil or cultural aspects of a social formation. Interests are operative at levels that transcend the individual. A theological liberationist epistemology must articulate the relation between these social conditions and systems of meaning.[175] Third, the best way to relate these is with a materialist rather than idealist conceptual frame. This means that images of making or practice are central to thinking about truth and are preferable to images of correlation. This model is important for attending to social location. Fourth, simplistic reflection theories where language or ideas are seen as reflections of social relations should not be accepted. Social forces converge in multiple ways on women, so that oppressions and possibilities for emancipation are signified in women's discourses in complicated ways. This is what many feminist liberation theologians have called the multiplicative character of women's oppression. And fifth, there must be a minimalist definition of the subject which allows us to respect the difference that attends the production of women. It is necessary to maintain both the individual and social aspects of this subject.[176]

172. Fulkerson 1994: 7.
173. Fulkerson 1994: 13-18.
174. Fulkerson 1994: 55-56.
175. Fulkerson 1994: 25-26.
176. Fulkerson 1994: 26-27.

The specific theological element in this construction is the 'social conception of finitude that gestures at what cannot be caused or proved but only witnessed to: its ultimate conditions, God's redemptive reality'. There is no false choice of either human agency or divine causality.[177]

Fulkerson's critique of certain tendencies in FT is similar to mine in Latin American LT (Chapter 1.4). Taking difference really seriously means that we first have to look at our own situation and especially how we as academic theologians create knowledge of the other. We must be able to see the ways our discourse *produces* the other as a result of where *we* are.[178]

According to Fulkerson, the processes of recognizing and respecting difference are more subtle and problematic than the mere notion that women are different, representing different races, classes, sexual preferences, and so on. We cannot 'see' the difference merely by 'looking' at the other.[179] Definitions of the 'other' that do not take seriously the radical instability of discourse and the intimate connection of power/knowledge are tempted to ignore the ways in which our definitions of the other do not allow us to really have an 'other'.[180]

Fulkerson recognizes two possible ways how theology can represent the other. First, we must concede how our discourse about the other does not in the philosophical and cultural sense 'represent' the other, but mediates difference. Second, we are called to represent (as in 'speak for') the outsider to well-being because of a vision of God's care for the Creation.[181] To be able to do this, she proposes a 'feminist theology of affinity' rather than identity or solidarity with the other.[182]

Morny Joy responds to both Rebecca Chopp's and Sheila Greeve Davaney's critique of FT.[183] From a postmodern paradigm any appeal to women's experience and God as an objective absolute are suspect.[184] As we saw earlier, Joy is not willing to interpret Ruether and Fiorenza as 'essentialists'. She proposes a political or feminist-tactical position. She says:

> for a time there should be a moratorium on theoretical pronouncements as to the death of God, the relativist nature of all knowledge, etc. From a feminist perspective, such theoretical postulates exclude women from a scene to which they have just gained access and where they need time/space to give expression to their experience.[185]

177. Fulkerson 1994: 29.
178. Fulkerson 1994: 377-81.
179. Fulkerson 1994: 381.
180. Fulkerson 1994: 382.
181. Fulkerson 1994: 383-84.
182. Fulkerson 1994: 384.
183. Joy 1995.
184. It should be noted, though, that there are feminists—in theology as well—on both sides: those who lean theoretically to postmodernist deconstructionist projects and those who are more suspicious of giving up modernity and its claims, especially those concerning subjectivity. See Nicholson (ed.) 1990.
185. Joy 1995: 140.

This project implies plurality and diversity of experiences. According to her, it is important to 'be aware that we are imbedded in concrete reality addressing issues of vital concern to the lives of everyday women'.[186] Here she comes close to those feminist liberation theologians, including Ruether and Fiorenza, who understand their theology as inherently practical and political. In order to avoid dogmatism, this position should not exclude more theoretical elaborations.

2.4 Conclusions

As this chapter has made clear, FT today is a pluralist, diverse, global and open theological project over which it is difficult to pronounce any definite claims. It is possible to analyse FT both as part of academic women's studies or feminist theory and as part of the liberation theology paradigm. FT looks different from these two angles.

FT shares similar methodological premises and point of departure with other liberation theologies. However, FT also functions as a critical corrective of other liberation theologies and differs from them in several aspects.

The most recent developments in FT are due to a greater theoretical debate within non-theological feminist theory. Younger-generation feminist theologians have been more eager than their foremothers to enter into debates with feminist epistemologies, postmodernist theories, French feminism, and others. This inter-action has given birth to theoretical and methodological questions in FT similar to those it has raised in other disciplines. In FT, too, the great question is how to speak from the realities of concrete women, obviously marginalized, albeit in different ways and to different levels, in all existing societies, and not fall into absolutist, essentialist positions which claim both a female essence and epistemo-logical privilege to 'women's experiences'.

In recent discussions on feminist theological methodology, feminist liberation theologians—especially Ruether and Fiorenza—have been both criticized and absent. Their work has been ground-breaking and foundational, but they have not taken part in the later debates concerning women's experience as an adequate tool of analysis in FT. The same can be said of Latin American feminist liberation theologians who, when touching methodological issues at all, often confess a closeness to the method of LT, without asking more fundamental theoretical questions which would concern them as much as liberation theologians in general.

The critique that has been aimed at the presupposed collective subject both in LT (the poor) and in FT (women, women's experiences) is similar. This is defi-nitely one area where FT and LT have methodologically had a lot in common, but where both of them also have to face new challenges. Both FT and LT are at a watershed, in at least two meanings. First, new generations are asking new questions, which sometimes are raised as a critique against the earlier generation. Whatever the future of the liberation theology paradigm, it is now time to give

---

186. Joy 1995: 140.

space to new definitions of it. Second, both the theoretical and political climate in which liberation theologies were created have changed. It is not only that new generations ask different questions *per se*. They also live in a different world.

Women from all parts of the Third World form the bridge between different discourses (feminist theory—including FT—, liberation theologies, postmodernism, postcolonialist critique, and so on), and it seems that this bridge is becoming more and more two-way. On the one hand, women in the Third World can critically use many of the insights of feminist theory developed in the First World setting. On the other hand, it is very much due to the critique presented by Third World women that the issue of difference, with all its theoretical and political weight, has entered not only feminist theories but other 'emancipatory discourses' in their own cultural climate, dominated by men.

Whatever the emphasis on women's experience, the commonalities or distinctiveness between different women, it is certain that the concept has come under fire mainly from two directions: first, from the part of those women who see the experience FT speaks about as the experience of 'white, middle-class, educated, heterosexual women'; and second, from the challenge to FT by postmodern views that reject modernity's claims to universal truth. [187]

'Women's experience' as the basis for FT has in a way become impossible because of its own premises. Even when women of different races, sexual orientations and classes correct the universalist tendency in the standard use of experience in FT, no criteria are given for which of all these experiences is closest to 'the truth'. It is the very call on experience that raises the question of how it is supposed to reflect 'reality'. Implicitly, there is a presupposition of an objective reality or truth about it which the different experiences try to make explicit.

In this sense, FT in its present phase is faced with challenges similar to those of Latin American LT concerning particularity as the base for critique, on the one hand, and the possible universality of these particular claims, on the other hand. The critique of one universalism, be it 'Eurocentrism', 'masculinity' or 'privileged women's experience', is not of much use if these universalisms are simply replaced by new ones or if all particular experiences are given the same status. This kind of relativism would make it impossible to deal critically with issues of power which, ethically and politically, form the basis of any feminist project.

It is not accidental that the challenges to the problems in FT's theoretical framework, presented in Chapter 2.3, all seem to point toward the same direction. As was said earlier, the critique of women's experience has also been a result of a dialogue with non-theological feminist theory, until recently almost non-existent in FT. The critique of women's experience as a solid point of reference also questions universal notions of womanhood. Issues of difference, to a far more radical extent than earlier, are central in the latest feminist theological discourses—difference between men and women, difference between women, and so on.

---

187. Introduction in Kim *et al.* (eds.) 1993: 2.

Non-theological feminist theory has for some time theorized such central issues as 'sex', 'gender' and 'women'. This discussion has been little reflected in FT which obviously is why it is easy to point out contradictions and lacunae in FT. However, even though I claim that more extensive use of non-theological feminist theory would serve FT in important, even central, issues, I would not rush to label feminist theologians, such as Rosemary Ruether and Elisabeth Schüssler Fiorenza, as essentialist or gynocentric. Their theology appears in a somewhat different light when analysed in the context of the liberation theology paradigm.

The meagreness of theoretical elaborations concerning the epistemological status of 'women's experience' in FT creates problems similar to those in Latin American LT concerning the role of praxis and 'the poor'. The category of 'women's experience' is as weak, analytically, as 'the poor', especially when used in a normative and uncritical way. Both are subject to a similar critique concerning universal truth claims, whatever the position of particularity they are expressed from. It is possible to interpret both LT and FT in ways that contradict their stated ideals. Both may in practice end up with a dogmatism contrary to the liberative and open character they claim to be based on.

It is important for the future development of FT that it would take up these issues. Since it is evident that there are similar problems in other theologies which take praxis or experience as their central points of departure, it seems that it is necessary for the liberation theological paradigm as such to take a more critical view on its own premises. Thus, it is not *only* in relation to non-theological feminist theory, but (intra-theologically) to the liberation theology paradigm as well, that FT should clarify its premises.

Even though the critique of the status of women's experience in FT comes from different theoretical positions, feminist theologians who are interested in epistemological questions in FT and in a dialogue with non-theological feminist theory emphasize *the concrete living conditions of different women in varying contexts* as a more fruitful starting point than theoretical unifying notions of common womanhood.

Anne-Louise Eriksson's proposal, as we saw, is that of the 'inner experience' of a historical and social 'I' who experiences herself as being marginalized because of her physical gender, as a starting point for FT, instead of a general 'women's experience'. Resistance to this marginalization does not presuppose an epistemological privilege for women but makes it possible to speak of women and from their own experiences.[188]

Rebecca Chopp speaks of the practical, historical experience of Christian feminism. Experience is particular and concrete rather than absolute and general. It is both structural and individual. It is defined by pluralism, the variety of experience.[189] Sheila Greeve Davaney also calls for 'a new pragmatism' instead of measuring which position is closer to 'truth' or 'reality'.[190]

188. Eriksson 1995: 134-44.
189. Chopp 1987: 242-45.
190. Davaney 1988: 93.

Mary McClintock Fulkerson actually does what she proposes: she lets the
voice of women outside the academic and feminist setting be heard in the centre
of FT. Feminist theologians must be especially self-critical when producing their
discourses of difference and representation. Social locations have to be taken
more seriously than they have been in FT. The relation between social conditions
and systems of meaning is best created in a materialist rather than idealist conceptual frame.[191] Similarly, Morny Joy says: 'We need to be aware that we are
imbedded in concrete reality addressing issues of vital concern to the lives of
everyday women'.[192]

For the Latin American feminist liberation theologians, everyday life (*la vida
cotidiana*) is an important point of departure. In many ways, Latin American
feminist liberation theologians respond to the demands of more diverse, concrete
experiences of women to be heard in theology. Not always theorized as such,
their perspective nevertheless brings forth a critical element to both FT and Latin
American LT. In fact, they bring the 'praxis' or 'experience' of the poor women of
Latin America as a critical corrective to both Latin American LT—the 'homogeneous poor'—and much of FT—the universal female subject. Implicitly,
questions of ethics, especially sexual ethics, are at the centre of these calls to take
into account the multiple forms of women's marginalization and oppression,
especially in the so-called Third World. We will now turn to these issues.

191. Fulkerson 1994: 25-26, 377-82.
192. Joy 1995: 140.

Chapter 3

Feminist Theology and Latin American Liberation Theology in Dialogue

3.1 The Irruption Within the Irruption: Latin American Feminist Liberation Theology

The dialogue between Latin American LT and FT has taken place until now mostly in the context of international ecumenical conferences. The EATWOT process, in particular, has been of great importance in bringing feminist perspectives into the Third World liberation theologies. On the level of individual theologians, it is mainly some feminist theologians who have made an effort to define their theologizing in both directions: the feminist and the liberational. Outstanding in this are a number of Latin American feminist liberation theologians. They also occupy the 'bridge' in the most 'natural' way—natural in the sense that as individuals they speak from both contexts simultaneously. FT in the Third World must be understood within the larger context of both FT and LT as well as that of a distinct Third World theology.[1]

Some, but strikingly few, of the Latin American male liberation theologians have entered into a serious dialogue with feminist theologians, be it their fellow Latin Americans or women from other continents.[2] The feminist agenda at international meetings of different liberation theologies has meant that gender issues must be taken into account, however superficially. Unfortunately, this is about it. Women are mentioned in the writings of male liberation theologians as the ones doubly or triply oppressed, and the need for their liberation is formally stated in 'the hit parade of oppression'.[3] Whatever more serious implications the feminist

---

1.   King 1994: 8.

2.   Since I will limit my discussion to the Latin American context, I will not touch at all on similar dialogue in other continents. In the EATWOT context, women from all continents have challenged their male colleagues both from their own continents and countries and from other latitudes.

3.   An expression by Rosemary Ruether, when she gave a lecture in San José, Costa Rica, 10 March 1993. By this, she points to the common habit among liberation theologians to add women to 'lists of the oppressed' in need of liberation. Usually, these are the blacks (race), the indigenous peoples (ethnicity), and women (gender). In spite of the irony in Ruether's statement,

perspective would have for Latin American LT is not treated by any of the most well-known male liberation theologians. By drawing a picture of the present situation, and especially by pointing towards possible areas of a more serious dialogue, I want to emphasize the possibility and need for such a dialogue.

It is not only that a dialogue between FT and Latin American LT has been rare. When taken up at all as an issue, it too often has also been superficial and cautious, aiming at avoiding conflicts. This again is understandable for both parties. Feminist liberation theologians do not want to create schisms, to be 'befoulers of one's own nest', with slightly different reasons for Latin Americans and those outside.

I will approach this problem in two ways. First, building on what was said in previous chapters about the praxis starting point in the two theologies, I will look at how some feminist liberation theologians, mostly Latin American, have criticized and reinterpreted Latin American LT (Chapter 3.2). Second, I will analyse what two major liberation theologians, Enrique Dussel and Leonardo Boff, have said about women and feminism (Chapter 3.3). Finally, I will touch on some of the themes that have been taken up in this dialogue, concentrating on Mariology (Chapter 3.4).

The first issue I will approach mainly by asking about the supposed subject of theology. In continuation of the discussion in Chapter 1.4 I will ask, Who are the 'the poor', the ideal subjects of LT? What happens to the poor when they are also seen as reproductive, gendered subjects? *Methodologically*, feminist critique seems to reinterpret and enlarge the concept of 'the poor' by giving it a more concrete appearance, although not only in the form of gender. The praxis itself is critically reinterpreted when 'everyday life' (*vida cotidiana*) is taken as an important point of reference. The separation of macro- and micro-level issues in LT is close to the much criticized distinction between the private and the public, central to any feminist concern.

These more methodological kinds of questions will be worked out in Chapters 3.2 and 3.3.

A more *thematical* approach will show how certain methodological pre-suppositions concerning the praxis and the subject(s) of LT are concretized in the content of LT. I will not do this by listing themes, but by taking one major example, Mariology. Both male and female liberation theologians seem to tie women's fate to a certain extent to Mariological reinterpretations. A feminist liberation theological Mariology will serve as an example of an already existing area of dialogue between LT and FT. Mariological reinterpretations also have an important link to feminist understanding of praxis as 'everyday life'. This is the link between methodological and thematical discourses, and will be analysed in Chapter 3.4.

Many of the themes concerning women('s presence) in LT, may be there in a very implicit form. There are male liberation theologians, such as Leonardo Boff,

this reflects a change of attitude in comparison to earlier stages of LT, when women and gender issues were not even mentioned.

who do write on women and 'women's issues' on a more substantial level. Nevertheless, a critical analysis reveals images of women and femininity that can hardly be taken as a common ground for a feminist liberation theology. Only a *critical* feminist perspective will both correct previous assumptions and create a space for a more constructive dialogue. This is for two reasons. First, the novelty of a feminist discourse on women has been the questioning of the naturalness of women's 'nature' and roles in the society and the church. This perspective further reveals differences between women, depending on factors other than their gender. Second, a feminist perspective is political to the extent that it aims at concrete changes. More specifically, up to now LT has formulated discourses on women that have not created spaces to discuss (poor) women's life conditions, most notably reproductive issues and sexual ethics. The supposed naturalness of women's subordinate role is especially clear in traditional Catholic sexual ethics. The Catholic Church nevertheless wields extensive political power concerning such areas as legislation in most Latin American countries. These questions will be worked out in more detail in Chapter 4.

The fact of women finding a voice of their own inside the global liberation theological movement has been described as 'the irruption within the irruption'.[4] It is during the last ten years that theological production by Third World women has grown to extensive proportions, both in quality and quantity.[5]

Women's concerns, expressed by feminist movements, have been 'the irruption within the irruption' in the context of socio-political—especially in Latin America, often Leftist—movements as well. This has been true both in secular movements and in religiously inspired movements such as LT and the popular church. Marxist-orientated male leaders and activists have been quick to see feminism and the critique of sexism as belonging 'to a minority of disgruntled, leisure-saturated, middle-class women of the capitalist West'.[6] This attitude has had serious effects on both the development of women's movements and on the fate of possible socialist experiments in Latin America. Even when seen as an issue, it has been supposed that as soon as a (socialist) revolution is a reality,

4.   Oduyoye 1994: 24. This paper was originally published in the compilation of papers from the EATWOT conference in New Delhi 1981. See Fabella and Torres (eds.) 1983. The irruption of the Third World and the poor into theology was described as a major historical event. The New Delhi meeting was a turning point in women's participation in the EATWOT organization and, concomitantly, in Third World liberation theologies.
5.   Since presenting works by individual theologians would be too laborious, I only mention here some of their collective works. The most representative of them are Fabella and Oduyoye (eds.) 1988 and King (ed.) 1994. The first is a selection of papers from an intercontinental EATWOT conference of women theologians held in Oaxtepec, Mexico, in 1986; the latter includes papers from the first but also a lot of other material. There are compilations of writings by Latin American, African and Asian women such as Tamez *et al.* 1986; Tamez 1989; Oduyoye 1986; Fabella and Park (eds.) 1990. For extensive bibliographies on Third World women's theology (including minorities in the First World, such as womanist and mujerista theologies in the United States), see King (ed.) 1994; Russell *et al.* (eds.) 1988.
6.   Oduyoye 1994: 27.

women's gender-specific problems will automatically be solved as well. The Sandinista Revolution in Nicaragua is one of the examples of this not being the case.[7]

The history of women's movements and feminism(s) in Latin America has been documented in various contexts.[8] Contemporary Latin American feminists form but one part of a larger, multifaceted, socially and politically heterogeneous women's movement. A distinction between 'feminine' and 'feminist' women's movement organizations is commonly made by both movement participants and social scientists.[9] The former, *movimientos de mujeres* or *movimientos femeninos*, cover everything from women-led human rights organizations (such as the mothers of the disappeared) to collective day-to-day survival strategies (communal kitchens, health and child care services, and so on). More often than not, they do not define themselves as feminist groups.

The conflicts and opposition between these two politically active women's movements have shaped the specific characteristics of Latin American feminism(s). In the 1990s, they have come closer to each other, creating a distinctive Latin American feminism with a political agenda far wider than the ones in the industrialized countries. Incorporating the demands of an increasingly feminist *movimiento de mujeres* for the construction of a more inclusive, racially aware, and class-conscious feminist transformational project is the biggest challenge facing Latin American and Caribbean feminisms in the 1990s.[10]

Thus, it may be unnecessary to draw such a clear-cut line between the two groups. According to Amy Conger Lind, it is through the making of a collective identity that Latin American women have come to take a stance against several forms of power represented in their daily lives. Women's struggle is not only a struggle to address their reproductive work and gender/class relations. It is also a struggle to overcome their lack of power, primarily through the transformation and politicization of identity. Basic needs are not tied solely to survival but rather to constructions of identity and relations of power.[11] As such, popular women's organizations have revealed and challenged unequal power relations as they are manifested in the everyday sphere, crossing in many ways traditional notions between 'private' and 'public'.[12]

---

7.   The contradictions between the Sandinista leadership and its feminist supporters are widely documented and analysed. An early analysis is by Molyneux 1985. See also Molyneux 1988; Stoltz Chinchilla 1992 and 1995. Some feminist analysts even claim that the Sandinista defeat in the 1990 elections was partially due to the loss of credibility of the Sandinista project among women. See Randall 1992 and 1994.

8.   See Jaquette (ed.) 1994; Jelin (ed.) 1994; Radcliffe and Westwood (eds.) 1993; Saporta Sternbach *et al.* 1992.

9.   Saporta Sternbach *et al.* 1992: 401.

10.   Saporta Sternbach *et al.* 1992: 433.

11.   Lind 1992: 147.

12.   Lind 1992: 134-35. Similar views are expressed by Jo Fisher and Jane S. Jaquette, who both identify *three* distinct patterns of women's mobilization in Latin America: women's human rights groups (such as the *Madres de Plaza de Mayo* in Argentina); organizations of poor urban

According to Arturo Escobar and Sonia E. Alvarez, a significant transformation has occurred in both reality and its forms of analysis concerning Latin American social movements. The 'old' is characterized by analysis couched in terms of modernization and dependency, traditional political actors being primarily the working class and revolutionary vanguard. The new theories see contemporary social movements as bringing about a fundamental transformation in the nature of political practice and theorizing itself. A multiplicity of social actors establish their presence and spheres of autonomy in a fragmented social and political space where old divisions between the bourgeoisie and the proletariat are being left behind.[13]

In the 'new' configuration, political struggle is not seen merely in terms of access to the mechanisms of power but also as cultural struggle in the search for different identities. Social movements have an impact on the democratization of cultural, social, economic and political life. According to Escobar and Alvarez, this is especially important with regard to the terrain of 'daily life' because it is at this level that many of today's forms of protest emerge and exert their action and influence.[14] They also say, 'At the most basic level, social movements must be seen as crucial forces in the democratization of authoritarian social relations. This influence is most evident, of course, in the cases of feminist, gay, and racial/ethnic movements'.[15]

I have quoted these social scientists at length, since I think they implicitly offer one valid explanation for the crisis of LT as a movement, on the one hand, and a potential common area of dialogue between the feminist movement and LT in Latin America. As was stated in Chapter 1, the CEBs and other circles close to LT are losing ground to other forms of religiosity, most notably Pentecostalism. Simultaneously, they evidently have lost much of the political influence they had two decades ago. As we saw, several researchers have offered as one explanation the inability of LT and CEBs to see 'domestic' or 'private' problems as 'real' problems, which is especially contradictory for many women[16] who comprise the great majority of active CEB members.[17] If I follow Escobar and Alvarez' definition, LT and the sections of the church close to it would thus represent the 'old' kind of social movement, with traditional notions of political activity and identity.

women (communal kitchens etc.); and feminist groups. Fisher brings up a fourth group, the activism of women in union organizing. According to Fisher, the military rule forced women (most of whom used to be housewives with no political experience) to take a more active role in public affairs (human rights groups) as the male breadwinners fell victims of either repressive violence (disappearance, death, imprisonment) or unemployment. In the name of motherhood and the family, women extended their domestic role into the public arena, and in the process they not only transformed politics, but also challenged traditional ideas about women. See Fisher 1993: 1-3; Jaquette 1994: 1-9. See also Chapter 3.4.3.

13. Escobar and Alvarez 1992: 3.
14. Escobar and Alvarez 1992: 4.
15. Escobar and Alvarez 1992: 326.
16. See Burdick 1992: 176-78.
17. See Drogus 1992: 67.

Religious feminists such as feminist liberation theologians would then find themselves caught between the two discourses, if feminism and other women's movements can be seen as representing the 'new' kind of politics and form of social movement. What Alvarez and Escobar termed as 'the terrain of daily life' is exactly what feminist liberation theologians mean by *vida cotidiana*. If it is true that new theoretical insights are needed in order to explain the variety of social movements and discourses in contemporary Latin America[18]—and religion, including LT, certainly forms a part of this scene—the intersection between progressive religious sectors and feminist concerns could prove to form one such area of new discourse. On the one hand, a deeper understanding of feminism and women's issues may help LT and grassroots religious (especially Catholic) groups to overcome their present crisis. On the other hand, taking religion and its moral weight in Latin America seriously may help to bridge the conflict between feminist and *movimientos de mujeres* types of women's groups. And last but not least, a broad perspective on (poor) women's realities may create a space where touchy issues such as reproductive rights can be discussed on a broader basis.

Escobar and Alvarez further point out how the 'developmentalist' notion that poor people's, especially women's, needs are exclusively or predominantly material is challenged in poor people's own discourses and activities. Thus, 'the politics of needs' must be retheorized. And it is especially the struggle of popular women's groups—those traditionally defined as non-feminist—that, according to Alvarez and Escobar, forces a reinterpretation of the politics of needs.[19] Implicitly, this view challenges the most traditional views of poverty in LT, even though liberation theologians—theologians as they are—have never considered poor people's needs as merely material. But it may be that narrow definitions of poverty and the poor (Chapter 1.4) have hindered the taking up of issues such as sexual ethics and individual identity which are central in feminist discourses and practices.

The very notion of what constitutes a 'survival struggle' must be expanded and reconceptualized to include non-economic dimensions, say Escobar and Alvarez. For women of all social sectors, struggling for survival necessarily encompasses the elimination of life-threatening violence against women.[20] This again implicitly points towards the need to critically examine issues of sexuality, sexual ethics and poor people's reproductive rights.

The distinction between 'feminine' and 'feminist' has been present in Latin American women's theological production, as well. Not all women liberation theologians have wanted to label their work as 'feminist'.[21] It is important to keep

18. Escobar and Alvarez 1992: 3.
19. Alvarez and Escobar 1992: 320.
20. Alvarez and Escobar 1992: 320.
21. For example, the Argentinian Nelly Ritchie says: 'Ante todo quiero decir que la frase teología feminista siempre me causa una cierta reacción. Acepto lo de muchas compañeras de que hay que usar el término feminista sin temores, pero también creo que está cargado de toda una connotación que tuvo en su momento la lucha feminista—que no se inició en la Iglesia—y que apuntó a la reivindicación de derechos de la mujer pero en confrontación con el compañero

in mind that Latin American feminist (theological, too) thinking and practice is as diverse as it is in other countries. Historically, the most common way of labelling women's theological work in the LT framework has been 'theology from women's point of view' (*teología desde [la perspectiva de] la mujer*). According to María Pilar Aquino,

> Although theological reflection from the perspective of women in Latin America does not describe itself as *feminist theology*, as it is called in the First World, there are important convergences with the works of significant North American and European women theologians; these should not be underestimated. These perspectives are aware of the different contexts, but their presuppositions, starting point, method and objectives bring them within liberation theology. Thus there are no serious reasons for not speaking of a *feminist liberation theology from Latin America*.[22]

However, at least since December 1993, when a gathering of Latin American women theologians took place in Río de Janeiro, Brazil,[23] there has been a group of theologians who explicitly define their work as *Latin American feminist theology of liberation* (*teología feminista latinoamericana de la liberación*).[24] They consciously depart from concepts such as 'feminine' and 'mujerista'. It is exactly here that they make the most critical move in relation to LT. The use of 'feminist' implies a critical analysis of the talk on 'women' and 'femininity' in LT. According to María Pilar Aquino, these are androcentric concepts which do not analyse critically how they are used to preserve and reproduce patriarchal relations and institutions. Their abstractness make them attractive to many liberation theologians, including women, who do not want to use concepts such as feminism/feminist.[25] Women have been included in LT's discourse, even extensively by some theologians. A *feminist* theology in that context will turn a critical eye even to the nature and degree of that inclusion.

In her book *Teólogos de la liberación hablan sobre la mujer*,[26] Elsa Tamez interviewed fifteen Latin American male and three female liberation theologians on

---

varón. Por lo tanto, a mí me gusta hablar de una teología liberadora, o de una teología liberadora desde la perspectiva de la mujer.' Quoted in Porcile Santiso 1991: 77-78.

22.   Aquino 1992a: 112 (emphasis in original). The original subtitle of Aquino's book in Spanish uses the term *teología latinoamericana desde la perspectiva de la mujer* whereas its English translation is 'feminist theology from Latin America'. Since Aquino lives and works in the US, she is probably more familiar with the North American feminist theological discourse than others who do not easily receive the latest books.

23.   The meeting was organized by the Latin American Commission of Women of EATWOT with the theme *Espiritualidad para la vida: mujeres contra la violencia*. About 40 women from different countries and denominations participated. A book is coming out containing the presentations of the meeting. See Aquino 1997: 24.

24.   See Aquino 1994b: 55 and 1997: 25-26. According to Aquino, the concept *teología feminista* was not used explicitly in Latin America before the end of the 1980s. Nevertheless, feminism as a secular ideology and movement has a much longer history on the continent. An entry on Latin American feminist theology written by Aquino is in Russell and Clarkson (eds.) 1996: 114-16.

25.   Aquino 1997: 26.

26.   Tamez 1986.

how they see the situation of women in Latin America, and how that should be incorporated into LT. The book offers an interesting picture of 1980's liberation theologians being, at least theoretically—when facing these questions directed at them by one of the most prominent female liberation theologians—both conscious about and open on many burning issues concerning Latin American women. They are also self-critical. It seems that there is a conflict of stated ideals and the lived reality. The legitimacy of feminist concerns is affirmed, but it is not taken as a serious challenge for theology, be it liberation theology or not. This is the same situation feminist theologians face everywhere. Still, there is a sensitivity to oppression and inequalities in Latin American liberation theologians one only rarely meets in mainstream male theologians in other parts of the world.

I shall give preference to those voices which combine the two perspectives, the liberationist and the feminist, and who consider themselves feminist liberation theologians. They maintain a critical dialogue with both Latin American LT and feminist liberation theologians from the First World who also see their work as an attempt to critically bridge LT and FT. For the sake of clarity, *I will call them all feminist liberation theologians*.

Those liberation theologians, both male and female, who have included women's concerns in LT seem to be closer to the political and ideological aims and presuppositions of the *movimiento de mujeres* than of an explicitly feminist movement. This becomes clear later in this chapter as we look at the kind of issues they have been considering and, even more so, what they have excluded from their discourse. There are several reasons why feminists inside the churches have felt more comfortable with the *movimiento de mujeres* type of women's movement.

Movimientos de mujeres have been both practically and ideologically tied to the Latin American Left, including the progressive part of the Catholic Church. Many of the day-to-day resistance strategies of Latin America's popular classes were in fact born in church-based organizations, besides the Leftist parties and labour unions.[27] Early Latin American feminists gave high priority to working with poor and working-class women active in the larger movement, helping women organize community survival struggles while fostering consciousness of how gender roles shaped their political activism.[28] Still today, in many popular women's organizations linked to the progressive Catholic Church or the secular Left, women are continually admonished against adopting 'bad' feminist beliefs, such as abortion rights and the right of sexual self-determination, as these are seen as intrinsically bourgeois and likely to 'divide' the united struggle of the working class.[29]

---

27.   See Castañeda 1993: 259.
28.   Saporta Sternbach *et al*. 1992: 402.
29.   Saporta Sternbach *et al*. 1992: 402. See also Peña 1995: 81. According to Jean Franco, 'The church…courageously sheltered and defended human-rights movements. Yet, as the case of Sandinista Nicaragua would show, the church could also prove to be a barrier that prevented

Because of liberation theologians' supposed concern for the poorest and the most vulnerable in society, they have felt closer to a women's movement that explicitly deals with such burning issues as living conditions, nutrition, work and health. But again, as we will see, they have been selective in seeing these as priorities over the issues taken up by more consciously feminist groups. The latter is probably more influenced by the international women's movement and feminist ideas, giving greater emphasis to 'classic' feminist issues such as sexuality, reproduction, violence and so on.[30]

Secular feminist movements are often of educated middle-class women who no longer have strong or any ties to the institutional churches. In fact, the church, especially the Catholic Church, is often considered as the archenemy. However, the progressive theologians, both male and female, keep silent about issues of sexual ethics, many of them as urgent for poor women as any other aspect of poverty. This creates a situation where a large group (if not the majority) of Latin American women—poor, uneducated and religious—find no one expressing their most intimate concerns.[31] For them religion plays an important, albeit in many ways contradictory, role.

Studies done on the contradictions of middle-class feminism and *movimientos de mujeres* usually do not see the missing link: Latin American feminist liberation theologians or feminists within existing churches, familiar with religious language and values, who would speak from the praxis of women from the popular classes. The practical base for doing this exists, for example in the form of Catholic sisters working with poor women. The Catholic monopoly in sexual ethics must be met with adequate tools of analysis and action. Neither secular feminist movements nor Catholic women without any formal education (especially in theology) meet this need. Very much the same can be said of the most prominent liberation theologians. They are hindered not only by the kind of political ideology they embrace but also by intraecclesiastical reasons.[32] This is why it is of extreme

women from debating sensitive issues such as reproductive rights. This is why…human-rights movements, particularly those dominated by the church, did not necessarily induct women into feminism. Survival movements are a different matter… It is in these movements that awareness of women's oppression has strengthened, although their activists often repudiate the label of feminism' (Franco 1992: 68).

30.   Saporta Sternbach *et al.* 1992: 401-402.

31.   It is important to bear in mind the critique expressed by some Third World feminist social scientists on the tendency of First World feminists to treat Third World women in a paternalistic way, where 'Third World women as a group or a category are automatically and necessarily defined as religious (read "not progressive"), family-oriented (read "traditional"), legal minors (read "they-are-still-not-conscious-of-their-rights"), illiterate (read "ignorant"), domestic (read "backward"), and sometimes revolutionary (read "their-country-is-in-a-state-of-war; they-must-fight!"). This is how the "third world difference" is produced' (Mohanty 1991: 72). Conscious of this stereotype, I will try to let Latin American women (also a generalization) speak as much as possible in their own voice. It is possible that some feminist theological interpretations by Latin American women themselves could be subject to Mohanty's critique, by creating the category 'poor Latin American women', for instance.

32.   See more about this in Chapter 4.1.2.

importance that there are such persons and groups who keep a critical distance to both middle-class secular feminist movements and traditional liberation theological discourse or who form alliances with the kind of 'new' social movements and their discourses presented by Escobar and Alvarez. The intersection of LT and FT could thus be the potential position from which to speak critically and constructively of issues of sexual ethics and gender on a theoretical level.

It is no wonder, then, that the first person to speak openly on abortion from within the church and the LT movement has been a Catholic nun working with poor women in Northeastern Brazil. Ivone Gebara, one of the most well-known Latin American feminist liberation theologians, was submitted to an ecclesiastical process of either retracting her statement that abortion is not always a sin or facing dismissal from her religious order.[33]

3.2 Option for the Poor as an Option for the Poor Woman

As has been said, Latin American LT holds as its ideal subject 'the poor', both collectively and individually, but with a definite emphasis on the collective nature of the concept. It is the poor who are the subjects of the praxis that liberation theologians take as their main point of reference.

It was also stated that 'the poor' as a concept has become more differentiated since the 1970s. The almost exclusive weight given to the poor as a class has given way to new ways of identity that reflect other forms of oppression besides the economic. Racism and sexism do not function as separate forms of oppression, but are interrelated.

In this chapter, I want to analyse critically some of the themes discussed in Chapters 1.3 and 1.4. How has the definition of 'the poor' and 'the option for the poor' changed in the dialogue between feminist theologians and liberation theologians? Has it changed?

The article 'Opción por el pobre como opción por la mujer pobre' (1987) by Ivone Gebara is one of the first attempts to interpret Latin American LT and some of its central concepts from the point of view of women. According to Gebara, 'The option for the poor is not something general and abstract but historical and concrete. That is to say that in different countries and cultures, the

---

33.   See Nanne and Bergamo 1993. Since then, Gebara was sent to Europe for two years to study European theology (this being her punishment). It is noteworthy that the same kinds of threats of dismissal and silencing were directed at Leonardo Boff in 1985, but whereas his case was met by strong international solidarity and public critique of the Vatican, there has been no such *public* community of support for Gebara. This is probably due both to her position as a feminist theologian (and woman) and to the difficulty of taking a stance on abortion. Supporting her would easily be interpreted as supporting her opinions.

What Gebara actually said in the interview, published in the Brazilian magazine *VEJA*, was that opting for abortion is not necessarily a sin for a poor woman. After being asked by her superior, Dom José Cardoso, archbishop of Recife, to retract her statement, she clarified her position for the legalization of abortion in Brazil.

poor has to be identified and historically situated as somebody from whom some-thing new can arise.'[34] There has been an extension of the term poor that makes it possible to include women as ones who are seeking elementary recognition in society. The woman is both subject and object of the option for the poor. As a subject, she represents the power of resistance, very much in order to survive.[35]

In another article, Gebara speaks of the way women have been shaping Latin American theology.[36] What is distinctive in women's way of doing theology in Latin America is how the elements of everyday life are intertwined with their speaking about God and how lived realities are their takeoff for theological elaboration.[37] Here she refers to some quite uncritically assumed 'feminine' qualities such as intuition and to women's reality as that of 'the person who gives birth, nurses and nourishes'.[38]

Two Brazilian theologians, Ana María Tepedino and Margarida L. Ribeiro Brandão, confirm explicitly the commitment of Latin American feminist liber-ation theologians to the larger movement of LT.[39] They, too, speak of 'concrete experiences' as the starting point for theology. Here, of course, they face the same problems as feminist theologians in other latitudes who found their theology in 'experience' without sufficient conceptual analysis of what is meant by that experience and how it possibly differs from other experiences. Nevertheless, in the context of LT, they want to concretize such concepts as the poor and the option for the poor.[40] 'The feminization of poverty', in Latin America as well as in other regions, including the First World, has created the situation where a pro-portionally large part of the poorest families is composed primarily of women and their dependents (children and elderly persons).[41]

Tepedino, in another text, specifies this 'concrete experience'. It is the experi-ence of oppression, both individually and collectively, with a special reference to the poorest persons.[42] She, too, gives emphasis to the realities of everyday life. In 1992, at the EATWOT General Assembly in Kenya, she stated:

> We from Latin America have an auto-critical attitude towards some aspects of the theology of liberation. Furthermore, we cannot speak of a theology of liberation but of theologies of liberation. Theology of liberation is the interpretation of the life we live, at least one part of life, the lives of the poor in general. Now we understand that this is not sufficient. The poor have many faces: Indian women, Blacks and other

---

34. Gebara 1987: 463.
35. Gebara 1987: 468. She refers primarily to the *movimientos de mujeres*, not as much to the feminist movement.
36. Gebara 1986.
37. Gebara 1986: 15, 19.
38. Gebara 1986: 15.
39. Tepedino and Ribeiro Brandão 1991: 289.
40. 'Las teólogas latinoamericanas, en su experiencia pastoral y cristiana, aprenden que la opción por el pobre se concreta en la opción por la mujer pobre, que hoy es la más pobre entre los pobres' (Tepedino and Ribeiro Brandão 1991: 295).
41. Tepedino and Ribeiro Brandão 1991: 296.
42. Tepedino 1988: 60.

persons are challenging the theology of liberation… There are problems which are still without solutions. For women the theology of liberation is patriarchal, and for Indians there is no real communication between the theology of liberation and Indian theology.[43]

The Colombian church historian Ana María Bidegain analyses the history of LT and the Catholic Action youth lay movement behind it from the perspective of the women who actively participated in it. She draws a picture of an anti-sexual and anti-feminist atmosphere that nevertheless gave rise to new theological insights—but not in sexual ethics nor from a feminist perspective:

we [women] had to become male, or at least present ourselves as asexual beings. This was also the framework in which the theology of liberation came into being. Obviously, then, that theology was not going to address the situation of women in the church and society. Nor would it concern itself with the male–female relationship.[44]

There is an emergent feminist theology within the current of LT which, according to her, needs to review the puritanical conception of sexuality as the ideological foundation of sexist oppression, and utter a prophetic denouncement of the feminization of poverty.[45]

In the same compilation of articles in honour of Gustavo Gutiérrez' sixtieth birthday, the Brazilian María Clara Bingemer joins her colleagues in affirming that

Out of the mass of faces of the great majority of Latin America, three types in particular are emerging and attracting attention, presenting new challenges to the church and society. They are the blacks, Amerindians, and women. These groups, oppressed for centuries by their color, race and sex, *are now essential for an evaluation of the theology of liberation and for any attempt to glimpse its future*, because they bring into theology new issues, a new method, and a new language.[46]

Bingemer wants to affirm the goodness of bodiliness and desire as the challenges women can bring into LT.[47] She even says, 'Moved by desire, a totalizing force, she [woman] does theology with her body, her heart and hands, as much as with her head.'[48]

These sorts of claims are based on a concept of womanhood that is quite debatable, as well as the method it supposedly contains. Similar expressions can be found in practically all Latin American feminist liberation theologians. They reflect the lack of critical theoretical elaboration of such central concepts as women, women's experience and sex vs gender. Very few Latin American feminist theologians make any theoretical differentiation between women as

43.   Tepedino 1994: 134.
44.   Bidegain 1989: 113-14. This is one of the few texts which openly and directly aims at creating alternative sexual ethics *inside the LT paradigm*, combining an explicit feminist analysis of the present situation with its historical roots.
45.   Bidegain 1989: 114.
46.   Bingemer 1989: 473 (emphasis added).
47.   Bingemer 1989: 477-78.
48.   Bingemer 1989: 478.

biological beings (sex) and the historical and cultural expressions of femininity or womanhood (gender). This may lead to a stereotyping of the very reality they want to talk about. They face theoretical problems similar to those of their colleagues who are not explicit enough about how they use their central concepts (Chapter 2.3). Nevertheless, *vida cotidiana* is not used by the Latin American feminist theologians in the same way that women's experience is used by primarily First World feminist liberation theologians. The call to take everyday life seriously may well be one particular response to the critiques presented against the uncritical use of 'women's experience'.

The everyday life of Latin American women varies according to the same variables as in other latitudes. Latin American societies are class societies in a much more traditional and strong sense than most industrialized societies. Latin American feminist liberation theologians' emphasis on *poor* women's life conditions is a conscious choice.[49] It is nevertheless sometimes confused with the very general, undifferentiated discourse of *women*, such as quoted above.

The most challenging and systematized analysis written on feminist theology from a Latin American perspective is the doctoral dissertation of the Mexican María Pilar Aquino.[50] She deals with the question of the subject of LT as well as giving a detailed overview of the work done by Latin American feminist liberation theologians up to today.[51] She is not proposing a new method of a Latin American feminist liberation theology, but an enlargement of the method in LT. She is both affirmative and critical of LT. Some of the factors for the enlargement of the understanding of praxis in LT are the praxis of *vida cotidiana*,[52] both publicly and privately, the sexual division of labour, gender stereotypes that affirm masculine superiority, and sexuality.[53] According to Aquino,

49.   Aquino 1994a: 59.

50.   Aquino 1992a. The book is an abridged edition of the original dissertation. Her later articles are also excellent in clarifying the feminist theological production in Latin America.

51.   This is a valuable work since it is commonly believed both inside and outside Latin America that there is no theological production by Latin American female liberation theologians or feminist theologians.

52.   The Spanish words *cotidiano* and *cotidianidad* do not refer only to the home or the private sphere as the other pole of the dualistic split between the private and the public but to everything that has to do with everyday life. The English words quotidian and quotidianness have the same connotations but I prefer translating *vida cotidiana* as 'everyday life'. In the English translation of M.P. Aquino's book, it is translated as 'daily life'.

In another text, Aquino speaks of 'the real' referring to Latin American women's experiences as 'women, poor and of subaltern race'. Latin American feminist theology opts for these women wanting to overcome the abstract character of androcentric theology and to lead towards greater honesty of the real of the socio-ecclesiastical reality. For her, this option is not merely an ethical option but the 'epistemological and hermeneutical position of the faith and theology'. See Aquino 1992b: 34. If liberative theologies such as the Latin American LT do not take the situation of women seriously, they 'demonstrate their ignorance of the *real reality*' (Aquino 1992b: 36 [emphasis in original]).

53.   Aquino 1992a: 36.

The incorporation of these previously neglected elements is closely linked to the emergence of a new historical and theological subject (*nuevo sujeto histórico y teológico*) among the popular subject (*sujeto popular*): women. Their commitment, activities, and reflections contribute enormous wealth to liberation theology, enabling it to broaden its horizon, method and content.[54]

According to Aquino, 'At the center of this theological perspective [Latin American feminist theology] is the preoccupation for the solution of women's oppressions, that is, a global and concrete transformation of the causes for their suffering'.[55] The incorporating of everyday life as a fundamental factor in the reflection of faith is one of the major contributions of Latin American feminist theology, says Aquino. 'For Latin American feminist theology, everyday life has been the prioritized sphere in which the present order of asymmetrical social relations is produced and reproduced, which acts against women in an organized manner'.[56]

The emphasis on everyday life is central to practically all Latin American feminist liberation theologians, and as such, presents an aspect that certainly has been lacking in the LT paradigm. It also opens space for questions concerning the private sphere (as well as questioning the very split into private and public spheres), which is of special importance when dealing with questions of sexual ethics. Similarly to her Latin American colleagues, Rosemary Ruether emphasizes the need for the analysis of the *concrete realities* of poor Latin American women.[57]

The specificity of a gendered subject inside the larger historical subject is necessary for several reasons. Aquino refers to an early article by Elsa Tamez.[58] According to Tamez, the specificity of women as historical subjects makes an allusion to the oppression of women as women inside their social class, family,

54. Aquino 1992a: 37. The *nuevo sujeto histórico* and *sujeto popular* are very much the same. She uses them in the same sense as do Gallardo and Hinkelammert (see Chapter 1.4.5).

55. Aquino 1994a: 61. And 'In Latin America, feminist theology is elaborated starting from the concrete realities' (Aquino 1994a: 65).

56. 'Para la teología feminista latinoamericana, la vida cotidiana ha sido el ámbito prioritario en que se produce y reproduce el orden presente de relaciones sociales asimétricas que actúan organizadamente contra las mujeres' (Aquino 1997: 30).

57. 'Yo conectaría la teología feminista con las realidades concretas de las mujeres pobres de América Latina, no hablándoles de teología abstracta o análisis social, sino de las realidades concretas de sus vidas... Significa ser violada en la calle..., ir a casa y ser abusada sexualmente..., significa no poder tomar decisiones sobre tu cuerpo o tu sexualidad... Los teologos de la liberación, sin excepción, jamás han discutido estas realidades concretas y no parecen entenderlas' (Ruether 1996a: 3). Nevertheless, it is important to keep in mind that the 'concrete realities' of poor women are not only abuse, lack and violence, in order not to reinforce stereotyped images of Third World women.

58. Tamez 1979: 106-107. This article appears in a compilation of articles called *Mujer latinoamericana: Iglesia y teología*, which brings together the voices of some Latin American women theologians gathered at the CELAM conference in Puebla in 1979, under the name *Mujeres para el diálogo*. They wanted to attract the bishops' attention to the situation of women in the church and society. These articles are probably the first public announcement on women's situation by a community of female theologians and lay women from within the LT movement. See *Mujer latinoamericana* 1981.

couple relationship, and in the society in general, which has been made invisible in movements otherwise critical of existent social structures. The (masculine) historical subject points to the rational, the objective, and so on, whereas the women even inside new social movements have been defined by a presupposed feminine subjectivity, including characteristics such as intuition and tenderness. This is also true of most theologians of liberation.[59] Already in 1979, Tamez demands including women's oppression as a constituent element of LT, and not just one more theme.[60]

According to Aquino, this process of incorporating women's theological reflection into the larger context of LT has been slow and late, and in fact, is still today something quite new.[61] This is due to the dichotomy of praxis and theory in LT itself.[62] Here Aquino uses the most central methodological claim of LT, the unity of theory and praxis, as a mirror for critical self-reflection of LT itself. There is an inner contradiction in LT.[63] 'As critical reflection, liberation theology ought to make a serious analysis of mechanisms operating to the detriment of the lives of the people and identify those that oppress women both as poor and as women', says Aquino.[64]

If LT wants to be the interpretation of the world of the poor and consciously assumes as its horizon of reflection the interests, hopes and struggles of the oppressed, it ought to promote women's self-expression.[65] If not, LT runs the risk of becoming merely rhetorical by abstracting itself from the concrete faces of the people who formally make it possible and verify it, including women. The suspicion of this *ideological slipping*, which left out or relegated the sexist and machista elements in society, church and theology, was made possible by the presence of women doing theology.[66] What it was and is about is a claim that *'deepens the hermeneutical position of LT, and represents, in this sense, a major enlargement of its epistemological field. This is why we can speak of a new stage in Latin American theology'.*[67]

---

59. Tamez 1979: 106-107.

60. Tamez 1979: 109. 'Ya que la teología de la liberación parte de una praxis liberadora y desde un contexto de opresión es lógico que considere el problema mujer también como elemento constituyente de su teología, y no como un tema más, de actualidad... No se trata, pues, de hablar de una teología de la mujer, ni de una teología feminista. Se trata de la misma teología de la liberación' (Tamez 1979: 109). The quotation makes it clear how Tamez has always insisted on including women's concerns inside LT, and not necessarily create a separate FT.

61. Aquino 1992a: 105. Rosemary Ruether shares this opinion when she states that the liberation theologians have not been capable of integrating the question of gender into their theology. LT continues to be 'very masculine' (Ruether 1996a: 3).

62. Aquino 1992a: 106.

63. Aquino 1992a: 109.

64. '...en cuanto reflexión crítica, debía hacer un análisis serio de los mecanismos que actúan en contra de la vida del pueblo y aquí, identificar los que oprimen a las mujeres como pobres y como mujeres' (Aquino 1992a: 109).

65. Aquino 1992a: 109.

66. Aquino 1992a: 109 (emphasis in original).

67. 'Se trataba y se trata, pues, de un reclamo que profundiza el lugar hermenéutico de la TL

How the concept of the option *for* the poor has changed because of a feminist critique becomes clear in Aquino's text. She says:

> it is not a matter of speaking *about women* as if they were an object of reflection external to the subject of LT and to the moment itself of doing theology. Neither is it about a discourse elaborated *for women* as if they were passively waiting for others—men, in most cases—to define their destiny. Neither is it about speaking *on behalf of women*, as if they were subjects incapable of intelligence and rationally limited to articulating the wisdom and justification of faith. It is not about speaking *in the name of women*, but about conceiving women as *subjects* of their own theoretical elaborations, from the point of view of their own consciousness and reality.[68]

Aquino agrees with Ivone Gebara when translating the option for the poor as an option for the impoverished woman.[69]

Here we can see how feminist liberation theologians accept and use the liberation theological method. The poor as subjects of theology is specified as the poor women as subjects of theology. None of the feminist liberation theologians question this central methodological claim in LT: the poor as subjects and their praxis as the starting point remain central even though the gender of this subject is changed. The quotation above by Aquino is a typical liberation theological formulation. It could be asked, though, if a more critical attitude to the methodological presuppositions of LT from a feminist perspective would more clearly reveal the difficulty of placing women as subjects at the centre of LT.

In another text, Aquino gives some characteristics of Latin American feminist theology. It is elaborated from the concrete realities, thus having contextuality as one of its central characteristics. By referring to the 'real world' and 'everyday life', Latin American FT wants to emphasize the structural unity between the intellect and the emotions, as well as between the private and the public. Latin

---

y representa, en este sentido, una ampliación mayor de su campo epistemológico… Por ello se habla de una nueva etapa en el quehacer latinoamericano y de una nueva manera de hacer teología' (Aquino 1992a: 109 [emphasis added]).

Aquino also states: 'la óptica de la mujer *re-asume* el sentido integral de la liberación produciendo dos efectos. Por una parte, provoca la crítica y transformación de las estructuras patriarcales, la visión androcéntrica y las actitudes machistas en el conjunto histórico-social opresivo y, por otro, incluye a las mujeres en la producción del conocimiento, la configuración de la teología y en la gestación de nuevas realidades liberadoras. Se trata de un cambio no sólo en el lenguaje, sino en el propio horizonte epistemológico de la TL' (Aquino 1992a: 190 [emphasis in original]).

68. '…no se trata de hablar *sobre las mujeres*, como si éstas fuesen un objeto de reflexión extrínseco al sujeto de la TL y al momento mismo del teologizar. Tampoco se trata de un discurso elaborado *para las mujeres*, como si éstas fuesen sujetos pasivos a la espera de que otros—varones, en la mayoría de los casos—definan su destino. Tampoco se trata de hablar *por las mujeres*, como si fuesen sujetos incapaces de inteligencia y limitadas racionalmente para articular la sabiduría y justificación de la fe. No es ya hablar *en su nombre*, sino concebir a la mujer como *sujeto* de su propia elaboración teórica, desde su propia conciencia y su realidad' (Aquino 1992a: 109-10 [emphasis in original]).

69. Aquino 1992a: 194. Note how Aquino, too, uses the term 'impoverished' (*empobrecido/a*) instead of 'poor', in a vein similar to Gallardo 1994: 15.

American FT also aims at incorporating the reality as it is presented to us in all its unity, complexity and diversity, in theology. Further, FT from Latin America emphasizes the transformative function of theology, as does LT. This kind of FT admits the confliction of the actual capitalistic patriarchal system, which is not orientated towards greater justice. Latin American FT has its centre in the life, human integrity, justice and liberation of all women. All this implies the necessity of naming the mechanisms of domination, as well as transforming them. Thus, Latin American feminist theology emphasizes the historical liberating praxis of women.[70]

In a recent text, Aquino is more concrete. She points out the dualistic anthropological notions in androcentric theologies, including Latin American LT, from which a Latin American feminist liberation theology must critically distance itself.[71] She also explicitly mentions women's health and reproductive rights, as well as domestic violence, as key issues for a Latin American feminist liberation theology.[72]

From this short presentation of some Latin American feminist liberation theologians' thinking, we could draw the following conclusions. First, they all seem to define their theologizing in the larger context of LT. Their own work is both an affirmation of the central claims of LT and a critical reinterpretation of it, which leads to a demand for a more self-critical reconstruction of the LT paradigm itself.[73]

Second, they all agree that even though their male colleagues seem to be well aware of the oppression of women, especially when it comes to the poorest women, this consciousness has not led liberation theologians to serious self-criticism of their theory and praxis. Latin American feminist theologians are also critical of those liberation theologians who, wishing to deal with the 'woman question', define women and femininity in a very traditional way, and apparently, are not familiar with feminist writings.[74] There is an apparent 'sexual division of theological labor' in LT, too.[75]

70.   Aquino 1992b: 37-38.
71.   Aquino 1997: 4-5, 8.
72.   Aquino 1997: 8, 30, 36.
73.   See Aquino 1995a: 108-109. 'Por ello creemos que la teología elaborada en el marco del pensamiento crítico feminista contribuye a *ampliar, profundizar y otorgar mayor radicalidad a los categorías epistemológicas fundamentales de la teología de la liberación* tanto en la mediación analítica, como en la hermenéutica y las prácticas [*sic*] pastorales. Este es el caso de los conceptos de praxis, experiencia, opresión, liberación, pobres, fe, humanidad, pecado, utopía, la tierra y su devenir histórico y escatológico' (Aquino 1995a: 112 [emphasis added]).
74.   Tamez 1989. This compilation of interviews with eleven Latin American women liberation theologians (and one man) is a reflection on Tamez' earlier interviews with well-known male liberation theologians (Tamez 1986). The women both credit their male colleagues for their openness to feminist concerns and criticize them. According to Tamez, the interviews summed up at least four important issues. First, it is clear that the category of class is necessary but not sufficient for the analysis of the situation of women. Second, there is a necessity for an analysis of feminist theories, including the ones developed in other parts of the world. Third, the question of women's ordination came up in almost all interviews. Fourth, even though the

Third, in spite of conceptual lack of clarity in central terms (such as women, women's point of view, and so on), these theologians seem to understand the women's point of view, or feminist critique, as an epistemological challenge to LT. They are asking LT to take seriously its central epistemological claims, both by making the subject of LT more concrete and more diversified and by demanding more self-criticism of the liberation theologians themselves as creators of theology. In this, the concrete everyday life experiences of poor women are emphasized.

Fourth, the subject in a feminist liberation theology is not 'a woman' as such, but the popular subject—the poor, the new historical subject, the Other—of LT with a more concrete face. This may refer to gender, but to other aspects as well, such as race and class. Those feminist theologians who define themselves as liberation theologians do not want to separate gender from other factors that affect people in a highly oppressive society. Thus, they speak of the poor in the same sense as do their male colleagues, but not as an undefined mass of people with no differentiation. They want to show how gender or race makes a difference even in how poverty affects people's real lives.

Fifth, and this is intimately tied to the question of the subject, is the emphasis given to everyday life, understood both in the most private sense of the word and in a more public sense. This emphasis on the concreteness of life conditions makes it possible to take up issues which have been avoided in LT, such as family and sexual violence, the unevenness of the work load between men and women, and to a certain extent, issues of sexual ethics. These are problems that touch women *as women*, as gendered subjects, but the negative effects of these problems seem to be intensified by poverty.

Nevertheless, the problems inherent in the praxis starting point itself are visible in the feminist liberation theology as well. This becomes clearest in how *both* male *and* female liberation theologians have been reluctant to openly discuss sexual ethics as an intrinsic part of their theologizing. How much does the female subject of feminist liberation theologians still remain the same as that of male

theologians use the term 'women's perspective', it is often done superficially. Tamez specifically refers to the use of the term 'feminine'. This is the same observation that I myself have made when reading Latin American women liberation theologians. According to my view, of the points Tamez mentions, the second and the fourth depend on each other, since it is exactly in feminist theory where the very definitions of 'women' and 'the feminine', and 'feminist', have been analysed critically. The necessity of liberation theologians to become familiar with Latin American feminist theological writings is shared by María P. Aquino: 'En esta línea, hemos enfatizado el llamado a los teólogos de la liberación para que amplíen sus recursos analítico-hermenéuticos e incorporen en su propio proceso intelectivo las herramientas críticas feministas... Este llamado a los teólogos, lanzado desde finales de la década de los setenta, en realidad ha sido escasamente escuchado como se demuestra en la producción teológica a nivel continental' (Aquino 1995a: 113). This opinion is shared also by María Teresa Porcile Santiso: 'De los teólogos (varones)...se puede decir que el tema de la mujer (y la teología feminista sobre todo), lo desconocen o lo conocen a un nivel tan superficial que la reacción resulta negativa' (Porcile Santiso 1991: 71). See also Biehl 1987: 94-95.

75. Aquino 1995a: 110.

liberation theologians? What does it really mean to 'change the gender' of the subject?

According to Carol Ann Drogus, the ecclesial base communities (CEBs) as the micro level communal expression of LT have given women (who form at least two-thirds of all and perhaps as many as 90 per cent of the most active members of the CEBs) practical skills and opened up a realm of new possibilities for participation in the public arena.[76] Nevertheless, we have already seen how gender may be one central reason for CEBs' decline. The church has encouraged women's activism, but did not help them to understand sexism or to deal with domestic problems. Many women are becoming increasingly aware of the problems they face as women.[77] Thus, on the one hand, if the CEBs and LT cannot respond to this situation seriously, they may further lose the ground of their support. On the other hand, feminist liberation theologians seem to be moving exactly in the direction where poor women's life conditions, in a very concrete manner, are being brought to the centre of LT. Issues of gender and women's specific problems may prove to be one of the core issues—if not *the* core issue—for the renewal or decline of LT in the future.

According to M.P. Aquino,

> The masculine theological focus has covered the oppressive relations lived in the private area, and concealed relationships of domination exercised in the domestic sphere, where it is the women who always carry the worse part. The everyday life for an androcentric vision does not have epistemological value, nor does it form part of its understanding horizon of reality, that is, it does not influence the doing of theology. What, in effect, happens here, is that the masculine theological focus grants a character of *naturality* to the private everyday life.[78]

76. Drogus 1992: 67.

77. Drogus 1992: 82. According to Drogus, 'Despite a growing literature by Latin American feminist liberation theologians…there has been extremely little reflection on gender in the CEBs' (Drogus 1992: 82).

In another article, Drogus point out how the CEBs, on the one hand, have been overtly political and maybe too despiritualized, but how they simultaneously, on the other hand, have strong similarities to traditional Catholicism. Referring to Burdick, Drogus maintains that Catholicism in general is a religion of continuity. This may be one reason why Pentecostal churches, even with all their traditional teaching on gender relations, may help women to solve their domestic problems more easily. A strong experience of conversion usually means drastic changes in (men's) lifestyles (drinking, extramarital affairs, domestic violence, etc.). LT has seen domestic problems too much as a result of class oppression, thus suggesting that women with domestic problems could solve them by working for class liberation. See Drogus 1995, especially p. 472.

I would point out that it is not only that LT would have seen domestic problems as class problems. Mostly they have not been seen as (real) problems at all. The church(es) have a long history of counselling women to stay even in the most destructive marriages, since the traditional teaching stresses the indissolubility of marriage and women's fidelity and obedience to their husbands.

78. Aquino 1991: 113 (emphasis in original).

In another text, referring to the use of the concept *vida cotidiana*, she says:

> [It] allowed the explicit recognition of the androcentric and sexist position of liberation theology, elaborated not exclusively but mainly by men, celibates, white, of comfortable social position, and some with a homophobic tendency; on the other hand, it generates a different mode of thinking and understanding the experience of faith starting from the real dynamics of socio-ecclesiastical life.[79]

This means greater realism and honesty.

As stated in Chapter 2.2.1, there are feminist theologians from the First World who explicitly identify themselves as feminist liberation theologians. It was also explained how this definition ties them, together with their colleagues from the Third World, to two major theological currents, namely feminist theology and liberation theology. Here I will take up mainly Rosemary Ruether and Elisabeth Schüssler Fiorenza, who have carried out an explicit critical dialogue with Latin American LT. They are also the theologians to whom Latin American feminist theologians most refer when speaking of their intellectual affinities in the First World.

According to Rosemary Ruether,

> It has often been said that women of the working class and Third World suffer from 'double oppression'—oppression both as women and as members of oppressed classist and racial groups. But the meaning of this phrase has not been fully explicated. 'Double oppression' does not mean simply one kind of oppression as women and another kind as members of oppressed groups, but, in addition, doubled kinds of *sexist* oppression that come from the multilayered oppression experienced by women of oppressed groups.[80]

In a lecture Ruether gave in March 1993 in San José, Costa Rica, she delineates four stages in the dialogue between Latin American LT and FT. First, from the mid-sixties to the end of that decade, there was a notable ignorance of issues of sexism in LT. The category 'poor' did not have any differentation of gender. Second, during the 1970s, the female theologians in EATWOT started to criticize some models of thought in LT. This is what Mercy Amba Oduyoye has called 'the irruption within the irruption'. In 1983, there was a common declaration by First World and Third World women at the EATWOT Geneva conference, where it was stated that even though feminism is a common preoccupation, it is only the Third World women who define their own feminisms. Since 1984 there has been an abundance of reflection (as well as international meetings) concerning FT in the Third World context. The existence and the challenge of feminist theologies of liberation cannot be negated. The third stage would be characterized

79. Aquino 1995a: 111.

80. Ruether 1985c: 69-70. This excerpt is from her paper at the meeting of Third World and First World liberation theologians in Geneva in 1983. In the final statement of the same conference, sexism is listed as one of the major issues of the conference. Because of the different viewpoints concerning women's status, it was also stated that 'Neither Third World men nor First World women can determine the Third World women's agenda. Third World women maintain that sexism must not be addressed in isolation, but within the context of the total liberation of their countries' (Fabella and Torres [eds.] 1985: 186).

by a more positive response on the part of male liberation theologians. This is when women 'are added to the list of the oppressed'. Women theologians are accepted but only in 'a feminine corner' where women's issues are seen literally as such. There is no real consciousness of the necessity of change in the content and method of LT.[81] The fourth and last stage would be characterized by a certain crisis in LT (from 1990 onwards) resulting from several factors, such as the collapse of socialism and the harsh attitude of the Vatican to LT. According to Ruether, Third World women theologians did not experience this crisis in a similar vein to that of their male colleagues since they did not share the same expectations. Thus, LT has a future only if it includes new protagonists (subjects) in their own right and with their own voice, which does not mean delegating them a specific corner of activity. There must be a transformation in the content and method of LT itself, and a new kind of vision of society.[82]

María Pilar Aquino points out how the EATWOT conference held in São Paulo, Brazil, in 1980 recognized the validity of the struggles of women insofar as they are inserted within the overall framework of the struggles of the poor, but not insofar as they represent women as a social group in their own right.[83] There is an awareness of the subordinate condition of women, but women are not acknowledged as social and ecclesiastical actors (women's movements in the society and the church).[84] Aquino, together with many others, point out the EATWOT New Delhi conference in 1981 as a watershed for gender issues in Third World theologies of liberation.[85] The new attitude involves understanding women as protagonists in society.[86] In 1985, the first Latin American women theologians' meeting was held in Buenos Aires, which Aquino sees as a starting point for a feminist theological reflection in the continent.[87] Another important meeting was the international Third World women theologians' conference in Oaxtepec, Mexico, in 1986, organized by the EATWOT Women's Commission, where women from Asia, Africa and Latin America came together.[88]

According to Elisabeth Schüssler Fiorenza,

> If liberation theologians make the 'option for the oppressed' the key to their theo-
> logical endeavors, then they must become conscious of the fact that 'the oppressed'

---

81.   Here Ruether refers to *Mysterium liberationis*, the 'Summa' of LT edited by Ignacio Ellacuría and Jon Sobrino (1991), where all the classical theological issues—God, Trinity, grace, etc.—are treated from an LT perspective. There are two articles by women: one on women and LT, the other on the Virgin Mary. By this Ruether wants to pay attention to the extent that LT wants to be taken seriously as 'classical theology'. Unfortunately, this sometimes carries very traditional, even conservative, connotations.

82.   Ruether 1993.

83.   Aquino 1994b: 46.

84.   Aquino 1994b: 47.

85.   Aquino 1994b: 48.

86.   Aquino 1994b: 50.

87.   Aquino 1994b: 50-52. The very first meeting of Latin American Christian feminists was actually in Puebla, Mexico, at the same time as the CELAM conference in 1979.

88.   Aquino 1994b: 52-55.

are women. Feminist theology, therefore, not only challenges academic theology to take its own intellectual presuppositions seriously, but *it also asks other liberation theologies to concretize their option for the oppressed*.[89]

She also reminds Latin American liberation theologians that they themselves are not poor, and thus for them the option is more an altruistic choice than an acknowledgement of their own oppression. The experience of oppression is different for women. This has far-reaching epistemological consequences, which Fiorenza analyses mainly in the context of biblical interpretation.[90] More generally, she claims that we cannot speak of human existence, nor of oppression, in general, without identifying whose human existence is meant. Thus, according to her, 'Liberation theologies, because of their option for a specific group of oppressed people, e.g. women or Native Americans, must develop, within the overall interpretative approach of a critical theology of liberation, more adequate heuristic interpretative models appropriate to specific forms of oppression'.[91]

Fiorenza calls her theology 'a critical feminist theology of liberation'.[92] It challenges

> all forms of liberation theology to take their preferential 'option' for the poor and oppressed seriously as the option for poor and Third World women because the majority of the poor and exploited today are women and children dependent on women for survival.[93]

LT should address the patriarchal domination and sexual exploitation of women,[94] and even more so, since 'religious obedience, economic dependence, and sexual control are the sustaining force of ecclesiastical patriarchy'.[95]

Saying all this is not a requirement for just incorporating 'women's questions' into the framework of LT but *calls for a different analysis and theoretical framework*.[96] This is very much the same as what Latin American feminist theologians have called the epistemological challenge of FT.

Fiorenza is also critical of 'the totalizing discourse of Western universalist feminism'. If 'the poor' have to be deconstructed in LT in order to unravel the complexity of oppressive realities, so has 'the woman'. Feminism requires a political commitment not only to the struggle against sexism but also to the struggles against racism, classism, colonialism and militarism as structures of women's

---

89.   Fiorenza 1984a: 92 (emphasis added).
90.   There are both commonalities and differences in experience and method between the hermeneutical proposals of liberation theologians and feminist theologians. Feminist theologians do not find an explicit feminist-critical principle or tradition in the Bible as do liberation theologians (God on the side of the oppressed and impoverished). The Bible is written in male language, which mirrors and perpetuates patriarchal culture and religion. See Fiorenza 1984b: xxi.
91.   Fiorenza 1984a: 95.
92.   Fiorenza 1986: 32.
93.   Fiorenza 1986: 35.
94.   Fiorenza 1986.
95.   Fiorenza 1985a: 8.
96.   Fiorenza 1989: 311.

exploitation and oppression.[97] In a similar vein, patriarchy must not be under-stood as a universal transcultural binary structure but as a historical political system of interlocking dominations. Fiorenza proposes a feminist agenda of simultaneously 'continuing critical deconstruction of the politics of otherness, in reclaiming and reconstructing our particular experiences, histories, and identities' and 'sustaining a permanent reflection on our common differences'.[98] Option for the oppressed is an *option for ourselves*.[99]

The German feminist liberation theologian Dorothee Sölle also brings questions of the subject and epistemology to the centre of the dialogue between FT and other liberation theologies. The question of the subject of theology is central in all liberation theologies, but it is of special importance for FT. Theology as 'God-talk' is both institutionally and substantially male-centred and andro-centric.[100] She, too, says that the de- and reconstruction of our theological traditions is more difficult for FT than for other liberation theologies, since patriarchal oppression is to be found in the Bible itself, which is, besides the foundational text of Christianity, a patriarchal document.[101]

The dialectical relationship of feminist critique with other liberation theologies is also stressed by the North American, theologically trained social ethicist Beverly Wildung Harrison. According to her, 'Feminism implies a specific critique of each particular Christian theological culture and tradition. Women within each tradition must develop these critiques... Over against the resistance of reputed liberation theologians, feminists must appeal to the pivotal thesis of liberation theological method'.[102] The former is a critical project, the latter a more constructive appeal to what is held central in LT, the method.

97. Fiorenza 1989: 316. See also Fiorenza 1994: 361-62.

98. Fiorenza 1989: 316. On a more conceptual level, these are issues that are the focus of most recent feminist theory. When Fiorenza asks 'How can women transcend our being socially constructed as *women* and at the same time become historical subjects as *women* struggling against patriarchal domination?' she joins feminist theorists from other fields and parts of the world (Fiorenza 1989: 317 [emphasis in original]).

99. Fiorenza 1989: 318.

100. Sölle 1990: 95-96.

101. Sölle 1990: 101-102. See also Ringe 1990; Fiorenza 1983, 1984a, 1984b and 1989.

102. Harrison 1985: 225-26. A sentimental liberal 'pro-woman' rhetoric may even be an obstacle for deeper understanding of sexism (Harrison 1985: 226). This could be interpreted to be very much the same as what Ruether calls 'the hit parade of oppression'. Francis Schüssler Fiorenza also traces the dialectical tension in the relationship between FT and LT: 'Feminist analyses of oppression have led feminist theologians to take positions that are both similar and dissimilar to those of Latin American liberation theologians. On the one hand, they begin, as other liberation theologians do, from the experience of oppression. *Yet because women interpret this oppression differently and because women have been traditionally excluded from the articulation of theology*, a critical feminist theology of liberation is forced, on the other hand, to take a much more complex and nuanced stance toward the religious tradition. It cannot locate a strand or principle or basis in the tradition that is free from ideological distortion. The pervasiveness and complexity of systemic patriarchy pushes a critical feminist theology *to go beyond the hermeneutical principles of Latin American liberation theology and to take a much more critical stance toward tradition*' (F. Fiorenza 1991: 98 [emphasis added]).

It is especially the interlocking of different forms of oppression that feminist liberation theologians from both the North and the South have emphasized. A demand for holism not just in theory and praxis but in theological anthropology and ethics as well is central. Relationality is central in feminist theology and ethics.[103] In this sense, feminist critique 'goes beyond the critical stance toward dominant Christianity that the most progressive male-generated liberation theology has developed'.[104] Taking sexism and its old historical roots into account makes it difficult to announce Christian scripture and tradition as the source of full human liberation.[105] The human body, especially in its female form, is at the centre of this critique of Christianity and its tendency to spiritualize life.[106] What Latin American feminist theologians call everyday life, Harrison calls 'concrete female experience, female modes of being, and women's culture'. This again is in clear contrast with what has traditionally been understood as 'femininity'.[107]

To say, as Milagros Peña does, that Christian feminists in Latin America would have 'rejected various versions of liberation theology, because liberation theology assumes women to be in the liberation process'[108] is not entirely correct and also contradictory in its argument. Latin American feminist liberation theologians do not consciously depart from LT, since they consider its basic insights both important and valid.[109] They *are* 'in the liberation process'. To criticize is not to reject. This dialectical way of approaching both traditional and liberation theology (critique *and* construction, de- and reconstruction) has been a feminist theological method since the beginning, and it is especially true for those feminist theologians who define themselves both as feminist and liberation theologians, be they from the North or from the South.

Peña is correct in emphasizing various feminist theologians' tenacious critical work, which is the only reason why feminist issues appear on liberation theology's agenda nowadays at all.[110] Nevertheless, it is still rare today to see a prominent male liberation theologian draw from feminist theological writings.

It is clear that those feminist theologians, whether from Latin America or from the industrialized countries, who are connected to the liberation theology paradigm in its wide meaning have very much in common with each other. Nevertheless, there are differences between those coming from Latin America and those

103. Harrison 1985: 240.
104. Harrison 1985: 241.
105. Harrison 1985: 31.
106. Harrison 1985: 242.
107. Harrison 1985: 31. 'it seems clear to me that all assumptions of essential, or ontic, difference will be as tainted by past oppression as all our concepts and languages are. The history of the subjugation of women is a *social history* that must be changed' (Harrison 1985: 31 [emphasis in original]).
108. Peña 1995: 81.
109. In the article right after Peña's, Peruvian feminist theologians themselves state this clearly. According to them, there is a *deficiency* in LT. It has not differentiated exploitation by gender and taken up issues of sexual ethics critically. See Gallagher 1995: 107-108.
110. Peña 1995: 92.

from the First World. On the one hand, the very fact that they come from very different contexts has shaped their form of theologizing. Theologians in the South have much less access to education, literature and international contacts than do their First World colleagues. They, especially women with families, have much less time and fewer financial possibilities to dedicate themselves to full-time research. On the other hand, Latin American feminist liberation theologians are in the most legitimate position for speaking with authority on issues concerning Latin American women. They are probably more listened to by their Latin American (male) colleagues. If LT can be interpreted as not only an intellectual but also deeply religious movement, feminist liberation theologians mostly share its basic presuppositions with their male colleagues. They understand themselves as belonging to the same cultural, religious and political community, which makes their critique both more difficult to deal with but also more serious. In this sense, Latin American feminist liberation theologians—at least the ones presented here—speak from a much more commonly shared context than do their colleagues in the industrialized countries.

And finally, Latin American feminist liberation theologians are in the difficult but privileged position of being able to speak of poor women's realities from inside, in a manner far different from their First World feminist colleagues or Latin American male colleagues.

3.3 Latin American Male Liberation Theologians and the Challenge of Feminist Theology

According to María P. Aquino, not only are most male liberation theologians not acquainted with feminist theological analysis, but there has also been active resistance to the acceptance of Latin American feminist theology as liberation theology. She calls this 'quality control'.[111] After an explicit commitment of most female liberation theologians to a feminist liberation theology, the split between 'women' and 'the feminine', on the one hand, and 'feminist', on the other hand, has nevertheless remained in much of the theological discourse of male liberation theologians (together with the official Catholic discourse and some female liberation theologians, whom she does not mention by name). This means women's theological discourse about women is acceptable as long as it does not call itself 'feminist'.[112]

Aquino, who is probably the most direct of Latin American feminist theologians in the critique of her male colleagues, mentions several 'myths' concerning feminism and FT in Latin American theology. Among them are: (1) Feminism is a product of the First World; (2) thus, feminism does not interest women of the popular (poor) sectors; (3) feminism is only about the interests of lesbian women; (4) FT represents a fracture in the common theoretical framework and leads to a division of generic liberative objectives; and (5) feminist

111. Aquino 1995a: 117.
112. Aquino 1995a: 117.

discourse inside LT is only partial, peripheral and reductive, and easily fragments a more universalized discourse.[113]

Those liberation theologians, both male and female, who are cautious about a feminist perspective usually presuppose that women and their gender-specific problems are already included among the central category 'the poor'. It is exactly at this point where the feminist critique gains its validity. The category in itself occults the 'multiple impoverishment, the structural inhumanism, and everyday violence directed at women'.[114] It omits the subjectivity of women *qua* women[115] and as an analytical framework does not do justice to women or to reality itself.[116] Aquino even says that the realization of unequal power structures between the sexes is 'the theological arena most ignored by Latin American liberation theologians'.[117]

It is practically only Leonardo Boff and Enrique Dussel of the male liberation theologians who have written more extensively and explicitly on women, which is exceptional among the liberation theologians, and important as such. Both of them treat this issue in the context of a larger intellectual framework, as one interesting theme among others, not as much as an epistemological challenge to the overall way of doing theology. Their knowledge and use of feminist (theological) research is scanty. Dussel, being a philosopher, historian, and philosophically orientated theologian, speaks of women's liberation in the context of his theory of Otherness and philosophy of liberation. Boff, who, among other things, has been interested in Mariology and spirituality, writes about women mostly in the context of Mariological reinterpretations.

First I will briefly present Dussel's thoughts, then Boff's, the latter also serving as a bridge to Chapter 3.4 on Mary.

3.3.1 *Enrique Dussel and the Woman as the Other*
In Chapter 1.4.4 I briefly presented Dussel's main thesis on the question of the Other and alterity, as well as some of the critique aimed at Dussel's philosophy. It was stated that the basic concretizations of the alterity are the relationships male–female, parent–child (also teacher–student) and brother–brother (including nation–nation). These correspond to three different levels: the erotic, the pedagogical and the political.[118]

The conquest of America was not only a political, economic and cultural enterprise, but also erotic: the *mestizaje* of the American peoples is the result of the violence of the European conquistador.[119] The modern ego of the conquistador also reveals itself as a phallic ego which is violent by nature: while the con-

113.   Aquino 1995a: 118-19.
114.   Aquino 1995a: 116.
115.   Aquino 1995a: 117.
116.   Aquino 1995b: 90.
117.   Aquino 1995b: 88.
118.   Dussel 1987: I, 97.
119.   Dussel 1974a: 118 and 1992a: 407.

quistador murders the male Indian or subdues him into servitude, he sleeps with the female, sometimes in the presence of the husband.[120] 'Spaniards vented their purely masculine libido through the erotic subjugation of the Other as Indian woman', says Dussel.[121] This 'unilateral machismo'[122] leads both to alienating erotics[123] and to the birth of modernity based on irrational praxis of violence.[124] If the conquest of America was the start of the modern era, as is often claimed, then, according to Dussel, we have to overcome modernity not through a postmodern attack on reason but by opposing modernity's irrational violence based on the reason of the Other.[125]

> To deny modernity's innocence and to affirm the alterity of the Other, the inculpable victim, reveals the other face hidden and yet essential to modernity. This Other encompasses the peripheral colonial world, the sacrificed Indian, the enslaved black, the oppressed woman, the subjugated child, and the alienated popular culture—all victims of modernity's irrational action in contradiction to its own rational ideal.[126]

Here the Other is the racially, culturally, politically and sexually oppressed. Dussel (as well as other philosophers and theologians of liberation) are strongly influenced by Emmanuel Levinas and his idea of the Other.[127]

Besides his historical-philosophical texts where the woman appears as one concretization of the Otherness, Dussel also writes on more practically orientated questions. He is actually one of the few male liberation theologians to touch issues of sexual ethics and the church at all.[128] He speaks of women as sexual objects educated to oppression,[129] but at the same time he has a surprisingly negative understanding of feminism.[130]

---

120. Dussel 1995: 46.
121. Dussel 1995: 46.
122. Dussel 1995: 138.
123. Dussel 1995: 48.
124. Dussel 1995: 136-37.
125. Dussel 1995: 137.
126. Dussel 1995: 46.
127. See Dussel 1992a: 397. According to Schutte, 'The categories of exteriority, totality, and alterity used by Dussel are borrowed directly from the work of the French philosopher Emmanuel Levinas, but these categories are then applied to a different and, indeed, contradictory end, insofar as they are subordinated to a political platform of national-popular liberation' (Schutte 1993: 188). In a recent Finnish dissertation, the philosopher Sara Heinämaa shows how the idea of the woman as the Other is especially clear in Levinas' *Le Temps et l'Autre*. For Levinas, alterity gets its absolute, immediate form in the feminine. Heinämaa points out how Simone de Beauvoir criticizes and reinterprets this understanding of the woman as the Other in *The Second Sex*. According to Heinämaa's interpretation of Beauvoir, woman is not the Other, but is comprehended as such. When Levinas writes that woman is a mystery, he forgets to say that she is a mystery to man. His description of woman is nothing else but the enforcement of masculine privilege. See Heinämaa 1996: 142-43.
128. See Chapter 4.1.1.
129. Dussel 1974a: 122-23.
130. Dussel 1974a: 124-26 and 1990: 25-33. In the new foreword to his *Filosofía ética de la*

When speaking of difference, Dussel implicitly touches several theoretical questions worked out in modern feminist theory. Since Dussel's use of the concept the Other—especially in the context of erotic alterity—is based on *difference*, it comes very close to definitions of women and femininity (versus men and masculinity) in recent Catholic theological anthropology, especially as expressed in official statements concerning women's role in the church and society.[131] It may be that this fact merely reflects Dussel's Catholic framework.

According to Dussel,

> Woman's liberation supposes that she is able to discern adequately her distinct functions, analogically diverse. One function is that of being a woman in the couple. Another is that of procreator of her son (*hijo*). Another is that of an educator. Another one is being a sister among sisters in the political society. And if one does not know how to discern each of these functions, tremendous errors are committed.[132]

He differentiates between 'femininity', 'woman' and 'human person'. A woman does not *equate* with femininity, but a woman as a human being 'carries with privilege the human femininity'.[133] Men and women equally share human personality, but femininity is different from masculinity even though there is something of the feminine in a man and something of the masculine in a woman.[134]

What Dussel calls 'the metaphysics of femininity'[135] is a dialectical notion which is not understandable in itself, but in relation to masculinity (the erotic heterosexual relationship), to the son (maternity) and to the brother (political

liberación (1987), he acknowledges this by saying that he cannot criticize feminism in the same way as he did at the beginning of the 1970s.

131.   See *Mulieris Dignitatem* 1988: 325-26, 383-384, 398. In his apostolical letter, Pope John Paul II affirms the equality between men and women based on ontological difference. There is a proper feminine 'originality', which is expressed in femininity. Masculinity and femininity are different and complementary to each other. A woman should not be masculine, a man should not be feminine. Femininity and masculinity have their origin in the ontological human nature. The former is best expressed in the two dimensions of a woman's vocation, maternity and virginity.

At the end of the letter, the statement on the impossibility of women's ordination in the Catholic Church is based exactly on this theological anthropology in which the priest acts *in persona Christi*. It is essentially a masculine function.

According to Anne Carr, 'While there are no longer assertions of the inferiority of women in Christian ecclesiastical or theological discourse, many official Catholic documents affirm a dual anthropology, the complementarity or "different but equal" status of men and women as inherent in nature, in the created order, and therefore as part of the divine plan' (Carr 1990: 125).

132.   'La liberación de la mujer supone que ésta sepa discernir adecuadamente sus distintas funciones analógicamente diversas. Una función es ser la mujer de la pareja. Otra es ser la procreadora de su hijo. Otra es ser la educadora. Otra ser una hermana entre los hermanos de la sociedad política. Y si cada una de estas funciones no se saben discernir, se cometen errores tremendos' (Dussel 1990: 28).

133.   Dussel 1990: 29.

134.   Dussel 1990: 29-30.

135.   Dussel 1990: 28.

realm).[136] All this is included in masculinity as well (woman–man relationship, paternity and political brother-sister relationship).[137] Dussel is careful not to absolutize what he calls femininity and not to identify it exclusively with the woman (nor human person with the male).

The difficulty in giving new meanings to these concepts (femininity and masculinity) while operating in the binary system they imply as concepts becomes clear when Dussel becomes more concrete. He says:

> The woman, human person, carries femininity essentially at the *sexed, erotic level in the couple,* in front of the man, human person as well, who carries his masculinity at the same level. The differences are clear and *equality in distinction (igualdad en la distinción)* must be defended concretely in all the details.[138]

In other texts, he says:

> What feminism proposes to us is an asexual angelism, even though it may not seem so, since it proposes to us the disappearance of sexual alterity and that each of us would fulfill love with himself... No. *The liberation of the woman is not through indistinction, but exactly through distinction.*[139]

> Liberation is not merely negation of domination by the negation of sexual diversity (as when feminism champions homosexuality, test-tube babies, etc.). *Liberation is real sexual distinction.*[140]

These excerpts could be from almost any recent Vatican document on women. It is exactly the 'equality in distinction', taken as naturally and uncritically as Dussel does, that has been criticized by Catholic feminist theologians.[141] Dussel's use of such problematic concepts as femininity and masculinity seems to imply a tendency towards traditional definitions of both actual gender relations and 'a

136.   Dussel 1990: 29. I have consciously used the exact English (masculine) equivalents of *hijo* and *hermano*.

137.   Dussel 1990: 30-31.

138.   'La mujer, persona humana, porta la femineidad esencialmente en su nivel *sexuado erótico en la pareja,* ante un varón, igualmente persona humana, que porta la masculinidad en ese mismo nivel. Las diferencias son claras y la *igualdad en la distinción* debe ser defendida en concreto en todos los detalles' (Dussel 1990: 32 [emphasis in original]).

139.   'El feminismo lo que nos propone es un angelismo asexual, aunque no parezca, porque nos propone que desaparezca la alteridad sexual y que cada uno cumpla consigo el amor... No. *La liberación de la mujer no es por indistinción, sino justamente por distinción*' (Dussel 1974a: 125 [emphasis added]).

140.   'La liberación no es negación pura de la dominación por la negación de la diversidad sexual (como cuando el feminismo propone la homosexualidad, los hijos en probetas, etc.). *La liberación es distinción real sexual*' (Dussel 1985: 101 [emphasis added]).

141.   See Carr 1990: 123-133; Ruether 1983: 94-99; 1987: 30-45; 1990 and 1991.

An interesting comparison could be made between Dussel and those feminists, both theologians and non-theologians, who also rely on essential difference between men and women. Are the projects of liberation they entail different from each other, and if yes, in which ways? Since feminist liberation theologians all reject essential binary oppositions as dualistic and sexist, I will not go into this discussion deeper.

Similarly, it is not possible in this research to analyse Dussel's reading of Merleau-Ponty and Freud, both of whom he extensively quotes in the context of erotic alterity.

female/male essence'. Or rather, as the recent discussion in feminist theory on difference makes clear, it is not notions of difference (whether between men and women or between women) in itself which would imply difference in value or certain hierarchical relations. It is the supposed naturality of difference and its social and political consequences that have been the targets of feminist critique.

Dussel's implicit implications of the naturality of the gender difference take him close to official Catholic statements where 'different but equal' and 'complementarity' of the differences form the basis of traditional arguments for clearly sexist notions of women and their role in society and church (maternity as women's principal vocation, women cannot be ordained, and so on).

Thus, it should not come as a big surprise that Dussel proposes 'women's liberation' as an alternative concept for 'feminism', which as we saw he understands in quite negative terms. He misunderstands that both historically and conceptually 'women's liberation' has been equated with 'feminism' *for feminist women*, on his own continent as well. In this context, he uses arguments against feminism that are similar to those often used against LT, especially on the part of the Vatican.[142]

Dussel has an idea of feminism as something that suppresses the difference between man and woman and inevitably leads to a homosexual definition of erotic relationships.[143] This, again, would lead (inevitably) to the suppression of biological motherhood.[144]

When speaking of feminism, Dussel explicitly refers to North American and European feminism.[145] This means two things. First, as has been the case in LT in general, by seeing feminism as something concerning primarily—or even

142.   Dussel 1990: 25-33 and 1987: I, 128-37. The Vatican Congregation of Faith has issued two reports on liberation in which the liberation theological use of the concepts is discredited and an alternative use is proposed. It has always been one of the main theological arguments of the Vatican against LT that 'liberation' is too narrow a term. Latin American liberation theologians have been quick—and often correct—in unmasking this 'taking over' and reinterpreting their central concepts for opposite aims. See *Libertatis Nuntius* in 1984 and *Libertatis Conscientia* in 1986. See Min 1989: 118-22, on the differences and similarities between the two documents.

143.   This view is still present in the latest edition of his *Liberación de la mujer y erótica latinoamericana* (1990). 'La mujer feminista, al ver a la mujer oprimida, pero sin salirse de la 'totalidad' como categoría fundamental, propone que la mujer remonte la corriente e iguale a varón; que suprima la di-ferencia, de tal manera que se hable de "hombres" sin más, ni de varones, ni de mujeres. Para llegar a eso habría que pensar en la homosexualidad, pues para que nadie dependiera de nadie, la relación debería ser homosexual; la mujer consigo misma, con la mujer; el varón con el varón' (Dussel 1990: 25).

Ironically, here he uses 'men' (*hombres*) in the generic meaning of 'human beings'. In another text, he says clearly; 'El feminismo en el fondo lo que quiere son *hombres*; no quiere varones ni mujeres... Cuando digo ahora hombre, quiero decir especie. El feminismo lucha para que todos seamos hombres, no varones ni mujeres' (Dussel 1974a: 124-25 [emphasis in original]).

144.   Here Dussel, probably unintentionally, coincides with some radical feminists of the early 1970s who saw biological motherhood as the main obstacle for women's liberation. See Firestone 1971.

145.   Dussel 1990: 26.

only—First World women, Dussel can ignore it by using anti-imperialist arguments (feminism being 'bourgeois' or 'foreign'). This way of avoiding the challenge of *Latin American* feminism is identified by Latin American feminist theologians as one expression of patriarchalism in LT.[146] Second, by speaking of feminism only as a European and North American phenomenon, Latin American male intellectuals ignore the history of Latin American feminism which has deep roots in the continent. This is especially questionable in the case of Dussel, who as a historian has mainly been interested in rewriting Latin American history, 'the unwritten history', giving credit to 'indigenous' forms of rebellion and cultural self-assurance.[147]

It is interesting to find this categorical understanding specifically in Dussel of feminists 'wanting to be men' (even though he uses 'men' for 'human beings'), effacing sexual difference (defined in very traditional terms) in favour of 'asexual angelism'[148] and not being feminine (which is practically the same as undoing sexual difference in his terms), since he so enthusiastically commits himself to women's liberation.

Many of the points he takes up are implicitly present in other liberation theologians' texts. As Latin American feminist liberation theologians have pointed out, the whole issue of feminism being omitted in LT is due to the very reasons that Dussel states explicitly: seeing feminism primarily as a phenomenon foreign to Latin American reality, and preferring an uncritical and undifferentiated use of concepts such as women and femininity. Thus, it is not totally incorrect to see Dussel's views as expressing a more widespread opinion among the liberation theologians.

I will deal with some of the practical consequences of Dussel's thinking in the area of sexual ethics in Chapter 4.1.1.

3.3.2 *Leonardo Boff and 'the Eternal Feminine'*

Leonardo Boff's view of women is both different from and similar to Dussel's. Boff is more theological, more spiritual, even mystical. He seems to tie women's fate to Mariological reinterpretations. He comes close to Dussel on a more philosophical level. They both share the ambiguity of defining women and women's reality from 'femininity' rather than from historical realities. They both hold to the binary structure of masculinity and femininity, without sufficient critical analysis of these concepts.

---

146.   See Aquino 1997: 11.

147.   Aquino notes that First World women also often operate with the idea that feminism is nonexistent in Latin America or that it is a mere reproduction of European or North American feminism (Aquino 1997: 11). Dussel not only ignores Latin American feminism, but he also defines European and North American feminism as something promoting 'indifferentiated individualism typical of English and North American societies', which is a very general and stereotypical statement. See Dussel 1990: 26.

148.   Dussel 1974a: 125.

Leonardo Boff has several texts on women, masculinity and femininity, human sexuality and the Virgin Mary.[149] I shall deal with the more explicitly Mariological issues (even though they are not always easily separable from his view of women and femininity) in Chapter 3.4.2. His fundamental starting point for both Mariology and gender issues in general is in an understanding of sexuality and sexual difference as ontological structures of the human being.

According to Boff,

> In the light of an ontological analysis, sexuality is not merely regional or genital quality of man. Consequently, it does not constitute only a biological dimension. It invades all layers of existence of the human being. Everything that a man is and does is marked by sexuality, anything as he is and does as a sexed being. Sex is not something that man *has*; he *is* a sexed being. In other words, man is man and woman. To be one or the other constitutes two different ways of being in the world.[150]

It seems that Boff identifies the existence of two sexes, men and women, with heterosexual sexuality. Sexuality is by definition something between men and women. Nothing is said about homosexuality.

Like Dussel, Boff too makes a leap from this ontological definition of sexuality to corresponding qualities of masculinity and femininity. These are defined by difference, reciprocity and complementarity. Whatever a man or a woman does, is done differently, because of the fundamental difference between them.[151] In Boff, too, the language of traditional Catholic anthropology is present.

Even though Boff claims, as does Dussel, that masculinity is not something belonging exclusively to men, nor femininity to women (in fact, 'everybody is man and woman at the same time'[152]), it does not become clear what this means. 'Masculinity' and 'femininity' seem to function to both Dussel and Boff as adequate terms which have a natural reference to existing men and women. This naturality is not questioned but taken for granted.

---

149. The most important of them are Boff 1978; 1980; 1985 (especially chapter 5); 1987a; 1990, and his interviews in Tamez 1986 and in Puleo 1994.

150. 'A la luz de su análisis ontológico, la sexualidad no es ninguna cualidad meramente regional o genital del hombre. Consiguientemente, no constituye sólo una dimensión biológica. Invade todas las capas existenciales del ser humano. Todo lo que el hombre es y cuanto hace está marcado por la sexualidad, ya que lo es y lo hace siempre como un ser sexuado. El sexo no es algo que *tiene* el hombre; éste *es* un ser sexuado. En otros términos: el hombre es varón y mujer. Ser lo uno o lo otro constituyen dos modos diferentes de ser y estar en el mundo' (Boff 1985: 158 [emphasis in original]). The generic use of 'man' (*hombre*) is notable in Boff's text(s), and leads to such terms as 'man-man' (*hombre-varón*) and 'man-woman' (*hombre-mujer*), when, ironically, what he wants to express by the term is the balance of both masculine and feminine qualities in an individual (Boff 1985: 162). Also, 'Man is not an existential reality, as are his concretizations, man and woman' (Boff 1985: 156).

Aquino comments: 'A woman does not sense being expressed in the term "man-woman", she prefers being recognized simply as "a woman"... To use the term "man-woman" to refer to women only expresses what men say of women, not what women say of themselves' (Aquino 1992a: 142-43).

151. Boff 1985: 158-59.

152. Boff 1985: 159.

Boff is more specific than Dussel in clarifying what he means by 'femininity' and 'masculinity'. His Jungian-based theological anthropology defines femininity and masculinity as two different poles or dimensions of human existence. The first expresses 'the obscurity and night, mystery and profoundness, interiority, earth, sentiment, receptivity, the generating power, human vitality', whereas the latter expresses 'the light, time, impulse, the provoking power, order, exteriority, objectivity and reason'. The feminine character entails 'repose, immobility, darkness that defies curiosity and investigation, the immanence, the longing for the past'. In opposition, the masculine entails all that is 'transformative dynamism, aggressivity, transcendence, clarity which is able to distinguish and separate, the capacity to order and project towards the future'.[153]

These 'lists' of feminine and masculine qualities have been carefully analysed as the symbolic structure of sexism in Western philosophy and theology. For example, according to Rosemary Ruether, this gendered dualistic structure has permeated the very core of Christian theology since the early church fathers.[154]

In the case of Boff, it does not become clear why he thinks it is necessary to use such concepts as 'masculinity' and 'femininity' if he also says they are not accurate because of their reductive potentiality and even possible serious social consequences.[155] The apparent tension is not solved by saying: 'What are the feminine and the masculine in their ultimate radicality? We do not know. It is a challenging mystery'.[156] It is not totally clear what Boff considers to be the relationship between masculinity and femininity, on the one hand, and existing men and women, on the other. 'The two different modes of being in the world' identified by Boff may or may not refer to essentialist notions of being male and female. When taken in the context of Boff's entire philosophical structure, it seems that he has a strong tendency to interpret men and women according to a dualistic notion of masculinity and femininity. It may also be that Boff contradicts himself at this point.

According to Beverly Wildung Harrison,

> A central contention of a feminist theological analysis is that the suppression of women and women's status as property of men are dialectically related to the mystification of women's 'nature'. Whenever it is claimed that women are 'opposite' or 'complementary' to men in their human nature, whether or not the implication is

153.   Boff 1985: 163. See also Boff 1987a: 67-68 and 1980: 17, 47. In the latter, there are more characteristics such as tenderness, delicacy, profundity, interiority, sentiment and donation for the feminine, as well as mystery. Actually, Boff states very clearly that 'For a man, the woman is always an abyss, a mystery, an interrogator'. See Tamez 1986: 112.

154.   See Ruether 1972: 62 and 1974: 150-83. See also Code 1992, especially pp. 117-26; Lloyd 1993 and McLaughlin 1974.

155.   Boff 1985: 163.

156.   Boff 1985: 170. In a later article, Boff holds to the same principle of the ontological character of sexuality. But probably because of his moving towards spiritual and ecological issues, he now enlarges his arguments from Jungian psychology to tantric yoga (Kundalini) and reinterpretations of the Holy Spirit as 'the human and cosmic vitality'. Sexuality and spirituality are expressions of radical cosmic energy, be it called Kundalini or Holy Spirit. Boff 1990: 561-65.

that women are therefore best suited to reproductive and domestic functions, such mystification is at work. Feminist analysis has revealed that the separation of mind and body lies at the core of Western Christian spirituality.[157]

In LT, this produces the difficulty of perceiving the concrete character of real oppression or human liberation, since all human suffering is subsumed under one analytic category: class oppression. For Harrison, a genuine liberation perspective is accountable to a praxis that gives priority to the concrete well-being of people.[158]

Some Latin American feminist liberation theologians have analysed critically Boff's presuppositions.[159] María Pilar Aquino is critical of Boff's use of sexist language, but shows also how he falls into the very trap he wants to avoid when not wanting to interpret 'masculinity' and 'femininity' as socio-cultural constructions and women's subordination as a historical process.[160] According to Aquino, the great difficulty in Boff's perspective is its biologism, which does not pay enough attention to historical, cultural and social factors.[161] 'The foundational problem with Boff's position is that *he transfers to an ontological dimension that which is a historically determined cultural creation*', says Aquino.[162]

Boff's use of the concepts 'masculinity' and 'femininity' faces similar problems to those in Dussel's case. Theoretically, it is very difficult—if not impossible—to tackle issues of sexism and male-female relationship from such uncritical ontological presuppositions where the 'I' almost by definition is a masculine subject, women being 'the Other' or the opposite pole of that subjectivity. Historically, femininity has been identified with subordination, masculinity with superiority. The presupposed biological differences between men and women are not free of their historical meaning.

When women as subjects refuse to symbolize this other 'feminine' pole of human existence and start to define what humanity means for them *qua* women, the concepts lose their 'naturalized' symbolic power. It is notable how all those feminist theologians who pay attention to Boff's ontology criticize him of ahistoricity, which implies the invisibility of women's oppression and feminist struggles against it.[163] Leonardo Boff was silenced by the Vatican in 1985 due to

---

157. Harrison 1985: 241-42.

158. Harrison 1985: 242-43.

159. See at least Aquino 1992a: 134-43; Carmen Lora and Leonor Aída Concha in Tamez 1989: 31-32 and 92-93 respectively and Porcile Santiso 1991: 72-74. For feminist theologians from the North, see Erickson 1993: 175-188 and Vuola 1993: 16-17.

160. Aquino 1992a: 137-39.

161. Aquino 1992a: 139-41.

162. Aquino 1992a: 142 (emphasis added).

163. For Aquino, 'sigue sin resolver la subordinación histórica de las mujeres y las relaciones sociales asimétricas' (Aquino 1992a: 137-38). Carmen Lora says about the mysteriousness of the woman which she traces not only in Boff, but in other male liberation theologians as well: 'A mí esto me sorprendió, porque para nosotras las mujeres muchas veces nuestra sensación de temor, por ejemplo, frente al hombre, nos es tanto por lo desconocido (la mujer aparece como misterio, y ligado a este misterio, está el temor) sino por la experiencia de dominación del hombre. Más

his ecclesiology. His critique of the hierarchical, authoritarian, and, yes, sexist church is perhaps the most radical ecclesiological critique by a liberation theologian.[164] In this, he is much closer to many feminist theologians than to his fellow Latin American male theologians who do not openly challenge the power structures *in the church itself.* He is not alone, though, in favouring women's ordination in the Catholic Church. When asked, most Catholic liberation theologians do favour it.[165]

Implications of Boff's image of women on sexual ethics will be dealt with in Chapter 3.4.2 (in a Mariological context) and in Chapter 4.1.1.

3.4 The Virgin Mary and Mariological Reinterpretations in Liberation Theology

Besides the more methodological kind of themes which were presented in Chapter 3.2, other more substantial themes have appeared in the discussion on women in LT. Roughly speaking, there are some very general kinds of works, such as the two books edited by Elsa Tamez, which critically raise the question of women in LT. Woman as 'the triply oppressed' is usually expressed by both male and female liberation theologians. Ecclesiological issues, as well as the question of women's ordination, appear regularly. Sexism is recognized as a critical issue in theology also, even though it usually does not imply (for the male theologians at

que lo desconocido que puede ser el hombre para nosotras como ser, el temor viene de la violencia que ejerce sobre la mujer, de la capacidad de dominio que puede tener...esa dimensión del misterio de la mujer tiene que ver, creo yo, con su [de los hombres] identidad sexual' (Tamez 1989: 31). I myself have criticized Boff's position as dualistic and ahistorical. The ontological opposition between 'the feminine' and 'the masculine' always leads to the identification of 'the feminine' with biological women and 'the masculine' with biological men. To try to change these oppositions without changing the anthropological dualism behind them probably does not result in a fresh or liberating reinterpretation. New perspectives are necessary which do not identify different human qualities with one or the other gender. See Vuola 1993: 16.

164.   See especially Boff 1986b and 1987b. In an interview in 1990, before he left the Franciscan order and priesthood (in 1992), Boff says: 'I'd like to see an inclusive church. It would be a church that integrates women, men, children, old people, persons with AIDS, sick people, healthy people. It would be a space where human beings could experience inclusion without taboos, exclusions, or scapegoats. This would be a non-hierarchical church' (Puleo 1994: 168-69). He also states that 'Rome lives in profound structural sin' and that sooner or later, there will be a schism, provoked by Rome, not by the people (Puleo 1994: 175, 178). According to Erickson, 'Boff is clearly attempting to combine the masculine, triangular, hierarchical church with the feminine, circular, community-building church'. Nevertheless, failing to stand with real women and seeing the poor as necessary for 'saving' the church, 'Boff's liberation theology implicitly and explicitly seeks to retain the hierarchical patriarchy of the institutional church, which continues to stand over and against communal life, women, and the poor' (Erickson 1993: 182, 185-86). Although this critique may not be totally correct, in the light of Boff's overall theological framework, it sheds light on the problematic question of subject and agency. As Erickson says, 'The poor and the oppressed do not have to address the "crisis in Christendom". It is not their crisis. Neither will the end of Christendom be their crisis' (Erickson 1993: 188).

165.   See Tamez 1986.

least) any use of feminist works done on sexism. The 'popular reading of the Bible' (*lectura popular de la Biblia*) as well as more scholarly exegetical works seem to be contexts easily suitable for feminist interpretations in LT as well. Besides these, more in-depth analyses on women are centred on questions of method and subject(s) of LT (Chapter 3.2) and Mariology. There are other issues that are notably missing in LT discourse concerning women, one of them being sexual ethics, which will be analysed in Chapter 4.

It seems that for the simple reason of Mary being the only woman in the 'divine hierarchy', theological speculations on women are easily tied to Mariological issues, at least in Catholic theology. This is also true in LT, where both male and female theologians explicitly tie women's fate (in the church) to Mary's fate and potential new Mariological reinterpretations. This is why I take a closer look at Mariology. I shall approach it by asking such questions as: Are there alternative Mariological reinterpretations in LT? How are they connected to concrete women? Are feminist interpretations of Mary possible in the context of LT? Could a 'liberation Mariology' open space for alternative ways of approaching gender issues in LT? What would this mean for sexual ethics?

3.4.1 *The Virgin as Queen of the Americas*

Hispanic colonization was Marian colonization.[166] The Marian cult was systematically encouraged in order to 'civilize' the indigenous peoples of America. The Spanish and Portuguese conquerors even saw Mary as the one who carried out the colonialist enterprise, as *La conquistadora*.[167] There were several Marian apparitions and miracles during the first years of the Conquest.[168] Thus, for the Indians, the Virgin Mary must have appeared as the principal symbol and protector of their enemies. The Virgin Mary became one of the most central and controversial symbols of the conquest of America.[169]

Mary came to incorporate the attributes of pre-Columbian feminine deities, as had happened in early Europe and the Near East with the pre-Christian goddesses. In the Andean region, there is still today the parallel cult of the Virgin Mary and *Pachamama*.[170] In other regions of Latin America, the most popular

166.   Perry and Echeverría 1988: 31; Gebara and Bingemer 1989: 129.

167.   González Dorado 1988: 38-39. He cites one of the early missionaries, Father Antonio de Santa María: 'Nadie puede dudar que el triunfo de esta conquista se debe a la Reina de los Angeles' (González Dorado 1988: 43).

168.   For example, there is a story from Cuzco, Peru, of a battle between the Spaniards and the Indians. At a crucial moment, the Virgin Mary herself appeared and threw sand in the eyes of the Indians. They were so shocked and astonished that they simply fled, and victory was guaranteed to the Spaniards.

169.   According to Virgilio Elizondo, 'It is an undeniable fact that Marian devotion is the most popular, persistent and original characteristic of Latin American Christianity' (González Dorado 1988: 49).

170.   *Pacha* (in Quechua and Aymara) means all vital space and time, Mama means Dame (*Señora*), woman with family. Thus, the usual translation of *Pachamama* into Mother-Earth may be too limited. According to Irarrazával, it could be translated as 'the globality of existence, life

Virgins often have clear continuity with their predecessors, not just visually but functionally as well.[171] In many places, the missionaries themselves actively promoted the syncretized Mary cults, in order to replace the pre-Columbian goddess cults and the continuation of idolatry.

Interestingly enough, these same Virgins have become some of the main symbols of *mestizo* nationalism in America. The most important of them have been declared patronesses of their respective countries. If there is a change from *María Conquistadora* to *María Liberadora,* as González Dorado claims, it passes through a phase of a nationalist 'Liberator Mary'. In 1810 the Virgin of Guadalupe was declared the Patroness and Queen of the Americas (*Nuestra Señora de América*). In some places, the Virgin Mary became the symbol of nationalism and independence. José de San Martín in the South declared the Virgin of Carmen to be a general of his army. In Mexico, it was two Catholic priests, Fathers Hidalgo and Morelos, who started the first independence rebellions. They declared the Virgin of Guadalupe the protector of their rebellion and patroness of Spanish American independence. Their slogan was '*¡Viva Nuestra Señora de Guadalupe! ¡Viva la Independencia!*'

It is exactly here where the 'Latinamericanized' Virgins play a national(ist) role: since they are not mere copies of Spanish Marian cults, they serve as representatives and symbols of the *mestizo* culture, as opposed to Spanish culture.[172] As early as the seventeenth century, the Virgin also served as a 'proof' of the level of Christianization of America. If the Indians venerated Mary, they could not be pagans. The numerous apparitions which appeared to ordinary, humble people must be a message from Mary (God) herself that she has chosen to speak directly to them, not through European missionaries and priests. This fact is emphasized in those cases in which Mary supposedly spoke the local indigenous language, not Spanish or Portuguese. Also racially, she identifies herself with the dark-skinned *mestizo* of mixed blood.

According to González Dorado, it is Mary's maternity that creates the affective and vital bond between her and her Latin American 'children'. Mary has 'adopted'

itself'. This totality is experienced as feminine and maternal. See Irarrazával 1989: 76-77. *Pachamama* does not merge into Mary. Rather, they co-exist, having common elements, but also characteristics of their own.

171.   Just to mention some of the most well-known and widely spread of the representations of Mary: *Nuestra Señora de la Aparecida* (Brazil) is a dark-skinned Virgin who appeared in 1717 to a poor fisherman called Juan Alves. She even contains elements of African goddesses. The legend of *Nuestra Señora del Rosario de Chiquinquirá* (Colombia) goes back to the end of the sixteenth century. The cult of *Nuestra Señora de Luján* (Argentina) is dedicated to a black slave called Manuel. *Nuestra Señora de Copacabana* (Bolivia) has her shrine at the site of an ancient pre-Columbian cult place at Lake Titicaca. She, too, is dark-skinned, and has close affinity to *Pachamama*. I shall deal later with the Virgin of Guadalupe more in detail, since she is the single most important Latin American Virgin. See Lafaye 1977.

172.   'El proyecto de convertir a la Virgen de Guadalupe en patrona nacional fue un proyecto no sólo antihispanista, sino de búsqueda de adhesión cultural entre los mestizos y los indígenas que le otorgaba a los criollos las riendas del poder político' (Zires 1993: 90).

the *mestizo* through her appearances. She is the universal mother, *La Moreñita*.[173]

But there are competing Virgins. The Virgin Mary serves as a national and military symbol for independent nation-states over practically all of modern Latin America. Since the times of the wars of independence, she has also served as a symbol of revolution or rebellion. It is important to emphasize here her use as a symbol, since neither militant nor military Mary has much to do with the historical Mary of Nazareth. Because of Mary's traditional role as the mediatrix between God and humanity, in a military and political context this role receives new connotations: it is as if she would mediate orders directly from God himself. In many battles, Mary was the only woman present—be it among the *zapatistas* in the Mexican revolution or in the Indian rebellion of the 1990s, guerrilla movements or highly repressive national armies and military dictatorships.

It is especially the Mexican Virgin of Guadalupe who has been interpreted in the context of Latin American (male) *mestizo* identity. The Mexican Nobel laureate Octavio Paz sees her as the 'good mother' in contrast to Doña Marina (Malinalli, Malinche), the Indian princess who was Cortés' interpreter, concubine and mother of his child. The Mexican/Latin American *male* identity is based on this conflict: he is *hijo de puta*, the son of a bitch (still today, one of the worst insults to any Latin American man), of the treacherous indigenous mother and the violent European father. According to Paz, this conflict of violent *mestizaje* is resolved in the figure of the Virgin of Guadalupe, who is the pure *mestiza* mother and who reconciliates the conflicting elements of Latin American culture.[174] Paz also explains how Mexican *machismo* is a result of the violent rejection of the rapist European father by the son.

All this may be very true from the male nationalist point of view. Woman as the symbol of nation is a universal phenomenon. What is so controversial in the figure of Mary is her function as 'the dominant symbol' in Latin American culture—thus capable of carrying multiple, even contradictory, meanings simultaneously.[175] 'The dark against the white, the indigenous against the Spanish, the Virgin without the child against the Virgin with the child, the one of Tepeyac[176]

173.   González Dorado 1988: 63, 119.

174.   Paz 1959. Similar views are expressed by other researchers as well, for example, Lafaye 1977 and Anzaldúa 1989. According to the former, 'Si Guadalupe fue la mediadora entre Dios y los hombres, entre Dios y los mexicanos, su mediación no se limitó a eso… Guadalupe hizo de los criollos, de los mestizos y de los indios un solo pueblo (al menos virtualmente), unido en la misma fe carismática' (Lafaye 1977: 403). The latter, a Chicana feminist, also interprets Mary's traditional role as the mediatrix in a wider context: 'She mediates between the Spanish and the Indian cultures…and between Chicanos and the white world. She mediates between humans and the divine, between this reality and the reality of spirit entities' (Anzaldúa 1989: 79). She also tells of the Virgin of Guadalupe in the context of a modern political conflict. During the 1965 grape workers' strike in California and in subsequent Chicano farmworkers' marches in Texas and other parts of the Southwest, her image on banners heralded and united the farmworkers (Anzaldúa 1989).

175.   See Zires 1993: 82.

176.   The hill where the Virgin of Guadalupe appeared to the Indian Juan Diego in 1531.

against the one of the Cathedral, the one of the people against the one of the powerful', according to Margarita Zires.[177] The Virgin Mary is a point of convergence of different social groups.[178]

Evidently, many of the Latin American Virgins contain pre-Columbian elements, the heritage of the great Mother Goddess, as in Europe. Many of them are dark-skinned, a fact that certainly does more justice to the historical Mary than the blond Marys of Western art. At several places in Latin America, Mary has replaced pre-Columbian goddesses, who continue to live in her in a syncretized form. The most famous and widely believed of these is the aforementioned Virgin of Guadalupe, who appeared—ten years after the conquest of Mexico—in a pilgrim site of the Aztec goddess Tonantzin where the actual Basílica Guadalupe now is situated.[179] The dark-skinned Latin American Virgins were encountered by simple people in situations of oppression and chaos.

The manipulation of these 'grassroot virgins' in the service of *mestizo* or white nationalism has little to do with their cultural origins. The conflict surrounding these extremely popular and meaningful symbols implies the need for a 'non-Westernized' Mary which has a strong and lively presence in the continents colonized by Europe, not just Latin America, but Africa and Asia as well.

3.4.2 *Leonardo Boff: Mary, the Archetype of the Feminine*
Practically all the texts by Catholic liberation theologians contain some reference to Mary, not necessarily as an alternative interpretation, but rather as an indication of Marian devotion.[180] Of the Latin American male liberation theologians, it is Leonardo Boff who most of all pays attention to Mary and Mariology.

As was said in Chapter 3.3.2, for Boff the feminine represents all the dimensions of tenderness, delicacy, interiority, sentiment, receptivity, giving, intuition and mystery. All this impregnates the concrete reality of every human being, and thus does not belong exclusively to the woman, but is nevertheless 'to be found more densely in her'.[181] This anthropological dualism in Boff's theology is transferred to his Mariological reinterpretations as well.

According to Boff, Mary is simultaneously the archetype of the feminine and a dimension of God, the 'maternal face of God'. Mary has a special relationship to the Holy Spirit, which represents the feminine principle of the Trinity. Thus, Boff locates Mary in a very important place in the history of salvation.[182]

Boff's main theological thesis concerning Mary is her being the place of incarnation of the Holy Spirit. He himself says this is 'heretical for normal theology',

---

177. Zires 1993: 81.
178. Zires 1993: 81.
179. Gebara and Bingemer 1991: 614; Rodríguez Sehk 1986: 82. There are several works—theological, anthropological, sociological etc.—written on the cult and meaning of the Virgin of Guadalupe.
180. Lozano Lerma 1991: 22.
181. Boff 1980: 17, 47.
182. See Boff 1980 and 1987a.

since it implies that Mary as well as Jesus can be adored.[183] Mary is not a mere collaborator of her son, but together with him the absolute mediatrix. Boff deifies Mary as much as does Latin American popular devotion.[184]

For Boff, this deified Mary has the anthropological implication of women being bearers of divinity. Boff accepts all the traditional Mariological doctrines, trying to give them new meaning and fresh interpretations. Thus, the Immaculate Conception (1854), according to which Mary was free of original sin, does not mean that Mary did not feel the different passions of life, but that she succeeded in directing those passions toward a holy plan. 'At last, a creature has appeared in the universe who is pure goodness', says Boff.[185] The Immaculate Conception is a mystery, a secret, and as such, gains its deepest meaning in 'the preparation for the future spiritualization of humanity'.[186]

The doctrine of the perpetual virginity (553 AD) has several meanings for Boff. It has to be analysed mainly in Christological and pneumatological not Mario-logical context.[187] For Boff, virginity is not a merely biological state (and here he comes close both to Jungian psychology and to some feminist theological Mario-logical interpretations), and as such, it is not a value in itself, but only in the service of Christ.[188] Nevertheless, the in partu virginity means absence of pain and that the hymen did not rupture even at delivery.[189] In sum, the perpetual virginity of Mary 'does not diminish her femininity, but elevates it, transforming it into fertile maternity'.[190]

In Boff's Mariology, there are many elements that do not affirm the traditional vision of the church. In a way, Boff radicalizes the traditional Catholic view on Mary, affirming theologically the divine character she actually has in popular piety, and partly in theology, too. Boff takes a clear position, which much of the Catholic teaching on Mary does not, because of her simultaneous exaltation and limitation. A closer study of Boff's Mariology would probably reveal affinities to some feminist theological interpretations as well, especially when it comes to the motivation of giving Mary a more significant position.

Boff has a sensitivity and openness towards what he himself calls 'the femin-ine', something that one rarely finds in other theologians, be they liberation theologians or not. Nevertheless, it is exactly his starting point, the exaltation of the feminine in the figure of Mary, that turns out to be quite problematic. Since Boff does not take a critical stance towards the anti-sexual context of the Mariological doctrines, he ends up confirming the very anti-sexual and anti-

---

183.   Boff in Puleo 1994: 173. Boff thinks it is curious that he has not been questioned by Rome because of his Mariology.
184.   Lozano Lerma 1991: 24.
185.   Boff 1987a: 158.
186.   Boff 1987a: 160.
187.   Boff 1987a: 169.
188.   Boff 1987a: 171.
189.   Boff 1987a: 175.
190.   Boff 1987a: 178.

woman (which is not the same as anti-feminine) character of traditional Catholic Mariology.[191]

For example, Boff does not explain the (anti)sexual origin of the doctrine of original sin. To accept and even reinterpret the doctrine without a critical analysis of its origins leads him to a devaluation of human sexuality. The 'spiritualization of humanity' after Mary's model affirms the classical anti-bodily and dualistic view of spirituality as something against bodily and sexual realities.

Most feminist liberation theologians depart from Boff, at least implicitly, in the exaltation of the feminine at the cost of real women and bodily womanhood. This devaluation of all the other women except Mary (who cannot be like her) is one of the consequences of classical Mariology. It is here exactly where Boff is unable to create new interpretations. If the bodily realities of sexuality, pregnancy and birth-giving—and their necessary interconnection—are taken seriously, it becomes impossible to accept the doctrine of perpetual virginity in its classical form. To claim, on the one hand, that virginity is not something exclusively biological and, on the other hand, that, biologically, Mary's hymen did not rupture at delivery, is to try to maintain two contradictory views simultaneously. At the symbolical level, these sorts of images of female bodiliness are probably some of the most violent in the Christian tradition. A simple and clear affirmation of human bodiliness, especially in its female form (in the Mariological context), makes the separation of Mary from all other women unnecessary.

The sort of image of woman that emerges from Boff's Mariology—even in a way which contradicts his explicit goal—is not only dualistic but also romantic, in the sense that in it woman appears more as an idea or fantasy than as a fellow human being of flesh and blood. According to Boff:

> The maternal potentiality impregnates all the fabrics of a woman's life. This is the dimension of receptivity, care and of being protected at home. Even though a woman would have no children, every woman is a mother, because it belongs to her to nurse and gestate.[192]

From the point of view of LT itself, 'to be protected at home' is not the situation of the majority of Latin American women. The reality certainly is that it 'belongs to her' to be responsible for the children. Nevertheless, this very reality is the major cause of the suffering of the poorest women, because on them alone depends the life of their children.

The praxis starting point in LT turns out to be quite empty regarding women. The ahistoricity of 'the feminine' (lo femenino) is visible in both traditional Mariology (not to speak of questions of sexual ethics) and LT. Even though 'the

---

191.   The Norwegian Catholic feminist theologian Kari Børresen speaks of 'socio-Mariology', by which she means that differences of attitude towards Mary seem to be determined more by socio-cultural than by confessional background. For her, as a Scandinavian Catholic, Mary means very little. She sees Mary as a contradiction of feminism. To make her a model for feminists is absurd if the essential ecclesiological and Mariological connection between femininity and subordination is ignored or not known. See Børresen 1983: 54-55.

192.   Boff 1980: 47.

feminine' could imply something of the characteristics listed by Boff, to be faithful to historicity and praxis, categories so central in LT, means starting with people's—in this case, women's—concrete reality and life conditions, not postulating them on an ontological level. This reality includes sexual violence, domestic violence and clandestine illegal abortions. 'The feminine' as a concept is by definition ahistorical and cannot reach the variety of realities faced by women of different times, cultures and realities.

Of course, this is not the entire and sole reality of women. To speak of the reality of especially the poorest women when it comes to work, to the survival of families and women's role in the community is to speak of what traditionally is considered as something 'masculine'. According to Boff, this is 'the movement towards transformation, aggressivity, transcendence, the capacity to command and project for the future'.[193] It is of extreme importance to take seriously what Latin American feminist liberation theologians call *la vida cotidiana*, everyday life, and its implications for LT. This means that liberation theologians should take feminist analysis (in theology as well as in other areas) seriously.

Boff aims at creating a Latin American Mariology that would be relevant and liberating for both women and men, as well as the socioeconomic situation of the continent. He fails to notice, though, that it is an extremely difficult project if one is not willing to break the old dualistic essentialism that traditional Mariology is built on. The binary sexual system on which Catholic anthropology is based on, according to which men and women are complementarily different, is the foundation of official Mariology, as well. The feminist emphasis on praxis takes human bodiliness, sexuality and the historical experiences of women seriously, and shows how these are often in clear contrast with 'femininity' exalted in theological anthropology and Mariology. It seems that exactly in these two, Latin American LT has been unable to challenge traditional teaching.[194] But, of course, if women's fate is tied to theological anthropology, on the one hand, and Mariology, on the other hand, in LT, this is a strong argument for the necessity of a critical feminist theological analysis of both.

In contrast with this view of Mary as somebody above and beyond all real women, it is interesting that feminist theologians both from the First World and Latin America seem to be aiming at the very opposite: finding a Mary that affirms and shares human womanhood. Even more, at least in women's everyday experiences, this very much *is* the image of the Mary of popular piety, in spite of the official teaching.[195]

Some of the Latin American feminist liberation theologians refer explicitly to Boff when criticizing certain traits of presenting women in LT. Leonor Aída Concha says of Boff's *El rostro materno de Dios*: 'My main preoccupation is that

193.   Boff 1987a: 67.
194.   M.P. Aquino notes that 'Until very recently the theme of women was dealt with in reflection upon Mary and in theological anthropology, but in neither case was it a discourse elaborated from the viewpoint of women's own understanding of faith' (Aquino 1992a: 113).
195.   See more about this in a cross-cultural context in Vuola 1993 and 1998.

when speaking of the maternal face of God, a valuation is introduced in which maternity appears as the only source of valuation of a woman. This happens without questioning the role of maternity experienced in the course of history among almost all peoples of the world'.[196] Boff's elaboration of 'feminine' and 'masculine' qualities is considered as sexist by two Brazilian theologians, Nancy Cardoso Pereira and Tania Mara Vieira Sampãio.[197] They also implicitly express a criticism of Boff when they state:

> We have to deconstruct the myth of a spirituality maintained by the negation of everyday life. [This spirituality] is based on celibacy, virginity, despiritualizing sexuality and maternity. The woman most directly included in the discourses on divinity and accepted as a symbol of spirituality was Mary—a mother deprived of her sexuality, exiled in virginity, addressed exclusively in the function of ministry and suffering and glory of the son.[198]

María Teresa Porcile Santiso pays attention to the same tension in Boff's thinking mentioned in the previous chapter. On the one hand, Boff speaks in favour of the ordination of women in the Catholic Church and the important role women play in the base communities. On the other hand, there is his mysterious and essentializing language concerning women on a more theological level. There is an obvious contradiction in his thinking between the theological (theoretical) and the pastoral (practical) level.[199]

There are male liberation theologians from other latitudes who have a more historicized view of Mary as well as of the relationships of Mariological reinterpretations to women's reality. The Sri Lankan Catholic theologian Tissa Balasuriya reworks the doctrine of original sin (which is behind the Marian doctrines, especially that of the Immaculate Conception) as anti-sexual and anti-woman, and its consequences (contempt for human maternity, celibacy and virginity as superior states of being, and the sanctification of masculine superiority).[200] Moreover, traditional Mariology has lacked a clear and systematic relationship to social transformation, which is exactly the same point I wanted to emphasize in my critique of Boff.[201]

According to Balasuriya, a new liberation theological Mariology has to be based on the actual and concrete experiences of individual human beings, especially of the poor women of the Third World. Thus, what is needed is the opposite of what Boff wants to do: to humanize, and not deify, Mary. The point of departure for this project can be found in the very concrete social, political, economic and sexual reality of the majority of the world's women, and more particularly, the poorest of them.

196.   Interviewed in Tamez 1989: 92-93.
197.   Tamez 1989: 111.
198.   Tamez 1989: 105.
199.   Porcile Santiso 1991: 72-74. I would add that the shortcomings at the theoretical level are reflected in the practical level, in the ahistorical and little practical understanding of (poor Latin American) women's everyday realities.
200.   Balasuriya 1990: 95, 98.
201.   Balasuriya 1990: 114.

3.4.3 *The Mary of Latin American Women*

Ivone Gebara and María Clara Bingemer describe how traditional Mariology speaks of Mary in 'feminine' terms, idealizing her on the basis of certain qualities said to be feminine, a determination which is made from a male point of view. A re-reading of Mary would entail a re-reading of the foundations of the patriarchal religious system.[202]

They also give certain assumptions for the re-reading of Marian dogmas, in order for them to be relevant in the Latin American context. First is the *anthropological assumption*, which aims at overcoming male-centrism, dualism, idealism and one-dimensionalism of traditional Western anthropology. Second, the *properly theological assumption* puts forward the idea of the Kingdom of God as being the unifying factor of Christian theology. It facilitates our seeing the potential of Marian dogmas for announcing the coming of the Kingdom of God. The *feminist assumption* implies a re-reading of the feminine concentrated in Mary. And fourth, the *pastoral assumption* starts from a Mary who is poor, dispossessed and simple, just like the Latin American poor whom she declared liberated in the *Magnificat*.[203] These assumptions lead Gebara and Bingemer to interpretations of the Marian dogmas quite different from those of Boff,[204] even though they also share many of the aspects of Boff's Mariology.

According to Gebara and Bingemer, the ecclesial base communities have a Mary which is present in the everyday life of the people. Besides heavenly mother, saint and compassionate, she is also seen as earthly sister, friend of the road (*compañera de camino*), mother of the oppressed, mother of the worthless. She is the protagonist and model for a new spirituality, born in the 'well' of life, in the sufferings and joys of Latin American people.[205]

The Mary of this theology of liberation is poor, prophetic and strong, mother of all, and she commits herself to justice and announcement of the Kingdom of God. The inspiration for this interpretation is found in the *Magnificat*:

> My soul magnifies the Lord, and my spirit rejoices in God my Savior, for he has regarded the low estate of his handmaiden. For behold, henceforth all generations will call me blessed; ... He has shown strength with his arm, he has scattered the proud in the imagination of their hearts, he has put down the mighty from their thrones, and exalted those of low degree; he has filled the hungry with good things, and the rich he has sent empty away.[206]

---

202.   Gebara and Bingemer 1989: 2. Even though not pointed out explicitly by the writers, what they say can easily be applied to Boff's Mariology.

203.   Gebara and Bingemer 1989: 91-93.

204.   Just to take an example of the doctrine of perpetual virginity, according to Gebara and Bingemer, 'far from limiting and reducing woman to sterility, far from denying her sexuality, the dogma of Mary's virginity forever declares a positive space where the Spirit of the Highest can repose and have a dwelling' (Gebara and Bingemer 1989: 107).

205.   Gebara and Bingemer 1991: 617.

206.   Lk. 1.46-53. Very few historical scholars believe that it was Mary herself who composed the text. See Brown *et al.* (eds.) 1978: 139-40.

In this text Mary appears in her traditional role as the symbol of the church. But what kind of a church? As an incarnation of the church, Mary represents a church that first of all is a community of the poor, the weak and the oppressed. Or, as Rosemary Ruether puts it, 'A poor woman of despised race is the head of the church'.[207] It is perhaps no coincidence that the Mariologist Boff has also been one of the strongest critics of the hierarchical and elitist model of the church.

Mary can be seen as the model of suffering motherhood,[208] but Latin American women also have this other Mary: poor like themselves, but elected by God, and whose personal suffering obtains a meaning and a horizon of hope in a larger socio-political context.[209]

It is interesting that both Leonardo Boff and Enrique Dussel have a more historical interpretation of Mary in the context of the *Magnificat*. As soon as 'the feminine principle' does not guide their interpretation, Mary becomes more concrete, more real and less isolated from human experience. When interpreting the Mary of the *Magnificat* as 'the liberating mother' and 'a prophetess committed to liberation' (Boff)[210] or 'free and liberating woman' and 'master of subversion' (Dussel),[211] they are also more in tune with the overall theological method of LT, giving priority to historical realities and the praxis.

According to M.P. Aquino, Mary is 'the paradigm of faith, prayer, and solidarity with all the oppressed and all women on earth'.[212] Referring to Boff, she says:

> Liberation theology from the perspective of women is now beginning to examine the figure of Mary in accordance with its own theological criteria for women's liberation. Current work does make certain key feminist points about the option for the poor, but it still moves in the context of the classical androcentric division between *the feminine* and *the masculine* and affirms Mary to be the feminine dimension of God.[213]

However, feminist liberation theology does not see Mary in terms of her feminine nature, in the roles of virgin, wife and mother. According to Aquino, in the base communities Mary is thought of not as an object of worship but as an active participant in liberation processes.[214] The stress is not on Mary's individual virtues but on her solidarity with the common project to create a new order. She is not seen exclusively in terms of her role as the mother of Jesus but in relation to God's reign that is bursting into history.[215]

---

207.   Ruether 1980: 21.
208.   See Marit Melhuus' interpretation later in this chapter.
209.   Gebara and Bingemer 1989: 163-64.
210.   Boff 1978: 70-71 and 1987a: 220-21.
211.   Dussel 1974a: 132-33.
212.   Aquino 1993a: 159. The chapter on Mary appears only in the English version of *Nuestro clamor por la vida*.
213.   Aquino 1993a: 172 (emphasis in original).
214.   Aquino 1993a: 173-74.
215.   Aquino 1993a: 175-76.

Aquino also stresses the same element in Mary that several other feminist theologians do, based on the actual experiences of ordinary women: Mary is not a heavenly creature but a woman like themselves who shares their lives as a comrade and sister in struggle.[216]

A central characteristic of the Latin American Mary is her quotidianness or ordinariness (*cotidianidad*). For example, one can see her images not only in every Catholic home, but also in women's hospitals and other places where women go to give birth. For a woman in labour, Mary is, on the one hand, a sister or mother with the same experience, and on the other hand, a divine figure whom one can ask for help in one of the most difficult situations in a woman's life. Mary can help even in birth pains. Thus, in women's everyday experience Mary shares and confirms but also transcends their experience. In the lived experience, Mary is 'she who listens to me', 'who understands me', 'she who suffered' and 'she who is a woman like myself'.[217]

The patroness of Costa Rica is the Virgin of Los Angeles, *La Negrita* ('Little Dark One') to the people. She is, materially, a tiny figure of a dark-skinned Mary in the basilica of Cartago, the former capital of the country. Around her cave-like sanctuary, the walls are covered by *exvotos*, miniature representations, mostly of metal, of different parts of the human body—legs, hands, eyes, lungs, even breasts and intestines—and trophies of soccer teams, anything that concretizes the every-day fears and hopes of the people. There are also several figures of the feminine pelvis, which may refer to infertility, fear of giving birth, maybe even clandestine abortions, against which there are posters on the columns of the same basilica.

Ivone Gebara and María C. Bingemer say: 'In the heart of the dialectical tension between anguish and hope, between love and pain, Mary and the Latin American people of the ecclesial base communities raise their prophetic cry to denounce injustices and to announce liberation'.[218]

Indirectly, the Virgin Mary, as one of the most powerful Latin American symbols, has also been taken up and reinterpreted by such non-feminist women's human rights movements as *Madres de Plaza de Mayo* (Argentina), *Grupo de Apoyo Mutuo* (Guatemala) and *COMADRES* (El Salvador). Their 'political mother-hood'[219] is a new form of the 'Suffering Mother' theme, universal but with special connotations in Latin America. These women are reclaiming a public space of resistance in extremely repressive and violent societies by openly

216. Aquino 1993a: 176-77. On the difficulty of changing the traditional image, a black Catholic Brazilian woman says: 'Mary as a woman who is white, virgin and mother, serene, delicate, straight and long hair, blue eyes, thin lips, a pious look on her face, young, slender, a halo on her head, with a white baby in her arms, submissive, who always says "yes"—never says "no". [...] For us black women, the church's image of Mary is a negation of our very being, a negation of our body' (Silvia Regina De Lima Silva's interview in Puleo 1994: 104).

217. These are all expressions that one can easily hear in conversations with Latin American Catholic women, especially women with children and difficult life situations—which can be of a continuous concrete experience of having nobody 'listening' or 'understanding'.

218. Gebara and Bingemer 1991: 617.

219. See Schirmer 1993: 61, and other articles in the same book.

mourning for their 'disappeared' children. But they do not just mourn, they also demand that those responsible for their children's fate must be judged. The feminine imagery of Catholicism guarantees them some, albeit limited, political and personal inviolability. Also, the very same symbolism that is used for repressive nationalism is given new critical meaning: the *Madres* question the private/public split by becoming 'subversive mothers'.[220] These women have taken the church and the state at their word. In trying to hold their families together, they have turned against the state the very symbols which the state claims to uphold and protect: motherhood and family. The church, with its long tradition of female obedience to and sacrifice for the family, has provided a basis for women's ability to challenge repressive regimes and exercise public power.[221]

In these women, several of the themes I have been dealing with come together, at least symbolically: Mary as the defender of the poor and oppressed, the identification of women with (the historical fate of) Mary, the suffering mother as a symbol with special meaning in Latin America, the controversiality of Mary as political and national(ist) symbol, and finally, the appropriation and reinterpretation of Mary by ordinary women in different social, cultural, religious and political situations. As a divine figure, Mary gives these women and their activities strength and transcendental hope.[222]

What is, then, the correlation between the veneration of Mary and the status of women in the church and in society? In the Protestant churches, the cult of Mary is not considered proper. The Marian doctrines are some of the obstacles in ecumenical dialogue. Nevertheless, it is the anti-Marian Protestant churches which have started to ordain women. It could be said that in countries with a strong veneration of Mary, the status of women is low, both in church and society.[223]

220.   Schirmer 1989: 25-26; Westwood and Radcliffe 1993: 18.
221.   Schirmer 1989: 26. She notes how the repressive state borrows heavily from Catholic ideology of familialism and in particular the image of woman as mother, as well as the family as the only proper sphere for women's conduct. It is the tension between competing ideologies of the repressive state and the Catholic Church which have provided the political space and language to these 'motherist' movements in Latin America (Schirmer 1989: 25-26).
222.   These human rights groups are a very interesting phenomenon among the social movements of Latin America. They consist predominantly (some exclusively) of women, mostly middle-aged and elderly, but they do not identify themselves with feminism or feminist groups. There are contradictory elements in their political practice, which probably explains why it is interpreted in conflicting ways by researchers. There are those who see them as reinforcing the traditional 'naturality' of women's roles as mothers; others see them as truly subversive when reinterpreting the most 'sacred' spaces (family, motherhood) in a new and concrete political way. As always, the truth may lie somewhere in between the two extremes. Recent investigation shows, though, that this sort of political activity by women often leads to 'gendered consciousness', be it formally labelled 'feminist' or not. One concrete reason for this may be that the repression faced by these groups is gender-specific, for example, in the form of rapes. See Schirmer 1993: 61-63.
223.   Campbell 1982: 21. It must be remembered, though, that a critical attitude is necessary when 'measuring' the status of women. This is of special importance in cross-cultural studies

According to M.P. Aquino,

> In the history of the Latin American church this [Mariological] tradition has been unable to eliminate the predominant machismo in our culture. *There is a convergence between the great reverence for Mary and the machista tendency of Latin American culture*, which the church itself has also helped to maintain. The theoretical and practical correspondence between these two phenomena is not accidental.[224]

Polarized sexual roles and idealization of the mother seem to be central traits in societies where women's social status is low.[225] These two characteristics are combined in the veneration of Mary. The reasons for this are probably very complicated. Michael P. Carroll gives us one explanation, at least from the male point of view, which of course is of special interest for this kind of study. According to his quite psychoanalytical arguments, the cult of Mary is at its strongest in regions such as Southern Italy and Spain, where one of the structuring factors of family is the lack or debility of the paternal figure. This is combined with exaggerated masculine behaviour (*machismo* complex, as he calls it) that demands aggressive or even violent sexual behaviour.[226] According to Carroll,

> The fervent devotion to the Mary cult on the part of the males is a practice that allows males characterized by a strong but strongly repressed desire for the mother to dissipate in an acceptable manner the sexual energy that is built up as a result of this desire.[227]

For an example of the female point of view, we could take Marit Melhuus, a Norwegian anthropologist, who has done research in Mexico, one of the most 'Marian' countries in the world. She sees the Virgin Mary, especially the Mexican Virgin of Guadalupe, as a symbol of maternity and suffering. According to Melhuus, there are at least two gender-specific and complementary moralities operating in Mexico, which she calls *machismo* and *marianismo*.[228] In a society which requires of women preservation of virginity (also in marriage, in the form of chastity) and of men the largest possible number of sexual conquests, the Virgin Mary can serve as a symbol in which this contradiction is reconciled. The Virgin of Guadalupe is the perfect incarnation of the ideal woman. An ordinary

---

when we speak of cultures that we actually cannot know from inside. This is why some Third World feminists are very critical of Western 'feminist imperialism', warning First World women about the danger of seeing Third World women only through the lenses of oppression and paternalism. See Mohanty 1991.

224.   Aquino 1993a: 172 (emphasis added).

225.   Campbell 1982: 21.

226.   Carroll 1986: 49-55.

227.   Carroll 1986: 56.

228.   There is a well-known and much-cited article by Evelyn P. Stevens called 'Machismo and Marianismo' (1973), from which these terms are probably taken even though Melhuus does not refer to her explicitly. On *marianismo* as the other side of *machismo* and as the cult of female spiritual superiority, see also Chaney 1979: 47; Fisher 1993: 3; Schirmer 1989: 25-26.

Some of Stevens' theses (for instance, how Latin American women seem to enjoy their martyrdom) are very stereotypical and reproduce what some Third World feminists have called 'the typical Third World woman' in the mentality of First World feminists.

woman sacrifices her virginity (since there is no other possibility for becoming a mother) and suffers shame. She can maintain her purity through chastity, even though she is no longer a virgin. Mary is perfect, but she too had to suffer on account of her son. These elements of maternity and suffering come together in one concept: suffering motherhood as the core of Mexican female identity.[229]

There is an article by Ivone Gebara in which she seems to be more critical of traditional popular devotion to Mary than in her earlier works. According to her, there is a rarely questioned 'dependence' on Mary which is seen as something positive and healthy. She wants to take a more critical attitude by asking if this 'dependence' can also sustain fatalism and lack of autonomy. There must be the possibility for a critical evaluation of the popular culture and religiosity, often promoted uncritically by sectors of the church committed to the defense of 'the popular'.[230]

According to Gebara, Mary of Nazareth is held captive by Mary Our Lady, who as a goddess of miracles is above all history and humanity. This view of Mary is sustained not only by the institutional church but by popular piety as well. Gebara says: 'In the category of a goddess, she [Mary] is distant from all the human beings, especially the women'.[231] She wants to historicize and humanize Mary, contrary to Leonardo Boff's Mariological project, for example.

It could be pointed out, though, that there are feminist Mariological interpretations which do not see Mary's divine nature in popular piety as a necessarily alienating factor. As I said earlier, it is her double character as both human and divine that women experience as both affirming their everyday experiences (as women) and transcendentalizing.[232] This image of Mary as being both close and distant, both 'like myself' (human) and 'above everybody else' (divine), is the core of the popular devotion of women in different cultures to Mary. I agree with Gebara that the popular religiosity should not be praised uncritically, but it is also true that it is exactly the 'grassroots' religiosity which has kept alive a tradition of exactly that human and historical Mary for which Gebara is looking.

According to Gebara and Bingemer,

> A Marian theology from the perspective of the Kingdom permits us to also perceive Mary's 'passion' for the poor, Mary's 'passion' for the justice of God, and through her, it is possible to recover the strength of the Spirit acting in women of all epochs. It is the recovering of the 'dangerous memory' or 'subversive memory' that is able to change things…and which makes a universal solidarity between women of the past, the present and the future possible.[233]

229.   Melhuus 1990: 58-60. This is a new and local interpretation of an old theme, the *Mater Dolorosa*.
230.   Gebara 1990: 137-40, 146.
231.   Gebara 1990: 145.
232.   See Vuola 1998.
233.   'Una teología mariana desde la perspectiva del reino permite percibir, también, la "pasión" de María por los pobres, la "pasión" de María por la justicia de Dios y, a través de ella, permite recuperar la fuerza del Espíritu actuante en las mujeres de todas las épocas. Es la recuperación de la "memoria peligrosa" o "memoria subversiva" capaz de cambiar las cosas…que

This critical but positive view is shared by Rosemary Ruether:

> Mariology becomes a liberating symbol for women only when it is seen as a radical symbol of a new humanity freed from hierarchical power relations, including that of God and humanity. It is here that the revolutionary side of the image of Mary appears, as the representative of the original and eschatological humanity that is repressed from existence within patriarchy, the culture of domination and subjugation.[234]

The feminist theological interest in Mary is international and ecumenical. This supports the notion that the official teaching and the negative image of women of the church have not been able to totally appropriate Mary. Independent of the doctrine, women have always given their own existential meanings to Mary.[235] Of course this does not negate the anti-female and anti-sexual anthropology mediated through her. Maybe it is this very tension that makes her such an interesting figure even for modern secularized women. Of course, it also reflects the high degree of ambiguity of Christianity vis-à-vis women today.

The search for a more human, more physical and more historical Mary has not produced alternative ways of thinking about sexual ethics in LT. Those who come closest are the theologians who emphasize the connection between theological anthropology and Mariology, and the necessity of seeing them through feminist theological analysis. This connection is not made explicit. Before closing this chapter, I want to point towards some possibilities of thinking about sexual ethics from Mariological reinterpretations in LT.

According to Elisabeth Schüssler Fiorenza, the myth of the virginal mother justifies the body-soul dualism of the Christian tradition. Whereas man in this tradition is defined by his mind and reason, woman is defined by her 'nature', that is, by her physical capacity to bear children. Motherhood, therefore, is the vocation of every woman regardless of whether or not she is a natural mother.[236]

---

permite que nazca y crezca una solidaridad universal entre las mujeres del pasado, del presente y del futuro' (Gebara and Bingemer 1991: 604).

234.   Ruether 1975: 58.

235.   See also Maeckelberghe 1989. She says, for example: ' "Mary" is, for women, always someone who is different from what the official statements and ideas might at first sight lead us to suspect... Women see "Mary" first and foremost as a woman and not as an exceptional being who is said to be both virgin and mother at the same time. "Mary" is, in other words, ...someone with whom they can speak as an equal, someone who knows their own difficulties... "Mary" is someone who resembles these women, someone who has experienced all that they have experienced and can therefore offer advice as a kind of maternal friend' (Maeckelberghe 1989: 125). This is in opposition to the male way of seeing her above all as an object that can be filled with all kinds of fantasies, which then has become the normative way of seeing her (Maeckelberghe 1989: 126).

236.   Fiorenza 1975: 622. In the same article, Fiorenza makes a reference to how Mary integrates aspects of the myth of the Great Mother Goddess. She does not mention that the virginal mother myth dates back to these ancient goddess mythologies. Thus, there are pre-Christian elements in it that cannot be reduced to the body-soul dualism of the *Christian* tradition. Also, if in the context of the goddesses, this virginal motherhood is not seen exclusively in negative terms, why should it be a totally destructive myth (for women) in the Christian image of Mary?

The mind-body dualism, its identification with male-female dualism, and their consequences in the Christian tradition have been widely documented and analysed by feminist theologians. In this early article, Fiorenza establishes a direct link between dualistic theological anthropology and (Catholic) sexual ethics: 'the official stance of the Roman Catholic Church on birth control and abortion demonstrates that woman in distinction from man has to remain dependent on her nature and is not allowed to be in control of her biological processes'.[237]

The critique of essentialism and dualism is central in feminist critique of traditional theological anthropology and Mariology in which Mary is seen as the perfect incarnation of 'femininity', defined in ontological opposition to 'masculinity', which again is taken as the normative humanity. This is what feminist theologians call androcentrism. Human masculinity is affirmed theologically whereas the female ideal represented by Mary, and only by her, is an impossible model for all women. The very same femininity that is exalted beyond earthly limits in Mary is the only obstacle to women's being ordained (in the Catholic Church). Since masculinity and femininity are understood as God-given and natural essences, they cannot be changed.

Against this essentialism, logically leading to two distinct anthropologies, one male and another female, Ivone Gebara and Maria Clara Bingemer say: 'The meaning of a feminine, or more precisely, a feminist anthropology, is closely connected to the historic moment in which women's consciousness is breaking out into awareness of their age-old oppression.'[238] This emphasis on the historical realities of women, their experiences of both oppression and liberation, is central in Latin American feminist liberation theology.[239] As was stated earlier, the concept *vida cotidiana* reflects well this more epistemologically, ethically and politically based women's perspective, over against romanticizing, essentializing and ahistorical definitions of 'femininity'. As such, it has direct consequences in the area of sexual ethics as well.

At the centre of the classical doctrine of incarnation, of God becoming human, is a woman who conceives, is pregnant, gives birth and becomes a mother. But not like any other woman. She must even have an asexual origin herself in order to be 'taintless' and 'pure'. The classical incarnation theology is actually contrary to incarnation. Jesus is 'conceived by the Holy Spirit' (without a sexual act) and 'born of the Virgin Mary' (perpetual virginity: before, at the moment and after the birth of Jesus) without pain (punishment to all other women because of Eve). No

237. Fiorenza 1975: 622.
238. Gebara and Bingemer 1989: 14. The distinction between the feminine and the feminist is crucial, even though made quite lightly here. See Tong 1993 for differences between feminine and feminist ethics and Alvarez 1990 for different ways in which gender becomes politicized (in Latin America).
239. '…our exploration in Marian theology does not highlight the qualities of Mary/woman, qualities idealized and projected from different needs and cultures, but rather aims at a re-reading of Mary from the needs of our age, and especially from the insights provided by the awakening of women's historical consciousness' (Gebara and Bingemer 1989: 16).

wonder, thus, that the biggest difficulty in Marian reinterpretations has been at the level of sexuality and sexual ethics. It is exactly the area where, by definition, no woman can be like Mary. Her fertility and maternity are not affirmations of human nature. But if it is true that women have a relationship to Mary which goes beyond these doctrinal limitations and in which they experience her as an understanding and affirming mother/sister/friend, it implies the possibility for a Mariology that would be affirmative of human sexuality, maternity and all the contradictions they entail.

The previously presented feminist interpretations of Mary, especially in the Latin American context, all point towards this possibility. Actually, an alternative sexual ethics, thought especially from the perspective of the poor women, is one logical consequence of such 'liberation Mariologies'. There are cultural, political and theological reasons why it has not been done.

3.5 Conclusions

The dialogue between Latin American LT and feminist liberation theology has, until now, very much centred on the inclusion of women in the concept of the poor, on the one hand, and on the critique of both the implicit and explicit images of women present in LT, on the other hand. Feminist liberation theologians' critique aims at challenging and deepening some of the most central methodological claims of LT, such as starting from the praxis and giving the poor a priority in theology as active subjects.

The problem in this dialogue has been both its certain superficiality and the avoiding of some important issues. The two issues are interdependent. The limited space open to feminist reflection within Latin American LT is subject to the same ecclesiastical and political pressure as any critical theology within the existing churches, especially the Catholic Church. After the political changes on the continent, direct political pressure on or repression of theologians is rare. Instead, several theologians have suffered from pressure from the church hierarchy.

Latin American feminist liberation theologians both agree with and depart from their male colleagues. They place their work in the overall framework of LT. They are asking LT to take seriously its central methodological claims. In a way, the feminist critique reveals that liberation theologians are really not doing what they claim to do: to start from the praxis of the poor and give the poor primacy as subjects of theology.

Leonardo Boff and Enrique Dussel are those male liberation theologians who have written more extensively and explicitly on women. Much of what they say is implicitly present in other liberation theologians' work, as well. The analysis of their thinking seems to point towards certain difficulties in LT's overall capacity to include feminist issues.

There is a tension between their explicit condemnations of sexism, in both the church and society, and their conceptual framework, which draws heavily on traditional Catholic teaching, especially concerning theological anthropology.

Conscious even of the shortcomings of a dualist anthropology, Boff himself very much reproduces it, as we have seen.[240]

The tension stems from two different sources. First, both Dussel and Boff apply a conceptual framework and have philosophical presuppositions in the area of theological anthropology which seem to contrast with their stated overall theological methodology. Second, there is an apparent lack of knowledge of feminist writing (especially in theology and ethics) in Dussel and Boff, although this material is available and both of them carry on a dialogue with other non-Latin American theorists. There is a whole tradition of feminist (theological) research done even inside Latin America.

It seems that those male liberation theologians who are most sensitive to feminist issues and who understand that the present situation is neither 'natural' nor equal get into trouble when they go beyond the most obvious level. It is exactly here where they could make use of feminist theorizing. This is the pivotal point for LT right now: there are new subjectivities, including women, who define what LT is to be in the future.

In the light of our two examples, it seems that the fact that somebody takes up women and feminism as issues does not necessarily imply any critical reinterpretation of them. It rather reflects the phase in LT which Ruether calls 'mere inclusion' of women and women's concerns. Women are taken as a homogeneous category to be added to the list of the oppressed, but since no feminist analysis is implemented, the possibilities for critical reinterpretations are left out.

As we have seen, the praxis starting point is the most central methodological claim liberation theologians make. They wish to reject idealistic and essentialist explanations of history and see it as a process open to human agency. They claim that it has been the cardinal sin of theologians to underestimate history as the central space for both human and divine action.

This methodology seems to be functioning in LT in all other areas of theology except theological anthropology, especially when the collective poor are translated into concrete human beings with gender, race, individual life histories and conflicting interests. Liberation theologians' sharp economic, political and religious critique has been possible because of the constant emphasis on praxis. Nevertheless, their concentration on macro-level issues or ones defined as such (sexism and racism certainly are macro-level issues, too) has made it possible for them not to apply this overall methodology in areas reduced to the more 'private' sphere.

This is exactly what feminist liberation theologians mean by the epistemological challenge of feminism and feminist theology to LT. The conflict between

---

240. 'The experience of women doesn't exist in the official discourse of the church, which is celibate, machista, patriarchal. And unfortunately the church isn't overcoming these differences but reproducing them—man/woman, cleric/non-cleric, inside/outside—always dualist! For me, this dualism betrays the utopia of Jesus' (Boff in Puleo 1994: 176). Men have to learn to listen to women (Boff in Puleo 1994: 177). It is ironical, compared to this overall (implicit) openness to feminism, that Boff himself, when writing on women and femininity, does not seem to listen to what women have to say about it.

praxis and theory in LT itself has been one of major feminist critiques. If liberation theologians want to take the praxis as seriously as they say they do, they should pay special attention to a critique which claims the classical liberation theological definition of praxis to be too reduced, and as such, prevent seeing the complicated reality of interrelated forms of oppressions.

It is also interesting that whereas the poor as a category are not defined by their 'real' difference as an oppressed group but as victims of historical realities—thus changeable—liberation theologians' analyses of gender issues take binary, even dualistic, gender differences as a starting point.

This kind of essentializing way of approaching questions of sexism and women in LT is in clear contrast with the more historical and practical method in other issues. The use of social sciences in theological analysis does not cover the research done on the history, character and critique of sexism. The idealized and uncritical way of speaking of femininity and masculinity makes it difficult to speak of real men and women, the uneven power structures between them, and, concomitantly, of issues of sexual ethics—all this being what Latin American feminist liberation theologians refer to broadly as *vida cotidiana*.

The woman appears in liberation theological texts, generally speaking, as one who is triply oppressed even though the character and nature of this triple oppression is not elaborated much further. In the case of Boff and Dussel, and even more so for the former, the woman appears as an idea or fantasy, an idealized being, even as a mystery, and not so much a fellow human being of flesh and blood. *This romanticizing image of woman becomes a serious ethical issue if it prevents speaking of the real-life conditions of women, especially poor women*. This is apparently a serious lack in a theology that claims that it *starts* from the real-life conditions of the people and makes ethical demands an essential part of both its epistemology and praxis.[241]

The ahistoricity of 'the feminine' (*lo femenino*) may partly explain the lack of sexual ethical elaborations in LT. To be faithful to historicity and praxis—categories so central in LT—would mean starting with people's—in this case, women's—concrete reality and life conditions, and not postulate them to an ontological level.[242] This is what Latin American feminist theologians mean when

---

241. According to B.W. Harrison, 'A central contention of a feminist theological analysis is that the suppression of women and women's status as property of men are dialectically related to the mystification of women's "nature". Whenever it is claimed that women are "opposite" or "complementary" to men in their human nature, whether or not the implication is that women are therefore best suited to reproductive and domestic functions, such mystification is at work' (Harrison 1985: 241). This analysis, taken together with the critique of (gender) dualism, is a 'standard' feminist theological starting point and appears, in one form or other, in all feminist theologians quoted in this research.

242. On this, Harrison says: 'The pseudo-objective use of the vague sexual dualisms "femininity" and "masculinity" will always reappear in a political counterattack against women's demands for full, uncompromised social, political, and economic justice, which is why "femininity" and "masculinity" are notions we must learn to live without' (Harrison 1985: 34). She claims that 'All assumptions of essential, or ontic, difference will be as tainted by past oppression

translating the option for the poor as an option for the poor woman. The kind of perspective on gender issues that Dussel and Boff have in a contradictory way prevents them from dealing with more concrete issues that shape poor women's realities, such as reproductive issues.

Traditional theological (especially Catholic) anthropology and seemingly new reinterpretations of it (Dussel and Boff) which actually presuppose the foundational dualistic categories of femininity and masculinity do not offer adequate tools for understanding the specific problems of Latin American women, especially the poorest of them.

From a feminist perspective, all the central concepts traditionally used of the 'subjects of liberation theology', such as the poor, the Other, and the new historical subject, seem to have the same kind of limitations. They all both start from and refer to a metaphysical rather than historical reality. Even when more historically rooted, such as 'the poor', the concept is too vague and homogeneous to address the multiplicity of *the real realities of the poor*. It is too bound to its origin as primarily a class concept. What all these concepts also have in common is that the supposed subjects are really no subjects at all. Somebody is naming them as such. What makes feminist claims different from all these, is that there is an oppressed subject voicing *her own oppression*, albeit also in a limited way. This is why feminist theologians prefer to speak of feminist theologies and feminisms in the plural, as well as of the multiplicity of women's experiences. Starting from the very concrete lived realities is seen as the best guarantee for an open and self-critical process. This is where we come back to LT and its notions of the importance and primacy of praxis.

The application of the overall praxis approach to gender issues as well and a critical elaboration of the concept itself, in dialogue with feminist theories of gender, would create room for a critical discussion of sexual ethics from a liberation theological perspective. At the same time, this would concreticize the emphasis on *vida cotidiana* by Latin American feminist liberation theologians and give it new critical meanings, almost non-existent until today.

It seems that the great difficulty in addressing women and feminism in LT lies in the disconnection between theory and praxis. On a more theoretical level, the oppression of women is acknowledged and the need for their liberation stated. This is true nowadays for practically all liberation theologians; Dussel is an exception only in dealing with the issue more extensively. When the move towards more practical questions is made, feminism—that is, women as subjects of their own liberation—is discredited, and 'woman' translates into 'femininity'.

In the context of LT, which critically reinterprets the Catholic tradition, a critical analysis of the anthropological presuppositions of one's theology seems to be of special difficulty for liberation theologians, too.

---

as all our concepts and languages are. The history of the subjugation of women is a *social history* that must be changed... What we must protest is not neglect of femininity but the exclusion of concrete female experience, female modes of being, and women's culture' (Harrison 1985: 31 [emphasis in original]).

Many liberation theologians, both men and women, Catholic and Protestant, seem to analyse gender questions in the context of Mariology. Even though traditional notions of sexuality and sexual ethics are at the centre of Mariology, the search for new Mariological interpretations in LT has not produced alternative ways of thinking about sexual ethics. Nevertheless, Latin American feminist liberation theologians' central concept *vida cotidiana*, when taken together with feminist interpretations of Mary and women's concrete, living relationship to Mary, points towards the possibility of thinking about sexual ethics from the perspective of Latin American (poor) women. A new theological anthropology is necessary for this task.

Ivone Gebara—the leading feminist Mariologist in Latin America—has been the first well-known liberation theologian, male or female, to defend the decriminalization of abortion (in certain situations) in public. In an interview, prior to her public announcement on abortion and the following ecclesiastical correction process, she said about the future of LT:

> From a feminist perspective, we need to keep working on the anthropological vision of liberation theology... Their [male liberation theologians'] anthropological perspective is male-centered. They include women, but women are never the starting point... Latin American liberation theology is done absolutely within the limits of the Catholic tradition, which is fundamentally male-centered. People don't break with this tradition, because to do so they'd have to touch upon things like power—power exercised by priests, bishops, the Pope. And touching this power is dangerous. I have a feeling it's not going to be the men who touch it, but the women.[243]

Issues of sexuality and sexual ethics seem to be sensitive in almost any given culture and especially in religious contexts. These issues have been critically analysed from women's point of view mainly as a consequence of a feminist movement and feminist theorizing. This is especially true in feminist studies of religion, because of the intimate connection between religious ideals and power and a culture's moral codes. These different factors have become reality in Latin America only in recent years, in spite of the long presence of a secular feminist movement.

Most liberation theologians, both male and female, agree (at least as private individuals) that there is an apparent need for new perspectives on sexual ethics in Latin America. This is especially true within the Catholic Church, which has a considerable amount of political, social and moral power in issues of sexual ethics almost everywhere on the continent. What I aim to do in the following chapter is to open up room for a critical and constructive dialogue between LT and religious feminists on issues of sexual ethics, based on what has been said in earlier chapters.

---

243.   Quoted in Puleo 1994: 211-13. In the same interview, she admits that this fear of breaking with the tradition is also visible in Latin American women theologians' writing, including her own (Puleo 1994: 213).

Chapter 4

Sexual Ethics and Liberation Theology

4.1 Moral Theology in Liberation Theology

In this chapter, I am not going to analyse the history of Christian sexual ethical teaching, nor am I going to go through the official Catholic teaching on sexual ethics. These have been done in several other contexts.[1] Considering the scope and purpose of this research, I will not argue for an alternative sexual ethics, either, although I claim that there is a necessity for such elaborations within LT. However, it is the liberation theologians themselves who should do it in their own context.

What I will do in this chapter is point out certain lacunae in LT and possibilities for filling them with critical but constructive alternatives. I will first go through the scant explicit material on sexual ethics, especially reproductive ethics, in the context of Latin American LT (4.1.1), then ask why this area of theology has been neglected in LT, deliberately or not, and what consequences this omission possibly has (4.1.2). There will be a definite emphasis on Catholic liberation theologians. Neither Protestant nor Catholic liberation theologians give sexual ethics much importance. Those who do, even to a limited extent, are Catholics. This is especially true of the male liberation theologians. It may be that, since the Catholic Church is globally so much more vocal and authoritative in issues of sexual ethics in comparison to most Protestant denominations, Catholic liberation theologians feel more necessity to deal with the issue. The social and political influence of the Catholic Church in Latin America is especially clear today in issues of sexual ethics. Direct ecclesiastical intervention in legislation is not rare, not to speak of the overall moral and political weight the church has, especially among ruling elites.

When speaking of sexual ethics, I refer mainly to questions concerning *reproductive rights* (not to marriage, divorce, sexuality in general, and so on). Reproductive rights as a concept was originally formulated by women activists or, more precisely, women's groups involved with health issues like reproductive health. The Women's Global Network for Reproductive Rights has defined reproductive rights as women's right to decide whether, when and how to have children—

---

1.   See Fox 1995; Harrison 1983; Ranke-Heinemann 1988.

regardless of nationality, class, ethnicity, race, age, religion, disability, sexuality or marital status—in the social, economic and political conditions that make such decisions possible.[2] The struggle for reproductive rights also contains a radical critique of patriarchal society and the dominant development model. Reproductive rights are human rights inseparable from other basic rights.[3] Feminists are united in their insistence that the moral agency of women seeking to shape their procreative lives must be respected.[4]

4.1.1 *Liberation Theologians and Sexual Ethics*
It was stated in Chapter 1.3.3 that Latin American LT could be seen as an intent to bridge dogma and morality, faith and Christian praxis. Even though there is really no distinctive ethical theory in LT, the central questions of LT are of an ethical nature. Thus, in an ideal situation, faith and ethics would not be separate. Theological reflection in itself would be an ethical act.

Those few Latin American theologians who consider themselves ethicists in the liberation theological context affirm this. According to Francisco Moreno Rejón,

> It is not exaggerated to affirm that in its disposition as well as in its methodology, [liberation theology] is the most moral of all theologies. In effect, on the one hand, it requires of the theologian the commitment to reflect from and on the praxis of Christian life. On the other hand, its methodology postulates the praxis as the starting point and as the goal of the hermeneutical circle. Therefore, we are faced with a theology in which the ethical connotations are something substantial and not merely peripheral derivations.[5]

According to Moreno Rejón, most Latin American moral theologians share the basic methodology and theses of LT.[6] The perspective of the poor is the starting point for any ethical theory within LT as well.[7] The option for the poor means incorporating the poor, the non-persons, as the preferential interlocutors in the theological-moral reflection.[8] Similarly, the three levels of liberation outlined by Gutiérrez are also central in the 'ethics of liberation'.[9] According to Bernardo Cuesta, an ethics of liberation does not differ from other forms of ethics as much in its themes as it does in its perspective.[10]

2.   Dutting 1993: 2.
3.   Dutting 1993; Petchesky 1995: 153.
4.   Andolsen 1996: 249. There are plenty of works done on reproductive issues from a feminist ethical—and also theological—perspective.
5.   Moreno Rejón 1991: 275. Similarly, see Cuesta 1987: 599; Moser 1984: 258; Vidal 1991.
6.   Moreno Rejón 1991: 277.
7.   'La ética de liberación afirma expresamente el lugar desde donde se elabora, esto es, su punto de vista, su situación y también cuál es su interlocutor, o sea, su toma de posición. Esto es lo que significa la expresión la *perspectiva del pobre*: explícitamente se pretende mirar la realidad desde el lugar y con los ojos del pobre' (Moreno Rejón 1991: 281 [emphasis in original]).
8.   Moreno Rejón 1991: 282; Cuesta 1987: 605.
9.   Moreno Rejón 1991: 283.
10.   Cuesta 1987: 612.

At least in those ethicists who explicitly affirm their affinities with LT, it is difficult to trace any clear difference between LT as fundamental theology and a specific ethical theory. Instead, they are making the ethical claims of LT more explicit and more systematic. Nevertheless, according to Marciano Vidal,

> It is possible to speak of an 'ethics of liberation', understood as a theological-moral discourse on the ethical implications of the liberating praxis of the Christians. It is not necessary to underline that this 'ethics of liberation' is nourished by the great theological orientations born of LT.[11]

It is almost impossible to find any explicit reference to issues of sexual ethics in the general presentations of the 'ethics of liberation'. The ethicists inside LT thus follow the general logic of LT, discussed in previous chapters, in which the poor do not appear as reproductive, gendered beings, nor are the implications of poverty to women discussed.

In a book which claims to be a systematic treatment of moral theology from the perspective of liberation theology, the pages which refer to sexuality or issues of sexual ethics add up to five, under the title 'the idol of pleasure', among other 'modern idolatries'.[12] The writers criticize the 'renewed morality' in recent Catholic moral theory of its personalism and individualism, social conservatism and being primarily applicable to the First World.[13] In contrast, even though a Latin American approach in moral theory is still in a fairly embryonic stage, its starting points are 'the impoverished as new social agents and their main problems'.[14] Moser and Leers ask, 'What are the moral problems raised by the irruption of the poor?'[15] Their answer is of a rather abstract nature: 'It is a question of redressing the balance, bringing the problems of the impoverished to the fore as well, making sure that all moral problems are approached in a fairer way'.[16] These specific problems of the impoverished include hunger, disease, lack of education, the struggle for land and housing, and unemployment.[17] The writers do not mention reproductive issues and how poverty may intensify problems having to do with reproduction.

There is a certain lack of concreteness in the book. How, in the end, does the 'liberative' moral theology differ from traditional Catholic moral theology? This is especially true in the short section on sexual ethics where pleasure (not necessarily or merely sexual) is portrayed as an idol and 'consumer good'. In other sections of the book, 'modern Western society' with its hedonism and individualism is usually contrasted with the totally different social reality of Latin America. In the section on pleasure, the writers nevertheless take the 'complication of the normal pattern of human relationships' produced by modern society as *the* sexual

11. Vidal 1991: 399-400.
12. Moser and Leers 1990: 193-97.
13. Moser and Leers 1990: 44-49.
14. Moser and Leers 1990: 59.
15. Moser and Leers 1990: 51.
16. Moser and Leers 1990: 61.
17. Moser and Leers 1990.

problem of Latin America. Nothing is said of the reality of illegal abortions and the high rates of domestic violence and households headed by women, which are some of the most burning problems for Latin American women.

The other author of the above-mentioned book, Antônio Moser, a Brazilian Franciscan brother, has an article on sexuality in the 'Summa' of LT (*Mysterium Liberationis*, in which all the classical themes of theology are dealt with from a liberation theological perspective).[18] In reality, there is very little in the article which would explain how LT proposes a different perspective or different sexual ethics from that of mainstream Catholic teaching. In the affirmation of the goodness of sexuality as God's gift,[19] in the concern for sexual liberty,[20] and in the critique of the most negative attitudes towards human sexuality in the history of theology[21] is nothing especially new. According to Moser, LT could offer a socio-political aspect in the discussion on sexuality.[22]

What are these socio-political dimensions of sexuality which LT could help to illuminate? First of all, according to Moser, sexual instrumentalization and alienation are results of an ideology which aims at keeping large proportions of people in the margins of decision processes (sexuality in the service of social and political status quo).[23] The commercialization of sex, especially of the female body, is another aspect of this ideological manipulation of sexuality.[24] Further, there are other problems, such as the campaigns in favour of birth control which use the 'ghost of demographic explosion' as an excuse for all kinds of brutalities— indiscriminate distribution of contraceptives, mass sterilizations, and incentives to abortion.[25] There are hidden ideological reasons behind these campaigns: they are directed to certain races and the most impoverished people. According to Moser,

> The secret presupposition is that these races and the most impoverished sectors of society, which are predominantly concentrated in the Third World, are those responsible for the economic, social and political problems. This is why they have to be decimated in a skilled and progressive manner. With this, the real problem, located in the unjust distribution of goods, remains in the shadow.[26]

According to him, another ideological dimension of the instrumentalization of sex is sexual liberation. 'Presenting virginity as a taboo, marriage as a thing of the past, forms part of this same ideological game', says Moser. The more the

18. Moser 1991.
19. Moser 1991: 112-13.
20. Moser 1991: 109.
21. Moser 1991: 114-15.
22. Moser 1991: 119-20.
23. Moser 1991: 121.
24. Moser 1991.
25. 'Blandiendo el fantasma de la "explosión demográfica" y de la consiguiente falta de recursos para atender a las necesidades básicas de todos, se señala el control sistemático de la natalidad como única salida. Y para garantizarlo, todos los medios se consideran válidos: desde la distribución indiscriminada de cualquier tipo de anticonceptivos, hasta la esterilización en masa y el incentivo al aborto' (Moser 1991).
26. Moser 1991: 121-22.

impoverished masses are 'distracted with sex', the less there is the possibility for a protest against unjust economic, social and political structures. He also states that 'As long as sex is one of the idols of the masses, nothing more profound can succeed in terms of restructuration [sic] of society'.[27] According to the analysis of Moser, speaking of 'sexual integration' or 'self-realization' to the poor is empty, since their problems have much more to do with mere survival.[28]

Much of what Moser says is in perfect mutual agreement with official Catholic teaching on sexual ethics. The praxis starting point of LT in the context of sexual ethics is not used for an analysis of uneven power structures (except in terms of Third World/First World inequity), sexual and domestic violence, machismo, or the real reproductive realities of poor women, including the lack of access to safe birth control and the high rate of illegal abortions.[29]

Of the most well-known liberation theologians, presented in previous chapters, only a few take up issues of sexual ethics and/or sexuality at all. As was said earlier, Enrique Dussel is exceptional among liberation theologians in speaking explicitly on issues of sexual ethics. As we saw, his Catholic background is reflected in how he theorizes sexual difference (masculinity/femininity). It seems that in issues of sexual ethics, too, he comes close to official church teaching, even though his argumentation may be different from that of the Vatican. There have also been changes in his thinking.

Even though not always explicitly stated, Dussel's ethical system presupposes heterosexuality as the normal and normative human sexuality. Dussel has a negative understanding of homosexuality as a 'totality' in which men are not men nor women women.[30] His rejection of homosexuality is combined with a rejection of feminism, defined as something that undoes the natural difference between male and female, leading to a homosexual definition of the erotic relationship.[31] Thus, 'The most extreme feminism, born and bred in the opulent North Atlantic world, interprets sexuality from Totality'.[32] Undoing the difference, this extreme feminism proposes homosexual autoeroticism in which nobody depends on anyone. This could mean lesbianism, elimination of maternity, as well as individualism and hedonism. Thus, it is the counterpart of machismo.[33] Homosexuality is 'indifferentiation' which cannot be the aim of erotic liberation.[34] He even says that 'Feminist homosexuality ends up summing up all

27.   Moser 1991: 122.

28.   Moser 1991: 123.

29.   I will deal with these realities more specifically in Chapter 4.2.2. They are issues that have been extensively dealt with by various women's organizations and feminist researchers all over the world.

30.   Dussel 1985: 97-98 and 1990: 25-26.

31.   Dussel 1990: 25.

32.   Dussel 1988: III, 116.

33.   Dussel 1988: III, 116-17.

34.   Dussel 1988: III, 117.

perversions'; it is, among other things, 'radical loss of sense of the reality of the Other and total schizophrenia'.[35]

In a later text, in which Dussel wants to make a critical evaluation of his philosophy of liberation, looking backwards, he presents a somewhat different view on homosexuality. He states that a homosexual person 'must be respected in the dignity of his/her personality'.[36] He seems to depart from his earlier understanding of the impossibility of encountering the Other in a homosexual relation, 'the Other' being defined exclusively in terms of heterosexual, genital sexual difference. There is the possibility of respect for the Other in a homosexual relationship, too. Nevertheless, he considers homosexuality as well as abortion situations of 'minor evil', which as such is an exception among the liberation theologians.[37]

When it comes to contraception and abortion, Dussel does not directly condemn them in the official Catholic way. Nevertheless, in his *Filosofía de la liberación*, he speaks of filicide, child murder, as alienation. The liberation of woman makes it possible that 'the couple permits the appearance of offspring'.[38] He also says that 'The child is the exteriority of all erotics, its metaphysical surpassing, its real fulfillment'.[39] Similarly, he says:

> the couple can again totalize itself, close itself in a hedonism without transcendence, without fecundity... The totalized couple negates the child because it invades as the Other who provokes to justice, interpellates for distinct rights and relaunches the couple into real history, responsible and fertile. The couple, because of its 'pulsation to totalization', would like to make its voluptuousity [*sic*] eternal without third parts.[40]

This is actually quite clearly the official Catholic position that sexual pleasure without the possibility of procreation is morally wrong. According to Dussel, *normal and human sexuality* is openness to a child. Fecundity is the seal of love.[41]

Although it does not become totally clear what Dussel means by all this, it is possible to read it, in the context of his general framework, as a rather traditional Catholic view.[42] In particular, together with his overall anti-imperialist tone

---

35. '...la homosexualidad feminista termina por sumar todas las perversiones, es la univocidad total de la sexualidad, es pérdida radical del sentido de la realidad (una esquizofrenia completa) del Otro, es el final solipsismo del *ego* cartesiano o europeo' (Dussel 1988: 117).

36. Dussel 1992a: 407.

37. Dussel 1992a: 407-408.

38. Dussel 1985: 102-103.

39. 'El hijo es la exterioridad de toda erótica, su superación metafísica, su cumplimiento real' (Dussel 1985: 107).

40. '...la pareja puede nuevamente totalizarse, cerrarse en un hedonismo sin trascendencia, sin fecundidad... El hijo es negado por la pareja totalizada porque viene a irrumpir como el Otro que pro-voca a la justicia, interpela por derechos dis-tintos y relanza a la pareja a la historia real, responsable, fecunda. La pareja, por la "pulsión de totalización", querría eternizar su voluptuosidad sin terceros' (Dussel 1988: III, 118).

41. Dussel 1988: III, 119.

42. Ofelia Schutte also pays attention to this: 'Despite his controversial and radical rhetoric, especially in the sphere of politics, Dussel's ethical principles do not contradict the magisterium

(Latin American and the Third World representing the Other in need of liberation), these 'pro-life' types of announcements come close to the official statements of Latin American Catholic bishops at their latest conference, in Santo Domingo in 1992. The bishops speak—in a modified language adopted from LT—of *contraceptive imperialism* (*imperialismo anticonceptivo*) against Latin America, of which women are the principal victims.[43] This is similar to Moser's view of 'decimating' poor peoples with the help of aggressive birth control campaigns.

In his earlier texts, Dussel mentions abortion explicitly only in the context of child murder:

> The physical or cultural death of the child is pedagogical alienation. The child is killed in the womb of the mother by abortion or in the womb of the people by cultural repression. This repression, evidently, will always be carried out in the name of freedom, and by means of the best pedagogical methods.[44]

In 1992, Dussel revised some of his earlier theses on abortion. There are two absolute rights—the right of the woman to her personality and body and the right of the new being to life—confronting each other. This dilemma can be solved through the old doctrine of 'minor evil'. Dussel bases his reasoning on the ethical responsibility of the woman as moral subject, who has the primary responsibility of decision.[45] Here he comes close to many feminist ethicists, who claim that it is the inability to see the woman as a moral subject which is behind an absolute condemnation of abortion. Thus, the critique presented by Ofelia Schutte is not totally justified when she says, 'He [Dussel] has equated abortion with murder (filicide)'.[46] As we saw, this reading is possible, but it is not the dogmatic stance of Dussel, whatever we think of his general reasoning on issues of sexual ethics.

According to my estimation, it is Dussel's overall unproblematized and uncritical use of such central concepts as the Other, alterity, difference, femininity and masculinity, and so on, which produces both the incoherence and anti-feminism in his ethics. Traditional Catholic teaching, especially in issues of sexual ethics,

---

or teaching authority of the Roman Catholic Church' (Schutte 1991: 277). Schutte's general estimation of Dussel is that he cannot be seen as a critical or progressive thinker, and this is especially true of his view of women. In that respect, Dussel's theory 'is as conservative as traditional patriarchal thought' (Schutte 1991: 284).

43.   *Nueva evangelización, promoción humana, cultura cristiana* 1992: 62.

44.   'La muerte física o cultural del hijo es la alienación pedagógica. Al hijo se lo mata en la vientre de la madre por el aborto o en el vientre del pueblo por la represión cultural. Esta represión, es evidente, se efectuará siempre en nombre de la libertad y con los mejores métodos pedagógicos' (Dussel 1985: 108). And, 'en conclusión la maldad del pro-yecto erótico, por su propia totalización, significa alienación del Otro (la mujer en nuestra sociedad machista), y, metafísicamente infecundidad (muerte del hijo, sea por no desearlo, sea por abortarlo ...). En cambio, la bondad erótica se despliega como servicio del Otro (en especial liberación de la mujer), y por apertura que esto significa y en esa misma apertura la bondad es *fecundidad*' (Dussel 1988: III, 108 [emphasis in original]).

45.   Dussel 1992a: 407.

46.   Schutte 1988–89: 64, referring to Dussel 1985; 1987 and 1988. In 1993, Schutte, too, recognizes a 'modification to some extent' in Dussel's views (Schutte 1993: 202).

apparently has a strong influence on his thinking. In his later texts, he nevertheless seems to be more aware of his earlier political conservatism and its possible consequences.

Dussel is an example of an overall rhetoric approval of women's liberation as part of the larger liberation project of Latin America (even though, as we saw, his artificial distinction between women's liberation and feminism is not what Latin American feminists would appreciate) but when put face-to-face with the concrete living conditions of women—and feminist theory and practice—his thinking appears abstract and contradictory, if not conservative. According to Schutte—and here I agree with her—'The process of appealing to the logic of exteriority can easily constitute an evasion when it comes to analysing the actual social relations of domination and the corresponding struggles for freedom found in human existence'.[47]

As we saw in the chapter on Mariology, Leonardo Boff comes closest to dealing with sexual ethical issues in the context of his reinterpretations of Mary. He is not as explicit as Dussel. He, too, deliberately or not, seems to presuppose much of his Catholic heritage, especially in questions of theological anthropology. In Boff, even more than in Dussel, the contradiction between the overall praxis starting point and the abstract character of his reasoning in theological anthropology and male–female relationships is notable. Issues of sexual ethics and women's realities are not analysed from their own practical perspective but rather derived from theological and philosophical abstractions.

In Boff's earlier writings, when he was still a priest, he claimed that celibacy is one concrete form of living out one's sexuality. Celibacy does not imply renunciation of love; to the contrary, the vow of chastity is a more radical vow of love and mutuality than marriage. This vow is not against 'ontological sexuality'.[48] His reasoning on celibacy and religious life is based on the dynamism between femininity and masculinity since chastity can be seen as the highest form of integration of these qualities.[49] Today, after leaving the priesthood and having married, Boff is a fierce critic of compulsory celibacy. On issues of contraception, abortion and divorce, he has not been explicit.

José Comblin is another example of a liberation theologian who, when treating the issue at all, speaks of sexual ethics mainly in the context of traditional Catholic teaching. He, similarly to Moser, sees issues such as divorce, contraception, sterilization and free expression of sexuality as products of bourgeois modernity, which he judges negatively. In Latin America, according to Comblin, it was primarily the Catholic bourgeoisie which started the anti-Catholic campaign in

---

47. Schutte 1993: 189. According to Schutte's argument, Dussel's ethics presupposes that the oppressed have to stay in the privileged position of exteriority in order to be able to speak to the established system of domination. Concretely, this could mean that women have to remain in their oppressed position, the poor have to remain poor, in order to maintain Dussel's pure, uncontaminated 'exteriority' (Schutte 1993: 189). 'One must remain on the periphery if one is to receive the moral blessings associated with alterity' (Schutte 1993: 201).

48. Boff 1985: 173-74.

49. Boff 1985: 173-74.

issues of sexual ethics, seeing the church as the main obstacle to sexual liberation.[50] Nevertheless, 'the popular masses' (that is, the poorest sectors of society)
do not resist traditional Catholic moral teaching in the same way, since 'they do
not experience it as oppression'. It is the mass media, controlled by the bourgeoisie, that spread the objections to Catholic morality to the poor masses, too.[51]

Comblin does not define what he means by sexual liberation, but it is obvious
that it is interpreted only in terms of bourgeois, modern individualism, 'as an
individual right',[52] which again is put in contrast with the Catholic teaching, supposedly based on love and communitarian understanding of the human person.[53]
Under the heading, 'the Catholic Church and sexuality', contraception is placed
in the long list of the detrimental effects of modernity on the Latin American
people, but nothing is said on issues such as abortion. Nevertheless, Comblin
treats sexuality in the larger context of theological anthropology, in which he
explicitly condemns *machismo*, the dualistic image of the human being, and even
the church's role in defining women as inferior to men.[54]

Once again it becomes clear that the formal approval of gender equality and
condemnation of anti-sexual elements in the Christian tradition does not make
Catholic liberation theologians reinterpret the official teaching on issues of sexual
ethics of their church. The same can, of course, be said of Catholic theology in
general, including the *magisterium*.[55]

Thus, moral theology or 'ethics of liberation' in the context of LT, or liberation
theology as such, first of all, does not address issues of sexual ethics extensively,
and second, when they are addressed, the reasoning very much follows traditional, official teaching, which also has been affirmed by Latin American Catholic
bishops.[56] This is true at least for the Catholic theologians. There is an apparent

50.   Comblin 1985: 104-105.
51.   Comblin 1985: 105.
52.   Comblin 1985: 105.
53.   Comblin 1985: 105-106.
54.   Comblin 1985: 74-101.
55.   In all recent Vatican documents concerning women, their oppression is stated and
condemned as well as their equality with men defended. Nevertheless, this is not applied to the
church itself (for example, women's ordination is not seen as an issue of equality, even though
the arguments against it are derived from a theological anthropology which makes women
unsuitable for the priesthood). Nor is the link between a theological anthropology which
unconditionally accepts women's full humanity and the traditional teaching on sexual ethics
made clear.
56.   See *Documentos de Medellín* 1969: 26-32, where the validity of the encyclical *Humanae
Vitae* is stated. There is nothing especially 'Latin American' in this part of the Medellín
documents, if 'antinatalist demographic politics' is not seen as such. This endorsing of the official
Catholic teaching in sexual ethics continues in the documents of Puebla (1979) and Santo
Domingo (1992).
    In December 1990, the state of Chiapas in Mexico decriminalized abortion in cases of rape
and serious genetic or other foetal malformation, as well as for reasons of family planning. As
such, the new legislation differs notably from most of Latin America. Chiapas is the poorest state
of Mexico, where the largest part of the indigenous population lives. In recent years, it has

conflict between the abstract reasoning in sexual ethical issues and the supposed praxis starting point, in which concrete problems of the poor form the base for ethics as well as theology. This again seems to point toward the lack of alternative reinterpretations in the area of theological anthropology, especially concerning male–female relationships and sexuality. 'The poor' as a homogeneous, primarily productive (not reproductive, gendered) category may even prevent such reinterpretations in LT.

Thomas C. Fox, quoting Charles Curran, presents two different models or approaches to moral theology in contemporary Catholicism, the classicist model and the historical consciousness model. The general movement in Catholic theology has been away from the former and toward the latter, although classicism is the approach to theology preferred by Rome.[57] Classicism understands reality in terms of the eternal, the immutable and the unchanging; historical consciousness gives more importance to the particular, the contingent, the historical and the individual. The latter recognizes the need for both continuity and discontinuity.[58] In sexual ethics, the classicism model has led to the teaching of absolutes in terms of right and wrong, natural *versus* unnatural.[59]

become internationally well-known as the base for the *zapatista* indigenous insurrection movement. The bishop of Chiapas, Samuel Ruiz García, is known for his sympathies for both the *zapatista* cause and liberation theology. Soon after the new legislation, he issued a pastoral letter condemning the decriminalization of abortion. He, too, pointed out how a demographic population policy (including mass sterilizations) on the part of the US and international agencies such as the International Monetary Fund can be interpreted as aggression against the predominantly indigenous population of his diocese. He strongly denounces *machismo* and violence against women, but he also judges some feminist demands as reflecting a similar mentality, as when women consider the new life they are carrying 'as their private property'. See Ruiz García 1994: 435-53. The pastoral letter of bishop Ruiz García is one more example of an argument which derives its contents simultaneously from the anti-imperialist discourse of LT in defence of the poor and from the traditional sexual ethical teaching of the Catholic Church. I will deal with the argumentation in Chapter 4.2.1.

In the United Nations International Conference on Population and Development in Cairo, September 1994, Latin American bishops—including Ruiz García—followed the Vatican and Muslim fundamentalists in their opposition to the proposed conference document, saying that its proposals would hurt the poorest of people, especially indigenous Indians. See Fox 1995: 285, 293.

See also Lepargneur for an extreme defence of the traditional Catholic position on abortion in a context of socio-political analysis. He maintains that the legalization of abortion may even increase the amount of abortions. He does not approve abortion in cases of rape. He condemns the socio-economic arguments for an abortion as 'egoism', similarly to when someone wants a new car or wants to travel instead of bearing a child. Needless to say, these 'choices' are not reality for poor Latin American women. Where modern culture tends to identify with the mother in the question of abortion, Lepargneur affirms the traditional Catholic identification with the unborn. It is sacred and as such untouchable. Lepargneur 1982: 82-109.

57. Fox 1995: 338-41.
58. Fox 1995: 339.
59. Fox 1995: 339-40.

It is clear that within these definitions, most of LT falls into the historical consciousness model. In a way, LT and other liberation theologies could even be seen as extreme versions of this model. Curiously, it is in questions of sexual ethics where both the Vatican teaching most leans on the absolute classicism model and centralizes its power and authority and where liberation theologians could be seen as *not* employing the historical consciousness model. This may be a sign of the low level of explicit statements on sexual ethics within Latin American LT, the overall history-centred model having not been applied in the area of sexual ethics.

In Chapter 1.4.1, it was explained how LT today has also been interpreted as *theology of life*. This is done in a context where the massive, real death of people in the Third World is seen as idolatry. Concrete human life must be defended against the powers of death, which the liberation theologians usually situate in 'the North'.[60] According to Pablo Richard, one of the major proponents of LT as a theology of life, the Third World is becoming a non-world, since the Third World in the classical sense is now less and less needed even for the production of cheap labour and raw materials.[61] The alternative between development and liberation has changed into a radical alternative between life and death. The only option for LT is to affirm life for everyone (*vida para todos*). The option for the poor translates into the option for life.[62] The fundamental ethical imperative in Latin America is human life, which in practice refers to work, bread, roof, education, justice and security.[63] The fundamental criterion for ethical discernment is the human life of the real concrete man (*hombre*).[64]

In a later text, Richard speaks of the same issue in absolute terms: LT must take the 'radical and absolute option for life',[65] 'Human life thus becomes a real criterion for discernment and an absolute and universal imperative',[66] and 'The denial of life is denial of truth, goodness, and beauty'.[67] The theology of life must 'guarantee the reproduction of human life and of nature'.[68] In the realm of ethics, 'Human life is an absolute value'.[69] Theologically, the soul is not saved from the body, as it was in Hellenistic philosophy, but rather the human being (body and soul) is saved from death.[70]

LT as theology of life takes seriously the concrete, corporal life of human beings in situations of oppression and death. It is not possible to discuss this perspective here in detail. I only want to point out one possible interpretation of this

60. See Richard 1987a: 93 and 1994: 104.
61. Richard 1991: 3.
62. Richard 1991: 3.
63. Richard 1981: 56 and 1988: 94.
64. Richard 1981: 56.
65. Richard 1994: 94.
66. Richard 1994: 95.
67. Richard 1994: 94.
68. Richard 1994: 94.
69. Richard 1994: 100.
70. Richard 1994: 106.

position. As we have seen, official church documents—for example, the CELAM Santo Domingo document of 1992—have adopted liberation theological language in issues of sexual ethics when the bishops speak of contraceptive imperialism. Some of the liberation theologians, such as Antônio Moser, combine this official Catholic view with the 'pro-life' language of LT, seeing birth control and abortion as the imperialist weapons of death against the Latin American poor. In the case of other liberation theologians, their silence on issues of sexual ethics, combined with a radical and absolutist overall defence of human life, opens up the possibility of reading liberation theologians as supporting the official Vatican teaching.[71]

Actually, in an article to a German audience, Pablo Richard comes quite close to such a view. He criticizes the way of thinking in which massive and effective birth control is seen as the solution to the problem (of poverty) in the Third World. He says: 'This solution does not have any other use than hiding the real problem and justifying the present power of death. This solution follows the logic of death of the dominating system.'[72] He states that family planning is necessary, but 'In Latin America, all birth control programs until today have been planned, financed, and finally, forced, by the USA'.[73] This is why there is deep distrust of all birth control politics from outside or from above.[74] In the same context, he takes up the central issue of defense of life in LT: 'The option for life means saying no to death, not accepting death, not permitting even a child to starve; it means radical and unyielded opposition to the death of the poor, not accepting the death of the poor'.[75] What he does not notice is how the death of poor women is intimately and directly connected to issues of unsafe or lacking contraception, illegal abortions and a high fertility rate. I will take up critically all the above-mentioned arguments in Chapter 4.2.1.

Franz Hinkelammert, one of the theorists of the theology of life, and a Catholic lay person, takes up the issue of abortion in a context where he speaks of 'the theology of the empire' in contrast to theology of life, that is, theology of liberation.[76] The theology of the empire needs to resort to the affirmation of life, but it does not do it in the concrete sense which LT does. Instead, this theology

---

71. Actually, Pope John Paul II's eleventh encyclical, *Evangelium Vitae* ('The Gospel of Life'), issued in 1995, sets out a moral vision aimed at overcoming what the Pope refers to as the modern 'culture of death'. The encyclical wishes to portray a consistent ethic of life, in which issues of abortion, euthanasia and capital punishment are treated. See Fox 1995: 317-18.

Thus, the language of morality in terms of life and death is present in both the Vatican teaching and LT, and in similar absolutist terms. The context and the contents differ, but less so in issues of sexual ethics than in other areas of moral theology. The least one can point out is that liberation theologians should be conscious of this potential dilemma.

72. Richard 1986: 16.
73. Richard 1986: 16.
74. Richard 1986: 16.
75. Richard 1986: 17.
76. Hinkelammert 1988: 27.

of the empire refers to the life of the unborn and declares the right to be born as the right to life.[77] This is a totally privatized meaning of a right to life, according to Hinkelammert, in order to avoid the recognition of the right to life of the human beings already being born.[78] He is for a defence of life for both the unborn and the born:

> the abortion is a product of an attitude in front of life which the theology of the empire itself promotes. It simply extends the treatment of men, used and legitimated by the system, to the unborn human life. The liberty of abortion is nothing else than the liberty to treat unborn human life in the same way as the life of already born human beings is being treated... [The liberal ethics] lets the unborn die and kills them in the same way as it preaches the letting to die and killing of the poor. Nevertheless, for ideological reasons, the right to be born is raised... Only an affirmation of the right to life of those already being born can create a new ethics which extends this recognition of life of men to unborn human life.[79]

Hinkelammert's argument is somewhat different from those who see abortion (and birth control) only as outside aggression against the poor, but he, too, ends up affirming the traditional absolutist Catholic position on abortion, implicitly affirming that human life starts at conception and seeing embryonic life and adult human life on the same continuum.

If 'concrete human life' and life of the poor which liberation theologians want to defend is not further concretized, problematized and differentiated, they may find themselves in rather surprising company. Does the defence of the life of the poor also translate into the defence of the life of poor women? If yes, one has to take seriously the fact that poor women die of causes directly related to reproduction. This, of course, is one argument in favour of the explication of sexual ethics within LT, from the perspective of those who suffer most from the consequences of the current situation, that is, poor women.

Latin American feminist theologians are not much more explicit on issues of sexual ethics than are their male colleagues. What was generally stated on sexual ethics being meagrely treated in LT very much concerns the women theologians as well.[80] Nevertheless, there are some who have pointed out sexual ethics as an issue to be raised. Already in 1979, a group of Christian women called *Mujeres para el Diálogo*, gathered at the CELAM Puebla conference, stated that in their meeting their biggest difficulties were in trying to deepen issues concerning sexuality even though there is an urgent necessity to think about even the most

---

77.   Hinkelammert 1988: 27.
78.   Hinkelammert 1988: 27.
79.   Hinkelammert 1988: 27.
80.   According to Phillip Berryman, 'Compared with their feminist colleagues in North America and Europe, Latin American women theologians are still rather timid, especially on reproductive issues' (Berryman 1995: 118). They do not necessarily have to be 'compared' with their colleagues in the industrialized countries. The whole issue must be treated in the historical and cultural context of Latin America—both the reasons why sexual ethics has not been high up on the feminist theological agenda and the ways it might be taken up.

thorny issues of traditional moral theology, such as the character of sexual relations, procreation, birth control, homosexuality and celibacy.[81]

As has been said earlier, Ivone Gebara from Brazil has been the first, and until today, the only liberation theologian, male or female, to publicly favour the decriminalization of abortion. In October 1993 she stated in an interview by the Brazilian magazine *VEJA* that if the mother is not in the psychological condition to face up to a pregnancy, she has the right to interrupt it.[82] According to her,

> The Catholic morality does not reach rich women. They abort, having the economic resources to guarantee a surgical intervention in human conditions. Therefore, the law which the church defends is detrimental to poor women. The abortion must be decriminalized and legalized. Even more, it must be realized at the expense of the state. Abortion is today the fifth cause of feminine mortality in Brazil. Those who die are the poorest women.[83]

Abortion is not a sin.[84]

She also states that what made her change her opinion on the issue was her living with the poor women of Camaragibe, a poor region on the outskirts of Recife, where she worked as a nun. After being ordered to retract her statement, she clarified her position in an article, 'La legalización del aborto vista desde el caleidoscopio social',[85] in which she says that her practical starting point is the reality of poor women who are the primary victims of the situation of 'violence against life' which numerous illegal abortions bring about.[86] A society which cannot guarantee employment, health, housing and schools is 'an abortive society' which forces women to choose between their work and the interruption of pregnancy. The millions of abortions and deaths of women is an existing reality which is not denounced in the same way as the 'innocent life' lost in an abortion.[87] She says her position is a denunciation of institutionalized violence, abuse and hypocrisy, a position stemming from the defence of life.[88] She uses the same language that her male colleagues use—that poverty is an issue of life and death—but in reproductive issues she seems to understand life quite differently from how other liberation theologians understand it. It is the life of poor women that is at stake.

Gebara does not discuss the Catholic teaching on birth control, nor does she enter a theological debate with the *magisterium*. Her position is very pragmatic, and as such, similar to a feminist position on abortion anywhere: there are always situations in which women resort to abortions. The issue is whether these are

81. *Mujer latinoamericana* 1981: iii-iv.
82. Nanne and Bergamo 1993.
83. Nanne and Bergamo 1993.
84. Nanne and Bergamo 1993.
85. Reprinted in *Revista Con-Spirando* 6 (1993).
86. *Revista Con-Spirando* 6 (1993).
87. *Revista Con-Spirando* 6 (1993).
88. 'Mi posición frente a la descriminalización y la legalización del aborto como ciudadana cristiana y miembra de una comunidad religiosa es una forma de denunciar el mal, la violencia institucionalizada, el abuso y la hipocresía que nos envuelven, es una apuesta por la vida, es pues en defensa de la vida' (*Revista Con-Spirando* 6 [1993]).

realized under decent conditions or not. Women die of illegal abortions. Nowhere has criminalization of abortion solved the problem.

Gebara, together with María Clara Bingemer, sees the area of theological anthropology as central for a Latin American feminist liberation theology.[89] This means at least four necessary changes in traditional theology: a shift from a male-centred to a human-centred anthropology, from a dualistic to a unifying anthropology, from an idealist to a realist anthropology, and from a one-dimensional to a pluri-dimensional anthropology.[90] They reject the binary model of specifically female/feminine and male/masculine modes of being and prefer speaking of a *feminist anthropology*, which is closely connected to the present historic moment 'in which women's consciousness is breaking into awareness of their age-old oppression and their age-old stance of compliance with and subjection to the oppressive structures of society and particularly of religion'.[91] This, together with the understanding of the option for the poor as an option for the poor woman,[92] is the larger framework for Gebara's public defence of legalization of abortion.

Gebara states how Christian churches have been afraid of the human body, especially the female body, which has led to the fear of sexuality. The traditional Christian anthropology is an anthropology of verbal equality, but with a patriarchal and hierarchical stamp.[93] The human body must become a new starting point for moral theology.[94] This implies accepting a unitary anthropology which intends to exceed dualisms and include the ambiguities inherent in human existence and history.[95] A new theology of sexuality should grow from a revised theology of creation, which must take into account the scientific knowledge of modern times and start from 'the wonder of the body'.[96]

Ana María Bidegain from Colombia is another Latin American feminist liberation theologian to openly discuss sexuality from a feminist perspective. She, too, is critical of speaking of 'a feminine nature' and wants to see the human body as the primary, indispensable means and principal element of social production.[97] LT has not been able to address the situation of women in the church and society

---

89.   See Gebara and Bingemer 1989: 1-19, 91.

90.   Gebara and Bingemer 1989: 3. Gebara and Bingemer propose this in a Mariological context, but the same anthropological principles can be seen guiding their overall theological approach. The pluri-dimensional anthropology 'takes into account the different dimensions of humankind as it has evolved through history and as countless elements have left their mark on it. The human being is not primarily a definition but rather a history within space and time…human beings are not first good and then corrupted, not first corrupted and then saved, but rather humans are this whole complex reality striving to explain themselves' (Gebara and Bingemer 1989: 10-11).

91.   Gebara and Bingemer 1989: 14.

92.   Gebara 1987.

93.   Gebara 1994: 80.

94.   Gebara 1994: 77.

95.   Gebara 1994: 82.

96.   Gebara 1994: 85-86.

97.   Bidegain 1989: 108.

nor to deal with the moral theology of sex.[98] According to Bidegain, there is an urgent need for a review of the puritanical conception of sexuality, which is the ideological foundation of the patriarchal mentality and sexist oppression in the Latin American society and church.[99] Bidegain does not consider concrete questions such as birth control and abortion.

María Pilar Aquino also emphasizes the need for reworking theological anthropology.[100] An egalitarian anthropology is opposed to the long tradition of anthropological perspectives based on asymmetrical models, both in male–female relationship and the split between the private and the public. The dualism and androcentrism present in, for example, Augustinian and Thomistic anthropologies need to be surpassed.[101] In LT, too, it has been common to identify man (*hombre*) with human being (*ser humano*).[102] Aquino agrees with the characterizations of Gebara and Bingemer concerning an egalitarian anthropology from a Latin American feminist theological perspective.[103]

Like other feminist liberation theologians Aquino, too, stresses the importance of restoring human corporality, especially in its humiliated female form. This corporal dimension is nothing less than existence itself. In Latin America, human existence is being threatened every day by malnutrition, sickness, unemployment and hunger. Women, especially, also live this threat to their existence as sexual beings, their sexuality being violated and destroyed.[104]

If some liberation theologians both implicitly and explicitly agree with official statements of the Catholic hierarchy, there are feminist theologians who strongly criticize the treatment of women in CELAM documents, for example. According to Gladys Parentelli, a Uruguayan Catholic lay woman, there is notorious indifference to women's sexual oppression in the Catholic Church.[105] She criticizes the way in which Latin American bishops condemn 'the attacks against life', such as abortion, sterilization and birth control programmes, as detrimental to the dignity of women.[106] According to Parentelli, the actual papacy of John Paul II has taken a step backwards in doctrinal issues concerning sexual ethics.[107] She

98.   Bidegain 1989: 113-14.
99.   Bidegain 1989: 114. See also Bidegain 1990, in which she points out the contradiction of the Catholic Church recognizing women's freedom of conscience and then subordinating this freedom and autonomy to a magisterium which has the sole authority to interpret this right. Questions of sexual ethics have centred on female sexuality. In the official declarations of the church, women are globally seen as lacking conscience and responsibility. The struggle for women's liberation is a necessary condition for a new understanding of human sexuality and new sexual ethics (Bidegain 1990: 119-20).
100. Aquino 1992a: 151.
101. Aquino 1992a: 154.
102. Aquino 1992a: 155.
103. Aquino 1992a: 156-61.
104. Aquino 1992a: 160.
105. Parentelli 1993: 4. María Pilar Aquino does not take up these questions in her analysis of the CELAM Santo Domingo conference. See Aquino 1993b: 212-25.
106. Parentelli 1993: 7.
107. Parentelli *et al.* 1990: 103.

mentions compulsory celibacy, homosexuality, prostitution, rape, incest, battering, abortion, birth control and divorce as issues which need to be reworked in the Latin American context, too.[108] She takes a clear stance in favour of birth control and legalization of abortion.[109]

The Brazilians Nancy Cardoso Pereira and Tania M. Vieira Sampãio raise the need for the 'subversion' of family and domestic life in Latin America. This includes the deconstruction of (the sacrality of) maternity, abortion, abandoned children, alienated sexuality and the privacy of the family.[110] They, too, see LT as the appropriate context for a feminist theological discourse in Latin America. Women's liberation should be seen as an essential part of the larger processes of liberation.[111]

María Clara Bingemer speaks of the oppression of Latin American women as 'real slavery'. She refers especially to the girls growing up in the poorest and most marginalized sectors of society whose childhood is threatened by sexual violence, prostitution, domestic labour and premature motherhood.[112]

In addition to these theologians who touch upon or openly discuss issues of sexual ethics from a feminist theological perspective, there are, of course, the secular feminist movements all over the continent which demand changes in legislation concerning issues like abortion. There are also some church-related groups, such as *Católicas por el Derecho a Decidir*, the Latin American branch of the US-based Catholics for a Free Choice, an organization which wants to reorient Catholic teaching on sexual ethics from within the church. In Latin America, the group is based in Montevideo, Uruguay, but has not gained major visibility even inside the Catholic Church. The organization has produced material dealing with sexual ethics from a feminist perspective in Latin America, such as the book *Mujeres e Iglesia: Sexualidad y aborto en América Latina*.[113]

According to the editor of this book, Ana María Portugal, the historical weight of Catholicism makes it very difficult to touch on such controversial issues as sexuality and abortion, even in presumably secular sectors of society or in groups which in theory support feminist demands on birth control and legalization of abortion.[114] The same is true of LT, which has 'a profoundly masculine look in avoiding a clear pronouncement on the validity of sexual demands such as the

---

108. Parentelli *et al.* 1990: 104-26.
109. Parentelli *et al.* 1990: 112-20.
110. Interviewed in Tamez 1989: 102-105.
111. Interviewed in Tamez 1989: 110.
112. Interviewed in Tamez 1989: 127.
113. Portugal (ed.) 1989. Another feminist group within the Catholic Church is the Peruvian *Talitha Cumi* which 'has assumed a responsibility for writing a statement criticizing the church from within', being aware of the continuing influence the church still has in Latin America. They also take up reproductive issues, defending a Christian feminist stance in public. They argue that most of the feminists in the women's movement are from a Catholic background and are products of Catholic schools, but they no longer identify with religion and religious practice. They have become indifferent to the church. See Gallagher 1995: 106-109.
114. Portugal 1989: 5.

right to birth control and voluntary abortion, pleasant sexuality as well as the question of women's ordination'.[115] If it is difficult to imagine a radical questioning of the church, it is *even more problematic* in the case of LT, since all inner critique is easily seen as 'reactionary' or 'counterproductive'. All the early feminist demands concerning abortion and birth control in Latin America were met with hostility by these groups. These were explained as problems alien to Latin American reality.[116] Even many feminist groups have been careful in taking up the issue of abortion, for the fear of losing support among poor, religious women.[117]

If there is not much open disagreement—with the exceptions mentioned above—on issues of sexual ethics between Catholic male and female liberation theologians, the same can be said of the Catholic and Protestant theologians. The silence on the part of the Catholic theologians apparently cannot be explained only by pressure on the part of the Vatican, if the Protestant theologians keep as silent. Rubem Alves, one of the most notable Protestant liberation theologians, says in an interview:

> It is significant that the Catholic bishops are divided on political issues—the bishops of the left and the right—but on sexual issues they reach an extraordinary agreement… When we speak of abortion and birth control, there is an amazing agreement, as if sexuality was the most crucial issue. Not one bishop would dare to doubt this or speak out!… In both the Catholic and Protestant churches,…we've built an ethical and political discourse, but we have repressed the discourse of sexuality and pleasure.[118]

Why this situation? Why are issues of sexual ethics not being discussed critically, neither by Catholic nor Protestant liberation theologians, not by men nor by women? As is made clear above, there are dissident voices, mostly of feminist Christian women who are close to LT but are not necessarily theologians. The overall situation is that of an almost total silence. This is especially true of a *theological* discourse on sexual ethics which would present an adequate alternative to the dominant Catholic discourse and practice. A situation is created in which the great majority of Latin American women find no one expressing their most intimate concerns. I will first analyse some possible reasons for the silence and then look at the consequences of it.

4.1.2 *The Silence Speaks: Reasons and Consequences*
The silence or neglect on the part of LT in issues of sexual ethics has not gone unnoticed in Latin America, even though it is not much discussed either. Secular feminists, especially, or feminists who do not act from within the churches, have been critical of the role religion—predominantly Catholicism—plays in defining

115. Portugal 1989: 6.
116. Portugal 1989.
117. Portugal 1989. Saporta Sternbach *et al.* 1992: 402.
118. Alves in Puleo 1994: 198.

the conditions and limits of the sexual ethical discussion in Latin America.[119]

Male liberation theologians—even those who touch upon issues of sexual ethics—have not offered any explanations for the minor importance of these issues in LT. Of the feminist liberation theologians, Elsa Tamez asks why 'women' is a delicate theme in the church—not only sexual ethics, but women's role(s) in the church on the whole, including the question of women's ordination both in Protestant denominations and in the Catholic Church. Tamez answers that the whole issue is one about power and concrete restructuring of the church, thus the delicacy.[120] The practice of celibacy creates fear of women in which women's personalities are reduced to their sex.[121]

According to María Pilar Aquino, feminist critique is met with much resistance in the sphere of popular religiosity. In the Catholic tradition, there is also a high level of tension due to ecclesiastical censorship and direct control of Latin American theologians.[122] There is still a fundamental incapacity in the church to

119.   Teresita de Barbieri, one of the most well-known Latin American feminist theorists, states, speaking of sexual ethics, especially abortion and Catholic doctrine: 'Ni siquiera las teólogas y teólogos que participan en el movimiento de la teología de la liberación han incorporado dentro de sus perspectivas la reflexión sobre los géneros y la opresión de las mujeres, o lo han hecho con exagerada timidez... Y quienes se atreven a hablar, no lo hacen con la fundamentación requerida: o doctrinal de peso, conocimiento fundado en los documentos, manejo adecuado de las fuentes, formación filosófica sólida' (De Barbieri 1990: 330).

Similarly, Frances Kissling, a North American theologian and president of the Catholics for a Free Choice, says: 'Deberíamos hacer una primera diferenciación entre la teología de la liberación masculina y la teología de la liberación feminista. Francamente nosotras vemos muy poca diferencia en los pronunciamientos públicos de los teólogos de la liberación aquí en Latinoamérica y el Vaticano, con respecto a la sexualidad femenina. Pero hay un movimiento muy fuerte de teólogas feministas que consideran que la sexualidad es buena, es saludable y por supuesto gratificante... La teología de la liberación en Latinoamérica, si bien es una teologia basada en los pobres, no ha reconocido a las mujeres en su discriminación específica y por lo tanto no tiene una especial preocupación por esa situación de discriminación. Concretamente, los teólogos de la liberación..., en relación al aborto, sostienen qu deben nacer niños aunque sean pobres y la pasen mal. Lo que la mujer quiere, piensa o siente no se considera prioritario'. See 'Conversando con Frances Kissling' (1989: 50). It is true that Latin American feminist liberation theologians present a different image of sexuality, especially women's sexuality, than do their male colleagues, but as we have seen, in most cases this does not lead them to explicit questioning of the teaching of the church in matters of sexual ethics. There are exceptions such as Ivone Gebara, who most probably will have followers in the near future.

120.   Tamez 1986: 174-75.

121.   Tamez 1986: 175.

122.   Aquino 1997: 9, 35. Phillip Berryman has a similar opinion: '... the general backlash in the Catholic Church encouraged by Pope John Paul II has put the [liberation] theologians on the defensive, making it even more difficult for them to explore openly issues that might create problems for themselves and also for priests and sisters working with the poor' (Berryman 1995: 115). Neither Aquino nor Berryman mentions sexual ethics, but it is clear that it is one such area of serious potential conflict with the hierarchy.

Rosemary Ruether, as well, sees the inner conflicts in the Catholic Church as one reason for the difficulty in dealing with gender issues in LT. She says: 'The situation of women in the Catholic Church is getting worse. There is an important reactive movement of the Vatican

accept the major advances of the contemporary world: autonomy of the person and democracy.[123] Of the Latin American feminist theologians, this control has been directly aimed at Ivone Gebara.

The censorship against Catholic liberation theologians has centred around overtly political issues (Marxism, for example) and ecclesiological issues (the fear of a parallel or new church, issues of obedience to church hierarchy). In this situation, it is understandable that liberation theologians have not been willing to complicate their situation by taking up issues of sexual ethics which has been exactly the area of control and censorship of Catholic theologians in other parts of the world. There is often a conflict between private beliefs and public announcements. Even though there would be a willingness to accept new sexual ethical reinterpretations, they are not discussed publicly. Mandatory celibacy seems to be an easier issue to take up than issues of birth control and abortion (Boff), even though the latter are issues that have a much more immediate relation to the everyday realities of the people, including the poor.

In spite of losing its colonial power, the Catholic Church is far from being a marginal institution in Latin America. The power of the Catholic Church is related to traditional ways of interaction of Latin American elites.[124] Catholicism is a kind of civil religion all over Latin America, independent of its formal status in relation to the secular state. In some countries, conservative Catholics and politically powerful elites are forming new alliances—as a kind of modern continuation of the colonial *patronato* system—between the church and the state in spite of the legal separation between the two.[125] In a way, Catholics close to LT and the CEBs have helped to reconstruct institutional Catholicism by playing a significant role in the revitalization of the faith of many Catholics.[126] Liberation theologians face a conflict between institution and renewal. Many of them have too much at stake, both personally and institutionally, in order to risk the limited institutional security they have.[127]

According to Rosa Dominga Trapasso, a Catholic sister from Peru,

> Women's cause is not going to be given priority because [liberation] theologians do not want to cause more difficulties for them in the church. I think that is a decision

concerning any form of democratization, which is taking space from the liberation theologians. And as they are losing space in what they were doing before, they are not going to risk anything now, especially if it is about women' (Ruether 1996a: 3).

123. Aquino 1997: 35.

124. Hynds 1993: 1.

125. Cadorette 1993: 2.

126. Cadorette 1993. This could also be the reason why the hierarchy is so eager to maintain the CEBs inside the church, by emphasizing their ecclesiastical character. The only alternative could be total secularization or the strengthening of Protestantism. This becomes clear, for example, in the CELAM Santo Domingo document.

127. As Thomas C. Fox says of the situation in the United States, 'Large numbers of U.S. bishops, even perhaps a sizable majority, are not pleased with how the Vatican is handling the birth control issue. To publicly say anything about it would constitute ecclesial suicide' (Fox 1995: 307).

that liberation theology has made, though perhaps not overtly… Any questioning of
the situation of women automatically means a questioning of the position of the
hierarchy in regard to women. You can't take a position in favor of women without
questioning religion and institutional church structures.[128]

She speaks explicitly of sexual ethics and women's reduced control of their reproductive capacity. In other words, she states the same problem that has been stated
in this research several times: liberation theology's theoretical position against
women's oppression and defence of their rights does not necessarily mean—and,
in effect, has not meant—any concrete steps in making their situation either in
society or in the church better.

   These reasons for the silence could be said to be 'church political', at least for
the Catholic theologians. The situation is somewhat different, of course, for
Protestant theologians. As was said above, liberation theologians' shyness in issues
of sexual ethics cannot be explained *only* by 'church politics' and fear of repression. If this would be the explanation, one might expect different elaborations
from the Protestant theologians. In spite of the low level of confessional disagreements in LT, one could easily expect differences between the Catholic and
Protestant theologians in the area of sexual ethics, both for doctrinal reasons
(Protestants have no such unified teaching on matters of sexual ethics as does the
Catholic Church) and practical reasons (theologians and pastors are usually
married, have children). The absence of Protestant as well as Catholic formulations in sexual ethics raises the question about the weight of Latin American
culture on theology in general.

   Patriarchal culture[129] and as part of it, patriarchal religion—in Latin America as
in any part of the world—make women and their concerns 'invisible'.[130] The

   128. Interviewed in Gallagher 1995: 108. Similarly, Ana María Portugal: 'Partidos de
izquierda, grupos y personas progresistas, aunque reconocen la validez de las reivindicaciones
feministas en lo tocante a la anticoncepción, al aborto y a la sexualidad, no están dispuestos a
apoyar y menos a acompañar a las mujeres en campañas de este tipo. Temen enfrentarse a las iras
de obispos y clérigos, y por consiguiente perder votos de simpatizantes católicos. *En esta misma
posición está la Iglesia progresista que sigue la línea de la Teología de la Liberación… Pero si por una parte la
Teología de la Liberación aboga por la condición de los oprimidos en general, su lectura de la condición
femenina no deja de estar sesgada, porque su mirada es profundamente masculina al evadir un pronunciamiento
claro sobre la validez de las reivindicaciones sexuales*: derecho a la anticoncepción y al aborto voluntario,
sexualidad placentera así como la cuestión del sacerdocio femenino' (Portugal 1989: 5-6
[emphasis added]).
   129. According to the *Dictionary of Feminist Theologies*, there are general characteristics usually
found in patriarchal societies, although one cannot define a single system that would be true of all
patriarchal societies at all times. The general characteristic of the status of women under
patriarchy is one of subjugation without legal status in their own right. Other aspects of this
subjugated status include, among other things, the lineage of children through the father, the
preferring of male children, the belonging of women's bodies, sexuality and reproductive
capacities to their husbands, and women's limited education. The exclusion of women from
public political and cultural offices and from higher education accounts for the almost exclusively
male elite formation of public culture. Women typically have had great difficulty gaining visibility
and credibility as creators of culture (Ruether 1996b: 205-206).
   130. 'The most simple and in many ways the most powerful criticism made of theory and

rigidity of traditional teaching in sexual ethics is just one more layer in this larger framework. Latin American *machismo*, however defined, makes its marks on theology, as well. In addition, most liberation theologians are academically trained men, clerics, often celibate, of a certain generation and racial stratum. The low level of higher education in theology among Latin American women is notable, even if it is true globally as well. As was stated in Chapter 2.2.1, the fact that so many female Third World theologians are including gender issues in their theology points towards a positive correlation between higher education and feminist consciousness, in LT as well.

Further, at least the older generation liberation theologians have extra difficulty in attending issues such as reproduction and sexuality because of their larger perception of society and social and political change. A Marxist-orientated political ethics—which informs many liberation theologians and especially their understanding of praxis, as we have seen—presupposes the change of (economic, political, social) structures.[131] A new ethics of sexuality and a new relationship between men and women would follow these changes almost automatically. Or, a hierarchy of necessary changes is established, in which 'women's issues' and reproductive questions are seen as less important than macro level economic changes.[132] Contemporary Latin America offers us several examples of this dynamic. The most notable and probably also the most analysed case is that of Sandinista Nicaragua.[133] The Latin American left in general has opposed birth

practice within the social sciences is that, by and large, they omit or distort the experience of women...although women are frequently massively present within whatever studied, we but rarely appear in the end products of this. This may be because women are simply not "seen" by researchers, are ignored by them or else our experiences are distorted by them' (Stanley and Wise 1993: 27). Referring primarily to sociology, they argue that it is a 'male profession' (most people within it are men) and that an 'ideology of gender' leads people to construct the world in sexually stereotyped ways. Also, where women's presence is not ignored it is viewed and presented in distorted and sexist ways (Stanley and Wise 1993).

All this could be said of most of the academic fields, including theology, which in addition has its peculiar ties to the sexist practices of religious institutions.

131.   According to Mary O'Brien, 'One of the great defects of Marx's work is the partial nature of his notion of history—mode of production follows mode of production in providing subsistence for the reproducing of man on a daily basis. The daily reproduction of the *species* in the birth of *individuals*, is not perceived as an essential dialectical moment of historical process, which of course it is' (O'Brien 1989: 10 [emphasis in original]). Thus, only productive labour counts for Marx in the reproduction of man's world. Marx defined labour as the creation of value, but he did not heed the value produced by women's reproductive labour (O'Brien 1989: 11, 303).

132.   In working with poor women, feminists learned that so-called taboo issues such as sexuality, reproduction or violence against women were interesting and important to working-class women—as crucial to their survival as the bread-and-butter issues emphasized by the male opposition. Latin American feminists began redefining and expanding the prevailing notion of revolutionary struggle, calling for a revolution in daily life (Saporta Sternbach *et al.* 1992: 404).

133.   See Molyneux 1985 and 1988; Randall 1992. The Sandinista government was not only reluctant to confront the Catholic Church. Its hierarchy already supported the political opposition. Many of the Sandinista leaders presented views on contraception and abortion which

control, considering it an imperialist strategy.[134] The influence of leftist party politics on LT can thus be seen here, too.

A further reason for the difficulty of creating spaces of critical dialogue on reproductive issues in Latin America in both religious and secular circles, including many feminists, is to be found in global perspectives on health and population policies. Many Latin American feminists insist on the importance of understanding how international organizations and multinational corporations determine national population policies in their countries.[135] As we saw, liberation theologians tend to see reproductive issues in the larger context of imperialist population control policy, aimed primarily at the poor nations. This is an extremely touchy and difficult area in which the clarification of positions and arguments supporting them is necessary. Many Third World countries, including Latin American, have been targets of aggressive, coercive, international population policies, including forced sterilizations (almost without exception on women), use of suspect hormonal contraceptives, and so on. It is understandable that those critical of Western notions of development—such as liberation theologians—and those defending poor women's right to control their reproductive capacities— such as Third World feminists—suspect any outside control of how issues of population, reproduction and women's health should be treated. Nevertheless, there is much confusion. On the one hand, liberation theologians joining the Vatican critique of 'contraceptive imperialism' may not want to share the premises behind the critique. On the other hand, Latin American feminists defending women's reproductive rights hardly want to endorse the Vatican policy, although both parties would criticize coercive population politics. This clarification of positions will be discussed in Chapter 4.2.1.

Naturally, there are specific, albeit not always explicit, theological thinking habits which make sexual ethics an especially difficult and complicated area and which are an obstacle for sexual ethical reinterpretations, not only in Latin America. Mostly these more theological reasons have to do with theological anthropology, especially the image of women. In the area of reproduction and sexual ethics, we have the traditional Catholic view of complementarity between men and women, which presupposes their different roles. The emphasis on motherhood and virginity as a woman's true vocations points, of course, to the Virgin Mary. I am not going into this discussion more deeply. Most Latin American feminist liberation theologians point out the necessity for a critical re-elaboration of theological anthropology. As we have seen, Mariological reinterpretations could serve as one possible way of realizing this task. It is, however,

---

contrasted with feminist organizations supportive of the government. The issue of population growth was seen by President Ortega as one of national interest, with the main problem being the genocide of Nicaraguans by the US and the *contras*.

134.   Monsivais 1991: 87. He quotes an 'ultrasexist song of the ultraleft' which says 'A parir madres latinas/a parir más guerilleros'.

135.   Saporta Sternbach *et al*. 1992: 403.

beyond the scope of this research to discuss the more theological arguments in the context of sexual ethics.

If liberation theologians have by and large been unable to discuss sexual ethical and reproductive issues, what consequences does it have?

As has been said, there are several secular women's movements in Latin America which also raise issues of reproductive rights, such as birth control and abortion. Feminist movements are often composed of educated, middle-class women who no longer have strong or any ties to the institutional churches. If liberation theologians, male and female, keep silent about issues of sexual ethics, this creates a situation where a large amount of Latin American women, to whom religion plays an important role in their lives, find no one expressing their most intimate concerns. This is especially true for poor, uneducated women who suffer most from the present situation. If tackling the theological arguments behind traditional sexual ethics is considered necessary, it must be done with adequate tools of analysis. To be able to do so implies a critical analysis of the controversial role of religion in the lives of women, taking its liberative potential seriously.

This again has to do with the very starting point of LT. If sexual ethics is not being treated in LT, what does this mean for the overall theological programme of LT?

As has been made clear, Latin American LT speaks of the poor as its context, its *locus*, its starting point, the subjects of the praxis, but understands the poor homogeneously, without taking into account how poverty affects people differently depending, for example, on their race and gender. Practically speaking, preventing the death of poor women has not been an explicit part of liberation theologians' agenda of 'defending the life of the poor'. To do so implies taking a critical look at how it is exactly in the area of reproduction where the violence and death produced by poverty affect women differently from men. Ninety-nine per cent of all maternal deaths in the world occur in the Third World.[136] What makes a difference in Latin America is its being still predominantly Catholic. The Catholic teaching on sexual ethics should thus be a special challenge to liberation theologians who wish to speak about the complex realities of the poor.

The scantiness of sexual ethics is an example of the insufficient conceptual analysis and its practical consequences in LT, pointed out in previous chapters. If the praxis, understood either in a traditional Marxist sense or as the homogeneous and general 'poor', does not offer tools for an analysis in one central practical area of life, that of reproduction, it no doubt is questionable as *a method* or as *a starting point*, which does not mean it does not serve at all. It means instead that it is insufficient.

There is an implicit presupposition of what is included in 'the praxis'. As we have seen, it is difficult to include women, especially as reproductive beings, in the supposed collective subject of LT. Feminist (theological) analysis and understanding of a female subject, which is both productive and reproductive, both

136. World Health Organization 1996: 2.

communitarian and individual, both public and private, reveals this breach in LT. The aspect of *vida cotidiana*, although not sufficiently explicated, of Latin American feminist liberation theologians, makes it clear that there are central areas of human life which not only challenge the liberation theological understanding of the praxis but questions the very usefulness of it as a norm for theology.

It seems that the praxis starting point in LT, as elaborated thus far, is a theoretical tool which has not been analysed enough. This creates difficulties in speaking of praxis as a new method as strongly as is usually done. From a feminist point of view, this method has much of the same restrictions and difficulties as other methods being used in modern theology: the omission of women, anthropological presuppositions which marginalize women, and so on. The conscious emphasis on praxis does not necessarily correct the sexist presuppositions of a method.

Similar methodological problems in FT, analysed in Chapter 2, concerning the status given to 'women's experience' point toward the difficulty of giving the praxis starting point the central methodological weight it is given in all liberation theologies. If 'the poor' can be seen as a context-bound Latin American application of a more general praxis starting point, 'women' and 'women's experience' in FT have a similar status. Thus, in order to be faithful to their most central methodological starting point, liberation theologians—including feminist theologians—should pay special attention to the difficulties in making praxis as overarching and determining as is usually done. Latin American feminist liberation theology faces problems similar to those of LT in general, because the praxis starting point is given a central status without much critical analysis of its limitations.

Thus, the scantiness of sexual ethics in LT is, first, a challenge to the supposed commitment to the praxis of the poor. Second, taken together with feminist theological notions of human agency or subjectivity, issues of sexual ethics also reveal the insufficiency of the praxis starting point as a method or norm of theology. Third, praxis not only as the starting point for theology but as its objective as well brings practical ethical issues to the centre of LT. The scant importance given to sexual ethics points toward an arbitrary omission of some ethical issues in favour of others. This omission happens without any explicit comments. And fourth, sexual ethics offers us a heuristic, albeit limited, perspective for analysing the weaknesses and blind spots, even certain dogmatism, in one of the major theological currents of our times. It reveals unexplicated thinking habits in LT, which influence the overall theological project. Since the praxis starting point also creates similar problems in another liberation theological current, FT, including the Latin American version of it, it could be maintained that it is the role given to the praxis in general that leads to certain incoherencies, omissions and contradictions in liberation theologies.

Next, I will discuss some of the specific conceptual difficulties liberation theologians, including feminist liberation theologians, have when discussing sexual ethics and reproductive rights in the Latin American context. I also will bring forth empirical data which points towards the great necessity of critical sexual ethical discourse on the continent, LT being the privileged context most suitable for it. Poor women's praxis, the poor woman as an integrated subject with reproductive capacities, has a weight that no discourse on praxis can ignore.

4.2 Sexual Ethics and Poor Women as Subjects of Theology

In Chapter 4.1, it was shown how issues of sexual ethics are being treated in LT. The issue is mostly avoided. When it is taken up, liberation theologians do not differ notably from the official Vatican teaching, even when this has not been their conscious aim. Moreover, in their discourse concerning the 'defence of the life of the poor' and their anti-imperialist critical stand towards population programmes defined and designed in the First World but aimed primarily at the Third World, liberation theologians have reached agreement with the Vatican and their own Latin American bishops. This is explicit and becomes clear in several official statements in which 'contraceptive imperialism' is denounced. Again, this may not be deliberate on the part of the liberation theologians, even though it would be so in the case of certain individual Latin American bishops, who both sympathize with LT and support the Vatican in issues of sexual ethics.

What is clear, though, is that in none of the cases do the poor Latin American women appear as subjects in their own right. They are, however, the ones who suffer most from the present situation. They are targets for both the absolutist teaching of the church and aggressive population control programmes. It is their perspective that lacks in both, and in LT, too.

In this section, I will first clarify the conceptual and practical confusion which is partly behind the situation of Catholic liberation theologians taking sides with the Vatican in issues of sexual ethics. Many Third World feminists, as well, are very critical of population control programmes and discourses on reproductive rights which do not take into account the specific circumstances of poor women in poor countries. Thus, they too may find themselves—at least on the level of rhetorics—denouncing 'demographic imperialism' together with the Vatican and Muslim fundamentalists. These clarifications will be made in Chapter 4.2.1.

Then I will discuss the real life conditions, the *vida cotidiana*, of poor Latin American women. I will show how this perspective, as brought forth by Latin American feminist liberation theologians, may serve as a bridge and critical element between the above-mentioned discourses and practices. Although the concept is not explicitly elaborated much in the context of sexual ethics, it nevertheless offers us tools for taking the praxis of the poor women seriously and, possibly, for a critical-constructive sexual ethical agenda in the setting of Latin American feminist liberation theology. Its definite starting point is in seeing the poor women as subjects of both their own lives and Latin American theology. However, the *vida cotidiana* perspective contains problems similar to those of the overall praxis starting point in LT. This will be analysed in Chapter 4.2.2. There will be an emphasis on the issue of abortion in which the life and death issues of poverty for women are crystallized and in which the Catholic Church and (Catholic) theologians have an especially important role to play.

4.2.1 *Clarification of Terms and Positions*

The International Conference on Population and Development, held in Cairo, Egypt, in September 1994, created strange bedfellows, such as the Vatican and fundamentalist Muslims, in order to prevent the inclusion of contraception and abortion as reproductive rights in the final document of the conference. However, the conference has also been characterized as 'enshrining an almost-feminist vision of reproductive rights and gender equality in place of the old population control discourse'.[137] Women's organizations from both the North and the South were successful in their lobbying, maybe for the first time in the history of such big international conferences, and as such, this represents a major historic achievement, won by women's efforts.[138]

Before the conference, Vandana Shiva from India said:

> The most important challenge facing the forthcoming UN Population Conference in Cairo is whether it will be able to transcend the 'demographic fundamentalism' of the US and the 'religious fundamentalism' of the Vatican and put Third World women at the centre of the population discourse.[139]

She refers to the history of the so-called 'population bomb' and the different measures taken to stop or control it, which more than often have ended up in coercive methods against the poor women of the Third World, considered as both the prime cause and solution of the problem.[140]

Thus, the critical view on Western 'demographic imperialism' is shared by such diverse groups as the Vatican, fundamentalist Muslims, feminist health activists and Third World development critics. As we saw in the previous chapter, various liberation theologians and sectors close to them *and* the hierarchy of the Latin American Catholic Church are also in this group. Nevertheless, feminist groups hardly endorse the Vatican agenda on reproductive issues. It is of utmost importance to understand the different positions and arguments behind the seemingly common agenda. A new agent in this already confusing discourse are different environmentalist groups which see the growing population in the Third World as the main cause for global environmental degradation, and eventually, ecological catastrophies.

In the course of international population policies, the nature of the problems perceived in the North has been expressed plainly: the growing population of the South is a threat to the supply of resources necessary to the economy; there is a potential of large protest movements against international economic order;[141] rapid population growth is a primary cause of the Third World's problems, notably hunger, environmental destruction, economic stagnation and political

---

137.   Petchesky 1995: 152. Also, 'A new definition of population policy was advanced, giving prominence to reproductive health and the empowerment of women while downplaying the demographic rationale for population policy' (McIntosh and Finkle 1995: 223).
138.   Petchesky 1995: 153-56.
139.   Shiva 1994: 4.
140.   See Amalric and Banuri 1994; De Barbieri 1993; Hartmann 1995; Kabeer 1994: 187-222.
141.   Koivusalo and Ollila 1996: 193.

instability.[142] Thus, people must be persuaded—or forced, if necessary—to have fewer children. Birth control services can be 'delivered' to Third World women in a top-down fashion, even in the absence of basic health-care systems.[143] According to Hartmann,

> When the overriding goal of family planning programs is to reduce population growth, rather than to expand the freedom of individuals to decide whether and when to have children, the results are often detrimental to women's health and well-being, and ineffective in terms of the stated goal of lowering birth rates.[144]

Against the argumentation of most population organizations and many international aid agencies, Hartmann says—joining feminist analyses both in the North and the South—that rapid population growth is *not* the root cause of development problems, but rather it is a symptom of them.[145] Improvements in the living standards and the position of women, via more equitable social and economic development, are the best ways to motivate people to want fewer children. And finally, safe, effective and voluntary birth control services cannot be 'delivered' in a top-down, technocratic fashion.[146] According to Hartmann, overpopulation is one of the most pervasive myths in Western society, which makes it possible to blame the poor for their poverty and make those who have the least power of all, the poor women and their children of the Third World, responsible for issues that are far beyond their control. It makes these women mere wombs to be controlled.[147]

This is an extremely broad and complicated discussion, and I am not going into it more deeply than what is necessary. Willingly or unwillingly, liberation theologians, too, are part of this discussion, as are feminist liberation theologians. This is why it is important that their positions be clarified. It is exactly in this discussion on population growth (and control) and women's reproductive rights—especially in the Third World—where the issue of sexual ethics in LT makes any sense. First, those liberation theologians who take up the issue at all explicitly join some of the voices in this discussion. Second, there is a feminist health and reproductive rights movement in the Third World, including Latin America, which has been an active participant in this global discussion. Its contacts with LT have been few and conflictive. Third, since the Vatican is one of the most powerful political actors in the formulation of global population policies and the

---

142.   Hartmann 1995: xix. See also Amalric and Banuri 1994: 699-700.

143.   Hartmann 1995: xix.

144.   Hartmann 1995: xix-xx.

145.   Hartmann 1995: xx. See also Amalric and Banuri 1994: 693, 696. They point out that population growth is a consequence of bad health, limited education and patriarchy, not the problem itself. At the local level, population growth is often a solution to problems, not a problem in itself.

146.   Hartmann 1995: xx.

147.   Hartmann 1995: 4; Koivusalo and Ollila 1996: 196-97. They point out that in discussions about sustainable development of the globe, the unsustainable patterns of consumption in the industrialized world usually get recognized alongside population growth in the Third World. Nevertheless, the actions required usually concentrate on reducing population growth.

concerned legislation in Catholic countries,[148] it is important that there are also (Catholic) theologians and lay people who are able to discuss sexual ethics in adequate terms.

As has been shown, the Catholic Church has officially adopted some of the language of LT (and feminism, as well) in its discourse on sexual ethics. When speaking of 'demographic imperialism' and condemning coercive birth control practices in the Third World—including dangerous contraceptives and forced or unconsulted sterilizations[149]—the Vatican joins many Third World intellectuals and activists who have good grounds for their suspicion of the motives behind global population policies. Nevertheless, in condemning both 'artificial' contraception and abortion and in adopting the absolute 'right-to-life' position only in the context of reproductive issues, the Vatican is a long way from the concerns of the women's movement. According to Hartmann,

> The population control and antiabortion philosophies, although diametrically opposed, share one thing in common: They are both antiwomen. Population control advocates impose contraception and sterilization on women; the so-called Right to Life movement denies women the basic right of access to abortion and birth control. *Neither takes the interests and rights of the individual woman as their starting point. Both approaches attempt to control women, instead of letting women control their bodies themselves*.[150]

Or, as Naila Kabeer puts it, 'The effects of pro-natalist policies that pressurize women to have more children than they want have been as repugnant as those which enforce lower fertility'.[151]

According to Rosalind Pollack Petchesky, the Cairo document is successful in many ways from women's point of view—for example, in identifying the elimination of all forms of discrimination against women as a prerequisite to ending poverty and promoting sustainable development. Nevertheless, with regard to global economic and political structures, development models and the enabling conditions necessary to realize reproductive and sexual rights, the programme is no achievement at all.[152] The practical implementation of Cairo's agenda will be impossible without the reallocation of resources globally and nationally to assure the full funding of social programmes, especially health—in other words, without

---

148.   According to Hartmann (1995: 53), in Latin America the Catholic Church has prevented many governments from establishing national family planning programmes. See also Kabeer 1994: 197; McIntosh and Finkle 1995: 224, 237; Pitanguy 1994: 113.

149.   On Latin American examples of coercive sterilization operations, see Hartmann 1995: 247-51. The most well-known cases are Puerto Rico, Colombia and Brazil. In the 1980s in Colombia female sterilization was the second most popular family planning method. See also Kabeer 1994: 195-98, 204-205, on examples of coercive practices and their concomitant indifference to human rights, and Molyneux 1988.

150.   Hartmann 1995: xviii (emphasis added).

151.   Kabeer 1994: 196.

152.   Petchesky 1995: 153, 156. In the document, there is no analysis of the impact of structural adjustment policies, foreign debt and transnational corporations on women's health, poverty and social programmes. There is a failure to address the real implications of privatization.

radically new development alternatives.[153] According to Petchesky, in spite of its progressive pro-woman language, the Cairo document promotes the very privatization, commodification and deregulation of reproductive health services that have led to diminished access and increasing mortality and morbidity for poor women.[154]

Petchesky does not separate her critique of the impact of market economies, privatization, structural adjustment policies, and the gap between the rich North and the poor South from her defence of full reproductive rights for women, especially the poorest of them. Liberation theologians and the Vatican criticize the former but count the latter among the same imperialist, foreign and coercive measures against the Third World poor. According to Petchesky,

> These fundamentalist forces (with the Vatican in the lead) also make a spurious claim to speak for the countries of the South in their struggle to change global economic relations and their opposition to cultural imperialism, including 'Western feminism'. In this way, moral conservatism and social and economic restructuring get oddly lumped together, and feminists who speak out in favour of reproductive and sexual rights or women's bodily self-determination, whatever country they are from, find themselves accused of fronting for the interests of Northern governments and donor agencies.[155]

Thus, 'women' and 'gender' become perceived as code words for imperialism, both cultural and economic.[156] However, it is exactly in the critical attitude towards the effects of neoliberalist economics for the poorest sections of society where liberation theologians and feminist health activists could approach one another.

Amalric and Banuri state that

> Starting by recognising that there is a conflict between people's strategies of livelihood at the local level and national priorities, between the North and the South with respect to the global environmental crisis, does not mean that nothing should be done to try to curb present fertility rates. It does not deny the importance of contraceptives, of education, and of health services. What it denies is the possibility to address the population issues outside a more global approach which would integrate these issues, notably economic and political ones. There is ample evidence that the conflicts mentioned above are part of the population issues. Remaining blind to them will only further exacerbate the problem, and might eventually lead to greater coercive measures against those who are silent: the poor and the powerless.[157]

---

153. Petchesky 1995: 156; Hartmann 1995: 138-39.
154. Petchesky 1995: 157. According to Wendy Harcourt, 'At the same time as women's health and education is seen as important for improving acceptance of contraceptive methods, structural adjustment programmes advocate cuts in primary health care and basic education' (Harcourt 1994: 11).
155. Petchesky 1995: 159.
156. Petchesky 1995: 160.
157. Amalric and Banuri 1994: 703.

According to Vandana Shiva, Third World women must be put at the centre of the population discourse as subjects by transcending patriarchal polarizations (of the state, religion and demographic establishment). This is also the way that women will be able to set an agenda for economic and social justice, environmental sustainability and women's right to health.[158]

The UN Conference on Environment and Development held in Rio de Janeiro, Brazil, in 1992 made popular the notion that the 'population explosion' is the cause of the environmental destruction of the planet. The environmental activists and researchers join women's groups in being critical of the mainstream arguments of population and environment. Both challenge the current development model by arguing that we need to move away from solutions based on infinite growth.[159] Nevertheless, alliances between women's groups and environmentalists falter because the policies proposed do not usually say anything about women.[160] Women fear that in order to 'save the planet' they may again become targets of coercive population programmes, which do not take women's empowerment as their starting point but rather see them as objects to be controlled.[161] Poor women are blamed for global consumption for which they are not responsible. Blaming environmental degradation on population growth may lay the groundwork for the re-emergence and intensification of top-down, demographically driven population policies and programmes deeply disrespectful of women, particularly women of colour, and their children.[162] The growing involvement of environmentalists in population debates is leading to new versions of the old link between population growth and global disaster.[163] The fact that a disproportionate amount of the world's resources are consumed by a small minority located mainly in the industrialized countries is often bypassed.[164]

The global feminist agenda on reproductive health issues and population policies has centred on an ethical critique of the demographic approach to population problems, on the one hand, and critique of the models of development that have systematically ignored women and destroyed the local environments, on the other.[165] According to Naila Kabeer, population policies in the past few decades offer an excellent illustration of why merely targeting women,

158. Shiva 1994: 6.

159. Harcourt 1994: 11.

160. Harcourt 1994: 11, 13.

161. Harcourt 1994: 13; Hartmann 1995: 131-55; Kabeer 1994: 187-88, 203-204; McIntosh and Finkle 1995: 237-38; Shiva 1994; Simons 1995.

162. Koivusalo and Ollila 1996: 196-97; McIntosh and Finkle 1995: 237.

163. Kabeer 1994: 188.

164. The population/environment lobby at Rio de Janeiro portrayed the women's actions against coercive population policies as playing into the hands of the Catholic Church. However, both in Rio and Cairo it became clear that feminist health activists strongly support women's access to safe, voluntary contraception and abortion as basic rights, but not as tools of population control, in clear opposition to the Vatican and religious fundamentalists (Hartmann 1995: 147; McIntosh and Finkle 1995: 237).

165. McIntosh and Finkle 1995: 236.

without considering the broader social relations in which they live, is unlikely either to change their lives or to achieve intended goals. As the pressure of population on limited resources becomes identified as the major cause of world poverty, women are being seen as both the cause and therefore the potential solution.[166]

When taking a critical stance on global population policies, Latin American liberation theologians, together with the Vatican, also take sides with left-wing movements, such as Sandinism in Nicaragua, failing, however, to distinguish between population control interventions from abroad and women's real need for birth control.[167] In his most recent encyclicals, *Veritatis Splendor* (1993) and *Evangelium Vitae* (1995), Pope John Paul II is critical of both imperialism—especially of what he considers 'demographic imperialism'—and the effects of neoliberal economics on the poor. It is easy to understand why liberation theologians and Latin American Catholic bishops can agree with him. They, too, hold the argument that the fundamental issue is not population growth but poverty and uneven distribution of the world's resources between the North and the South.[168]

'The culture of death' is now one of the favourite concepts for the Pope, Latin American Catholic bishops, liberation theologians and feminists. They share with each other the critique of a development model, which is based on unlimited growth, and its impacts especially in the Third World. In reproductive issues, they share the conviction that many of the population programmes realized in the South, including Latin America, have not served human ends. There are racist presuppositions behind the view that there are 'too many dark babies being born' in the world, instead of the view that it is mainly the white minority of the globe which causes global environmental problems. Further, they can also agree that it is the poor women and children of the Third World who suffer most.

Nevertheless, none of the first three looks at the concrete situation of those women and children. They do not take a critical look at the limits of real possibilities of choice women have in a patriarchal culture. They want to defend the rights of the poor to education, health, employment and a decent standard of living, but without asking how poverty is connected to reproduction and women's status. They fail to make the connection between aggressive population programmes, racism, poverty and sexism. It is the very interconnection of these factors that informs the feminist point of view, both in the secular feminist

166. Kabeer 1994: 187. According to her, a population policy that is concerned with the needs of the poor, as well as with the preservation of the natural environment, has to break finally with the narrow fertility-reduction goals of the past and address the social conditions in which reproductive choices can be enhanced. Birth rates have declined in countries where socio-economic development has been relatively advanced and family planning services strong. For example, in countries with high infant mortality, people are likely to want more children (Kabeer 1994: 204-205).

167. Hartmann 1995: 53.

168. On Pope John Paul II's advocacy in social issues, see Fox 1995: 313-21; McIntosh and Finkle 1995: 243-44.

movement and in FT. This is the central point where the feminist perspective differs drastically from the other three, and which I claim to be of importance if we want to tackle environmental and reproductive issues simultaneously.

When liberation theologians speak of 'the radical and absolute option for life'[169] and of human life being 'an absolute value',[170] they do not specify what they mean by 'life'. This is of specific importance in the abortion issue, where the principle of absolute right to life informs the Catholic and 'pro-life' Protestant view. It is not my intention to discuss the abortion debate here. I merely want to point out that if liberation theologians want to create a coherent ethics—which includes sexual ethics—this kind of specification would be necessary.

Most feminists, including Ivone Gebara,[171] when speaking of the reproductive realities of poor women, consider the issue of life and death from another angle. Illegal abortions, too many pregnancies too often, and undernourishment are the main causes of death of poor women all over the Third World. There will be no solution as long as the life of the woman and the life of her (potential) child are put against each other.[172]

Mary O'Brien points out that the parameters of the abortion debate have come from two abstractions: 'life' on the one hand and the 'right' to free choice on the other hand. It is mostly men who have defined what constitutes life itself, without having the experience of conceiving new life, carrying it and giving birth to it.[173] This is, of course, a statement that excludes all those women who have not been pregnant from definitions of life. Nevertheless, most feminist ethicists agree with O'Brien that whereas only women get pregnant, men, almost exclusively, interpret the morality of and make the laws about abortion.[174]

According to Beverly Wildung Harrison, a theologically trained ethicist, almost nothing, especially in the literature in Christian ethics, has been written on the morality of abortion that fully reflects women's experience.[175] Much of what has been written reflects an open misogyny and lack of concern for women.[176] Misogyny in Christian discussions of abortion is evidenced clearly in the fact that the abortion decision is never treated in the way it arises as part of the female agent's life process.[177] According to Harrison, the discussion on abortion treats abortion as if it were an isolated act or deed having no relation to the lived world other than its involvement with prospective birth.[178] For her, as well as for most other

---

169. Richard 1994: 94.
170. Richard 1994: 100.
171. See Chapter 4.1.1.
172. On feminist theological perspectives on abortion, see especially Harrison 1983 and 1985: 115-34 (together with Shirley Cloyes).
173. O'Brien 1989: 301-303.
174. Harrison 1983: 2.
175. Harrison 1983: 6.
176. 'We have a long way to go before the sanctity of human life will include genuine regard and concern for every female already born' (Harrison 1985: 115).
177. Harrison 1985: 123.
178. Harrison 1983: 9.

feminist ethicists, 'The well-being of a woman and the value of her life plan always must be recognized as of intrinsic value in any appeal to intrinsic value in a moral analysis of abortion'.[179]

According to Harrison,

> If we are ever to become genuinely serious about reducing the need for abortions…, we must cut through the miasma of fear and suspicion about women's sexuality and confront, by concrete analysis of women's lives, the conditions that lead women to resort to frequent abortion.[180]

Only uncompromising, extensive support for a feminist agenda of social justice for women can hold out any hope of reducing the need for abortions.[181] In other words,

> Our moral goal should be to struggle against those real barriers—poverty, racism, and antifemale cultural oppression—that prevent authentic choice from being a reality for every woman. In this process we will be able to minimize the need for abortions only insofar as we place the abortion debate in the real lived-world context of women's lives.[182]

Finally, there must be concrete respect for women as fully autonomous, unconditionally valuable members of the moral community.[183]

Harrison also joins secular feminist opinions of reproductive rights when she states that

> Under the most adverse conditions, women have had to try to control our fertility—everywhere, always. Women's relation to procreation irrevocably marks and shapes our lives… Women's lack of social power, in all recorded history, has made this struggle to control procreation a life-bending, often life-destroying one for a large percentage of females.[184]

Concretely, this means that women have always resorted and always will resort to abortions. The issue is not whether they are legal or illegal, but whether they are performed in decent conditions.

What both secular and religious feminists share is their emphasis on the real-life conditions of real women, especially the most vulnerable of them. Conceptually, this is very much what Latin American feminist liberation theologians mean by *vida cotidiana*, although they do not discuss it in the context of sexual ethics, for reasons that have been pointed out. Nevertheless, much of what Harrison says on the contradiction between abstract discussion of life, especially

179. Harrison 1983: 16. She also discusses at length how the understanding of when life begins has been changing through the history of theology.
180. Harrison 1983: 245.
181. Harrison 1983: 249.
182. Harrison 1985: 126.
183. Harrison 1983: 251.
184. Harrison 1983: 122. Similarly, Naila Kabeer: 'Abortion remains a major means of fertility control in the world…throughout history women have resorted to abortion, whether legal or not, for the sake of themselves and for their children and that restrictive laws do not stop abortions—they simply make them unsafe' (Kabeer 1994: 207).

in the context of abortion, on the one hand, and the inability to speak of women's life in concrete terms, on the other hand, also applies to those liberation theologians who defend the life of the poor in rather abstract terms. And as has been said, the poorer the women we are talking about, the more the issues of life, death and reproduction are bound together.

4.2.2 La vida cotidiana: Feminist Theology and the Realities of Poor Women in Latin America

Taking all the above considerations into account and remembering that the liberation theologians and the so-called progressive church in Latin America have always taken a critical distance to feminist issues, especially those concerning sexuality or reproductive rights,[185] it becomes understandable why those liberation theologians who take up these issues at all seem to agree with the official Vatican teaching.

Nevertheless, I have been claiming that LT offers the privileged, albeit difficult and contradictory, space for a critical discussion of issues of sexual ethics. This is especially true of Latin American feminist liberation theology, which by its very nature is able to speak to several audiences and shares interests with different actors who may be in open conflict with each other, such as the Catholic hierarchy and feminist movements. Could Latin American feminist liberation theology present a critical voice to both mainstream LT and to feminist concerns over reproductive rights?

According to Maura O'Neill, the interreligious, global dialogue between women is revealing that for women, as well as for other people seeking liberation, there seems to be a vital connection between social justice and religion. Many women are realizing that an understanding of religious issues is basic to changing the situation of women. A culture's religious traditions *are* its basis for meaning-making, image-making and creating an ordered world. Religious images, including images of women, are profoundly influential in determining attitudes toward women. The fight for women's rights in the secular arena will be weakened if it fails to acknowledge the religious dimension of the problem.[186]

Although I am not going to go through the specifically religious or theological issues behind both traditional and feminist sexual ethics, I do agree with O'Neill that it is of utmost importance. There are plenty of works written on theological ethics from a feminist perspective, with a specific focus on issues of sexual and reproductive ethics. Nevertheless, O'Neill holds the same view as I do on why feminist liberation theologians are in an especially important position in Latin America. As has been said, the secular feminist movement, in Latin America and elsewhere, is unable to adequately and profoundly question the Vatican teaching on contraception and abortion because of the 'feminist blindness' to the importance of religion for many women. Feminist theologians have the tools to dialogue with both secular feminism and the church. Theological arguments have to be

185. See Pitanguy 1994: 107-109.
186. O'Neill 1990: 54-55.

countered theologically. Since this project undoubtedly will be different in Latin America than elsewhere—including European Catholic countries—it must be the Latin American women themselves who take it up. In spite of similarities and mutual learning, a sexual ethics from the perspective of poor women will look different from a feminist theological ethics in the First World setting.

The kind of theorizing Latin American feminist liberation theologians have been doing until now offers tools for a new sexual ethical discourse, which moves in the minefield among the official Catholic teaching, liberation theology, secular feminism, patriarchal culture, and the often brutal realities of the poor women of the continent. It is especially the perspective of *vida cotidiana* which I claim to be the most adequate tool and even prerequisite for the creation of a sexual ethics in LT, which does not mean that there would not be others as well. However, the *vida cotidiana* contains problems that need to be surpassed in order to adequately address issues of sexual ethics.

María Pilar Aquino points out how sexual ethics and sexuality constitute some of the major challenges to the Catholic Church today. The perspective of sexual liberation must be included in all emancipatory projects.[187] More concretely, she takes up the issue of sexual violence and battering.[188] The central notion of *vida cotidiana* as a general corrective of male perspectives in LT acquires more specific connotations in issues of sexual ethics. It means, among other things, returning to everyday life its political aspect, questioning the traditional split between the private and the public,[189] restoring women's strength, authority, leadership and wisdom as constitutive aspects of their identity,[190] and bringing women's everyday struggle for life and for their own right to life to the centre of all emancipatory practices and reflections.[191]

The option for the poor woman of Latin American feminist liberation theology leads towards greater realism and honesty concerning the reality (*lo real*). The real significance of liberation is better understood from the perspective of poor women.[192] It is about affirming everyday life in the midst of so much everyday death.[193]

Aquino, too, stresses the importance of life and the right to life as central categories for new Christian ethics.[194] Even though she does not explicitly discuss concrete issues such as abortion and birth control,[195] it is obvious that her overall theoretical and practical context differs from that of her male colleagues mentioned above. At the centre of the right to life is the threatened life of women as

187. Aquino 1992a: 174, 175.
188. Aquino 1992a: 175-77. Also in Aquino 1997: 30.
189. Aquino 1992a: 177 and 1997: 30.
190. Aquino 1992a: 179.
191. Aquino 1992a: 178-79.
192. Aquino 1992b: 34-35.
193. Aquino 1992b: 34-35.
194. Aquino 1992a: 232-33; 1992b: 35, 39 and 1994a: 61, 69.
195. In a later text, Aquino refers to health and reproductive rights as important aspects that Latin American feminist liberation theology has to take into account (Aquino 1997: 8, 36).

human subjects.[196] Women and children (foetuses) are not put into opposition with each other. They are seen instead as co-dependent in a system of oppression. The operative anthropological presuppositions of the Latin American feminist theologians are different from the more traditional perspective, also represented by many liberation theologians. A feminist theological anthropology stresses women's bodiliness and concrete everyday experiences—including violence, sexuality and survival—and not specific transhistorical feminine qualities or complementarities between men and women.

Nevertheless, it seems that this discourse on life and death (of the poor), the threat to human life in Latin America, the right to life as a central theological and ethical category, needs to be specified, concretized and differentiated in LT, from a feminist perspective as well. If not, there is the possibility of using this discourse to quite opposite ends, as we have seen. For a feminist sexual ethics, it is hardly desirable.

The perspective of *vida cotidiana*, if it is further concretized, could be a corrective for these tensions in LT. If too abstract theorizing on 'femininity' and 'masculinity'—instead of concrete women and men and their life conditions— seems to make it impossible to speak of subjects like sexual ethics in new terms, holding up the *vida cotidiana* merely as a theoretical tool may have the same result. Concreteness is of special importance in the context of a praxis-based theology, which aims at creating new ethical principles. Such a project is needed in order to take effective steps in improving women's situation in Latin America, including legislation which in most countries still follows Catholic reasoning in issues of sexual ethics.

The statistics concerning women's realities in the Third World show the interconnection between poverty, lack of reproductive rights and women's mortality. Globally some 585,000 women died from pregnancy-related causes in 1990, 99 per cent of them in developing countries.[197] Some 23,000 of these maternal deaths occurred in Latin America and the Caribbean, with strong variation within the region.[198] According to the World Health Organization,

---

196.   For example, 'una de las tareas que enfrenta la reflexión de las mujeres en el ámbito de la ética cristiana liberadora es, precisamente, criticar y desmantelar los fundamentos del orden socio-religioso actual que subordina a las mujeres. Se trata de desbrozar el camino hacia un orden nuevo, cuyo criterio ético primordial sea la afirmación de la vida en plenitud y la integridad de toda persona humana' (Aquino 1992a: 228). She also says: 'No se trata aquí…de un principio que legitima el estereotipo patriarcal sobre las mujeres según el cual, ellas, por sus funciones biológicas, deban dedicarse a la exclusiva función procreativa. La comprensión liberadora de la vida supone el rescate y "des-cubrimiento" de todas las energías espirituales, físicas y sociales concentradas en la condición de la mujer' (Aquino 1992b: 39).

197.   World Health Organization 1996: 2. Because measuring maternal mortality is difficult and complex, reliable estimates of the dimensions of the problem are not generally available (World Health Organization 1996: 1). In poor countries, as much as 21 to 46 per cent of women's deaths in the age group between 15 to 49 years can be maternal deaths. See Henshaw 1990.

198.   World Health Organization 1996: 3, 10-15.

Maternal mortality is a particularly sensitive indicator of inequity. Of all the indicators commonly used to compare levels of development between countries and regions, levels of maternal mortality show the widest disparities. Maternal mortality offers a litmus test of the status of women.[199]

The majority of maternal deaths in developing countries is preventable. Women in their prime reproductive period (20 to 35-year age group) number among these deaths. These women also have the most young, dependent children whose own survival and well-being may be seriously compromised by the death of their mother.[200]

It has been estimated that there are 36 to 53 million abortions per year world-wide, of which 30 to 50 per cent are illegal.[201] In 1993, 41 per cent of the world's population lived in countries with legislation allowing abortion on request, and 25 per cent where an abortion is allowed only if the woman's life is in danger.[202]

---

199.   World Health Organization 1996: 2. According to the International Classification of Diseases, a maternal death is defined as the death of a woman while pregnant or within 42 days of termination of pregnancy, irrespective of the duration and the site of the pregnancy, from any cause related to or aggravated by the pregnancy or its management but not from accidental or incidental causes (Graham and Airey 1987: 324). Thus, abortions, legal and illegal, are counted among these causes.

200.   Graham and Airey 1987: 323.

201.   Henshaw 1990: 62-64. According to Kabeer, about 33 million safe, legal abortions are carried out each year. Clandestine procedures raise the total to between 45 to 60 million (Kabeer 1994: 207).

202.   Henshaw 1990: 59. Restrictive laws do not necessarily mean that safe abortion services are unavailable. In Latin America, virtually all major cities have physicians who perform abortions. Because of the cost of these services and their scarcity outside of major cities, most abortions in Latin America are probably self-induced or performed by nonmedical practitioners, with Cuba as a notable exception. On the other hand, the absence of restrictions does not guarantee that services will be available. In India and Bangladesh, the overall shortage of medical facilities makes legal abortion unavailable to most women (Henshaw 1990: 60-61, 64). In both cases, it is the poorest women who fall outside the services.

Nevertheless, when access to safe abortion has been introduced in a country, maternal mortality has decreased. The provision of abortion under modern medical conditions has reduced abortions mortality to an extremely low level in countries that have legalized the procedure (Henshaw 1990: 64).

In contrast, experience in Romania shows the dramatic rise in maternal mortality which can occur when abortion is made illegal. In 1966, President Nicolae Ceaucescu introduced pro-natalist policies, outlawed abortion and contraception, and took measures to enforce the law (mandatory pelvic examinations at places of employment, introduction of security police in maternity hospitals, and so on). These policies resulted in the highest maternal mortality rate in Europe and in thousands of unwanted children in institutions. In the 23 years of its enforcement, the anti-abortion law in Romania resulted in over 10,000 deaths of women from unsafe abortions. The Romanian experience demonstrates the futility and folly of attempts to control reproductive behaviour through legislation. A law that forbids abortion does not stop women from aborting unwanted pregnancies. Criminalizing abortion has never prevented it; it simply increases its human and material costs to women. See Stephenson et al. 1992. See also Henshaw 1990: 61, 64; Kabeer 1994: 197; Koivusalo and Ollila 1996: 202.

The Romanian case also makes clear that the ideological reasons behind restrictive abortion

Thus, whether legal or illegal, abortion remains a major means of fertility control
in the world.[203]

Abortion is the leading cause of death for Latin American women between 15
and 39 years of age.[204] In spite of the difficulty in obtaining exact estimations,
Stanley Henshaw states: 'Complications of nonmedical abortions are a major
cause of maternal mortality, and their treatment absorbs a large share of the
medical resources devoted to obstetrics and gynecology'.[205] According to Naila
Kabeer, an estimated 200,000 or more Third World women die needlessly each
year due to botched abortions.[206]

According to Kabeer,

> It is important to bear in mind that maternal health and well-being requires atten-
> tion to women's status long before they become pregnant… The constraining factors
> that help to perpetuate women's low status, high fertility and maternal mortality/
> morbidity rates across generations are closely intertwined and have to be dealt with
> simultaneously.[207]

Thus, a health-care policy that only recognizes women in their capacity as repro-
ducers is unlikely to promote a social perception of women as empowered social
actors.[208]

According to Barroso and Bruschini, in Latin America the Catholic Church is
considered the most important pressure group against governmental support of
family planning programmes.[209] Their case study is Brazil, but much of what they
say is valid in other parts of the continent as well. However, there are differences
between countries. The Brazilian church is simultaneously highly dependent on
the Vatican and strongly influenced by LT. This has led to a curious combination
of a great tolerance for birth-control practices at the individual level and an absolute rejection of any kind of official family-planning policy. This rejection is a
point of consensus in a church otherwise quite divided with regard to political
and doctrinal issues.[210] The writers draw the conclusion that the importance of
the issue of family planning is inflated in order to overshadow disagreements in
other areas. This becomes clear when one looks at the 'progressive wing of the
church' (liberation theologians).[211] They also note how the arguments against

laws may differ, but the results are the same. A Communist state apparatus can enforce laws
similar to those in Catholic Latin American countries.

203. Kabeer 1994: 207.
204. Sihvo and Kajesalo 1994: 117. Cuba is the only country in Latin America with legalized
abortion (Henshaw 1990: 60).
205. Henshaw 1990: 65.
206. Kabeer 1994: 207.
207. Kabeer 1994: 218.
208. Kabeer 1994: 219.
209. Barroso and Bruschini 1991: 154; Hartmann 1995: 51, 53. For concrete examples of
recent direct interventions of the Catholic Church into national legislation policies concerning
family planning, see Chauvin 1995 (Peru) and Pitanguy 1994 (Brazil).
210. Barroso and Bruschini 1991: 154.
211. Barroso and Bruschini 1991: 155.

family planning are political, rather than religious.[212] This again is notably true especially of the liberation theologians, as we saw in Chapter 4.1.1.

If liberation theologians want to maintain their discourse on defending the life of the poor, they should also take these realities of the poor into account. Defending the life of poor women implies defending their reproductive rights, stemming from a sexual ethics that is able to start from the concrete realities of these women. Whatever this means in questions of legalization of abortion, for example, is up to Latin Americans themselves. However, closing one's eyes to the reality of poor women is inconsistent with liberation theologians' overall emphasis on praxis and their defence of the life of the poor.

Because of the difficulty in finding a consistent liberation theological sexual ethics and because of the confusing statements of single theologians, I would claim that in spite of concentrating on a discourse between life and death, the perspective of *vida cotidiana* serves as a better starting point for the creation of constructive sexual ethics in LT. The statistics clearly state that defending the life and possibility of choice of an adult woman best serves as the guarantee of defence of life more generally, that is, potential and existing children.[213] According to the World Bank,

> Women's own health and their efficiency in using available resources have an important bearing on the health of others in the family, particularly children... Education greatly strengthens women's ability to perform their vital role in creating healthy households... A child's health is affected more by the mother's schooling than by the father's schooling... Data from thirteen African countries between 1975 and 1985 show that a 10 percent increase in female literacy rates reduced child mortality by 10 percent, whereas changes in male literacy had little influence.[214]

Any discourse on issues concerning abortion, life and death, contraceptive imperialism, and so on, should thus start from women's realities, especially the poorest of them, since they are the ones with least possibility of choice and they are also the prime victims of coercive policies. According to Naila Kabeer, 'Surely any notion of social justice, and certainly any notion of gender equity, demands that those who bear the main burden of reproductive responsibilities should also enjoy a measure of reproductive choice'.[215]

---

212.   Barroso and Bruschini 1991.

213.   According to Graham and Airey, 'Maternal deaths are now frequently described as family tragedies with wide-reaching repercussions... When a woman dies in childbirth, the death sentence of the child she carries is almost certainly written. Often the children she leaves behind suffer the same fate, and the family stands a good chance of disintegration' (Graham and Airey 1987: 332).

According to Linda M. Whiteford, 'Infant mortality increases with increases in maternal undernutrition, contributing to low birth weight and the provision of little resistance to disease... Evaluations of infant mortality both by age and cause of death suggest that poor maternal health and nutritional status during pregnancy heavily contribute to the high infant death rate' (Whiteford 1993: 1393).

214.   The World Bank 1993: 42-44.

215.   Kabeer 1994: 204.

Theologically, this points toward the necessity of rethinking theological anthropology in the context of LT. Feminist theologians in both the North and the South emphasize the historical, concrete realities of women, including their body and bodiliness, as a more accurate starting point for theological anthropology than is a female *essentia*. This pragmatic starting point in the context of Latin American LT is what feminist liberation theologians call *vida cotidiana*.

This pragmatic perspective challenges the traditional understanding of praxis in Latin American LT and ahistorical women's experience in FT. The limits of sexual ethical elaborations in LT even propose a critical perspective on the limits of praxis as a theological method. To maintain the praxis starting point as strongly as liberation theologians wish implies re-elaborations in the area of theological anthropology. From the poor women's point of view, this especially means reworking the understanding of the poor as the *locus* of LT. The poor must also be understood as heterogeneous, bodily, gendered and reproductive subjects, if LT is to maintain praxis as its starting point and expand its vision of liberation.

If Latin American feminist liberation theologians want the *vida cotidiana* perspective to realize its critical potential—which certainly would take LT in new directions—they may have to distance themselves from some of the methodological presuppositions of both LT and FT. As was shown in Chapter 2, 'women's experience' in FT has theoretical problems similar to the 'praxis starting point' in LT. When Latin American feminist liberation theologians place their *vida cotidiana* uncritically between these two discourses, they face the same problems. Thus, it is this very 'fixation' with praxis—be it defined as the realities of the poor, women's experiences or *vida cotidiana*—without paying attention to its limitations which creates the contradictory situation of not being able to critically analyse the very reality (praxis) one wishes to give such central status. A more critical reflection of the limitations of the starting point itself is necessary in order to avoid the strange combination of elevating some areas of the supposed praxis to an almost dogmatic position, on the one hand, and omitting other areas without any further explanations, on the other.

A critical Latin American feminist theology could overcome these conflicts by paying attention to the critique aimed at FT, especially from the perspective of recent feminist theory, and at LT from the feminist perspective.

4.3 Conclusions

There is a notable scantiness of issues of sexual ethics, especially in the area of reproduction, being treated in Latin American LT. Only a few liberation theologians and ethicists take it up as an issue at all. There are theological, political and cultural reasons for this overall silence. Neither Catholic nor Protestant liberation theologians give issues of sexual ethics much importance. Nevertheless, those who do are mainly Catholics. They seem to agree with the official teaching of the Catholic Church, especially in the area of theological anthropology: men and women are complementary to each other, which implies different roles in church and society. Liberation theologians tend to treat issues of gender, male–female relationship, and sexuality with less emphasis on history and praxis than in other areas. This again is reflected in their treatment of sexual ethics.

Willingly or unwillingly, liberation theologians end up agreeing in large part with the Vatican in issues of sexual and reproductive ethics. This becomes especially clear in the context of 'demographic imperialism', which both liberation theologians and the church hierarchy denounce, albeit for different reasons. There are also strong feminist groups which are critical of the coercive methods of international population programmes, aimed primarily at poor Third World women. The clarification of these different positions is important, because they stem from very different arguments. The silence of the liberation theologians, on the one hand, and their defence of the absolute value of life—mostly without further clarifications—in the context of sexual ethics, on the other hand, make it possible to interpret them as supporting the official teaching in issues of birth control and abortion. Thus, if this is not what liberation theologians want, they should pay more attention to explicit clarification of their position.

At the same time, the Catholic Church as an institution wields significant power in Latin American societies concerning legislation in issues of sexual ethics, most notably the criminalization of abortion. Direct intervention in national legislation on the part of the Catholic hierarchy is not rare. Thus, abortion remains illegal in all but one country (Cuba) in Latin America. Some countries allow abortion in cases of rape and when the continuation of the pregnancy produces a health risk for the mother. The rates of illegal abortions are extremely high and produce a danger for the poorest women, who cannot pay for and have access to a medically safe, albeit illegal, operation. Abortions are practised by qualified doctors in all countries of the region, but it is the poorest women in the countryside who must resort to botched abortions.

'The defence of the life of the poor' in LT is maintained at a somewhat abstract level. The death of poor women is intimately and directly connected to issues of reproduction (unsafe and lacking birth control, high rate of risk pregnancies and illegal abortions) which are the main causes of maternal mortality in Latin America as well as in other areas of the Third World. Preventing the death of poor women has not been an explicit part of liberation theologians' agenda for defending the life of the poor. The reason is that 'the poor' are seen mainly as productive subjects, understood in the framework of Marxist class analysis, and not as bodily, gendered and reproductive subjects as well. To see them as such would necessarily imply examining issues of sexual ethics in a more critical way. Catholic liberation theologians are also unwilling to risk their already difficult position in the church by taking a stance in favour of birth control and decriminalization of abortion.

It is not only that these issues are important in themselves: women, especially the poorest and most vulnerable of them, deserve more humane treatment. It is also that the little attention given to issues of sexual ethics is even more serious in LT than in some other—more theoretically orientated—form of modern theology because of the fundamental self-definition of LT as theology of praxis.

LT as praxis-orientated theology which considers ethical reasoning and action as central to its self-understanding as a theology starting from and aiming at changing unjust structures in church and society could be understood as giving—explicitly or implicitly—some guiding principles for a Christian life. If in some significant area an almost total silence rules, there must be powerful reasons for it.

Sexual ethics is an area in which liberation theologians are far from their stated ideals and method. Sexual ethics can thus serve as an example of insufficient conceptual analysis and its practical consequences in LT. It is questionable if the praxis starting point can be maintained as strongly as *the* starting point and method of LT, as it usually is. How the praxis model in fact can be realized in theology is, however, something to be clarified by further research.

Sexual ethics is an example of how 'the new way of doing theology' remains an ideal which has not become effective in LT in its entirety. There is a huge discrepancy within LT between praxis as an ideal and the ways in which it has been realized. If the praxis starting point would really have as determining a status in LT as it is claimed to have, one would expect this to be true in all areas of theology, including ethics, and when not, weighty reasons for this would be given.

Our case study seems to reveal that when praxis is given as definitive a status in theology as it gets in both LT and FT, more theoretical kinds of elaborations, especially concerning the status of one's truth claims, are not evaluated critically. This, in turn, leads to certain impotence of the chosen point of departure itself. When it comes to sexual ethics it becomes especially clear how liberation theologians simultaneously hold contradictory views. On the one hand, they claim to present the perspective of the Latin American poor which is not taken into account by the Vatican and First World theology. On the other hand, they end up presenting very traditional views in one area of ethics—the area that maybe in the most authoritarian and centralized way is created in Rome and given as instructions to the rest of the world. And even more seriously, it is an area of ethics which directly deals with issues concerning the life and death of the poor, who are the ones who die of reasons related to reproduction. The lack of a critical analysis of what is really meant by the praxis starting point may lead to uncritical and dogmatic attitudes even in issues which are said to have utmost importance and be in need of reinterpretation.

In sum, the scantiness of sexual ethics in LT is both a *challenge* for the supposed commitment to the praxis and a *critique* of the actual importance of praxis for the liberation theological method. Further, it critically *questions the content* of the praxis as being defined in LT up to now.

Can the concept *vida cotidiana* of the Latin American feminist liberation theologians open up possibilities for a critical-constructive sexual ethics in the context of LT? Although not explicitly elaborated as such, the perspective of *vida cotidiana* implies a different anthropology and sees the threatened life of poor women as a central ethical question. Latin American feminist liberation theology sees poor women as subjects who must be included in the formulation of LT. Feminist liberation theologians are in the important position of being able to speak to several, even opposing, audiences simultaneously. A secular feminist movement does not understand the critical role of religion—especially Catholicism—for many women. Nor does it have the adequate tools of analysis in order to employ a dialogue with the official teaching.

Latin American feminist liberation theologians are critical of the anthropological presuppositions in much of LT and see the necessity of new theological anthropology which takes the real life conditions of women, especially the poorest of them, seriously. Catholic Mariology has always served as the privileged area of both anti-female and anti-sexual anthropological underpinnings, which feminist theologians have tried to reveal. Latin American feminist liberation theologians point to a different Mary, which many women experience as a close and understanding figure. The *vida cotidiana*, taken together with Mariological reinterpretations, from the perspective of poor Latin American women, could thus serve as a critical corrective of both LT and traditional sexual ethics, and take LT in a direction in which both *liberation* and its *subjects* are understood in a more inclusive and heterogeneous way. Up to today, feminist liberation theologians have not touched upon issues of sexual ethics any more than have their male colleagues, with the exception of Ivone Gebara.

However, Latin American feminist liberation theology faces problems similar to those of LT in general as well as a FT which is not critical of its own presuppositions. Since Latin American feminist liberation theologians so eagerly endorse the methodological presuppositions of LT and take them as their central starting point as well, it is logical that similar critical questions can be asked of them, too. Even though *vida cotidiana* is understood as a critical corrective for the more general praxis starting point in LT, it is not given so much concreteness and critical status that this aim could be fully achieved. Even though the concept certainly specifies some central claims of LT and brings a new critical element to the core of LT, it simultaneously contains the very same problems as the more general praxis starting point.

The least liberation theologians, including feminist liberation theologians, should do is to specify and explicate their position on issues of sexual ethics. If their particular context, that of the impoverished people of Latin America, is held as the basis for truth claims about reality in such manner that all attempts to solve some of the problems poor women face as women are judged as 'contraceptive imperialism', it is clear that this very starting point is turned against itself, both theoretically and practically. Some of these problems could be solved by an explicit and critical analysis of the relation between the universal and the particular in theology. It may be that it is easier to hold an essentialist view of women in a context that gives so much emphasis to particularity. In fact, this has happened: not only liberation theologians but other Latin American intellectuals as well have been quick to place 'our', that is, Latin American, women against European or North American women. Particularity thus becomes a theoretical trap with practical consequences which may not have been foreseen.

The other side of this theoretical discussion is that according to the statistics, some 585,000 women die annually from pregnancy-related causes, 99 per cent of them in the Third World. Illegal abortion is the leading cause of death for Latin American women between 15 and 39 years of age. There is a clear inter-connection between poverty, lack of reproductive rights and women's mortality. If these facts do not form part of liberation theologians' discourse on praxis and the poor, serious questions about the coherence and credibility of LT are raised.

Chapter 5

Final Conclusions

At the beginning of this research, it was assumed that a broad definition of liberation theology makes it possible to analyse Latin American liberation theology and feminist theology together. This is based on methodological commonalities in different liberation theologies. It is even possible to speak of a liberation theological method. Especially in Latin American LT, it is assumed that the chosen praxis-based point of departure makes LT 'a new way of doing theology'. This praxis in FT is most commonly called 'women's experience', taken as the methodological premise in most of FT until today. However, this concept has become criticized by a new generation of feminist theologians as well as by economically and racially disadvantaged women.

The reality of poverty and the immersion of Christians in different actions in order to change the situation has given birth to both the ecclesial base communities and liberation theology in Latin America. However, the present situation on the continent is quite different from that of the 1970s. LT is facing new challenges. One of them seems to be the question of how (poor) women's issues are taken into account in the theory and practice of LT.

In Latin American LT, the ideal subjects of the praxis are 'the poor'. LT and the church make a preferential option for the poor, giving them both theoretical and practical primacy in theology. The question of the subject was analysed critically as was liberation theologians' understanding of what actually forms the praxis. Less importance was given to the historical roots of liberation theologians' use of the concept. However, it is of importance that they mainly use it in the Marxist sense. Thus, the poor refers primarily to a class, even though there has been some expansion of the concept beyond mere economic aspects. This move towards more heterogeneity is very much on a level of inclusion, in the sense that it is stated that it is important to take issues of race and gender into account in the analysis of poverty.

'The poor' as the subject of LT turned out to be a vague and homogenizing concept. There is an obvious lack of theorizing about an integral subject in LT which is also an individual, corporal, gendered and reproductive subject.

There are similar methodological problems in FT. However, as liberation theology, FT serves as a critical corrective for the sexist presuppositions of other

liberation theologies. The most recent developments in FT are due to a greater
theoretical debate with non-theological feminist theory, even though its influence
on FT is still rather modest. The critique aimed at the presupposed collective
subject both in LT (the poor) and in FT (women, women's experience) is similar,
although not usually presented together, as is done in this study. In its present
phase, FT faces challenges similar to those of Latin American LT concerning
particularity as the base for critique, on the one hand, and the possible universality of these particular claims, on the other hand. It was shown how 'women's
experience' has gained the status of a 'new universal' in FT, raising important
questions about the role of experience and praxis in liberation theologies, leading
eventually to dogmatism. The concrete living conditions of different women is
seen nowadays as a more fruitful point of departure for FT than are the unifying
and abstract notions of a supposed common womanhood.

For Latin American feminist liberation theology, everyday life (*vida cotidiana*) is
an important point of departure. Although not theorized as such, this perspective
nevertheless brings forth a critical element to both Latin American LT and FT.
Latin American feminist liberation theologians bring the 'praxis' or 'experience' of
poor Latin American women as a critical corrective to both the homogeneous
poor in LT and the universal female subject in FT.

The dialogue between Latin American LT and FT has, until recently, been
meagre and to some extent superficial. There are some ground-breaking works,
though, which all point in the same direction. The *vida cotidiana* questions the
absence of women and their realities in LT. Feminist liberation theologians
demand that LT take more seriously its central methodological claims. Of the
male liberation theologians, Leonardo Boff and Enrique Dussel were analysed in
more detail, since they are the ones who have written more extensively and explicitly on women. The analysis of their thinking seems to point towards certain
difficulties in LT's overall capacity to include feminist concerns. Their work
reflects the phase in LT that has been called 'mere inclusion' of women and their
concerns. The area of theological anthropology is important.

The essentializing way of approaching questions of sexism and women in LT is
in clear contrast with the more historical and practical method in other issues.
The idealized and often uncritical way of speaking of femininity and masculinity
makes it difficult to speak of sexism and real women and men as historical beings.

The ahistoricity of 'the feminine' may again partially explain the lack of sexual
ethical elaborations in LT. Traditional theological, especially Catholic, anthropology which most liberation theologians seem to adopt, at least to a certain
extent, does not offer adequate tools for understanding the specific problems,
such as reproductive issues, of Latin American women, especially the poorest of
them.

The application of the overall praxis approach to gender issues, in dialogue
with feminist theories of gender, would create room for a critical discussion of
sexual ethics in LT. This would also concretize the emphasis on *vida cotidiana* by
Latin American feminist liberation theologians and give it new critical meanings.
In addition, the *vida cotidiana* aspect, taken together with feminist interpretations

of Mariology and women's living, existential relationship to the Virgin Mary, points towards one possibility of thinking about sexual ethics from the perspective of (poor) Latin American women.

It seems that the great difficulty in addressing women and feminism in LT lies in the disconnection between theory and praxis, thus, it is about the very core of LT. This became especially clear when it was analysed how and why issues of sexual ethics are omitted, on the one hand, and traditionally treated, on the other hand, in LT. Willingly or unwillingly, Catholic liberation theologians seem to end up agreeing with the Vatican on issues of sexual ethics. The least what can be said of liberation theologians' position on sexual ethics, especially concerning reproductive rights, is that this position should be explicitly clarified.

Tied together with issues of reproduction, most poor women's living conditions are characterized by a high rate of maternal mortality, a high incidence of botched, illegal abortions, and their overall lack of power concerning their reproductive capacities. The death of these women has not been dealt with in LT as part of the general agenda of 'defending the life of the poor'.

The scant attention given to sexual ethics and reproductive issues is more serious in LT than in some other branch of theology because of the fundamental self-definition of LT as a theology of praxis. Sexual ethics is an area in which liberation theologians are far from their stated ideals and method. The analysis of sexual ethics revealed the insufficient conceptual analysis and its practical consequences at the theoretical core of LT. It is questionable if the praxis starting point can be maintained as strongly as *the* point of departure and method of LT as is usually done. Very much the same can be said of FT.

Further, our case study—sexual ethics—reveals that when praxis is given such a definitive status in theology as is done in LT and FT, more theoretical kinds of elaborations concerning the status of one's truth claims are not evaluated critically. This leads to a certain impotence of the chosen point of departure itself.

Thus, issues of sexual ethics—as (not) treated in LT up to now—are both a challenge for the supposed commitment to praxis and a critique of the actual importance of praxis for the liberation theological method. Further, it critically questions the content of the praxis as defined in LT. It seems that serious questions can—and, indeed, should—be asked about the status of praxis in theology, that is, about how the praxis model can, in fact, be realized. This is an issue to be clarified by further research.

Even though Latin American feminist liberation theologians are probably in the best position to rework these problems, they have not been explicit in issues of sexual ethics, with one notable exception, that of Ivone Gebara. She took a clear stance in favour of decriminalization of abortion in her home country, Brazil, but she did not tackle the issues theologically. Looking at Latin American feminist theological writings, however, it is clear that it is only a matter of connecting the more theological (theoretical) kind of critique with the political and practical positions held by liberation theologians that issues of sexual ethics will be discussed more on this highly Catholic continent.

Bibliography

Primary Sources

Aquino, María Pilar

1991   ' "Sin contar las mujeres" (Mt. 14.21). Perspectiva latinoamericana de la teología feminista', in Dolores Aleixandre *et al.*, *La mujer en la iglesia* (Madrid: Editorial Popular): 103-22.

1992a   *Nuestro clamor por la vida: Teología latinoamericana desde la perspectiva de la mujer* (San José: Editorial DEI).

1992b   'Y Dios creó a la mujer: Teología y Mujer en América Latina', *Reflexión y Liberación* 15: 27-40.

1993a   *Our Cry for Life: Feminist Theology from Latin America* (translated from the Spanish by Dinah Livingstone; New York: Orbis Books).

1993b   'Santo Domingo Through the Eyes of Women', in Alfred T. Hennelly (ed.), *Santo Domingo and Beyond: Documents and Commentaries from the Fourth General Conference of Latin American Bishops* (New York: Orbis Books): 212-25.

1994a   *La teología, la iglesia y la mujer en América Latina* (Bogota: Indo-American Press Service-Editores).

1994b   'Trazos hacia una antropología teológica feminista', *Reflexión y Liberación* 23: 43-55.

1995a   'Teología feminista latinoamericana: Evaluación y desafíos', *Tópicos* 7: 107-22.

1995b   'Evil and Hope: A Response to Jon Sobrino', in Paul Crowley (ed.), *The Catholic Theological Society of America: Proceedings of the Fiftieth Annual Convention* (CTSA Proceedings, 50; Santa Clara: Santa Clara University Press): 85-92.

1997   'Lateinamerikanische Feministische Theologie', in Raúl Fornet-Betancourt (ed.), *Befreiungstheologie: Kritischer Rückblick und Perspektiven für die Zukunft*, II (Mainz: Grünewald): 291-323.

Aquino, María Pilar (ed.)

1988   *Aportes para una teología desde la mujer* (Madrid: Editorial Biblia y Fe).

Assmann, Hugo

1971   *Opresión–liberación: Desafío a los cristianos* (Montevideo: Tierra Nueva).

1976   *Teología desde la praxis de la liberación: Ensayo teológico desde la América dependiente* (Salamanca: Ediciones Sígueme, 2nd edn).

Bidegain, Ana María

1989   'Women and the Theology of Liberation', in Marc H. Ellis and Otto Maduro (eds.), *The Future of Liberation Theology: Essays in Honor of Gustavo Gutiérrez* (New York: Orbis Books, 2nd edn): 105-20.

1990   'Mujer y poder en la Iglesia', in Milagros Palma (ed.), *Simbólica de la feminidad: La mujer en el imaginario mítico-religioso de las sociedades indias y mestizas* (Quito, Ecuador: MLAL y Ediciones Abya-Yala): 97-120.

Bingemer, María Clara

1988   'Chairete: Alegrai-vos (Lc 15, 8-10) ou a Mulher no Futuro da Teologia da Libertação', *Revista Eclesiástica Brasileira* 191 (September): 565-87.

1989	'Women in the Future of the Theology of Liberation', in Marc H. Ellis and Otto Maduro (eds.), *The Future of Liberation Theology: Essays in Honor of Gustavo Gutiérrez* (New York: Orbis Books, 2nd edn): 473-90.

Boff, Clodovis

1987	*Theology and Praxis: Epistemological Foundations* (translated from the Portuguese by Robert R. Barr; New York: Orbis Books).
1991	'Epistemología y método de la teología de la liberación', in Ignacio Ellacuría and Jon Sobrino (eds.), *Mysterium Liberationis: Conceptos fundamentales de la teología de la liberación* (San Salvador: UCA Editores), I: 79-113.

Boff, Leonardo

1975	*Teología desde el cautiverio* (translated from the Portuguese by Luis Gabriel Alejo; Bogota: Indo-American Press Service).
1976	'¿Qué es hacer teología desde América Latina?', in *Liberación y cautiverio: Debates en torno al método de la teología en América Latina* (Mexico City: Comité organizador): 129-54.
1978	'Maria, Mulher Profética e Libertadora: A Piedade Mariana na Teologia da Libertação', *Revista Eclesiástica Brasileira* 149 (March): 59-72.
1980	*El Ave María: Lo femenino y el Espíritu Santo* (Bogota: Indo-American Press Service).
1981	*La fe en la periferia del mundo: El caminar de la Iglesia con los oprimidos* (translated from the Portuguese by Jesús García-Abril; Santander: Editorial Sal Terrae, 2nd edn).
1985	*Testigos de Dios en el corazón del mundo* (translated from the Portuguese and adapted by M. Díez Presa; Madrid: EDITA, Publicaciones Claretianas, Instituto Teológico de Vida Religiosa, 3rd edn).
1986a	*Teología desde el lugar del pobre* (translated from the Portuguese by Jesús García-Abril; Santander: Editorial Sal Terrae, 2nd edn).
1986b	...*Y la Iglesia se hizo pueblo. 'Eclesiogénesis': La Iglesia que nace de la fe del pueblo* (translated from the Portuguese by Jesús García-Abril; Santander: Editorial Sal Terrae, 2nd edn).
1987a	*El rostro materno de Dios: Ensayo interdisciplinar sobre lo femenino y sus formas religiosas* (translated from the Portuguese by Alfonso Ortiz; Madrid: Ediciones Paulinas, 2nd edn).
1987b	*Iglesia: carisma y poder: Ensayos de eclesiología militante* (Bogota: Indo-American Press Service). *Church: Charism and Power: Liberation Theology and the Institutional Church* (translated from the Portuguese by John W. Dierksmeier; New York: Crossroad).
1990	'Espiritualidade e sexualidade: uma perspectiva radical', *Revista Vozes* 84.5: 554-65.

Boff, Leonardo, and Clodovis Boff

1989	*Cómo hacer teología de la liberación* (translated from the Portuguese by María Antonieta Villegas; Bogotá: Ediciones Paulinas). *Introducing Liberation Theology* (translated from the Portuguese by Paul Burns; New York: Orbis Books, 4th edn).

Chopp, Rebecca S.

1987	'Feminism's Theological Pragmatics: A Social Naturalism of Women's Experience', *The Journal of Religion* 67: 239-56.
1989	*The Praxis of Suffering: An Interpretation of Liberation and Political Theologies* (New York: Orbis Books, 2nd edn).
1993	'From Patriarchy into Freedom: A Conversation Between American Feminist Theology and French Feminists', in C.W. Maggie Kim, Susan M. St.Ville and Susan M. Simonaitis (eds.), *Transfigurations: Theology and the French Feminists* (Minneapolis: Fortress Press): 31-48.

1996   'Praxis', in Letty M. Russell and J. Shannon Clarkson (eds.), *Dictionary of Feminist Theologies* (Louisville: Westminster/John Knox Press): 221-22.

Christ, Carol P.
1989   'Embodied Thinking: Reflections on Feminist Theological Method', *Journal of Feminist Studies in Religion* 5.1 (Spring): 7-15.

Davaney, Sheila Greeve
1988   'Problems with Feminist Theory: Historicity and the Search for Sure Foundations', in Paula M. Cooey, Sharon A. Farmer and Mary Ellen Ross (eds.), *Embodied Love: Sensuality and Relationship as Feminist Values* (San Francisco: Harper & Row): 79-95.

Dussel, Enrique
1974a   'Alienación y liberación de la mujer en la iglesia (Un tema de la erótica teologal)', in *Caminos de liberación latinoamericana* (Buenos Aires: Latinoamérica Libros): 113-34.
1974b   'Dominación–liberación: Un discurso teológico distinto', *Concilium* 96: 328-52.
1980   'Historical and Philosophical Presuppositions for Latin American Theology', in Rosino Gibellini (ed.), *Frontiers of Theology in Latin America* (London: SCM Press): 184-212.
1981   *History of the Church in Latin America: Colonialism to Liberation (1492–1979)* (Grand Rapids: Eerdmans).
1982   'La iglesia latinoamericana en la actual coyuntura (1972–1980)', in Sergio Torres (ed.), *Teología de la liberación y comunidades cristianas de base. IV Congreso Internacional Ecuménico de Teología, São Paulo 1980* (Salamanca: Ediciones Sígueme): 93-122.
1985   *Filosofía de la liberación* (Buenos Aires: Ediciones La Aurora, 3rd edn). *Philosophy of Liberation* (translated from the Spanish by Aquilina Martinez and Christine Morkovsky; New York: Orbis Books).
1987–88   *Filosofía ética de la liberación* (3 vols.; Buenos Aires: Ediciones La Aurora).
1990   *Liberación de la mujer y erótica latinoamericana* (Bogota: Editorial Nueva América).
1992a   'Filosofía de la liberación como praxis de los oprimidos', *Carthaginensia* 8: 395-413.
1992b   'Lateinamerikanische Konzile. II. 19. und 20. Jahrhundert', in Erwin Fahlbusch *et al.* (eds.), *Evangelisches Kirchenlexikon: Internationale theologische Enzyklopädie*, III (Göttingen: Vandenhoeck & Ruprecht, 3rd edn): 29-31.
1995   *The Invention of the Americas: Eclipse of 'the Other' and the Myth of Modernity* (translated from the Spanish by Michael D. Barber; New York: Continuum).

Fiorenza, Elisabeth Schüssler
1975   'Feminist Theology as a Critical Theology of Liberation', *Theological Studies* 36: 605-26.
1979   'Feminist Spirituality, Christian Identity, and Catholic Vision', in Carol P. Christ and Judith Plaskow (eds.), *Womanspirit Rising: A Feminist Reader in Religion* (New York: Harper & Row): 136-48.
1983   *In Memory of Her: A Feminist Theological Reconstruction of Christian Origins* (New York: Crossroad).
1984a   'Toward a Feminist Biblical Hermeneutics: Biblical Interpretation and Liberation Theology', in Brian Mahan and L. Dale Richesin (eds.), *The Challenge of Liberation Theology: A First World Response* (New York: Orbis Books, 2nd edn): 91-112.
1984b   *Bread Not Stone: The Challenge of Feminist Biblical Interpretation* (Boston: Beacon Press).

1984c   'Claiming the Center: A Critical Feminist Theology of Liberation', in Janet
             Kalven and Mary I. Buckley (eds.), *Women's Spirit Bonding* (New York: The
             Pilgrim Press): 293-309.
1985a   'Breaking the Silence—Becoming Visible', *Concilium* 202: 3-16.
1985b   'Reivindicación de nuestra autoridad y poder', *Concilium* 200: 57-69.
1986   'For Women in Men's Worlds: A Critical Feminist Theology of Liberation', in
             Claude Geffré, Gustavo Gutiérrez and Virgil Elizondo (eds.), *Different
             Theologies, Common Responsibility: Babel or Pentecost?* (Edinburgh: T. & T. Clark):
             32-39.
1988   'The Ethics of Biblical Interpretation: Decentering Biblical Scholarship',
             Journal of Biblical Literature 107.1 (March): 3-17.
1989   'The Politics of Otherness: Biblical Interpretation as a Critical Praxis for
             Liberation', in Marc H. Ellis and Otto Maduro (eds.), *The Future of Liberation
             Theology: Essays in Honor of Gustavo Gutiérrez* (New York: Orbis Books, 2nd
             edn): 311-25.
1992   *But She Said: Feminist Practices of Biblical Interpretation* (Boston: Beacon Press).
1994   *Discipleship of Equals: A Critical Feminist Ekklesia-logy of Liberation* (New York:
             Crossroad).

Gebara, Ivone
1986   'La mujer hace teología: Un ensayo para la reflexión', in Ma. Clara Bingemer *et
             al.*, *El rostro femenino de la teología* (San José: Editorial DEI): 11-23.
1987   'La opción por el pobre como opción por la mujer pobre', *Concilium* 214: 463-
             72.
1990   'El cautiverio de María en el cautiverio de los pobres', in *Teología y liberación.
             Escritura y espiritualidad. Ensayos en torno a la obra de Gustavo Gutiérrez*, II (Lima:
             Centro de Estudios y Publicaciones): 137-54.
1994   *Teología a ritmo de mujer* (translated from the Portuguese by Miguel Angel
             Requena Ibáñez; Madrid: San Pablo).

Gebara, Ivone, and María Clara Bingemer
1989   *Mary: Mother of God, Mother of the Poor* (translated from the Portuguese by
             Phillip Berryman; New York: Orbis Books).
1991   'María', in Ignacio Ellacuría y Jon Sobrino (eds.), *Mysterium Liberationis: Con-
             ceptos fundamentales de la teología de la liberación*, I (San Salvador: UCA Editores):
             601-18.

Gutiérrez, Gustavo
1973   'Evangelio y praxis de libéración', in *Fe cristiana y cambio social en América Latina*
             (Salamanca: Ediciones Sígueme): 231-45.
1977   *Teología desde el reverso de la historia* (Lima: Centro de Estudios y Publicaciones).
1982   *La fuerza histórica de los pobres* (Salamanca: Ediciones Sígueme). *The Power of the
             Poor in History* (translated from the Spanish by Robert R. Barr; New York:
             Orbis Books, 4th edn, 1988).
1984   'Teología y ciencias sociales', *Revista Latinoamericana de Teología* 3 (September–
             December): 255-74.
1986   *Hablar de Dios desde el sufrimiento del inocente: Una reflexión sobre el libro de Job*
             (Lima: Instituto Bartolomé de las Casas y Centro de Estudios y Publicaciones).
1990   *Teología de la liberación: Perspectivas* (Salamanca: Ediciones Sígueme, 14th rev.
             edn). *A Theology of Liberation: History, Politics, and Salvation* (revised edition with
             a new introduction; translated from the Spanish and edited by Caridad Inda
             and John Eagleson: New York: Orbis Books [1988]).
1993   *Las Casas: In Search of the Poor of Jesus Christ* (translated from the Spanish by
             Robert R. Barr; New York: Orbis Books).

Harrison, Beverly Wildung
    1983   *Our Right to Choose: Toward a New Ethic of Abortion* (Boston: Beacon Press).
    1985   *Making the Connections: Essays in Feminist Social Ethics* (ed. Carol S. Robb; Boston: Beacon Press).
Portugal, Ana María
    1989   'Introducción', in *idem* (ed.), *Mujeres e Iglesia: Sexualidad y aborto en América Latina* (Washington, DC: Catholics for a Free Choice y Distribuciones Fontamara): 1-8.
Portugal, Ana María (ed.)
    1989   *Mujeres e Iglesia: Sexualidad y aborto en América Latina* (Washington, DC: Catholics for a Free Choice y Distribuciones Fontamara).
Richard, Pablo
    1981   'La ética como espiritualidad liberadora en la realidad eclesial de América Latina', *Cristianismo y Sociedad* 69-70: 51-59.
    1986   'Vorwort: Mit den Augen der Dritten Welt', in Bernd Päschke, *Befreiung von unten lernen: Zentralamerikanische Herausforderung theologischer Praxis* (with a Foreword and Afterword by Pablo Richard; Münster: Edition Liberación).
    1987a   *La fuerza espiritual de la Iglesia de los pobres* (San José: Editorial DEI).
    1987b   *Death of Christendoms, Birth of the Church: Historical Analysis and Theological Interpretation of the Church in Latin America* (translated from the French and Spanish by Phillip Berryman; New York: Orbis Books).
    1988   'El fundamento material de la espiritualidad', *Christus* 613-14 (March–April): 88-95.
    1990   *La iglesia latinoamericana entre el temor y la esperanza* (San José: Editorial DEI, 5th edn).
    1991   'La Teología de la Liberación en la nueva coyuntura: Temas y desafíos nuevos para la década de los noventa', *Pasos* 34 (March–April): 1-8.
    1992   'La Iglesia Católica después de Santo Domingo', *Pasos* 44 (November–December): 1-10.
    1993   'Las Comunidades Eclesiales de Base en América Latina (después de Santo Domingo)', *Pasos* 47 (May–June): 1-8.
    1994   'A Theology of Life: Rebuilding Hope from the Perspective of the South', in K.C. Abraham and Bernadette Mbuy-Beya (eds.), *Spirituality of the Third World: A Cry for Life* (Papers and Reflections from the Third General Assembly of the Ecumenical Association of Third World Theologians, January 1992, Nairobi, Kenya; New York: Orbis Books): 92-108.
Richard, Pablo (ed.)
    1981   *Materiales para una historia de la teología en América Latina* (VIII Latin American Meeting of CEHILA, Lima; San José: Editorial DEI).
Richard, Pablo *et al.*
    1989   *La lucha de los dioses: Los ídolos de la opresión y la búsqueda del Dios liberador* (San José: Editorial DEI, 3rd edn). *The Idols of Death and the God of Life: A Theology* (translated from the Spanish by Barbara E. Campbell and Bonnie Shepard; New York: Orbis Books, 1983).
Ruether, Rosemary Radford
    1972   *Liberation Theology: Human Hope Confronts Christian History and American Power* (New York: Paulist Press).
    1974   'Misogynism and Virginal Feminism in the Fathers of the Church', in *idem* (ed.), *Religion and Sexism: Images of Woman in the Jewish and Christian Traditions* (New York: Simon & Schuster): 150-83.

1975   *New Woman/New Earth: Sexist Ideologies and Human Liberation* (San Francisco:
            Harper & Row).
1979   *Mary—the Feminine Face of the Church* (London: SCM Press).
1980   'She's a Sign of God's Liberating Power', *Other Side* (May): 17-21.
1981a   'The Feminist Critique in Religious Studies', *Soundings* 64: 388-402.
1981b   *To Change the World: Christology and Cultural Criticism* (London: SCM Press).
1982   *Disputed Questions: On Being a Christian* (Nashville: Abingdon Press).
1983   *Sexism and God-Talk: Towards a Feminist Theology* (London: SCM Press).
1985a   'The Future of Feminist Theology in the Academy', *Journal of the American
            Academy of Religion* 53: 703-13.
1985b   'Feminist Interpretation: A Method of Correlation', in Letty M. Russell (ed.),
            Feminist Interpretation of the Bible (Oxford: Basil Blackwell): 111-24.
1985c   'A Feminist Perspective', in Virginia Fabella and Sergio Torres (eds.), *Doing
            Theology in a Divided World* (Papers from the Sixth International Conference of
            the Ecumenical Association of Third World Theologians, 5–13 January 1983,
            Geneva, Switzerland; New York: Orbis Books): 65-71.
1987   *Contemporary Roman Catholicism: Crises and Challenges* (Kansas City: Sheed and
            Ward).
1988   *Women-Church: Theology and Practice of Feminist Liturgical Communities* (San
            Francisco: Harper & Row).
1990   'Catholicism, Women, Body and Sexuality: A Response', in Jeanne Becher
            (ed.), *Women, Religion, and Sexuality: Studies on the Impact of Religious Teaching on
            Women* (Geneva: WCC Publications): 221-32.
1991   'Diferencia y derechos iguales de las mujeres en la iglesia', *Concilium* 238: 373-
            82.
1992   'Feminist Theology and Interclass/Interracial Solidarity', in Lorine M. Getz
            and Ruy O. Costa (eds.), *Struggles for Solidarity: Liberation Theologies in Tension*
            (Minneapolis: Fortress Press): 49-61.
1993   'El feminismo y la crisis de la izquierda' (A lecture given at the Departamento
            Ecuménico de Investigaciones, San José, Costa Rica, 10 March, 1993).
1996a   'La teología de la liberación sigue siendo muy masculina. Entrevista con la
            teóloga feminista', *Noticias Aliadas* 33.36 (October): 3.
1996b   'Patriarchy', in Letty M. Russell and J. Shannon Clarkson (eds.), *Dictionary of
            Feminist Theologies* (Louisville: Westminster/John Knox Press): 205-206.
Segundo, Juan Luis
1973   'Teología y ciencias sociales', in *Fe cristiana y cambio social en América Latina:
            Encuentro de El Escorial, 1972* (Salamanca: Ediciones Sígueme): 285-95.
1975   *Liberación de la teología* (Buenos Aires: Ediciones Carlos Lohlé). *The Liberation of
            Theology* (translated from the Spanish by John Drury; New York: Orbis Books,
            5th edn, 1988).
1976   'Condicionamentos actuales de la reflexión teológica en Latinoamérica', in
            Liberación y cautiverio: Debates en torno al método de la teología en América Latina
            (Mexico City: Comité organizador): 91-101.
1982   *El hombre de hoy ante Jesús de Nazaret. I. Fe e ideología* (Madrid: Ediciones
            Cristiandad). *Jesus of Nazareth Yesterday and Today. I. Faith and Ideologies*
            (translated from the Spanish by John Drury; New York: Orbis Books, 1984).
1985a   'The Shift Within Latin American Theology', *Journal of Theology for Southern
            Africa* 52 (September): 17-29.
1985b   *Theology and the Church: A Response to Cardinal Ratzinger and a Warning to the
            Whole Church* (translated from the Spanish by John W. Diercksmeier; Winston
            Press: Minneapolis).

Sobrino, Jon
 1976   'El conocimiento teológico en la teología europea y latinoamericana', in
          Liberación y cautiverio: Debates en torno al método de la teología en América Latina
          (Mexico City: Comité organizador): 177-207.
 1988   'Teología en un mundo sufriente. La teología de la liberación como "Intel-
          lectus amoris"', *Revista Latinoamericana de Teología* 15 (September–December):
          243-66.
 1993   'The Winds in Santo Domingo and the Evangelization of Culture', in Alfred
          T. Hennelly (ed.), *Santo Domingo and Beyond: Documents and Commentaries from
          the Fourth General Conference of Latin American Bishops* (New York: Orbis
          Books): 167-83.

Tamez, Elsa
 1979   'La mujer como sujeto histórico en la producción teológica', in *Mujer
          latinoamericana: Iglesia y teología* (Mexico City: Mujeres para el Diálogo): 105-12.
 1986   *Teólogos de la liberación hablan sobre la mujer* (San José: Editorial DEI).
 1988   'Women's Rereading of the Bible', in Virginia Fabella and Mercy Amba
          Oduyoye (eds.), *With Passion and Compassion: Third World Women Doing Theo-
          logy* (New York: Orbis Books): 173-80.
 1989   *Las mujeres toman la palabra* (San José: Editorial DEI).

Tamez, Elsa *et al.*
 1986   *El rostro femenino de la teología* (San José: Editorial DEI).

Tepedino, Ana María
 1988   'Mujer y teología: Apuntes para el quehacer teológico de la mujer en América
          Latina', in María Pilar Aquino (ed.), *Aportes para una teología desde la mujer*
          (Madrid: Editorial Biblia y Fe): 60-69.
 1994   'Response from Latin America', in K.C. Abraham and Bernadette Mbuy-Beya
          (eds.), *Spirituality of the Third World: A Cry for Life* (Papers and Reflections from
          the Third General Assembly of the Ecumenical Association of Third World
          Theologians, January, 1992, Nairobi, Kenya; New York: Orbis Books): 133-
          35.

Tepedino, Ana María, and Margarida L. Ribeiro Brandão
 1991   'Teología de la mujer en la teología de la liberación', in Ignacio Ellacuría and
          Jon Sobrino (eds.), *Mysterium Liberationis: Conceptos fundamentales de la teología de
          la liberación*, I (San Salvador: UCA Editores): 287-98.

Vidales, Raúl
 1974   'Logros y tareas de la teología latinoamericana', *Concilium* 96: 423-30.
 1976   'Acotaciones a la problemática sobre el método en la teología de la liberación',
          in *Liberación y cautiverio: Debates en torno al método de la teología en América Latina*
          (Mexico City: Comité organizador): 255-60.
 1978   *Desde la tradición de los pobres* (Mexico City: Ediciones CRT).
 1985   'La teología de la liberación: una opción histórica', *Cristianismo y Sociedad* 84:
          69-80.

Secondary Sources

Acosta, Yamandú
 1992   'Pensamiento crítico en América Latina: La constitución del "sujeto" como
          alternativa en los noventa. Observaciones a un paradigma en construcción',
          Pasos 44 (November–December): 18-29.

Adolf, Felipe
 1992   'Lateinamerikanischer Rat der Kirchen (Consejo Latinoamericano de Iglesias,
          CLAI)', in Erwin Fahlbusch *et al.* (eds.), *Evangelisches Kirchenlexikon: Inter-*

nationale theologische Enzyklopädie, III (Göttingen: Vandenhoeck & Ruprecht, 3rd edn): 41-42.

Ahmed, Leila
    1992   *Women and Gender in Islam: Historical Roots of a Modern Debate* (New Haven: Yale University Press).

Alcoff, Linda
    1988   'Cultural Feminism versus Post-Structuralism: The Identity Crisis in Feminist Theory', *Signs* 13 (Spring): 405-36.

Alvarez, Carmelo
    1987   'El pensamiento protestante en América Latina 1969–1982', in Pablo Richard (ed.), *Raíces de la teología latinoamericana: Nuevos materiales para la historia de la teología* (San José: Editorial DEI and CEHILA): 253-60.

Alvarez, Sonia E.
    1990   *Engendering Democracy in Brazil: Women's Movements in Transition Politics* (Princeton: Princeton University Press).

Alvarez, Sonia E., and Arturo Escobar
    1992   'Conclusion: Theoretical and Political Horizons of Change in Contemporary Latin American Social Movements', in Arturo Escobar and Sonia E. Alvarez (eds.), *The Making of Social Movements in Latin America: Identity, Strategy, and Democracy* (Boulder, San Francisco: Westview Press): 317-29.

Alves, Rubem
    1969   *A Theology of Human Hope* (Washington DC: Corpus Books).

Amalric, Frank, and Tariq Banuri
    1994   'Population: Malady or Symptom?', *Third World Quarterly* 15.4: 691-706.

Andolsen, Barbara Hilkert
    1996   'Rights, Reproductive', in Letty M. Russell and J. Shannon Clarkson (eds.), *Dictionary of Feminist Theologies* (Louisville: Westminster/John Knox Press): 248-50.

Anna, Timothy
    1986   'The Independence of Mexico and Central America', in Leslie Bethell (ed.), *The Cambridge History of Latin America*, III (repr.; Cambridge: Cambridge University Press): 51-94.

Anzaldúa, Gloria
    1989   'Entering Into the Serpent', in Judith Plaskow and Carol P. Christ (eds.), *Weaving the Visions: New Patterns in Feminist Spirituality* (San Francisco: Harper-Collins): 77-86.

Araya, Victorio
    1987   *God of the Poor: The Mystery of God in Latin American Liberation Theology* (translated from the Spanish by Robert R. Barr; New York: Orbis Books).

Audi, Robert
    1996   *The Cambridge Dictionary Of Philosophy* (repr.; Cambridge: Cambridge University Press).

Balasuriya, Tissa
    1978   'The Latin American Theology of Liberation: An Asian View', in *The Church at the Crossroads: Christians in Latin America from Medellín to Puebla (1968–1978)* (Rome: IDOC International): 130-36.
    1984   *Planetary Theology* (London: SCM Press).
    1986   'Why Planetary Theology?', in Deane William Ferm (ed.), *Third World Liberation Theologies: A Reader* (New York: Orbis Books): 324-35.
    1990   'Mary and Human Liberation', *Logos* 29.1, 2 (March–July).

Barnadas, Josep M.
1986   'The Catholic Church in Colonial Spanish America', in Leslie Bethell (ed.), *The Cambridge History of Latin America*, I (repr.; Cambridge: Cambridge University Press): 511-40.

Barroso, Carmen, and Cristina Bruschini
1991   'Building Politics from Personal Lives: Discussions on Sexuality among Poor Women in Brazil', in Chandra Talpade Mohanty, Ann Russo and Lourdes Torres (eds.), *Third World Women and the Politics of Feminism* (Bloomington and Indianapolis: Indiana University Press): 153-72.

Batllori, M.
1967   'Latin America, Church and Independence in', in *New Catholic Encyclopedia*, VIII (New York: McGraw-Hill): 441-42.

Benhabib, Seyla
1990   'Epistemologies of Postmodernism: A Rejoinder to Jean-François Lyotard', in Linda J. Nicholson (ed.), *Feminism/Postmodernism* (New York: Routledge): 107-30.
1992   *Situating the Self: Gender, Community and Postmodernism in Contemporary Ethics* (New York: Routledge).

Beozzo, José Oscar
1992   'Lateinamerikanischer Bischofsrat (Consejo Episcopal Latino-Americano, CELAM)', in Erwin Fahlbusch *et al.* (eds.), *Evangelisches Kirchenlexikon: Internationale theologische Enzyklopädie*, III (Göttingen: Vandenhoeck & Ruprecht, 3rd edn): 39-41.

Berryman, Phillip
1987   *Liberation Theology: The Essential Facts about the Revolutionary Movement in Latin America and Beyond* (New York: Pantheon Books).
1995   'Is Latin America Turning Pluralist? Recent Writings on Religion', *Latin American Research Review* 30.3: 107-22.

Beteta, Ramón
1950   *Pensamiento y dinámica de la revolución mexicana* (Mexico City: Editorial México Nuevo).

Bethell, Leslie
1986   'A Note on the Church and the Independence of Latin America', in Leslie Bethell (ed.), *The Cambridge History of Latin America*, III (4 vols.; repr.; Cambridge: Cambridge University Press): 229-34.

Bevans, Stephen B.
1994   *Models of Contextual Theology* (New York: Orbis Books, 2nd edn).

Beverley, John, and José Oviedo (eds.)
1993   *The Postmodernism Debate in Latin America*, Special Issue of *Boundary: International Journal of Literature and Culture* 2.3 (Fall).

Biehl, João Guilherme
1987   *De Igual Pra Igual: Um diálogo crítico entre a Teologia da Libertação e as Teologias Negra, Feminista e Pacifista* (Petrópolis e São Leopoldo: Editora Vozes e Editora Sinodal).

Bonino, José Míguez
1992   'The Dimensions of Oppression', in Lorine M. Getz and Ruy O. Costa (eds.), *Struggles for Solidarity: Liberation Theologies in Tension* (Minneapolis: Fortress Press): 27-35.

Børresen, Kari
1983   'Mary in Catholic Theology', *Concilium* 19: 48-56.

Bottomore, Tom (ed.)
1988   *A Dictionary of Marxist Thought* (repr.; Oxford: Basil Blackwell).

Braidotti, Rosi
   1993   *Riitasointuja* (trans. and ed. Päivi Kosonen; Tampere: Vastapaino).
   1994   *Nomadic Subjects: Embodiment and Sexual Difference in Contemporary Feminist Theory* (New York: Columbia University Press).
Brock, Rita Nakashima
   1996   'Feminist Theories', in Letty M. Russell and J. Shannon Clarkson (eds.), *Dictionary of Feminist Theologies* (Louisville: Westminster/John Knox Press): 116-20.
Brown, Raymond E. *et al.* (eds.)
   1978   *Mary in the New Testament: A Collaborative Assessment by Protestant and Roman Catholic Scholars* (Philadelphia: Fortress Press; New York: Paulist Press).
Bruneau, T.C.
   1979   'Latin America, Church in', in *New Catholic Encyclopedia*, XVII Supplement (Washington, DC and New York: Publishers Guild, Inc. in association with McGraw–Hill): 332-35.
Burdick, John
   1992   'Rethinking the Study of Social Movements: The Case of Christian Base Communities in Urban Brasil', in Arturo Escobar and Sonia E. Alvarez (eds.), *The Making of Social Movements in Latin America: Identity, Strategy, and Democracy* (Boulder, San Francisco: Westview Press): 171-84.
   1993   *Looking for God in Brazil: The Progressive Catholic Church in Urban Brazil's Religious Arena* (Berkeley: University of California Press).
   1994   'The Progressive Catholic Church in Latin America: Giving Voice or Listening to Voices?', *Latin American Research Review* 29.1: 184-97.
Butler, Judith
   1990   *Gender Trouble: Feminism and the Subversion of Identity* (New York: Routledge).
   1993   *Bodies That Matter: On the Discursive Limits of 'Sex'* (New York: Routledge).
Cadorette, Curt
   1993   'Trascender creativamente el pasado', *Noticias Aliadas* 30.38 (October 21): 2-3.
The Cambridge History of Latin America
   1986   (ed. Leslie Bethell; 4. vols.; Cambridge: Cambridge University Press).
Campbell, Ena
   1982   'The Virgin of Guadalupe and the Female Self-Image: A Mexican Case History', in James J. Preston (ed.), *Mother Worship: Themes and Variations* (Chapel Hill: University of North Carolina Press): 5-24.
Cannon, Katie G.
   1988   *Black Womanist Ethics* (Atlanta: Scholars Press).
Cannon, Katie G. *et al.* (The Mudflower Collective)
   1988   *God's Fierce Whimsy: Christian Feminism and Theological Education* (New York: Pilgrim Press, 3rd edn).
Carr, Anne E.
   1990   *Transforming Grace: Christian Tradition and Women's Experience* (San Francisco: Harper & Row).
Carroll, Michael P.
   1986   *The Cult of Virgin Mary: Psychological Origins* (Princeton: Princeton University Press).
Casanova, José
   1994   *Public Religions in the Modern World* (Chicago: University of Chicago Press).
Castañeda, Jorge A.
   1993   *La utopía desarmada: Intrigas, dilemas y promesa de la izquierda en América Latina* (Mexico City: Joaquín Mortiz y Grupo Editorial Planeta).

Castillo, Fernando
    1978   *Theologie aus der Praxis des Volkes: Neuere Studien zum lateinamerikanischen Christentum und zur Theologie der Befreiung* (Munich: Chr. Kaiser Verlag).
Cerutti Guldberg, Horacio
    1988–89 'Actual Situation and Perspectives of Latin American Philosophy for Liberation', *The Philosophical Forum*, XX.1-2 (Fall–Winter): 43-61.
    1992   *Filosofía de la liberación latinoamericana* (Mexico City: Fondo de Cultura Económica).
    1996   'Pensamiento y compromiso social' (unpublished manuscript).
    1997   *Filosofías para la liberación: ¿liberación o filosofar?* (Toluca: Universidad Autónoma del Estado de México).
Chaney, Elsa M.
    1979   *Supermadre: Women in Politics in Latin America* (Austin: University of Texas Press).
Chauvin, Lucien
    1995   'Fujimori versus Iglesia', *Noticias Aliadas* 32.34 (September): 1-3.
Christ, Carol P., and Judith Plaskow (eds.)
    1979   *Womanspirit Rising: A Feminist Reader in Religion* (San Francisco: Harper & Row).
Chung, Hyun Kyung
    1990   *Struggle to Be the Sun Again: Introducing Asian Women's Theology* (New York: Orbis Books).
Cleary, Edward L.
    1985   *Crisis and Change: The Church in Latin America Today* (New York: Orbis Books, 2nd edn).
    1992   'Conclusion: Politics and Religion—Crisis, Constraints, and Restructuring', in Edward L. Cleary and Hannah Stewart-Gambino (eds.), *Conflict and Competition: The Latin American Church in a Changing Environment* (Boulder: Lynne Rienner Publishers): 197-221.
Code, Lorraine
    1992   *What Can She Know? Feminist Theory and the Construction of Knowledge* (Ithaca, NY: Cornell University Press, 2nd edn).
Comblin, José
    1979   *The Church and the National Security State* (New York: Orbis Books).
    1985   *Antropología cristiana* (Buenos Aires: Ediciones Paulinas).
Cone, James H.
    1969   *Black Theology and Black Power* (New York: Seabury Press).
    1970   *A Black Theology of Liberation* (Philadelphia: Lippincott).
    1984   *For My People: Black Theology and the Black Church* (New York: Orbis Books).
'Conversando con Frances Kissling'
    1989   in Cotidiano Mujer (ed.), *Yo aborto, tú abortas, todos callamos…* (Montevideo: Editorial Cotidiano Mujer): 49-52.
Cooey, Paula M., William R. Eakin and Jay B. McDaniel (eds.)
    1994   *After Patriarchy: Feminist Transformations of the World Religions* (New York: Orbis Books, 5th edn).
Copeland, M. Shawn
    1996   'Theologies, Contemporary', in Letty M. Russell and J. Shannon Clarkson (eds.), *Dictionary of Feminist Theologies* (Louisville: Westminster/John Knox Press): 283-87.
Costa, Ruy O.
    1992   'Introduction', in Lorine M. Getz and Ruy O. Costa (eds.), *Struggles for Solidarity: Liberation Theologies in Tension* (Minneapolis: Fortress Press): 15-24.

Costello, G.M.
1979   'Latin America, Evangelization in', in *New Catholic Encyclopedia*, XVII Supple-
         ment (Washington, DC and New York: Publishers Guild, Inc. in association
         with McGraw–Hill): 335-37.
Couture, Pamela D.
1996   'Feminization of Poverty', in Letty M. Russell and J. Shannon Clarkson (eds.),
         Dictionary of Feminist Theologies (Louisville: Westminster/John Knox Press):
         120-21.
Cox, Harvey
1988   *The Silencing of Leonardo Boff* (Oak Park: Meyer-Stone).
Cuesta, Bernardo
1987   'Nuevo enfoque de la moral: la perspectiva de la moral latinoamericana',
         Ciencia tomista 114 (September–December): 595-621.
Daly, Mary
1974   *Beyond God the Father: Toward a Philosophy of Women's Liberation* (Boston:
         Beacon Press, 2nd edn).
1975   *The Church and the Second Sex* (New York: Harper & Row).
1984   *Gyn/Ecology: The Metaethics of Radical Feminism* (London: Women's Press).
De Barbieri, Teresita
1990   'Mujeres, Iglesia y Aborto', *Debate feminista* 1.1 (March): 329-33.
1993   'Gender and Population Policies: Some Reflections', *Reproductive Health Matters*
         1 (May): 85-92.
Di Stefano, Christine
1990   'Dilemmas of Difference: Feminism, Modernity, and Postmodernism', in
         Linda J. Nicholson (ed., and with an introduction), *Feminism/Postmodernism*
         (New York: Routledge): 63-82.
Dillon, E.J.
1979   'Medellín Documents', in *New Catholic Encyclopedia*, XVII Supplement
         (Washington, DC and New York: Publishers Guild, Inc. in association with
         McGraw–Hill): 399.
Documentos de Medellín: IIa Conferencia General del Episcopado Latinoamericano
1969   (San José: Ludovico).
Drogus, Carol Ann
1992   'Popular Movements and the Limits of Political Mobilization at the Grassroots
         in Brazil', in Edward L. Cleary and Hannah Stewart-Gambino (eds.), *Conflict
         and Competition: The Latin American Church in a Changing Environment* (Boulder:
         Lynne Rienner Publishers): 63-86.
1995   'The Rise and Decline of Liberation Theology: Churches, Faith, and Political
         Change in Latin America', *Comparative Politics* 4: 465-77.
Dunkerley, James
1990   *Power in the Isthmus: A Political History of Modern Central America* (London: Verso,
         2nd edn).
Dutting, Gisela
1993   'The Concept of Reproductive Rights: Reflections from Experiences', *Women's
         Global Network for Reproductive Rights Newsletter* 44 (July-September): 2-3.
Eagleson, John, and Philip Scharper (eds.)
1980   *Puebla and Beyond: Documentation and Commentary* (translated from the Spanish
         by John Drury; New York: Orbis Book, 2nd edn).
Eck, Diana L., and Devaki Jain (eds.)
1986   *Speaking of Faith: Cross-Cultural Perspectives on Women, Religion, and Social Change*
         (London: Women's Press).

Ellacuriá, Ignacio
  1976   'Hacia una fundamentación filosófica del método teológico latinoamericano',
          in *Liberación y cautiverio: Debates en torno al método de la teología en América Latina*
          (Mexico City: Comité organizador): 609-35.
  1984   *Conversión de la Iglesia al Reino de Dios: Para anunciarlo y realizarlo en la historia*
          (Santander: Editorial Sal Terrae).
Ellacuriá, Ignacio, and Jon Sobrino (eds.)
  1991   *Mysterium Liberationis. Conceptos fundamentales de la teologie de la liberación* (2 vols.;
          San Salvador: UCA Editores).
Engel, Mary Potter, and Susan Brooks Thistlethwaite
  1990   'Introduction: Making the Connections among Liberation Theologies around
          the World', in Susan Brooks Thistlethwaite and Mary Potter Engel (eds.), *Lift
          Every Voice: Constructing Christian Theologies from the Underside* (San Francisco:
          Harper & Row): 1-15.
Erickson, Victoria Lee
  1993   *Where Silence Speaks: Feminism, Social Theory, and Religion* (Minneapolis:
          Fortress Press).
Eriksson, Anne-Louise
  1995   *The Meaning of Gender in Theology: Problems and Possibilities* (Acta Universitatis
          Upsaliensis. Uppsala Women's Studies. Women in Religion, 6; Stockholm:
          Almqvist och Wiksell International).
Escobar, Arturo, and Sonia E. Alvarez (eds.)
  1992   'Introduction: Theory and Protest in Latin America Today', in *idem*, *The
          Making of Social Movements in Latin America: Identity, Strategy, and Democracy*
          (Boulder, San Francisco: Westview Press): 1-15.
Fabella, Virginia, and Mercy Amba Oduyoye (eds.)
  1988   *With Passion and Compassion: Third World Women Doing Theology* (New York:
          Orbis Books).
Fabella, Virginia, and Sun Ai Lee Park (eds.)
  1990   *We Dare to Dream: Doing Theology as Asian Women* (New York: Orbis Books).
Fabella, Virginia, and Sergio Torres (eds.)
  1983   *Irruption of the Third World: Challenge to Theology* (Papers from the Fifth Inter-
          national Congress of the Ecumenical Association of Third World Theologians,
          17-29 August, 1981, New Delhi, India; New York: Orbis Books).
  1985   *Doing Theology in a Divided World* (Papers from the Sixth International Con-
          ference of the Ecumenical Association of Third World Theologians, January 5-
          13, 1983, Geneva, Switzerland; New York: Orbis Books).
Ferm, Deane William
  1981   *Contemporary American Theologies: A Critical Survey* (New York: Seabury Press).
  1986   *Third World Liberation Theologies: An Introductory Survey* (New York: Orbis
          Books).
Fiorenza, Francis Schüssler
  1991   'Roundtable Discussion: The Influence of Feminist Theory on My Theo-
          logical Work', *Journal of Feminist Studies in Religion* 7.1 (Spring): 95-105.
Firestone, Shulamith
  1971   *The Dialectic of Sex: The Case for Feminist Revolution* (New York: Bantam Books).
Fisher, Jo
  1993   *Out of the Shadows: Women, Resistance, and Politics in South America* (London:
          Latin America Bureau).
Fonseca, Elizabeth
  1996   *Centroamérica: su historia* (San José: Flacso and Educa).

Fornet-Betancourt, Raúl
    1988   *Philosophie und Theologie der Befreiung* (Frankfurt am Main: Materialis Verlag).
Foulkes, Irene (ed.)
    1989   *Teología desde la mujer en Centroamérica* (San José: Ediciones SEBILA).
Fox, Thomas C.
    1995   *Sexuality and Catholicism* (New York: George Braziller).
Franco, Jean
    1992   'Going Public: Reinhabiting the Private', in George Yúdice, Jean Franco and Juan Flores (eds.), *On Edge: The Crisis of Contemporary Latin American Culture* (Minneapolis: University of Minnesota Press): 65-83.
Frank, André Gunder
    1969   *Capitalism and Underdevelopment in Latin America: Historical Studies of Chile and Brazil* (New York: Monthly Review Press, revised and enlarged edn).
Fraser, Nancy, and Linda J. Nicholson
    1990   'Social Criticism without Philosophy: An Encounter between Feminism and Postmodernism', in Linda J. Nicholson (ed. and with an introduction), *Feminism/Postmodernism* (New York: Routledge): 19-38.
Fulkerson, Mary McClintock
    1994   *Changing the Subject: Women's Discourses and Feminist Theology* (Minneapolis: Fortress Press).
Gallagher, Nancy E.
    1995   'Compañeras in the Peruvian Feminist Movement: A Conversation with Rosa Dominga and Timotea, Maryknoll Sisters', *Journal of Feminist Studies in Religion* 11.1 (Spring): 95-109.
Gallardo, Helio
    1992   'Radicalidad de la teoría y sujeto popular en América Latina', *Pasos especial* 3: 27-42.
    1994   'La Teología de la Liberación como pensamiento latinoamericano', *Pasos* 56 (November–December): 12-22.
García, Ismael
    1987   *Justice in Latin American Theology of Liberation* (Atlanta: John Knox Press).
Gatens, Moira
    1991   'A Critique of the Sex/Gender Distinction', in Sneja Gunew (ed.), *A Reader in Feminist Knowledge* (London: Routledge): 139-57.
Gibellini, Rosino
    1988   *The Liberation Theology Debate* (translated from the Italian by John Bowden; New York: Orbis Books).
Gibellini, Rosino (ed.)
    1994   *Paths of African Theology* (New York: Orbis Books).
Goizueta, Roberto S.
    1988   *Liberation, Method and Dialogue: Enrique Dussel and North American Theological Discourse* (Atlanta: Scholars Press).
Goldstein, Horst
    1991   *Kleines Lexikon zur Theologie der Befreiung* (Düsseldorf: Patmos Verlag).
González Dorado, Antonio
    1988   *De María conquistadora a María liberadora: Mariología popular latinoamericana* (Santander: Sal Terrae).
Gössmann, Elisabeth *et al.* (eds.)
    1991   *Wörterbuch der Feministischen Theologie* (Gütersloh: Gütersloher Verlagshaus Gerd Mohn).

Graham, Wendy, and Pauline Airey
    1987   'Measuring Maternal Mortality: Sense and Sensibility', *Health Policy and Planning* 2.4: 323-33.
Grant, Jacquelyn
    1989   *White Women's Christ and Black Women's Jesus: Feminist Christology and Womanist Response* (Atlanta: Scholars Press).
Grosz, Elizabeth
    1994   *Volatile Bodies: Toward a Corporeal Feminism* (Bloomington: Indiana University Press).
Guralnik, David B. (ed.)
    1984   *Webster's New World Dictionary of the American Language* (New York: Simon & Schuster, 2nd edn).
Hale, Charles A.
    1986   'Political and Social Ideas in Latin America, 1870–1930', in Leslie Bethell (ed.), *The Cambridge History of Latin America*, IV (repr.; Cambridge: Cambridge University Press): 367-441.
Halkes, Catharina J.M.
    1980   'Teología feminista: Balance provisional', *Concilium* 154: 122-37.
Hampson, Daphne
    1990   *Theology and Feminism* (Oxford: Basil Blackwell).
Hanke, Lewis
    1965   *The Spanish Struggle for Justice in the Conquest of America* (Boston: Little, Brown and Company, 2nd edn).
Harcourt, Wendy
    1994   'Dangerous Liaisons: Population and Development Dialogues', *Development* 1: 10-13.
Harding, Sandra
    1987   'Introduction: Is There a Feminist Method?', in Sandra Harding (ed.), *Feminism and Methodology: Social Science Issues* (Bloomington: Indiana University Press): 1-14.
Hartmann, Betsy
    1995   *Reproductive Rights and Wrongs: The Global Politics of Population Control* (Boston: South End Press, revised 2nd edn).
Heinämaa, Sara
    1996   *Ele, tyyli ja sukupuoli: Merleau-Pontyn ja Beauvoirin ruumiinfenomenologia ja sen merkitys sukupuolikysymykselle* (Tampere: Gaudeamus).
Hennelly, Alfred T.
    1977a   'Theological Method: The Southern Exposure', *Theological Studies* 38: 709-35.
    1977b   'The Challenge of Juan Luis Segundo', *Theological Studies* 38: 125-35.
Hennelly, Alfred T. (ed.)
    1990   *Liberation Theology: A Documentary History* (New York: Orbis Books).
    1993   *Santo Domingo and Beyond: Documents and Commentaries from the Fourth General Conference of Latin American Bishops* (New York: Orbis Books).
Henshaw, Stanley K.
    1990   'Induced Abortion: A World Review, 1990', *International Family Planning Perspectives* 16.2 (June): 59-76.
Hewitt, Marsha Aileen
    1990   *From Theology to Social Theory: Juan Luis Segundo and the Theology of Liberation* (New York: Peter Lang).
Heyward, Carter
    1989a   *Speaking of Christ: A Lesbian Feminist Voice* (ed. Ellen C. Davis; New York: Pilgrim Press).

1989b   *Touching Our Strength: The Erotic as Power and the Love of God* (San Francisco: Harper & Row).

Hinkelammert, Franz

1988   'La teología del imperio', *Pasos* 15 (January–February): 21-28.

1990   *Democracia y totalitarismo* (San José: Editorial DEI, 2nd edn).

1991a   *La fe de Abraham y el Edipo Occidental* (San José: Editorial DEI, 2nd edn).

1991b   *Sacrificios humanos y sociedad occidental: Lucifer y la bestia* (San José: Editorial DEI, 2nd edn).

1995   'La teología de la liberación en el contexto económico-social de América Latina: economía y teología o la irracionalidad de lo racionalizado', *Pasos* 57 (January–February): 1-15.

Hodges, Donald C.

1986   *Intellectual Foundations of the Nicaraguan Revolution* (Austin: University of Texas Press).

Hofmann, Manfred

1978   *Identifikation mit dem Anderen: Theologische Themen und ihr hermeneutischer Ort bei lateinamerikanischen Theologen der Befreiung* (Stockholm: Verbum).

Houtart, François

1990   'CELAM: The Forgetting of Origins', in Dermot Keogh (ed.), *Church and Politics in Latin America* (New York: St Martin's Press): 65-81.

Humm, Maggie

1990   *The Dictionary of Feminist Theory* (Columbus: Ohio State University Press).

Hynds, Patricia

1993   'Poder y gloria: La Iglesia católica en América Latina', *Noticias Aliadas* 30.38 (October): 1.

Irarrazával, Diego

1989   'Pachamama—vida divina para gente abatida', *Iglesias, pueblos y culturas* 4.14 (July–September): 73-91.

Isasi-Díaz, Ada María

1988   'A Hispanic Garden in a Foreign Land', in Letty M. Russell *et al.* (eds.), *Inheriting Our Mothers' Gardens: Feminist Theology in Third World Perspective* (Louisville: Westminster Press): 91-104.

Isasi-Díaz, Ada María, and Yolanda Tarango

1988   *Hispanic Women: A Prophetic Voice in the Church* (New York: Harper & Row).

Jaquette, Jane S.

1994   'Introduction: From Transition to Participation—Women's Movements and Democratic Politics', in Jane S. Jaquette (ed.), *The Women's Movement in Latin America: Participation and Democracy* (Boulder, San Francisco: Westview Press, 2nd edn): 1-11.

Jaquette, Jane S. (ed.)

1994   *The Women's Movement in Latin America: Participation and Democracy* (Boulder, San Francisco: Westview Press, 2nd edn).

Jelin, Elizabeth (ed.)

1994   *Women and Social Change in Latin America* (translated from the Spanish by J. Ann Zammit and Marilyn Thomson; London, Atlantic Highlands; Geneva: UNRISD and Zed Books, 2nd edn).

Johnson, Elizabeth A.

1994   *She Who Is: The Mystery of God in Feminist Theological Discourse* (New York: Crossroad).

Joy, Morny

1995   'God and Gender: Some Reflections on Women's Invocations of the Divine', in Ursula King (ed.), *Religion and Gender* (Oxford: Basil Blackwell): 121-43.

Kabeer, Naila
1994   *Reversed Realities: Gender Hierarchies in Development Thought* (London: Verso).
Kasper, Walter
1986   'Die Theologie der Befreiung aus europäischer Perspektive', in Johann Baptist Metz (ed.), *Die Theologie der Befreiung: Hoffnung oder Gefahr für die Kirche?* (Düsseldorf: Patmos Verlag): 77-98.
Katoppo, Marianne
1979   *Compassionate and Free: An Asian Woman's Theology* (New York: Orbis Books).
Kay, Cristóbal
1989   *Latin American Theories of Development and Underdevelopment* (London: Routledge).
Keen, Benjamin, and Mark Wasserman
1988   *A History of Latin America* (Boston: Houghton Mifflin Co., 3rd edn).
Keogh, Dermot
1990   'Catholicism in Latin America: Conclusions and Perspectives', in Dermot Keogh (ed.), *Church and Politics in Latin America* (New York: St Martin's Press): 398-403.
Keogh, Dermot (ed.)
1990   *Church and Politics in Latin America* (New York: St Martin's Press).
Kilminster, Richard
1993   'Praxis', in William Outhwaite and Tom Bottomore (eds.), *The Blackwell Dictionary of Twentieth-Century Social Thought* (Oxford: Basil Blackwell): 507-509.
Kim, C.W. Maggie, Susan M. St.Ville and Susan M. Simonaitis (eds.)
1993   *Transfigurations: Theology and the French Feminists* (Minneapolis: Fortress Press).
King, Ursula
1994   'Introduction', in Ursula King (ed.), *Feminist Theology from the Third World: A Reader* (London: SPCK; New York: Orbis Books): 1-20.
King, Ursula (ed.)
1994   *Feminist Theology from the Third World: A Reader* (London: SPCK; New York: Orbis Books).
Koivusalo, Meri, and Eeva Ollila
1996   *International Organizations and Health Policies* (Saarijärvi: STAKES and HEDEC).
Koyama, Kosuke
1974   *Waterbuffalo Theology* (New York: Orbis Books).
1985   *Mount Fuji and Mount Sinai: A Critique of Idols* (New York: Orbis Books).
Kwok, Pui-lan
1992   'Speaking from the Margins'. Special Section on Appropriation and Reciprocity in Womanist/Mujerista/Feminist Work. *Journal of Feminist Studies in Religion* 8.2 (Fall): 102-105.
Lafaye, Jacques
1977   *Quetzalcóatl y Guadalupe: La formación de la conciencia nacional en México* (translated from the French by Ida Vitale and Fulgencio López Vidarte (Mexico City: Fondo de Cultura Económica).
Lehmann, David
1990   *Democracy and Development in Latin America: Economics, Politics and Religion in Postwar Period* (Cambridge: Polity Press).
Lehmann, Karl *et al.*
1977   *Theologie der Befreiung Internationale Theologenkommission* (Einsiedeln: Johannes Verlag).

Lepargneur, Hubert
    1982   'Avaliação Moral do Abortamento Voluntário', *Revista Eclesiástica Brasileira* 165
                (March): 82-109.
Levine, Daniel H.
    1986   'Religion, the Poor, and Politics in Latin America Today', in Daniel H. Levine
                (ed.), *Religion and Political Conflict in Latin America* (Chapel Hill: University of
                North Carolina Press): 3-23.
    1990   'How Not to Understand Liberation Theology, Nicaragua, or Both', *Journal of
                Interamerican Studies and World Affairs* 32.3 (Fall): 229-45.
    1992   *Popular Voices in Latin American Catholicism* (Princeton: Princeton University
                Press).
Levine, Daniel H. (ed.)
    1986   *Religion and Political Conflict in Latin America* (Chapel Hill: University of North
                Carolina Press).
Libertatis Conscientia: Instruction on Christian Freedom and Liberation
    1986   (Vatican City: Vatican Polyglot Press).
Libertatis Nuntius: Instruction on Certain Aspects of the 'Theology of Liberation'
    1984   (Rome: Sacred Congregation for the Doctrine of the Faith).
Lind, Amy Conger
    1992   'Power, Gender, and Development: Popular Women's Organizations and the
                Politics of Needs in Ecuador', in Arturo Escobar and Sonia E. Alvarez (eds.),
                The Making of Social Movements in Latin America: Identity, Strategy, and Democracy
                (Boulder, San Francisco: Westview Press): 134-49.
List, Elisabeth
    1991   'Feministische Forschung. II. Feministische Wissenschaftskritik', in Elisabeth
                Gössman *et al.* (eds.), *Wörterbuch der Feministischen Theologie* (Gütersloh: Güters-
                loher Verlagshaus Gerd Mohn): 99-102.
Lloyd, Genevieve
    1993   *The Man of Reason: 'Male' and 'Female' in Western Philosophy* (Minneapolis:
                University of Minnesota Press, 2nd edn).
Lois, Julio
    1988   *Teología de la liberación: Opción por los pobres* (San José: Editorial DEI).
    1991   'Opción por los pobres: Síntesis doctrinal', in José Ma. Vigil (ed.), *La opción por
                los pobres* (Santander: Editorial Sal Terrae): 9-18.
Lozano Lerma, Betty R.
    1991   *En búsqueda de perspectivas liberadoras para la mujer en la teología de la liberación
                latinoamericana* (unpublished thesis, Universidad del Valle, Colombia).
Lynch, John
    1986   'The Catholic Church in Latin America, 1830–1930', in Leslie Bethell (ed.),
                The Cambridge History of Latin America, IV (repr.; Cambridge: Cambridge
                University Press): 527-95.
Maduro, Otto
    1991   'Some Theoretical Implications of Latin American Liberation Theology for the
                Sociology of Religion' (A paper presented at the 21st International Conference
                on the Sociology of Religion: Religion and the Economic Order, 19–23 August
                1991, Maynooth, Ireland).
Maeckelberghe, Els
    1989   ' "Mary": Maternal Friend or Virgin Mother?', *Concilium* 206: 120-27.
Mainwaring, Scott, and Alexander Wilde
    1989   'The Progressive Church in Latin America: An Interpretation', in Scott Main-
                waring and Alexander Wilde (eds.), *The Progressive Church in Latin America*
                (Notre Dame: University of Notre Dame Press): 1-37.

Mananzan, Mary John (ed.)
 1992   *Woman and Religion: A Collection of Essays, Personal Histories and Contextualized*
             Liturgies (Manila: Institute of Women's Studies, St Scholastica's College, 2nd
             edn).
May, Melanie A.
 1996   'Feminist Theologies, North American', in Letty M. Russell and J. Shannon
             Clarkson (eds.), *Dictionary of Feminist Theologies* (Louisville, KY: Westminster/
             John Knox Press): 106-108.
Mbiti, John S.
 1970   *Concepts of God in Africa* (New York: Praeger Publishers).
 1990   *African Religions and Philosophy* (Oxford: Heinemann, 2nd revised and enlarged
             edn).
McGovern, Arthur F.
 1989   *Liberation Theology and its Critics: Toward an Assessment* (New York: Orbis
             Books).
McHugh, Francis P.
 1993   'Christian Social Theory', in William Outhwaite and Tom Bottomore (eds.),
             The Blackwell Dictionary of Twentieth-Century Social Thought (Oxford: Basil
             Blackwell): 70-73.
McIntosh, C. Alison, and Jason L. Finkle
 1995   'The Cairo Conference on Population and Development: A New Paradigm?',
             Population and Development Review 21.2 (June): 223-60.
McLaughlin, Eleanor Commo
 1974   'Equality of Souls, Inequality of Sexes: Woman in Medieval Theology', in
             Rosemary Radford Ruether (ed.), *Religion and Sexism: Images of Woman in the
             Jewish and Christian Traditions* (New York: Simon & Schuster): 213-66.
Mecham, J. Lloyd
 1936   'The Church in Colonial Spanish America', in Curtis Wilgus (ed.), *Colonial
             Hispanic America* (Studies in Hispanic American Affairs, 4; Washington, DC:
             George Washington University Press): 200-39.
Meléndez, Guillermo (ed.)
 1992   *Sentido Histórico del V Centenario (1492–1992)* (San José: Editorial DEI).
Melhuus, Marit
 1990   'Una vergüenza para el honor, una vergüenza para el sufrimiento', in Milagros
             Palma (ed.), *Simbólica de la feminidad: La mujer en el imaginario mítico-religioso de
             las sociedades indias y mestizas* (Quito, Ecuador: MLAL and Ediciones Abya-Yala):
             39-71.
Metz, Johann Baptist
 1986   'Thesen zum theologischen Ort der Befreiungstheologie', in Johann Baptist
             Metz (ed.), *Die Theologie der Befreiung: Hoffnung oder Gefahr für die Kirche?*
             (Düsseldorf: Patmos Verlag): 147-57.
Meyer, Michael C., and William L. Sherman
 1987   *The Course of Mexican History* (Oxford: Oxford University Press, 3rd edn).
Miguelez, Xosé
 1976   *La teología de la liberación y su método: Estudio en Hugo Assmann y Gustavo Gutiérrez*
             (Barcelona: Editorial Herder).
Min, Anselm Kyongsuk
 1986   'Praxis and Theology in Recent Debates', *Scottish Journal of Theology* 39: 529-49.
 1989   *Dialectic of Salvation: Issues in Theology of Liberation* (Albany: State University of
             New York Press).

Mires, Fernando
    1991   *La colonización de las almas: Misión y conquista en Hispanoamérica* (San José: Editorial DEI, 2nd edn).

Mohanty, Chandra Talpade
    1991   'Under Western Eyes: Feminist Scholarship and Colonial Discourses', in Chandra Talpade Mohanty, Ann Russo and Lourdes Torres (eds.), *Third World Women and the Politics of Feminism* (Bloomington: Indiana University Press): 51-80.

Molyneux, Maxine
    1985   'Mobilization Without Emancipation? Women's Interests, the State, and Revolution in Nicaragua', *Feminist Studies* 11.2 (Summer): 227-54.

    1988   'The Politics of Abortion in Nicaragua: Revolutionary Pragmatism—or Feminism in the Realm of Necessity?', *Feminist Review* 29 (Spring): 114-32.

Monsivais, Carlos
    1991   'De cómo un día amaneció Pro-Vida con la novedad de vivir en una sociedad laica', *Debate feminista* 2.3 (March): 82-88.

Moreno Rejón, Francisco
    1991   'Moral fundamental en la teología de la liberación', in Ignacio Ellacuría and Jon Sobrino (eds.), *Mysterium Liberationis: Conceptos fundamentales de la teología de la liberación*, I (San Salvador: UCA Editores): 273-86.

Moser, Antônio
    1984   'Como se faz Teologia Moral no Brazil Hoje', *Revista Eclesiástica Brasileira* 174 (June): 243-64.

    1991   'Sexualidad', in Ignacio Ellacuría and Jon Sobrino (eds.), *Mysterium Liberationis: Conceptos fundamentales de la teología de la liberación*, II (San Salvador: UCA Editores): 107-24.

Moser, Antônio, and Bernardino Leers
    1990   *Moral Theology: Dead Ends and Alternatives* (translated from the Portuguese by Paul Burns; New York: Orbis Books).

Mujer latinoamericana: Iglesia y teología
    1981   (Mexico City: Mujeres para el diálogo).

Mulieris Dignitatem
    1988   'Mulieris Dignitatem. Carta Apostólica del Sumo Pontífice Juan Pablo II sobre la dignidad y la vocación de la mujer con ocasión del año mariano', in *Encíclicas y otros documentos de Juan Pablo II* (San José: Libro Libre): III, 285-406.

Nanne, Kaike, and Mónica Bergamo
    1993   'Entrevista a Ivone Gebara: "El aborto no es pecado"' (reprinted in *Revista Con-Spirando* 6).

Nash, Margaret
    1975   *Ecumenical Movement in the 1960s* (Johannesburg: Ravan Press).

Navarro García, Luis (ed.)
    1991   *Historia de las Américas* (4 vols.; Madrid: Alhambra Longman).

Nessan, Craig L.
    1989   *Orthopraxis or Heresy: The North American Theological Response to Latin American Liberation Theology* (American Academy of Religion, Academy Series, 63; Atlanta: Scholars Press).

Nicholson, Linda J.
    1990   'Introduction', in Linda J. Nicholson (ed.), *Feminism/Postmodernism* (New York: Routledge): 1-16.

Nicholson, Linda J. (ed. and with an introduction)
    1990   *Feminism/Postmodernism* (New York: Routledge).

Nueva evangelización, promoción humana, cultura cristiana
   1992   Fourth General Conference of Latin American Bishops (Santo Domingo, 12–
             28 October. Conclusiones. A conference draft).
Nuñez, Emilio A.
   1986   *Teología de la liberación* (San José: Editorial Caribe).
O'Brien, Mary
   1989   *Reproducing the World: Essays in Feminist Theory* (Boulder: Westview Press).
Oduyoye, Mercy Amba
   1986   *Hearing and Knowing: Theological Reflections on Christianity in Africa* (New York:
             Orbis Books).
   1994   'Reflections from a Third World Woman's Perspective: Women's Experience
             and Liberation Theologies', in Ursula King (ed.), *Feminist Theology from the
             Third World: A Reader* (London: SPCK; New York: Orbis Books): 23-34.
   1995   *Daughters of Anowa: African Women and Patriarchy* (New York: Orbis Books).
Oliveros, Roberto
   1989   'Teología de la liberación: su génesis, crecimiento y consolidación (1968-
             1988)', in *Teología y liberación. Perspectivas y desafíos: Ensayos en torno a la obra de
             Gustavo Gutiérrez*, I (Lima: Centro de Estudios y Publicaciones): 89-107.
O'Neill, Maura
   1990   *Women Speaking, Women Listening: Women in Interreligious Dialogue* (New York:
             Orbis Books).
Pakkasvirta, Jussi
   1992   'Stereotypia yhdestä Latinalaisesta Amerikasta', in Jussi Pakkasvirta and Teivo
             Teivainen (eds.), *Kenen Amerikka? 500 vuotta Latinalaisen Amerikan valloitusta*
             (Jyväskylä: Gaudeamus): 22-45.
   1996   *Nationalism and Continentalism in Latin American History* (Working Paper, 14;
             Helsinki: Institute of Development Studies, University of Helsinki).
Pakkasvirta, Jussi, and Teivo Teivainen (eds.)
   1992   *Kenen Amerikka? 500 vuotta Latinalaisen Amerikan valloitusta* (Jyväskylä:
             Gaudeamus).
Parentelli, Gladys
   1993   'Teología feminista en América Latina' (paper presented at the Fifth Inter-
             national Interdisciplinary Congress on Women, San José, Costa Rica, 22–26
             February).
Parentelli, Gladys, Giovanna Mérola and Elsa Tamez
   1990   *Mujer, Iglesia, Liberación* (Caracas: Edición de la autora).
Paz, Octavio
   1959   *El laberinto de la soledad* (Mexico City: Fondo de Cultura Económica).
Peña, Milagros
   1995   'Feminist Christian Women in Latin America: Other Voices, Other Visions',
             Journal of Feminist Studies in Religion 11.1 (Spring): 81-94.
Perry, Nicholas, and Loreto Echeverría
   1988   *Under the Heel of Mary* (London: Routledge).
Petchesky, Rosalind Pollack
   1995   'From Population Control to Reproductive Rights: Feminist Fault Lines',
             Reproductive Health Matters 6 (November): 152-61.
Pitanguy, Jacqueline
   1994   'Feminist Politics and Reproductive Rights: The Case of Brazil', in Gita Sen
             and Rachel C. Snow (eds.), *Power and Decision: The Social Control of Reproduction*
             (Boston: Harvard University Press): 101-22.
Pobee, John S.
   1996   *Christ Would Be an African Too* (Geneva: WCC).

Porcile Santiso, María Teresa
    1991   *La mujer, espacio de salvación: Misión de la mujer en la Iglesia, una perspectiva antro-pológica* (Montevideo: Ediciones Trilce).

Prien, Hans-Jürgen
    1978   *Die Geschichte des Christentums in Lateinamerika* (Göttingen: Vandenhoeck & Ruprecht).

Puebla: La evangelización en el presente y en el futuro de América Latina
    1979   Third General Conference of Latin American Bishops (San José: CELAM and the Costa Rican Bishops' Conference, 3rd edn).

Puleo, Mev
    1994   *The Struggle Is One: Voices and Visions of Liberation* (Albany: State University of New York Press).

Pulkkinen, Tuija
    1996   *The Postmodern and Political Agency* (Helsinki: Department of Philosophy, University of Helsinki).

Quesada, Juan Rafael, and Magda Zavala (eds.)
    1991   *500 años: ¿Holocausto o descubrimiento?* (San José: EDUCA).

Radcliffe, Sarah A., and Sallie Westwood (eds.)
    1993   *'ViVa': Women and Popular Protest in Latin America* (London: Routledge).

Randall, Margaret
    1992   *Gathering Rage: The Failure of 20th Century Revolutions to Develop a Feminist Agenda* (New York: Monthly Review Press).
    1994   *Sandino's Daughters: Feminism in Nicaragua* (New Brunswick: Rutgers University Press, rev. edn).

Ranke-Heinemann, Uta
    1988   *Eunuchen für das Himmelreich: Katholische Kirche und Sexualität* (Hamburg: Hoffmann & Campe).

Ringe, Sharon H.
    1990   'Reading from Context to Context: Contributions of a Feminist Hermeneutic to Theologies of Liberation', in Susan Brooks Thistlethwaite and Mary Potter Engel (eds.), *Lift Every Voice: Constructing Christian Theologies from the Underside* (San Francisco: Harper & Row): 283-91.

Rivera Pagán, Luis N.
    1991   *Evangelización y violencia: la conquista de América* (San Juan, Puerto Rico: Editorial CEMI).

Rodríguez, Raquel
    1991   'La Marcha de las mujeres... Apuntes en torno al movimiento de mujeres en América Latina y el Caribe', *Pasos* 34 (March–April): 9-13.

Rodríguez Sehk, Penelope
    1986   'La virgen-madre: Símbolo de la feminidad', *Texto y Contexto* (January–April): 73-90.

Rubiolo, Eugenio
    1990   'Aportes para el debate en torno a la teología de la liberación: Un enfoque epistemológico de la cuestión', *Stromata* 3/4 (January–June): 176-86.

Ruiz García, Samuel
    1994   'Documento pastoral sobre el aborto' (reprinted in *Debate feminista* 5.9 [March]): 435-53.

Russell, Letty M., and J. Shannon Clarkson (eds.)
    1996   *Dictionary of Feminist Theologies* (Louisville: Westminster/John Knox Press).

Russell, Letty M. *et al.* (eds.)
    1988   *Inheriting Our Mothers' Gardens: Feminist Theology in Third World Perspective* (Louisville, KY: Westminster Press).

Santa Ana, Julio de
	1988	'La teología latinoamericana (1982–1987)', *Concilium* 219 (September): 231-41.
Saporta Sternbach, Nancy *et al.*
	1992	'Feminisms in Latin America: From Bogotá to San Bernardo', *Signs* 17.2 (Winter): 393-434.
Scannone, Juan Carlos
	1990	'Cuestiones actuales de epistemología teológica: Aportes de la teología de la liberación', *Stromata* 3/4 (July–December): 293-336.
	1991	'Ciencias sociales, ética política y doctrina social de la Iglesia', in *Teología y liberación. Religión, cultura y ética. Ensayos en torno a la obra de Gustavo Gutiérrez*, III (Lima: Centro de Estudios y Publicaciones): 263-93.
Schirmer, Jennifer
	1989	'"Those Who Die for Life Cannot Be Called Dead": Women and Human Rights Protest in Latin America', *Feminist Review* 32 (Summer): 3-29.
	1993	'The Seeking of Truth and the Gendering of Consciousness: The CoMadres of El Salvador and the CONAVIGUA widows of Guatemala', in Sarah A. Radcliffe and Sallie Westwood (eds.), *'ViVa': Women and Popular Protest in Latin America* (London: Routledge): 30-64.
Schreiter, Robert J.
	1986	*Constructing Local Theologies* (New York: Orbis Books, 2nd edn).
Schutte, Ofelia
	1988–89	'Philosophy and Feminism in Latin America: Perspectives on Gender Identity and Culture', *The Philosophical Forum* 20.1-2 (Fall–Winter): 62-84.
	1991	'Origins and Tendencies of the Philosophy of Liberation in Latin American Thought: A Critique of Dussel's Ethics', *The Philosophical Forum* 22.3: 270-95.
	1993	*Cultural Identity and Social Liberation in Latin American Thought* (Albany: State University of New York Press).
Seed, Patricia
	1993	'"Are These Not Also Men?": The Indians' Humanity and the Capacity for Spanish Civilisation', *Journal of Latin American Studies* 25.3 (October): 629-52.
Serbin, Ken
	1992	'Latin America's Catholics: Postliberationism? Emerging Structures: Sharpening Issues after Santo Domingo', *Christianity and Crisis* 52.18 (December 14): 403-407.
Shaull, Richard
	1991	*The Reformation and Liberation Theology: Insights for the Challenges of Today* (Louisville, KY: Westminster/John Knox Press).
Shiva, Vandana
	1994	'Whose Choice? Whose Life? Whose Security?', *Third World Resurgence* 49: 4-6.
Sihvo, Sinikka, and Kristiina Kajesalo
	1994	'Ehkäisymenetelmät ja oikeus perusterveydenhuoltoon', in Eeva Ollila *et al.* (eds.), *Vallaton väestö: Kansallisia ja kansainvälisiä väestöpoliittisia kysymyksiä* (Juva: WSOY): 109-24.
Silva Gotay, Samuel
	1983	*El pensamiento cristiano revolucionario en América Latina y el Caribe. Implicaciones de la teología de la liberación para la sociología de la religión* (Río Piedras, Puerto Rico: Cordillera/Ediciones Sígueme).
Simons, Helen
	1995	'Cairo: Repackaging Population Control', *International Journal of Health Services* 25.3: 559-66.

Slater, David
1994   'Power and Social Movements in the Other Occident: Latin America in an
            International Context', *Latin American Perspectives* 21.2 (Spring): 11-37.
Smith, Ruth L.
1989   'The Evasion of Otherness: A Problem for Feminist Moral Construction',
            Union Seminary Quarterly Review 43.1-4: 145-61.
Sölle, Dorothee
1990   *Gott denken: Einführung in die Theologie* (Stuttgart: Kreuz Verlag, 3rd edn).
Song, Choan-Seng
1989   *Tell Us Our Names: Story Theology from an Asian Perspective* (repr.; New York:
            Orbis Books).
1991   *Third-Eye Theology: Theology in Formation in Asian Settings* (New York: Orbis
            Books, rev. edn).
Spivak, Gayatri Chakravorty
1994   'Can the Subaltern Speak?', in Patrick Williams and Laura Chrisman (eds.),
            Colonial Discourse and Post-Colonial Theory (New York: Harvester Wheatsheaf,
            2nd edn): 66-111.
Stanley, Liz, and Sue Wise
1993   *Breaking Out Again: Feminist Ontology and Epistemology* (London: Routledge, 2nd
            edn [1983]).
Stephenson, Patricia *et al.*
1992   'Commentary: The Public Health Consequences of Restricted Induced
            Abortion—Lessons from Romania', *American Journal of Public Health* 82.10
            (October): 1328-31.
Stevens, Evelyn P.
1973   'Machismo and Marianismo', *Society* 10.6 (September/October): 57-63.
Stewart-Gambino, Hannah
1992   'Introduction: New Game, New Rules', in Edward L. Cleary and Hannah
            Stewart-Gambino (eds.), *Conflict and Competition: The Latin American Church in
            a Changing Environment* (Boulder, San Francisco: Lynne Rienner Publishers):
            1-19.
Stoll, David
1990   *Is Latin America Turning Protestant?* (Berkeley: University of California Press).
1993   'Introduction: Rethinking Protestantism in Latin America', in Virginia
            Garrard-Burnett and David Stoll (eds.), *Rethinking Protestantism in Latin America*
            (Philadelphia: Temple University Press): 1-19.
Stoltz Chinchilla, Norma
1992   'Marxism, Feminism, and the Struggle for Democracy in Latin America', in
            Arturo Escobar and Sonia E. Alvarez (eds.), *The Making of Social Movements in
            Latin America: Identity, Strategy, and Democracy* (Boulder, San Francisco: West-
            view Press): 37-51.
1995   'Revolutionary Popular Feminism in Nicaragua: Ideologies, Political Tran-
            sitions, and the Struggle for Autonomy', in Christine E. Bose and Edna
            Acosta-Belén (eds.), *Women in the Latin American Development Process* (Philadel-
            phia: Temple University Press): 242-70.
Tamayo-Acosta, Juan José
1990   *Para comprender la teología de la liberación* (Estella [Navarra]: Editorial Verbo
            Divino, 2nd edn).
1994   *Presente y futuro de la teología de la liberación* (Madrid: San Pablo).

Teivainen, Teivo
    1992   'Kansainvälinen Valuuttarahasto: moderni pappi', in Jussi Pakkasvirta and Teivo Teivainen (eds.), *Kenen Amerikka? 500 vuotta Latinalaisen Amerikan valloitusta* (Jyväskylä: Gaudeamus): 182-200.
    1994   'El Fondo Monetario Internacional: un cura moderno', *Pretextos* 6: 79-107.

Thistlethwaite, Susan Brooks
    1989   *Sex, Race and God: Christian Feminism in Black and White* (New York: Crossroad).

Thistlethwaite, Susan, and Mary Potter Engel (eds.)
    1990   *Lift Every Voice: Constructing Christian Theologies from the Underside* (San Francisco: Harper & Row).

Todorov, Tzvetan
    1984   *The Conquest of America: The Question of the Other* (translated from the French by Richard Howard; New York: Harper & Row).

Tomm, Winnie
    1992   'Ethics and Self-Knowing: The Satisfaction of Desire', in Eve Browning Cole and Susan Coultrap-McQuin (eds.), *Explorations in Feminist Ethics: Theory and Practice* (Bloomington: Indiana University Press): 101-10.

Tong, Rosemarie
    1993   *Feminine and Feminist Ethics* (Belmont: Wadsworth).

Torres-Rivas, Edelberto (ed.)
    1993   *Historia general de Centroamérica*, I–VI (Madrid: Sociedad Estatal Quinto Centenario and FLACSO).

Touraine, Alain, and Sergio Spoerer
    1978   'The Present Socio-Political Situation', in *The Church at the Crossroads: Christians in Latin America from Medellín to Puebla (1968–1978)* (Rome: IDOC International): 1-13.

Vargas, Virginia
    1989   *El aporte de la rebeldía de las mujeres* (Lima: Centro Flora Tristán).

Vidal, Marciano
    1991   'Resituar la teología moral a la luz de la teología de la liberación. Aportes fundamentales de la "ética de la liberación" al discurso teológico-moral general', in *Vardagskulturens teología y liberación. Religión, cultura y ética. Ensayos en torno a la obra de Gustavo Gutiérrez*, III (Lima: Centro de Estudios y Publicaciones): 399-415.

Vuola, Elina
    1992   '1500-luvun espanjalainen keskustelu Amerikan valloituksen oikeutuksesta', *Teologinen Aikakauskirja* 97.6: 537-47.
    1993   'La Virgen María como ideal femenino, su crítica feminista y nuevas interpretaciones', *Pasos* 45 (January–February): 11-20.
    1998   'Jungfru Maria och alla övriga kvinnor: Om möjligheterna av en feministisk befrielsemariologi', in Sigurd Bergmann and Carl Reinhold Bråkenhielm (eds.), *Vardagskulturens teologi i nordisk tolkning* (Falun: Nya Doxa): 45-81.

Walker, Alice
    1983   *In Search of Our Mothers' Gardens: Womanist Prose* (New York: Harcourt, Brace & Jovanovich).

Wallerstein, Immanuel
    1980   *The Capitalist World-Economy* (repr.; Cambridge: Cambridge University Press).

Westwood, Sallie, and Sarah A. Radcliffe
    1993   'Gender, Racism and the Politics of Identities in Latin America', in Sarah A. Radcliffe and Sallie Westwood (eds.), *'ViVa': Women and Popular Protest in Latin America* (New York: Routledge): 1-29.

Whiteford, Linda M.
    1993   'Child and Maternal Health and International Economic Policies', *Social Science and Medicine* 37.11: 1391-1400.

Witvliet, Theo
    1985   *A Place in the Sun: An Introduction to Liberation Theology in the Third World* (New York: Orbis Books; London: SCM Press).

World Bank, The
    1993   *World Development Report 1993: Investing in Health* (Oxford: Oxford University Press).

World Health Organization
    1996   *Revised 1990 Estimates of Maternal Mortality: A New Approach by WHO and UNICEF* (WHO).

Young, Iris Marion
    1985   'Humanism, Gynocentrism and Feminist Politics', *Women's Studies International Forum* 8: 173-83.

Young, Pamela Dickey
    1990   *Feminist Theology/Christian Theology: In Search of Method* (Minneapolis: Fortress Press).

Zires, Margarita
    1993   'Reina de México, Patrona de los Chicanos y Emperatriz de las Américas: Los mitos de la Virgen de Guadalupe—Estrategias de producción de identidades', *Iberoamericana. Lateinamerika–Spanien–Portugal* 17.3/4: 76-91.

Index of Subjects

Index of Authors